INDEX

TO AMA RESOURCES

1977–1981

Compiled by Elizabeth A. Keegan
Management Information Service

RESEARCH AND INFORMATION SERVICE
AMERICAN MANAGEMENT ASSOCIATIONS

Suggestions or corrections will be appreciated.
Please address the Management Information Service.

Library of Congress Cataloging in Publication Data

Main entry under title:

Index to AMA resources, 1977–1981.

Continues: Index to AMA resources of the seventies:
1970–1976. c1977.
   1. Management—Indexes. I. Keegan, Elizabeth A.
II. American Management Associations. Management
Information Service. III. Title: Index to A.M.A.
resources, 1977–1981. IV. Title: Index to American
Management Associations resources, 1977–1981.
Z7164.07I29 1982 [HD31]   016.658   82-8743
ISBN 0-8144-3508-4   AACR2

This *Index* has been distributed without charge to official representatives of firms holding Company membership in the AMA as well as to those enrolled as Library and Professorial members. Additional copies are available to members at $10.00. Price to non-members, $13.50.

INTRODUCTION

SINCE 1915, the American Management Associations and its predecessor organizations have published a wealth of material on all aspects of management. To help members identify publications bearing on specific managerial questions, comprehensive indexes to AMA publications have been issued for the years 1954 through 1976. Informal indexes, in some cases combined with a publications catalog, were prepared intermittently in earlier years.

The present *Index* includes, with a few exceptions, all AMA materials published in the years 1977 through 1981. The periodicals and other materials included are described in the "AMA Resources" section which begins on page 145. Omitted are many short reportorial items, and digests of books and articles.

This new edition of the *Index* includes for the first time articles and reports of the National Association of Corporate Directors, one of the American Management Associations since 1979.

HOW TO USE THE INDEX

To find what publications are available on a given subject, turn to the appropriate heading in the SUBJECT INDEX. These headings are arranged alphabetically in dictionary style. For a preview of the subject headings, see pages vii–ix.

Entries under each subject heading are listed alphabetically by title. They show, in addition to the customary information, the company with which the author is affiliated. Where several authors have contributed to an entry, the company affiliations are listed in the same order as the authors' names. If no company name is listed, the writer is a professional (such as an attorney, a physician, or a consultant), a free-lance writer or a member of the AMA staff. In a very few cases the author has used a pseudonym.

The abbreviations used to identify the periodicals and reports are explained on page 1. Descriptions of the various kinds of publications, full titles, lengths, and prices for books and reports are shown in the TITLE/SERIES INDEX, pages 148–166.

To find the contributions of a specific author, consult the AUTHOR INDEX beginning on page 167.

"BY PURCHASE ONLY" MATERIAL

In order to acquaint managers with the full range of AMA management tools and materials, the *Index* also includes some AMA materials available only through purchase and not available in the AMA library or other libraries. In this category are reports of the Executive Compensation Service, Evaluation Tools and Skill Series, Extension Institute home-study programs, audio cassette programs, courses and audio books, multimedia courses for in-company training, and special studies of the Presidents Association (an AMA division). The reminder phrase "By purchase only" follows the citation of each of these items in the *Index*.

HOW TO OBTAIN THE ITEMS INDEXED

Members will already have many of the AMA publications in their files or company libraries. They may borrow from the Associations' library for a period of ten days any other material not specifically identified as "By purchase only." Books, reports and other materials may also be purchased. See p. 145 for guidance in ordering. If a publication is no longer available for purchase, "O.P." (out of print) appears after the citation in the TITLE/SERIES INDEX on pages 148–166. Most AMA publications that are out of print are available in xerographic form from University Microfilms, 300 North Zeeb Road, Ann Arbor, Michigan 48106.

Although Elizabeth A. Keegan spearheaded the effort to identify, assemble and classify all of the AMA publications and other resources for this *Index*, the *Index* is the result of the combined efforts of the AMA Management Information Service staff.

Robert N. Carpenter
Manager, Information Service

John W. Enell
Vice President for Research

CONTENTS

Subject Headings	vi
Explanation of Abbreviations	1
Subject Index	1
AMA Resources	145
Title/Series Index	148
Author Index	167

LISTING OF SUBJECT HEADINGS

A Word about the Headings

The principal headings to be found in the subject section are grouped below, allocated to management functions and subfunctions in essentially the same manner as these subjects are allocated to AMA program divisions. These headings, appear in alphabetical order in the subject section of the *Index*, supplemented by "see" and "see also" references. Below the headings, all titles, whether periodical or book, are listed in alphabetical order. Note that a few of the headings below are labeled "heading only" to indicate that they are merely in use for classification purposes. They do not appear in the subject section and therefore no page number appears.

FINANCIAL MANAGEMENT — 47

Accounting — 2
Auditing — 5
Budgeting — 9
Cash Management — 14
Cost Control — 31
Credit Management — 33
International Operations—
  Finance — 63
Investor Relations — 68
Leasing — 73
Management Controls — 80
Mergers and Acquisitions — 91
Reports — 123

FINANCIAL MANAGEMENT (cont.)

Return on Investment — 125
Taxation — 136

GENERAL MANAGEMENT
(heading only)

Executives — 43
Executive Skills and
Qualifications — 44
Change — 14
Communications — 17
Cooperation, Coordination
  and Conflict Resolution — 29
Creativity — 32

GENERAL MANAGEMENT
(heading only) (cont.)

Decision-making 36
Delegation 37
Ethics 43
Human Relations 56
Leadership 71
Motivation .... 92 ✓
Productivity 113
Superior—Subordinate
 Relations 133
Supervision 134
Team Management 137
Time Management 138

Management 76

**Organizational Forms, Units
and Relationships** (heading only)
Assistants and Assistants to 4
Board of Directors 7
Charts and Graphs 15
Committees 16
Consultants 29
Decentralization 35
Line-Staff 76
Matrix Management 90
Meetings 90
Organization 95
 Job Descriptions 69
 Job Design/Job Enlarge-
 ment/Job Enrichment 70
Organizational Development 97
Organizational Effectiveness 99
Participative Management 101
President's Job 110
Public Relations 117
 Community Relations 23
 Company Image 23

Planning and Control (heading
only)
Contracts 29
Management by Objectives 78
Management Controls 80
Planning 106
Policies 109
Security 128
 Dishonesty 39

**Public Service and Non-Profit
Management** 117

Small Company 129

Socio-Economic Conditions 131
Government and Business 51
Legislation and Regulation 73
Social Responsibility 131

**GENERAL & ADMINISTRATIVE
SERVICES** (heading only)
Libraries 75
Manuals 86
Office Layout 94
Office Management 94
Secretaries 127
Word Processing 143
Work Measurement 143

**HUMAN RESOURCES
MANAGEMENT** 57

**Employee Attitudes and Work-
ing Conditions** (heading only)
Absenteeism .... 1 ✓
Attitudes—Employee .... 4 ✓
Data Processing—Staffing
 and Human Effects .... 35 ✓
Discipline 38
Discrimination 38
Handicapped Workers 53
Health (including Transcen-
 dental Meditation) 53
 Alcoholism 3
 Drug Abuse 40
 Health Maintenance Organi-
 zations .... 55 ✓
 Health—Mental .... 53 ✓
Hours .... 55 ✓
Quality of Work Life .... 121 ✓
Safety 125

**International Operations—
Human Resources** 65

**International Operations—
Personnel Surveys** 67

Labor Management Relations 71
Arbitration 4
Collective Bargaining 16
Grievances 52
Strikes 133
Unions 141

Manpower Planning 85
Affirmative Action 3
Equal Employment Opportunity 42
Interviewing 67
Older Workers and Retirement 95
Orientation 100
Recruitment 121
Relocation 122
Selection 128
Termination 137
Testing—Personnel 138
Turnover 141

Personal Affairs 105

**HUMAN RESOURCES
MANAGEMENT** (cont.)

Suggestion Systems   133
Training and Development   139
  Career Management—Individual
    Development   10
  Career Management—Job Search   13
  Coaching and Counseling   15
  Education   40
  Management Development
    (including assessment
    centers)   81
  Performance Appraisal   102
  Performance Standards   104
  Supervisory Training   135

**Wage and Salary Administra-
tion** (heading only)
  Compensation   23
  Job Evaluation   70
  Wage Incentives   142
Women Workers   142
Young Adults   144

INFORMATION SYSTEMS
(heading only)
  Data Processing   33
  Glossaries   50
  Management Information
    Sources & Systems   83
  Management Science and
    Statistics   85
  Scheduling Techniques   127
  Simulation   129
  Systems Analysis   135
  Work Simplification   143

**INSURANCE AND EMPLOYEE
BENEFITS** (heading only)
  Employee Benefits   40
  Insurance   59
  Insurance—Life—Health—
    Accident   59
  Pensions   101
  Product Liability   112

INTERNATIONAL OPERATIONS   59
  International by Region—
    Asia   61
  International by Region—
    Europe   62
  International by Region—
    Latin America   62

INTERNATIONAL OPERATIONS
(cont.)
  International by Region—
    Other Regions   62
  International Finance   63
  International Human
    Resources   65
  International Marketing   66
  International Personnel
    Surveys   67

MANUFACTURING MANAGEMENT
(heading only)
  Engineers   42
  Energy Management   41
  Inventory Control   68
  Maintenance   76
  Materials Management   89
  Metrication   91
  Plant and Equipment   109
  Pollution Control   110
  Production Management   112
  Production Planning and
    Control   113
  Quality Circles   120
  Quality Control   120

MARKETING MANAGEMENT   86
  Advertising and Sales
    Promotion   3
  Competitive Intelligence   28
  Forecasting Methods   49
  International Operations—
    Marketing   66
  Marketing Research   89
  Pricing   111
  Sales Management   126
  Sales Training   126
  Salespeople   127
  Servicing   129

PACKAGING   100
  Packaging Design and Mer-
    chandising   100

**PURCHASING, TRANSPORTATION
AND PHYSICAL DISTRIBUTION**
(heading only)
  Distribution   39
  Purchasing   119
  Transportation   140

RESEARCH AND DEVELOPMENT   123
  Engineers   42
  Product Development   111
  Project Management   116

SUBJECT INDEX

Explanation of Abbreviations

AMJ	Advanced Management Journal	MRev.	Management Review
BPM	Board Practices Monograph	OD	Organizational Dynamics
CDSR	Corporate Directors' Special Report	PA	Presidents Association Special Study
CR	Compensation Review	Pers.	Personnel
DM	Director's Monthly	RS	Research Study
ES	Executive Skills	SM	Supervisory Management
HSM	Health Services Manager	SR	Survey Report
MB	Management Briefing	SS	Supervisory Sense

For a description of the various series of AMACOM publications, please see TITLE/SERIES INDEX.

ABSENTEEISM

The Absenteeism Culture: Becoming Attendance Oriented. Robert F. Allen, Michael Higgins. Pers., Jan.–Feb. 1979, pp. 30–39. Human Resources Institute, Hoffman-La Roche, Inc.

Curb Excessive Absenteeism: Bolster Self-Confidence. Harris Odell, Jr. HSM, March 1977, pp. 1–4. Memorial Medical Center.

Curing Problem Absenteeism. SS, Feb. 1981, 24 pp.

Dear Personnel Manager. Sam Witchel. SM, July 1978, pp. 18–20.

How Good Is Your Absenteeism Control System? Frank E. Kuzmits. AMJ, Winter 1980, pp. 4–15. Univ. of Louisville.

Limit Absenteeism: Try a Back-to-Basics Approach. J. M. McDonald, Ann V. Shaver. HSM, March, 1978, pp. 1–5. Clemson Univ., Stephens County Hospital.

Managing Absenteeism. Frank E. Kuzmits. Pers., May–June 1977, pp. 73–76. Atlanta Univ.

Managing Employee Absenteeism. Louis V. Imundo. *The Effective Supervisor's Handbook,* 1980, pp. 147–165. Management Perspectives.

A New Look at Absenteeism. Richard M. Steers, Susan R. Rhodes. Pers., Nov.–Dec. 1980, pp. 60–65. Univ. of Oregon, Syracuse Univ.

Time Off with Pay. An Illusive Reward. J. H. Foegen. SM, June 1978, pp. 26–30. Winona State College.

To Cut Casual Absenteeism: Tie Benefits to Hours Worked. Clarence R. Deitsch, David A. Dilts. CR, First Quarter 1981, pp. 41–46. Ball State Univ., Kansas State Univ.

What Is Your Absenteeism I.Q.? J. Michael McDonald. Pers., May–June 1980, pp. 33–37. Clemson Univ. (Also in reprint collection *Leadership on the Job: Guides to Good Supervision* (third ed.), 1981).

ACCIDENT PREVENTION. See Occupational Safety and Health Act., Safety

ACCOUNTING. See Also Financial Management

Accounting for Managers (sec. ed.). George J. Chorba. 1978. (Extension Institute Course) By purchase only.

AT&Ts New Accounting System Charges for Office Services. MRev., April 1981, pp. 29, 31–32.

The Changing Business Scene. Warren Chippindale, Philip L. Defliese. *Current Value Accounting,* 1977, pp. 1–4. Coopers & Lybrand.

Cost Accounting for Profit Improvement. Raymond Jordan. 1979. (Extension Institute Course) By purchase only.

Current Value Accounting. Warren Chippindale, Philip L. Defliese (editors). 1977, 184 pp. Coopers & Lybrand.

A Current Value Approach. Kenneth P. Johnson. *Current Value Accounting,* 1977, pp. 43–64. Coopers & Lybrand.

Direct Costing. William E. Arnstein, Frank Gilabert. 1980, 280 pp. Main Hurdman & Cranstoun.

Financial Reporting Under Changing Values: An Introduction to Current Value Accounting. Morley P. Carscallen, Kenneth P. Johnson. 1979, 47 pp. Coopers and Lybrand. MB.

Fund Accounting. James M. Patton. *Management Principles for Nonprofit Agencies and Organizations,* 1979, pp. 433–476. Univ. of Pittsburgh.

How Cost Accounting Systems Can Affect Organizational Behavior. Ray G. Funkhouser. MRev., Oct. 1979, pp. 71–73. Booz, Allen & Hamilton, Inc.

How Financial Reporting Has Responded to Changing Values. Morley P. Carscallen. *Current Value Accounting,* 1977, pp. 27–42. Coopers & Lybrand.

Inflation Accounting: Which Method Is Best? Robert K. Mautz. MRev., Nov. 1977, pp. 11–17. Ernst & Ernst.

Is This Strategy Working? A New Role for Accountants. Felix Pomeranz, James C. Gale. MRev., March 1980, pp. 14–18. Coopers & Lybrand.

Management and Accounting. Billy E. Goetz, Dennis J. Gaffney. *The Evolving Science of Management,* 1979, pp. 450–456. Florida Atlantic Univ., Michigan State Univ.

New Partners in National CPA Firms: A Profile. Mary Zippo. Pers., March–April 1981, p. 42.

Operational Considerations in Implementing and Maintaining the Current Value Approach. John N. Miles, Derek W. Williams. *Current Value Accounting,* 1977, pp. 93–112. Coopers & Lybrand.

Some Notes on Accounting. Merritt L. Kastens. *Redefining the Manager's Job: The Proactive Manager in a Reactive World,* 1980, pp. 130–140.

Standard Cost Accounting. Robert E. Nolan, Richard T. Young, Ben C. DiSylvester.

Improving Productivity Through Advanced Office Controls, 1980, pp. 357–368. Robert E. Nolan Co., Inc.

What Accounting Managers Do. Arthur S. O'Neill, Jr., 1980. (Extension Institute Course) By purchase only.

ADVERTISING AND SALES PROMOTION. See Also Data Processing Applications

Advertising. Lucille A. Maddalena. *A Communications Manual for Nonprofit Organizations,* 1981, pp. 151–173. Fairleigh Dickinson Univ.

Advertising. William R. Osgood. *Basics of Successful Business Management,* 1981, pp. 116–136.

Advertising Pure and Simple. Hank Seiden. 1977, 198 pp. Hicks & Greist, Inc· (Also available as AMACOM audio cassette book. By purchase only)

Advertising: Strategy and Design (fourth ed.). Elizabeth Trotman. 1979. (Extension Institute Course) Revised by Gertrude Salaway. By purchase only.

Advertising Your Skills. Richard J. Rinella, Claire C. Robbins. *Career Power! A Manual for Personal Career Advancement,* 1980, pp. 61–112. Management Resource Associates.

Building a Successful Professional Practice with Advertising. Irwin Braun. 1981, 289 pp. Braun Advertising, Inc.

Corporate Advertising. Gerald J. Voros, Paul Alvarez (editors). *What Happens in Public Relations,* 1981, pp. 200–209. Ketchum MacLeod & Grove.

Developing a Low Cost Promotion Strategy. William A. Cohen, Marshall E. Reddick. *Successful Marketing for Small Business,* 1981, pp. 145–174. California State Univ.

The Direct Marketing Approach to Capital Formation. Andrew H. Field, Carol Field. MRev., March 1980, pp. 37–41. Capital Formation. Ltd.

How to Develop an Advertising Plan. ES, Sept. 1980, 16 pp.

How to Develop an Industrial Advertising Budget for Smaller Companies. David Hosman, Donald L. Fugate. MRev., March 1981, pp. 43–46. Trend Graphics, Inc., Pittsburgh State Univ.

How to Write Sales Copy. Herman R. Holtz. *Profit from Your Money-Making Ideas: How to Build a New Business or Expand an Existing One,* 1980, pp. 157–204.

An Introduction to Direct Marketing. Chaman L. Jain, Al Migliaro. 1978, 67 pp. St. Johns Univ., Glenwood Associates. MB.

Marketing and Sales Promotion. Herman R. Holtz. *Profit from Your Money-Making Ideas: How to Build a New Business or Expand an Existing One,* 1980, pp. 125–156.

The 27 Most Common Mistakes in Advertising. Alec Benn. 1978, 156 pp. Benn & MacDonough, Inc.

AFFIRMATIVE ACTION PROGRAMS. See also Discrimination, Equal Employment Opportunity, Handicapped

AAP and OD: Not Such an Odd Couple. Gopal C. Pati. MRev., May 1980, pp. 58–62. Indiana Univ. Northwest.

Affirmative Action and the Woman Worker. Jennie Farley. 1979, 225 pp. Cornell Univ.

Affirmative Action: Take Aim at Discrimination. Robert Thayer HSM, April 1980, pp. 1–3. Rush-Presbyterian-St. Lukes Medical Center.

Affirmative Action—What It Is and What It Means for Your Company. ES, Dec. 1980, 16 pp.

Conducting an Internal Compliance Review of Affirmative Action. Kenneth E. Marino. Pers., March–April 1980, pp. 24–34. Univ. of Kentucky. (Also in reprint collection *Leadership on the Job: Guides to Good Supervision* (third ed.), 1981)

A Manager's Guide to Affirmative Action. Mary E. Fulton. 1979. (Extension Institute Course) By purchase only.

Using Survey Feedback to Achieve Enlightened AA/EEO. George Neely, Fred Luthans. Pers., May–June 1978, pp. 18–23. Univ. of North Carolina, Univ. of Nebraska.

ALCOHOLISM. See also Health

Alcoholic Employees Beget Troubled Supervisors. Donald A. Philips, Harry J. Older.

SM, Sept. 1981, pp. 2–9. Cope, Inc. (Also in reprint collection *Leadership on the Job: Guides to Good Supervision* (third ed.), 1981)

Hospitals: A Link To Alcoholism Treatment. Anna L. Checkett. HSM, March 1980, pp. 4–5. Comprehensive Care Corporation.

Supervising the Alcoholic. Joseph J. Walker. SM, Nov. 1978, pp. 26–32. Training Materials, Inc.

What the Supervisor Should Know About Employer Liability for Intoxicated Employees. Brent E. Zepke. SM, Part 1. July 1977, pp. 32–39. Part 2. Aug. 1977, pp. 35–40.

Women, Work, and Alcohol: A Disturbing Trend. Edith S. Gomberg. SM, Dec. 1977, pp. 16–20.

APPRAISAL. See Performance Appraisal

APTITUDE TESTS. See Testing—Personnel

ARBITRATION

Arbitration in One Easy Lesson: A Review of Criteria Used in Arbitration Awards. Donald Austin Woolf. Pers., Sept.–Oct. 1978, pp. 70–78.

If You Were the Arbitrator. Morris Stone, Charlotte Gold, Earl Baderschneider. SM, monthly feature beginning July 1960. American Arbitration Assn.

ASSESSMENT CENTERS. See Management Development—Techniques—Assessment Centers

ASSISTANTS AND ASSISTANTS TO. See also Line-Staff

How to Be an Assistant-To. C. Connie Firm. AMJ, Summer 1981. pp. 25–30, 35–36. Executive Assistants Assn.

Preface to the Revised Edition. Joseph J. Famularo. *Organization Planning Manual* (rev. ed.), 1979, pp. ix–x. McGraw-Hill, Inc.

ASSOCIATION MANAGEMENT. See Public Service and Non-profit Management and headings for individual functions

ATTITUDES—EMPLOYEE

Action-Oriented Attitude Surveys. Louis A. Allen. *Human Resources Management: The Past Is Prologue,* 1979, pp. 319–334.

All About Job Satisfaction. Gene Milbourn, G. James Francis. SM, Aug. 1981, pp. 35–43. Univ. of Baltimore, Colorado State Univ.

Attitude Surveys: A Diagnostic Tool. Ernest C. Miller. Pers., May–June 1978, pp. 4–11.

The Business-Media Relationship: Countering Misconceptions and Distrust. David Finn. 1981, 92 pp. Ruder & Finn, Inc. RS.

Charting and Changing the Organizational Climate. Melvin Sorcher, Selig Danzig. *Human Resources Management: The Past Is Prologue,* 1979, pp. 356–361.

Commitment Is Too Easy! Gerald R. Salancik. OD, Summer 1977, pp. 62–80. Univ. of Illinois.

Communication: A Study on Conflict in Two Hospitals. Harry A. Washing. HSM, Dec. 1978, pp. 1–3, 9. Univ. of Dayton.

Company Loyalty: A Zero-Based Asset? William D. Heier. MRev., April 1980, pp. 57–61. Arizona State Univ.

Conducting a Successful Survey. Robert E. Pitts. HSM, March 1980, pp. 6–7. Univ. of Notre Dame.

Conversation with Rensis Likert. William Dowling (editor). *Effective Management and the Behavioral Sciences,* 1978, pp. 52–74.

Dealing with Nurse Dissatisfaction: A Management Tool that Works. Paula L. Stamps,

Gretchen Ramirez-Sosa. HSM, Dec. 1980, pp. 3–6. Univ. of Massachusetts, Univ. of Puerto Rico.

Decades: Lifestyle Changes in Career Expectations. Edith M. Lynch. 1980, 144 pp. American Employers for Free Enterprise.

The Employee Attitude Survey: Cure for Labor/Management Blues? Mary Zippo. Pers., March–April 1980, pp. 75–76.

Employee Values in a Changing Society. Mark G. Mindell, William I. Gordon. 1981, 72 pp. Abbott Laboratories, Kent State Univ.

Factors Influencing Industrial Morale. Mason Haire, Josephine S. Gottsdanker. *Human Resources Management: The Past Is Prologue,* 1979, pp. 335–348.

How Men and Women View Their Jobs—and What This Means to the Supervisor. Mildred Golden Pryor, R. Wayne Mondy. SM, Nov. 1978, pp. 17–24. East Texas State Univ.

How to Assess Your Managerial Style. Charles Margerison. 1980, 151 pp. Cranfield School of Management, England.

Improving the Effectiveness of Survey Feedback. Jerome L. Franklin. Pers., May–June 1978, pp. 11–17. Rensis Likert Associates.

Leadership and the Work Ethic. James L. Hayes. MRev., Dec. 1977, pp. 2–3.

The Manager and Self-Respect: A Follow-up Survey. Preston G. McLean, M.D., Katherine Jillson. 1977, 28 pp. N.Y. Univ. SR.

Manager to Manager II: What Managers Think of Their Managerial Careers. Robert F. Pearse. 1977, 65 pp. Boston Univ. SR.

Managers and Heroes: How Maturity Levels Influence Managerial Values. Ross Arkell Webber. MRev., May 1980, pp. 43–45. Univ. of Pennsylvania.

Men and Machines: An Assembly-Line Worker Looks at His Job. Robert H. Guest. *Human Resources Management: The Past Is Prologue,* 1979, pp. 98–108.

Mind-to-Mind Management. Stanley Peterfreund. 1977, 34 pp. MB.

The Ongoing Feedback System: Experimenting with a New Managerial Tool. David Nadler, Philip Mirvis, Cortlandt Cammann. *Organizational Development: Theory and Practice,* 1977, pp. 107–124. Columbia Univ., Univ. of Michigan.

Opinion Surveys: The Results Are In—What Do We Do with Them? David Sirota. *Human Resources Management: The Past Is Prologue,* 1979, pp. 349–355.

Organizational Seduction: Building Commitment to Organizations. Roy J. Lewicki. OD, Autumn 1981, pp. 5–21. Duke Univ.

Professional Lives Vs. Private Lives—Shifting Patterns of Managerial Commitment. Fernando Bartolome, Paul A. Lee Evans. OD, Spring 1979, pp. 3–29. European Institute.

Rekindling Corporate Loyalty. Mary Zippo. Pers., Sept.–Oct. 1981, pp. 48–49.

Surveying Employee Attitudes. Roger J. Howe. *Building Profits Through Organizational Change.* 1981, pp. 154–173. Donaldson Co., Inc.

The Technique of Measuring Employee Attitudes. Arthur W. Kornhauser. *Human Resources Management: The Past Is Prologue,* 1979, pp. 309–318.

Uncovering Organizational Problems Through Employee Surveys. Ken Thompson. HSM, May 1980, pp. 6–8. Univ. of Notre Dame.

Watch Your Attitude! James L. Hayes. MRev., April 1979, pp. 2–3.

What Do Executives Really Think About Their Organizations? Frank J. Smith, Lyman W. Porter. OD, Autumn 1977, pp. 68–80.

What to Expect from Your First Survey of Employee Morale. Sandra L. Holmes. Pers., March–April 1979, pp. 69–73. Santone Industries.

What Today's Employee Wants from You. William C. Waddell. *Overcoming Murphy's Law,* 1981, pp. 14–30. California State Univ., Los Angeles.

Why Motivational Theories Don't Work. Kenneth A. Kovach. AMJ, Spring 1980, pp. 54–59. George Mason Univ. (Also reprinted in *Making Successful Presentations,* 1981)

The Work Ethic: Working Values and Values That Work. David J. Cherrington. 1980, 288 pp. Brigham Young Univ.

AUDITING. See also Financial Management
Administrative Audit and Oversight: Low-cost Benefits for the Smaller Company.

Philip D. Ameen, S. Thomas Moser. MRev., June 1978, pp. 8–13. Peat, Marwick, Mitchell & Co.

Assessing Computer Center Effectiveness. Frank Greenwood, Lee A. Gagnon. 1977, 38 pp. Univ. of New Haven, Peat, Marwick, Mitchell & Co. MB.

Auditing the Data Processing Function. Richard W. Lott. 1980, 214 pp. Bentley College.

Developing In-House EDP Auditing Capabilities. Robert F. Reilly, John A. Lee. MRev., April 1981. pp. 57–61. Huffy Corp.

Evaluating the Personnel Department's Internal Functioning. R. Bruce McAfee. Pers., May–June 1980, pp. 56–62. Old Dominion Univ.

Evaluation. William R. Tracey. *Human Resource Development Standards,* 1981, pp. 3–15. U.S. Army Intelligence Training School.

The FCPA and the Emerging Role of the Internal Auditor. Robert L. Richmond. *Corporate Governance Review,* 1981, pp. 58–63. Institute of Internal Auditors, Inc.

The General Management Survey: A Diagnostic Tool for Managers. John Quay. MRev., March 1981, pp. 12–15. Quay Associates.

A Guide to Operational Auditing. Archie McGhee, Mary Etzel Fleischer, 1979. (Extension Institute Cassette Program) By purchase only.

How PAR Can Save $100,000 Annually. Morton M. Kaplan, John W. Gifford. HSM, March 1981, pp. 4–6. Kent General Hospital, Middle Atlantic Shared Services.

How to Audit Finance. J. McConnell. 1979. (An AMACOM Evaluation Tool) By purchase only.

How to Audit General Management. J. McConnell. 1979. (An AMACOM Evaluation Tool) By purchase only.

How to Audit Marketing and Sales. J. McConnell. 1978. (An AMACOM Evaluation Tool) By purchase only.

How to Audit Operations. J. McConnell. 1980. (An AMACOM Evaluation Tool) By purchase only.

How to Audit the Personnel Department. J. McConnell. 1977. (An AMACOM Evaluation Tool) By purchase only.

How to Audit the Purchasing Function. J. McConnell. 1981. (An AMACOM Evaluation Tool) By purchase only.

How to Audit Your EEO Compliance. J. McConnell. 1979. (An AMACOM Evaluation Tool) By purchase only.

How to Conduct an Energy Audit. T. Hollen, R. Redd. 1980. (An AMACOM Evaluation Tool) By purchase only.

How to Plan and Track Your Personal Finances. H. Moore. 1980. (An AMACOM Evaluation Tool) By purchase only.

Making Use of Operational Auditing. ES, Aug. 1981, 16 pp.

Management Auditing: A Questionnaire Approach. Robert J. Thierauf. 1980, 239 pp. Xavier Univ.

The Manager and the Modern Internal Auditor: A Problem-Solving Partnership. Lawrence B. Sawyer. 1979, 466 pp.

Monitoring Emergency Department Management. Robert Inglis. HSM, Feb. 1979, pp. 1–3, 10. Touche Ross & Co.

Nuts and Bolts Methods for Achieving Quality Assurance. Martin R. Smith. *Qualitysense: Organizational Approaches to Improving Product Quality and Service,* 1979, pp. 99–154. Capital Manufacturing Co.

Operational Auditing: A Key to Cost Containment. William L. Werner. HSM, May 1979, pp. 4–6. The Toledo Hospital.

Performing the Operations Audit (sec. ed.). Archie McGhee. 1978. (Extension Institute Course) By purchase only.

Preemptive Auditing: Future Shock or Present Opportunity? Felix Pomeranz. MRev., Aug. 1979, pp. 18–21.

The Product-Line Audit: An Approach to Profit-Oriented Marketing. H. M. Tibbetts. MRev., March 1977, pp. 14–17. Thomas J. Lipton, Inc.

Research and Communications Audits. Gerald J. Voros, Paul Alvarez (editors). *What Happens in Public Relations,* 1981, pp. 1–10. Ketchum MacLeod & Grove.

Risk Analysis Guide to Insurance and Employee Benefits. A. E. Pfaffle, Sal Nicosia. 1977, 71 pp. EBASCO Risk Management. MB.

Role of the Audit Committee: Update and Implementation. Lawrence J. Trautman, James H. Hammond, Jr. BPM 13, Nov. 1980, 10 pp. OZMA Corp., Peat Marwick, Mitchell & Co.

The Role of the Internal Auditor. Elizabeth Trotman. 1977. (Extension Institute Course) By purchase only.

Safe: Security Audit & Field Evaluation for Computer Facilities and Information Systems (rev. ed.). Leonard I. Krauss. 1980, 308 pp.

What a Management Audit Can Do for You? Theodore Barry. MRev., June 1977, pp. 41–43. Theodore Barry & Associates.

AUTOMATION. See Data Processing, Plant & Equipment

BANKING. See Financial Management

BENEFIT PLANS. See Employee Benefits

BOARD OF DIRECTORS

Board Functions. CDSR II, 1978, 24 pp.

Board Meetings: Let's Get Together More Often . . . or Should We? Peter G. Scotese. DM, Aug. 1981, pp. 1–3. Springs Mills, Inc.

Board Models. CDSR III, 1978, 24 pp.

The Board of Directors. J. Keith Louden. *Managing at the Top: Roles & Responsibilities of the Chief Executive Officer*, 1977, pp. 117–133. Corporate Director, Inc.

Board Practices Monographs: Objectives and Scope. Stephen I. Cummings. BPM 1, April 1979, 5 pp. Stanford Univ.

Boardroom Evolution in the Small and Mid-Sized Company? William Chisholm. DM, June 1981, pp. 1–2. Boardroom Consultants, Inc.

Boardroom Roots: The Early American Experience. Stanley C. Vance. *Corporate Governance Review*, 1981, pp. 2–7. Univ. of Tennessee.

Boards of Directors of Nonprofit Corporations. Glen A. Wilkinson. BPM 10, July 1980, 9 pp. Wilkinson, Cragun & Barker.

Building and Operating an Effective Board of Directors. Milton C. Lauenstein. PA #70, 1979, 64 pp. Ventron Corp. By purchase only.

Building Better Relations with the Hospital Board. Terry O. Hartshorn. HSM, Nov. 1978, p. 5. PacifiCare, Inc.

Business Leadership on Nonprofit Boards. John Carver. BPM 12, Oct. 1980, 9 pp.

A Busy Board Is Never Bored. David L. Woodrum. HSM, March 1979, pp. 5–6. Ryan Advisors

The Catch-22 in Reform Proposals for Restructuring Corporate Boards. S. Prakash Sethi, Bernard Cunningham, Carl Swanson. MRev., Jan. 1979, pp. 27–28, 38–41. Univ. of Texas.

A Compendium of Monographs on Board Practices. National Association of Corporate Directors (editor). 1981, 86 pp. (A reprint collection of *Board Practices Monographs*)

Corporate Confrontations: A 3-Year Retrospect. National Association of Corporate Directors (editor). 1981, 147 pp. (A collection of reprints from DM)

Corporate Directors Legal Case Books (Vol. 1–4) and 1980 Update. National Association of Corporate Directors (editor). 1981.

Corporate Governance Issues and the Corporate Secretary. National Association of Corporate Directors (editor). 1981, 111 pp.

Corporate Governance Review. National Association of Corporate Directors (editor). 1981, 63 pp.

The Crisis of the American Board. Warren Bennis. 1978. (AMACOM audio cassette) By purchase only.

Director Information Systems. Donald R. Jackson. CDSR X, 1979, 24 pp. The Barlow Corp.

Director Qualifications and Selection. William H. Chisholm. CDSR IX, 1980, 11 pp. Boardroom Consultants, Inc.

Director Selection Considerations. Ira G. Corn, Jr. BPM 2, May 1979, 6 pp. Michigan General Corp.

Directors' and Officers' Liability: How to Avoid Personal Liability. Robert M. Shafton Randy E. Nonberg. DM, Sept. 1980, pp. 6–7. Tyre & Kamins.

Evolution in the Boardroom. CDSR I, 1978, 24 pp. By purchase only.

Guidelines for Information Flow to Directors. Richard S. Maurer. BPM 6, March 1980, 9 pp. Delta Air Lines.

Guidelines with Respect to "Board Influences on Company Organization Structure." James W. Fisher. BPM 11, Aug. 1980, 5 pp. Ford Motor Co.

How to Manage the Management Bureaucracy. W. Stanton Halverson, Jr. MRev. July 1978, pp. 26–28, 39–40. Milton Roy Co.

In Search of Better "Boardsmanship": Helping Trustees Assess Their Role. Richard A. Reif, Jr. HSM, Oct. 1981, pp. 13–14. Jeanes Hospital.

Inside vs. Outside Directors. Stanley C. Vance. CDSR IV, 1978, 24 pp. The Univ. of Tennessee.

Keeping Directors Informed: The Role of the Corporate Secretary. John B. Megahan. BPM 8, May 1980, 7 pp. El Paso Co.

Liabilities of Directors Under State Law. Michael D. Goldman. BPM 7, April 1980, 6 pp. Potter, Anderson & Corroon.

The New Look in European and American Boards. Lawrence W. Hill. *The International Essays for Business Decision Makers, Vol. V,* 1980, pp. 316–322. Heidrick & Struggles.

The 1979 Proxy Season Analysis of the Newly Required Board and Director Proxy Disclosures. National Association of Corporate Directors (editor). 1979, 216 pp.

A Performance Model for Boards of Directors. Bruce C. Sherony, Philipp A. Stoeberl. BPM 5, Jan. 1980, 7 pp. North Michigan Univ., St. Louis Univ.

Planning for Change: Bank Directorship in the '80s. National Association of Corporate Directors (editor). 1981, 86 pp.

The Role of the Chairman of the Board. Ira G. Corn, Jr. CDSR VI, 1979, 23 pp. Michigan General Corp.

Satisfying Corporate Accountability: The Roles of the Board, the Corporate Secretary, and the SEC Disclosure Rules. Victor Futter. BPM 4, Dec. 1979, 10 pp. Allied Chemical Corp.

The SEC in the Boardroom. Pearl Meyer. MRev., July 1978, pp. 23–27. Handy Associates.

A Shield for Directors: The Outside Consultant. Wallace F. Forbes. MRev., Dec. 1977 pp. 26–28, 37–39. Standard Research Associates.

The Strategic Planning Committee: Focus on the Future. Lawrence J. Trautman. DM, Sept. 1980, pp. 2–5.

Tailoring the Board to Your Size and Circumstances. S. John Loscoco. DM, Dec. 1981, pp. 1–5. Acquivest Group, Inc.

Using the Business Acumen On Your Board of Trustees. Alfred R. Stern. HSM, Oct. 1979, pp. 5–6. Warner Communications.

What Every Director Should Know About Computer Security. Jack Bologna. BPM 9, June 1980, 6 pp. George Odiorne Associates.

Why a Board of Directors? John M. Nash. *Corporate Governance Review,* 1981, pp. 48–57. National Assn. of Corporate Directors.

Why Corporate Boards Need Independent Directors. Paul B. Firstenberg, Burton G. Malkiel. MRev., April 1980, pp. 26–28, 37–38. Children's TV Workshop, Princeton Univ.

Why Corporate Officers Should Not Be on Their Own Board. C. Courtney Brown. MRev., Aug. 1978, pp. 29–30. Columbia Univ.

Why Managers Should Serve on Their Board of Directors. Richard R. West. MRev., Aug. 1978, pp. 29–30. Dartmouth College.

BUDGETING

Break-Even Analysis for Higher Education. R. Keith Larimore. *Managing Nonprofit Organizations*, 1977, pp. 95–101. Missouri Southern State College.

Budgeting Basics for Supervisors. SS, July 1981, 24 pp.

Budgeting by Department and Functional Area (third ed.). Wayne G. Bremser. 1981 (Extension Institute Course) By purchase only.

Budgeting Strategy: A Meaningful Mean. Carl Joiner, Brad J. Chapman. AMJ, Summer 1981. pp. 4–11. Univ. of Nebraska.

Capital Budgeting: Plan Your Work and Work Your Plan. A. E. Young. SM, Jan. 1979, pp. 31–38.

Direct Costs in Budgeting, Forecasting, and Business Modeling. William E. Arnstein, Frank Gilabert. *Direct Costing*, 1980, pp. 72–91. Main Hurdman & Cranstoun.

Discounted Cash Flow Analysis for Capital Budgeting Decisions. Robert E. Pritchard, Thomas J. Hindelang. *The Strategic Evaluation and Management of Capital Expenditures*, 1981, pp. 96–109. Glassboro State College, Drexel Univ.

The Fine Art of Budgeting. Gerald J. Voros, Paul Alvarez (editors). *What Happens in Public Relations*, 1981, pp. 24–40. Ketchum MacLeod & Grove.

Flexible Budgets: The Next Step in Healthcare Financial Control. Steven A. Finkler, HSM, May 1981. pp. 6, 11. The Wharton School.

Forecast Budgeting. William R. Osgood. *Basics of Successful Business Management*, 1981, pp. 55–75.

Fundamentals of Budgeting. Kenneth M. Lizotte. 1979. (Extension Institute Cassette Program) By purchase only.

How to Budget and Control Costs. William A. Cohen. *Principles of Technical Management*, 1980, pp. 132–159. California State Univ.

How to Use Your Budget As a Control Tool. ES, Aug. 1980, 16 pp.

Managing Discretionary Organizational Expenses: Applying the Hospital's Goals to Department Services. Ken Thompson, Ann Marie Wesley. HSM, Jan. 1980, pp. 3–4. Univ. of Notre Dame.

Murphy's Law Vs. Zero-Base Budgeting. Donald N. Anderson. MRev., Oct. 1977, pp. 53–54. Executive Action, Inc.

The Personnel Activity Index: A New Budgeting Tool. W. C. Jackson. *Human Resources Management: The Past Is Prologue*, 1979, pp. 285–292.

Planning and Administering the Company Budget (sec. ed.). Reginald L. Jones, H. George Trentin. 1977. (Extension Institute Course) By purchase only.

Planning and Administering the Company Budget (third ed.). Wayne G. Bremser. 1981. (Extension Institute Course) By purchase only.

Programming and Budgeting. William R. Tracey. *Human Resource Development Standards*, 1981, pp. 64–77. U.S. Army Intelligence Training School.

Public Budgeting Systems. James L. Mercer, Edwin H. Koester. 1978, pp. 68–78. *Public Management Systems: An Administrator's Guide*, 1979, Battelle Southern Operations, C. R. Drew Postgraduate Medical School.

R&D on a Minimum Budget. Donatas Tijunelis, Nancy Miles Clausen. 1979, 37 pp. Borg-Warner Corp. MB.

Range Estimating for Reduced Risk. Lou Lewis. AMJ, Summer 1981, pp. 37–41. Decision Sciences Corp.

Salary Budgeting. Stanley B. Henrici. *Salary Management for the Nonspecialist*, 1980, pp. 186–205. Heinz, U.S.A.

Some Thoughts on the Human Side of Budgeting. Owen B. Mosely. SM, April 1981, pp. 27–29. Murray State Univ.

Spending for Its Own Sake: Time for a Change. J. H. Foegen. AMJ, Autumn 1980, pp. 16–20. Winona State Univ.

Strategic Budgeting: How to Turn Financial Records into a Strategic Asset. Edmund J. Luksus. MRev., March 1981, pp. 57–61. San Jose Police Dept.

A Total Approach to Hospital Budgeting and Financial Planning. Bruce J. Wright. HSM, Nov. 1981, pp. 3–4. B. Wright & Associates.

What the Supervisor Should Know About Measuring Profits. Narendra C. Bhandari, Charles C. McCubbin, Jr. SM, Nov. 1978, pp. 33–38. Pace Univ.

ZBB Without Paperwork: An Informal Approach to Budget Planning. H. Henry Goldman. MRev., Oct. 1977, pp. 51–53. Norris Industries.

Zero-Base Budgeting: A Decision Package Manual. L. Allan Austin, Logan M. Cheek. 1979, 207 pp. Xerox Corp.

Zero-Base Budgeting Comes of Age. Logan M. Cheek. 1977, 314 pp. Xerox Corp.

The Zero-Base Budgeting Misconception. Frederick W. Harvey. MRev., July 1978, pp. 33–34. Towers, Perrin, Forster & Crosby.

Zero-Base Budgeting: Organizational Impact and Effects. L. Allan Austin. 1977, 33 pp. Austin & Lindberg, Ltd. SR.

Zero-Base Budgeting: What Is It? How Does It Work? ES, Dec. 1979, 16 pp.

Zero-Base Planning & Budgeting. L. Allan Austin, Edward Ritvo. 1978. (Extension Institute Course) By purchase only.

Zero-Based Budgeting: Implications for Social Services. Gerard L. Otten. *Management Principles for Nonprofit Agencies and Organizations*, 1979, pp. 523–534. United Way of the Midlands.

BUSINESS CONDITIONS. See Socio-Economic Conditions

CAREER MANAGEMENT—INDIVIDUAL DEVELOPMENT

The Ambitious Woman's Guide to a Successful Career (rev. ed.). Margaret V. Higginson, Thomas L. Quick. 1980, 276 pp. The Research Institute of America.

Analysis Before Commitment: The Career-Strategy Wheel. Andrew H. Souerwine. MRev., Sept. 1977, pp. 53–60. (Also in reprint collection *Career Strategies: Planning for Personal Achievement*, 1977)

Assertiveness for Career and Personal Success. Robert A. Moskowitz. 1977. (Extension Institute Cassette Program) By purchase only.

Becoming an Information Manager. Morton F. Meltzer. *Information: The Ultimate Management Resource: How to Find, Use and Manage It*, 1981, pp. 121–137. Martin Marietta Corp.

The Boss: Committing Power to Help You Win. Andrew H. Souerwine. MRev., Feb. 1978, pp. 57–65. Univ. of Connecticut. (Also in reprint collection *Career Strategies: Planning for Personal Achievement*, 1977)

Campus to Corporate Careers. Karen Greenberg. AMJ, Summer 1981, pp. 23–24.

The Career Contract: Quid Pro Quo Between You and Your Boss. John J. Leach, William A. Murray. MRev., Oct. 1979, pp. 20–28, 51–52. Univ. of Chicago.

Career Crisis for the High Achiever. Sigmund G. Ginsburg. MRev., Aug. 1977, pp. 57–59. Adelphi Univ.

Career Development: An Integration of Individual and Organizational Needs. John C. Aplin, Darlene K. Gerster. Pers., March–April 1978, pp. 23–29. Indiana Univ.

Career Development Programs. Daniel C. Morgan. Pers., Sept.–Oct. 1977, pp. 23–27. The Fidelity Bank.

Career Development Strategies in Industry—Where Are We and Where Should We Be? Marilyn A. Morgan, Douglas T. Hall, Alison Martier. Pers., March–April 1979, pp. 13–30. Univ. of Pennsylvania, Northwestern Univ.

Career Development: What Organizations Are Doing About It. Albert R. Griffith. Pers., March–April 1980, pp. 63–69. Boston Univ.

Career Development: Whose Responsibility? Robert Barkhaus, Charles Bolyard. AMJ, Summer 1978, pp. 51–55. Indiana Univ., Lincoln National Life Insurance Co.

Career Identity Crisis. Ben S. Graham, Jr. *The Amazing Oversight: Total Participation for Productivity*, 1979, pp. 177–188. The Ben Graham Corp.

Career Life Planning for Americans: Agenda for Organizations and Individuals. Patrick J. Montana, Margaret V. Higginson. 1978, 204 pp.

Career Management: How to Make It Work. Edward O. Joslin. Pers., July–Aug. 1977, pp. 65–72. U.S. Department of Agriculture.

Career Negotiation: Trading Off Employee and Organizational Needs. James F. Wolf, Robert N. Bacher. Pers., March–April 1981, pp. 53–59. Virginia Polytechnic Institute.

Career Planning for the Younger Manager. P. Philip Sidwell. AMJ, Winter 1981, pp. 59–63.

Career Planning: Help Your Organization Grow. Lee R. Ginsburg. SM, June 1977, pp. 9–16. Miller/Ginsburg & Brien.

Career Planning Practices. James W. Walker, Thomas G. Gutteridge. 1979, 40 pp. Arizona State Univ., State Univ. of New York. SR.

Career Planning: Sparks? Yes. Fire? No. Ernest C. Miller. Pers., March–April 1978, pp. 4–9.

Career Planning: Steps You Can Take for Yourself. Lee R. Ginsburg. SM, May 1977, pp. 2–10. Miller/Ginsburg & Brien.

Career Prospects for Managers-to-Be: A Look to the 1980's. Eli Ginzberg. AMJ, Fall 1977, pp. 50–60. Columbia Univ.

Career Satisfaction and Success: How to Know and Manage Your Strengths (rev. ed.). Bernard Haldane. 1981, 210 pp. Univ. of Washington.

Career Strategies: Planning for Personal Achievement. Andrew H. Souerwine. 1978, 292 pp. Univ. of Connecticut. (Also in reprint collection *Career Strategies: Planning for Personal Achievement*, 1977)

Career Strategies: Planning for Personal Achievement. Andrew H. Souerwine. 1977, 63 pp. (A collection of reprints from MRev.)

Career Success. Eugene Emerson Jennings. 1980. (AMACOM audio cassette) By purchase only.

Characteristics of Career Strategy. Andrew H. Souerwine. MRev., July 1977, pp. 55–59. (Also in reprint collection *Career Strategies: Planning for Personal Achievement*, 1977)

Climbing the Corporate Success Ladder: A Self-Marketing Program for Executives. Richard R. Conarroe. MRev., Feb. 1981, pp. 25–28, 42–44. Walden Public Relations, Inc.

Confronting Nonpromotability: How to Manage a Stalled Career. Edward Roseman. 1977, 244 pp. Answers & Insights, Inc.

The Content of Career Strategy. Andrew H. Souerwine. MRev., Aug. 1977, pp. 49–56. (Also in reprint collection *Career Strategies: Planning for Personal Achievement*, 1977)

The Corporate Casino: How Managers Win and Lose at the Biggest Game in Town. Dean P. Peskin. 1978, 243 pp. Joseph George Distributors.

Decades: Lifestyle Changes in Career Expectations. Edith M. Lynch. 1980, 144 pp. American Employers for Free Enterprise.

The Dual Career Couple: Benefits and Pitfalls. Nancy Lee. MRev., Jan. 1981, pp. 46–52. Lee Associates.

Dual Careers—How Do Couples and Companies Cope with the Problems? Francine S. Hall, Douglas T. Hall. OD, Spring 1978, pp. 57–77. Organization Research, Inc., Northwestern Univ.

Enjoy Work? Douglas H. Eads. SM, Sept. 1978, pp. 37–39. M.A. Management.

The Executive Look and How to Get It. Mortimer Levitt. 1979, 76 pp. MB.

The First Job: Making the Transition to Manager. AMJ, Autumn 1978, pp. 54–60.

From Manpower Planning to Human Resources Planning Through Career Development. Lynda L. Moore. Pers., May–June 1979, pp. 9–16.

Getting Started: Problems, Concepts, Action. Andrew H. Souerwine. MRev., Oct. 1977, pp. 59–65. (Also in reprint collection *Career Strategies: Planning for Personal Achievement*, 1977)

How Managers View Promotions. Donald DeSalvia, Gary Gemmill. AMJ, Summer 1977, pp. 40–47. Syracuse Univ.

How to Change Careers. Paula I. Robbins. AMJ, Summer 1980, pp. 46–57. Fitchburg State College.

How to Conquer the Panic of Change. Robert E. Levinson, MRev., July 1977, pp. 20–24.

How to Feather Your Nest When It's Time to Talk Turkey. Robert Jameson Gerberg. AMJ, Winter 1979, pp. 15–20. Performance Dynamics Intl. (Also reprinted in *Making Successful Presentations*, 1981)

How to Get to the Top ... and Stay There. Robert J. McKain. 1981, 210 pp.

How to Make Your First Big Chance Count for More. Robert E. Levinson. AMJ, Winter 1978, pp. 49–57. Steelcraft Manufacturing Co.

How to Succeed in Business and Marriage. Richard W. Ogden. 1978, 161 pp. Seminole Manufacturing Co.

How to Survive and Market Yourself in Management. Andrew Pleninger. 1977, 238 pp. Group V Consultants. (Also AMACOM audio cassette book. By purchase only)

How's Your Managerial Momentum. Rudolf E. Sirny. HSM, Aug. 1981, pp. 7–10. Univ. of Wisconsin.

Human Resources Management. William H. Wagel. Pers., Sept.–Oct. 1977, pp. 40–42.

Implementing a Career Life Planning Program. Patrick J. Montana. Pers., Sept.–Oct. 1979, pp. 66–71.

Interpersonal Relations in Career Strategies. Andrew H. Souerwine. MRev., Jan. 1978, pp. 55–62. (Also in reprint collection *Career Strategies: Planning for Personal Achievement*, 1977)

Invitation to Achievement: Your Career in Management (rev. ed.). Elizabeth Marting. 1981, 52 pp.

The Job: Commitment to Activities. Andrew H. Souerwine. MRev., March 1978, pp. 52–61. (Also in reprint collection *Career Strategies: Planning for Personal Achievement*, 1977)

Learning and Career Strategy. Andrew H. Souerwine. MRev., Dec. 1977, pp. 46–54. (Also in reprint collection *Career Strategies: Planning for Personal Achievement,* 1977)

Make Up Your Mind! The 7 Building Blocks to Better Decisions. John D. Arnold. 1978, 210 pp. Executrak Systems.

Manager to Manager II: What Managers Think of Their Managerial Careers. Robert F. Pearse. 1977, 65 pp. Boston Univ. SR.

Managing Your Career. Brian H. Kleiner. SM, March 1980, pp. 17–21. California State Univ.

The Midcareer Conundrum. Manfred F. R. Kets de Vries. OD, Autumn 1978, pp. 45–62. McGill Univ.

A Model Career Planning Program. Philip G. Benson, George C. Thornton, III. Pers., March–April 1978, pp. 30–39. Colorado State Univ.

More Trouble on the Horizon? William H. Wagel. Pers., March–April 1978, pp. 41–42.

Motivation and Career Strategy: Giving Direction to Commitment. Andrew H. Souerwine. MRev., Nov. 1977, pp. 54–60. (Also in reprint collection *Career Strategies: Planning for Personal Achievement*, 1977)

Moving Up: Women and Leadership. Lois Borland Hart. 1980, 229 pp. Mountain States Employers Council, Inc.

A Mythology of Career. Andrew H. Souerwine. MRev., June 1977, pp. 55–60. (Also in reprint collection *Career Strategies: Planning for Personal Achievement*, 1977)

Organizational Independence: Taking Charge. Bruce D. Sanders. SM, March 1981, pp. 29–33.

Out of the Classrooms and into the ...? William H. Wagel. Pers., March–April 1978, pp. 40–41.

Overcoming Mid & Late Career Crises. Patrick J. Montana. 1978, 43 pp.

Paying Your Dues: How and for How Long? Lois B. Hart, Karen Stolz. MRev., Oct. 1980, pp. 19–24. Leadership Dynamics, United Banks of Colorado.

Periodic Audits Keep Your Career on the Road. Allan D. R. Stern. MRev., Sept. 1979, p. 34. Haskell & Stern Associates.

Picking the Fastest Route to the Top. Karen Greenberg. AMJ, Spring 1978, pp. 58–64.

Planning Job Progression for Effective Career Development and Human Resources Management. Harry L. Wellbank, Douglas T. Hall, Marilyn A. Morgan, W. Clay Hamner. Pers., March–April 1978, pp. 54–64.

The Present Power of Hope. James L. Hayes. MRev., May 1980, pp. 2–3.

Professionalizing the Workforce. Bruce McEwan. AMJ, Winter 1981, pp. 53–58. Hawaii Pacific College.

A Ray of Hope. William H. Wagel. Pers., March–April 1978, pp. 42–43.

Research: The Four Stages of Professional Careers—A New Look at Performance By Professionals. Gene W. Dalton, Paul H. Thompson, Raymond L. Price. OD, Summer 1977, pp. 19–42.

The Results: How Career Planning Pays Off. Andrew H. Souerwine. MRev., April 1978, pp. 56–61. Univ. of Connecticut. (Also in reprint collection *Career Strategies: Planning for Personal Achievement,* 1977)

Satisfaction with Your Job: A Life-Time Concern. Jeffrey L. Jacobs. AMJ, Spring 1977, pp. 44–50. U.S. General Accounting Office.

Self-Assessment and Career Planning: Matching Individual and Organizational Goals. Irving R. Schwartz. Pers., Jan.–Feb. 1979, pp. 47–52.

Self Development. Paul W. Cummings. *Open Management: Guides to Successful Practice,* 1980, pp. 185–198.

Successful Midlife Career Change: Self-Understanding and Strategies for Action. Paula I. Robbins. 1978, 268 pp. Fitchburg State College.

Taking Off for the Top . . . How Much Acceleration for Career Success? Lotte Bailyn. MRev., Jan. 1979, pp. 18–23. Sloan School of Management, Massachusetts Institute of Technology.

Taking the Mystery Out of Career Development. Fazel Mohammed. Pers., March–April 1978, pp. 46–53. Purdue Univ.

Toot Your Own Horn. David K. Lindo. *Supervision Can Be Easy,* 1979, pp. 227–237.

Two Careers—One Marriage. William M. Jones, Ruth A. Jones. 1980, 229 pp. Univ. of Missouri.

Up Is Not the Only Way. Beverly L. Kaye. SM, Feb. 1980, pp. 2–9.

What to Do When Their Skills Aren't Up to Par. *Leadership on the Job: Guides to Good Supervision* (third ed.), 1981, pp. 246–249.

Who Is Responsible for Employee Career Planning? . . . A Personnel Symposium. Pers., March–April 1978, pp. 10–22. (Also in reprint collection *The Human Resources Function: Its Emergence and Character,* 1978)

Why Develop a Career Strategy? Andrew H. Souerwine. MRev., May 1977, pp. 24–28. Univ. of Connecticut. (Also in reprint collection *Career Strategies: Planning for Personal Achievement,* 1977)

Yes, Virginia, There Really Is . . . A Career Development Program That Works. William C. Thomas. MRev., May 1980, pp. 38–40. Univ. of Minnesota.

You Can Be a Winner, Too! Donald R. Dean. SM, Dec. 1978, pp. 31–33.

CAREER MANAGEMENT—JOB SEARCH

Aiming for the "Right" Company: Choosing from Among Job Offers. Thomas J. Kosnik. AMJ, Spring 1979, pp. 44–54.

Career Power! A Manual for Personal Career Advancement. Richard J. Rinella, Claire C. Robbins. 1980, 167 pp. Management Resource Associates.

The Executive's Guide to Finding a Superior Job. William A. Cohen. 1978, 166 pp. Global Associates.

Getting Down to Basics About Landing That Job. William F. Brady. AMJ, Winter 1977, pp. 47–54. Northeastern Univ.

Help Wanted—On How to Find the Right Job. Richard Rinella, Claire Robbins. MRev., May 1981, pp. 34–35. Management Resource Associates.

How to Find a Job When Jobs Are Hard to Find. Donald R. German, Joan W. German. 1981, 242 pp.

How to Look for a Job. Edward L. McClendon. AMJ, Autumn 1978, pp. 48–53. Vesper Hospital of San Leandro.

Job Search: The Complete Manual for Jobseekers. H. Lee Rust. 1979, 258 pp.

Making the Job Connection: Four Steps to Career Power. Richard J. Rinella, Claire C. Robbins. 1981. (AMACOM audio cassette) By purchase only.

A Marketing Approach to the Professional Hiring Process. Gopi R. Jindal, Carl H. Sandberg. AMJ, Winter 1978, pp. 58–64. Comp/Tech Search Corp., Sycor, Inc.

Preparing for a Successful Job Interview. Darlene L. Paris, Milton E. Stinson, Jr. AMJ, Winter 1980, pp. 45–52. ASI Personnel Service.

Preparing for an Entry-Level Position in Personnel. Thomas J. Bergmann, M. John Close. AMJ, Summer 1980, pp. 58–63. Univ. of Minnesota, Univ. of Wisconsin-Eau Claire.

Resume Vibes—Reading Between the Lines. Deslie Beth Lawrence, Iris D. Rosendahl. Pers., March–April 1979, pp. 53–56.

Sacked! What to Do When You Lose Your Job. Dean B. Peskin. 1979, 177 pp. Joseph George Distributors.

Want a Job? Get Some Experience. Want Experience? Get a Job. Don Berliner. 1978, 184 pp.

Writing a Skills Résumé—Translating Nonwork Experience into Highly Marketable Skills. Michele Stimac. AMJ, Summer 1977, pp. 52–64. Pepperdine Univ.

CASH MANAGEMENT. See also Financial Management

Cash Management: Principles and Practices for the 80s. Paul J. Beehler. 1980, 67 pp. Wells Fargo Bank. MB.

Computing Cash Flows to Evaluate Capital Investment Decisions. Robert E. Pritchard, Thomas J. Hindelang. The Strategic Evaluation and Management of Capital Expenditures, 1981, pp. 55–68. Glassboro State College, Drexel Univ.

Corporate Cash Management (Including Electronic Funds Transfer). Alfred L. Hunt. 1978, 232 pp.

Evaluatig Customer Profitability: Key to Effective Cash Flow Management. Michael Schiff. MRev., Oct. 1981, pp. 18–20. New York Univ.

Managing Cash Flow. Kenneth M. Lizotte. 1978. (Extension Institute Cassette Program) By purchase only.

Managing Corporate Cash (sec. ed.). Joseph E. Finnerty. 1980. (Extension Institute Course) By purchase only.

Planning Cash Flow (third ed.). Leslie P. Anderson, John Heptonstall, Joseph E. Finnerty. 1980. (Extension Institute Course) By purchase only.

Problem: What Do We Do with All That Cash. Gary B. Rappaport, Frank D. Trestman. MRev., May 1981, pp. 32–33. Napco Industries Inc.

A Second Look at Corporate Cash Management. G. M. Dobson. MRev., Aug. 1977, pp. 33–35. Warner-Lambert Co.

Understanding Cash Flow Planning. ES, June 1980 16 pp.

CHANGE. See Also Organizational Development

Applications. Beverly A. Potter. Turning Around: The Behavioral Approach to Managing People, 1980, pp. 220–249.

Building Profits Through Organizational Change. Roger J. Howe. 1981, 264 pp. Donaldson Co., Inc.

Conversation with Chris Argyris. William Dowling (editor). Effective Management and the Behavioral Sciences, 1978, pp. 75–97.

Deliberate Methods Change: Its Concepts and Application. Arthur Spinanger. The Amazing Oversight: Total Participation for Productivity, 1979, pp. 155–166. Spinanger Methods.

The Effect of Continuing Technological Change on Corporate Organization and Management. Harold Smiddy. The Evolving Science of Management, 1979, pp. 229–246.

An Empirical Approach to Change. Howard L. Smith. SM, Jan. 1979, pp. 2–8. San Diego State Univ.

Employee Resistance to Change. Laird W. Mealiea. SM, Jan. 1978, pp. 16–22.

How to Handle Change. William F. Christopher. Management for the 1980's (rev. ed.—former title: The Achieving Enterprise), 1980, pp. 130–150.

How to Overcome Organizational Resistance to Change. Irving G. Calish, R. Donald Gamache. MRev., Oct. 1981, pp. 21–28. Innotech Corp.

Human Energy for Innovation. Glenn R. Cowan. *The Amazing Oversight: Total Participation for Productivity*, 1979, pp. 127–138. SUNY.

Making Change Productive: Do You Optimize or Compromise? James J. Cribbin. *Leadership: Stragegies for Organizational Effectiveness*, 1981, pp. 190–205. St. John's Univ.

Making Waves: Change Management that Works. Gerald L. Arffa. SM, June 1981, pp. 19–24. Purdue Univ.

Managing Change in Organizations. Robert A. Cooke. *Management Principles for Nonprofit Agencies and Organizations*, 1979, pp. 154–209. Univ. of Michigan.

That's Okay in Theory, But . . . Ronald H. Gorman, Kent Baker. Pers., July–Aug. 1978, pp. 48–54. American Univ.

CHARTS AND GRAPHS. See also Reports

The Business of People. Linda A. Roxe. *Personnel Management for the Smaller Company*, 1979, pp. 1–15. Rox Associates.

How to Organize the EDP Department. Michael R. Frank. 1980, 47 pp. MB.

Management, Governance & Leadership: A Guide for College and University Administrators. John D. Millett, 1980, 208 pp. Academy for Educational Development.

The Master Gantt Chart. Lois B. Hart, J. Gordon Schleicher. *A Conference and Workshop Planner's Manual*, 1979, pp. 11–19. Organizational Leadership, Inc., Michigan Department of Social Services.

Organising for International Operations. Derek F. Channon with Michael Jalland. *Multinational Strategic Planning*, 1978, pp. 22–50. Manchester Business School.

Product Service Planning: Service-Marketing-Engineering Interactions. William H. Bleuel, Henry Bender. 1980, 84 pp. AM International. RS.

Production Planning. Darryl J. Ellis, Peter P. Pekar, Jr. *Planning for Nonplanners: Planning Basics for Managers*, 1980, pp. 66–69. Resource Technology Development Corp., Michael Allen Co.

The Properties of MMP. Lawrence A. Appley, Keith L. Irons. *Manager Manpower Planning: A Professional Management System*, 1981, pp. 75–90.

Q-Charts: How to Give New Perspective to the Organizational Picture. Ronald Fraser. MRev., Dec. 1979, pp. 28, 38, 39. Appalachian Regional Commission.

Sample Organization Charts. Joseph J. Famularo. *Organization Planning Manual* (rev. ed.), 1979, pp. 17–183. McGraw-Hill, Inc.

COACHING AND COUNSELING. See also Performance Appraisal

Clergy as Counselors. J. H. Foegen. Pers., July–Aug. 1979, pp. 70–78. Winona State Univ.

Coaching: A New Look at an Old Responsibility. Will Lorey. SM, May 1977, pp. 26–31. The Drawing Board.

Coaching and Counseling. James F. Evered. *Shirt-Sleeves Management*, 1981, pp. 95–106. Redman Industries, Inc.

Coaching and Development Opportunities. Paul E. Illman. *Developing Overseas Managers—and Managers Overseas*, 1980, pp. 239–262. Management Training, Inc.

Coaching the Troubled Employee. Terry L. Smith. SM, Dec. 1981, pp. 33–36. City of Tacoma, Washington.

Counseling: Helpful Understanding. Ray A. Killian. *Managers Must Lead!* (rev. ed.), 1979, pp. 165–172. Belk Stores.

Counseling Leavers. Edward Roseman. *Managing Employee Turnover: A Positive Approach*, 1981, pp. 197–204. Answers & Insights, Inc.

Curbside Conferences. John Fenton. *The A to Z of Sales Management*, 1979, pp. 19–23. Sales Augmentation International Group.

Employee Counseling. Louis V. Imundo. *The Effective Supervisor's Handbook*, 1980, pp. 203–217. Management Perspectives.

Employee Counseling Services. Hermine Zagat Levine. Pers., March–April 1981, pp. 4–11.

The Leader as Counselor. Lois Borland Hart. *Moving Up: Women and Leadership*, 1980, pp. 108–124. Mountain States Employers Council, Inc.

The Manager as Coach. Margaret V. Higginson, Thomas L. Quick. *Leadership on the Job: Guides to Good Supervision* (third ed.), 1981, pp. 124–126. Research Institute of America. (From *The Ambitious Woman's Guide to a Successful Career*, 1980)

Preventive Measures Against Marginal Performance. Charles D. Lein. *Leadership on the Job: Guides to Good Supervision* (third ed.), 1981, pp. 239–245. Weber State College.

Ten Basic Counseling Skills. Richard J. Walsh. SM, July 1977, pp. 2–9.

Why Won't They Accept Help from Supervisors? Kent Baker, Ronald H. Gorman. SM, March 1978, pp. 16–22. American Univ. (Also reprinted in HSM, Sept. 1980)

COLLECTIVE BARGAINING

Bargaining Units. John G. Kilgour. *Preventive Labor Relations*, 1981, pp. 60–88. California State Univ.

Collective Bargaining: When Is a Supervisor a Manager? George Munchus III. HSM, Oct. 1980, pp. 1–3. Univ. of Alabama.

Conflict Resolution—or Agreement Making? . . . An Interview with Theodore Kheel. Deslie Beth Lawrence. Pers., July–Aug. 1979, pp. 28–37.

"Good Faith" Bargaining: What Does It Mean? Kenneth A. Kovach. SM, Oct. 1979, pp. 18–22. George Mason Univ.

How to Calculate the Manufacturer's Costs in Collective Bargaining. Frederick L. Sullivan. 1980, 68 pp. Sullivan & Hayes. MB.

Management's Rights in Labor Relations. Norman Metzger. HSM, Nov. 1978, pp. 1–4. The Mount Sinai Medical Center.

COLLEGE GRADUATES. See Recruitment—College

COMMITTEES. See also Quality Circles

Appendix II. Vijay Sathe. *Controllership in Divisionalized Firms: Structure, Evaluation and Development*, 1978, pp. 43–45. MB.

Audit Committee Interface with the Internal Auditor. National Association of Corporate Directors, Institute of Internal Auditors. 1979, 154 pp.

Audit Committee Interface with the Internal Auditor. National Association of Corporate Directors, Institute of Internal Auditors. 1980, 150 pp.

Board Committee Trends. Robert W. Lear. DM, July 1981, pp. 1–3. Columbia Graduate Business School.

Board Compensation Committees at Work: A Compensation Review Symposium. CR, Second Quarter 1978, pp. 24–33. (Also in reprint collection *The Human Resources Function: Its Emergence and Character*, 1978)

Bringing Out the Best in Committee Members. J. W. Gilsdorf, M. H. Rader. SM, Nov. 1981, pp. 6–11. Arizona State Univ.

The Chief Executive Officer and the Nominating Committee. J. Robert Harman, Jr. DM, April 1981, pp. 1–3. Booz, Allen & Hamilton, Inc.

Committees of the Board. *The Corporate Directorship Report*, pp. 104–119. Executive Compensation Service. By purchase only.

The Compensation Director and the Board's Compensation Committee. Frederic W. Cook. CR, Second Quarter 1981, pp. 37–41. Frederic W. Cook & Co., Inc.

Coordinating Package Development Activities. Edmund A. Leonard. *Managing the Packaging Side of the Business*, 1977, pp. 46–50. General Foods Corp. MB.

Evaluation Committees. Stanley B. Henrici. *Salary Management for the Nonspecialist*, 1980, pp. 58–59.

Eyes on the Audit Committee. Thomas W. McMahon, Jr. BPM 3, June 1979, 5 pp. Interracial Conference for Business Opportunity.

Internal Consulting Groups: Catalysts for Organizational Change. Jay Spechler, John

Wicker. MRev., Nov. 1980, pp. 24–28, 37–41. Florida Power & Light Co., Theodore Barry & Associates.

Management Committees. Joseph J. Famularo. *Organization Planning Manual* (rev. ed.), 1979, pp. 276–280, 338–343. McGraw-Hill, Inc.

Position Description for a Board of Directors. J. Keith Louden. *Managing at the Top*, 1977, pp. 146–159. Corporate Director, Inc.

The Review Board. Lawrence A. Appley, Keith L. Irons. *Manager Manpower Planning: A Professional Management System*, 1981, pp. 61–74.

Role of the Audit Committee: Update and Implementation. Lawrence J. Trautman, James H. Hammond, Jr. BPM 13, Nov. 1980, 10 pp. OZMA Corp., Peat Marwick, Mitchell & Co.

Security Committee. Leonard I. Krauss. *Safe: Security Audit & Field Evaluation for Computer Facilities and Information Systems* (rev. ed.), 1980, pp. 10–11.

The Strategic Planning Committee: Focus on the Future. Lawrence J. Trautman. DM, Sept. 1980, pp. 2–5.

The Value of a Compensation Committee. MRev., Dec. 1978, p. 31.

COMMUNICATIONS—EMPLOYEE-MANAGEMENT. See also Meetings

The Abuse of "Cooling Out": Recognition and Prevention. Norma L. Chaska. HSM, Jan. 1980, pp. 5, 9. Univ. of Illinois.

Achieving Cooperation and Mutual Understanding. Ernest C. Miller. Pers., Sept.–Oct. 1977, pp. 4–7, 10–11.

Are You a Closet Sexist? Christine B. Stiegler. SM, May 1979, pp. 38–41. Northern Kentucky Univ.

The Art of Filtering. W. A. Delaney. SM, July 1979, pp. 9–12. Analysis & Computer Systems, Inc.

Becoming an Effective Listener. Marion E. Haynes. SM, Aug. 1979, pp. 21–28.

The Believable Corporation. Roger M. D'Aprix. 1977, 211 p.

Better Communication for Managers. Sally Bulkley Pancrazio, James J. Pancrazio. SM, June 1981, pp. 31–37. Illinois State Board of Education, Sangamon State Univ.

Chances Are You're Not Communicating. Wayne Sanders. SM, Oct. 1979, pp. 33–35. Sanders Associates, Inc. (Also in reprint collection *Effective Communication on the Job* (third ed.), 1981)

Communicating Expectations. V. Clayton Sherman. HSM, July 1979, pp. 7–8. Mark Silber Associates.

Communicating for Improved Motivation and Performance. Larry E. Penley, Brian L. Hawkins. *Making Successful Presentations*, 1981, pp. 226–230. Univ. of Texas.

Communicating for Productivity. Lawrence A. Appley, Gabriel Stillian, 1981. (An AMA multimedia program) By purchase only.

Communicating Up and Down and All Around. Lois Borland Hart. *Moving Up: Women and Leadership*, 1980, pp. 23–59. Mountain States Employers Council, Inc.

Communicating with Impact: Do You Build Bridges or Chasms? James J. Cribbin. *Leadership: Strategies for Organizational Effectiveness*, 1981, pp. 173–189. St. John's Univ.

Communication and Managerial Functions. Gerard P. Boe. HSM, Jan. 1977, pp. 8–10. Eisenhower Army Medical Center.

Communication Barriers: Individual Quirks and Corporate Personalities. Joseph A. Rice, John B. Colby. *Effective Communication on the Job* (third ed.), 1981, pp. 19–26. Univ. of Houston, Exxon Production Research.

Communication in the Organization. Lois B. Hart. *Effective Communication on the Job* (third ed.), 1981, pp. 85–95. Leadership Dynamics. (From *Moving Up: Women and Leadership*, 1980)

The Communication Matrix: Ways of Winning with Words. Georgette F. McGregor, Joseph A. Robinson. 1981, 230 pp. Joseph A. Robinson Associates.

Communication . . . or Getting Ideas Across. J. Thomas Miller, III. AMJ, Summer 1980, pp. 32–38. Leadership Seminars Associates. (Also in reprint collection *Leadership on the Job: Guides to Good Supervision* (third ed.), 1981)

Communication Problems on the Job. Marion E. Haynes. HSM, March 1980, pp. 1–3, 10. Shell Oil Co.

Communication Skills for Managers (sec. ed.). Brook Taliaferro. 1980. (Extension Institute Course) By purchase only.

Communication Skills for Secretaries. Kathleen J. Hansell. 1981. (Extension Institute Cassette Program) By purchase only.

Communications. Lawrence B. Sawyer. *The Manager and the Modern Internal Auditor: A Problem-Solving Partnership*, 1979, pp. 161–186.

Communications—The Art of Getting Through to People. John D. Drake. *Corporate Planning Techniques and Applications*, 1979, pp. 359–369. Drake-Beam & Associates.

Controlling the Syncophant: Policies and Techniques of Corporation Presidents. Robert P. Newman, Lyle Sussman. AMJ, Autumn 1978, pp. 14–21. Univ. of Pittsburgh.

Create a Communication Climate. Lena Seidel. HSM, Dec. 1977, pp. 5–6. Wausau Hospitals.

Develop Communication Skills. David K. Lindo. *Supervision Can Be Easy*, 1979, pp. 35–83.

Effective Communication on the Job (third ed.). William Fallon (editor). 1981, 328 pp. (A collection of reprints from AMACOM publications)

Employee Communications. Gerald J. Voros, Paul Alvarez (editors). *What Happens in Public Relations*, 1981, pp. 83–94. Ketchum MacLeod & Grove.

Face-to-Face Communication. Paul W. Cummings. *Open Management: Guides to Successful Practice*, 1980, pp. 17–31.

Feedback on Feedback. Philip L. Quaglieri. SM, Jan. 1980, pp. 34–38. Univ. of New Brunswick. (Also in reprint collection *Effective Communication on the Job*, 1981)

Freedom of Speech in Office and Shop . . . How to Gain from Give-and-Take Sessions with Employees. Robert J. Dulsky. MRev., Aug. 1979, pp. 32–33. Tax Corp. of America.

Get Things Done by Improving Your Communication Skills. Mark B. Silber. HSM, Oct. 1977, pp. 6–7. Hume, Mansfield, Silber, Ltd.

Getting the Word to the Top. John B. McMaster. MRev., Feb. 1979, pp. 62–65.

The Give and Take of Communication. Marion M. Wood. *Effective Communication on the Job* (third ed.), 1981, pp. 1–7. Univ. of Southern California, Los Angeles.

Giving Effective Directions. SS, Oct. 1981, 24 pp.

How Do You Rate as a Listener? Jean W. Wining, Augusta C. Yrle. SM, Jan. 1980, pp. 22–25. Univ. of New Orleans. (Also in reprint collection *Effective Communication on the Job* (third ed.), 1981)

How to Communicate in the Business Organization. ES, Sept. 1981, 16 pp.

How to Communicate in the Tongue-Tied Organization. Edward J. Giblin. MRev., Oct. 1978, pp. 69–73.

How to Improve Your Managerial Communications. James L. Hayes. 1980. (An AMA multimedia program) By purchase only.

How to Inspire Your Subordinates. Thomas L. Quick. 1981. (AMACOM audio cassette book) By purchase only.

How to Plan Your Communications. David Emery. *Effective Communication on the Job* (third ed.), 1981, pp. 29–33.

'Impractical' Education Produces Vital Corporate Skills. Philip Lesly. MRev., Sept. 1979, p. 33.

Improving Communications with Employees, Peers, and Superiors. Louis V. Imundo. *The Effective Supervisor's Handbook*, 1980, pp. 72–93. Management Perspectives.

Improving Managerial Productivity: The Key Ingredient Is One-on-One Communication. Gerard Tavernier. MRev., Feb. 1981, pp. 12–16.

Increasing Human Potential Through Communicative Effectiveness. J. Duane Hoover. SM, Oct. 1977, pp. 8–15.

Issues in Upward Communication. Russel W. Driver. SM, Feb. 1980, pp. 10–13. Univ. of Oklahoma.

Let's Talk: Breaking Down Barriers to Effective Communication. Edward Levine. SM, June 1980, pp. 2–12. Univ. of South Florida. (Also in reprint collection *Let's Talk: The*

Art of One-to-One Communication, 1981)

Let's Talk: Communicating with the New Worker. Edward L. Levine. SM, Aug. 1980, pp. 12–23. Univ. of South Florida. (Also in reprint collection *Let's Talk: The Art of One-to-One Communication*, 1981)

Let's Talk: Effectively Communicating Praise. Edward L. Levine. SM, Sept. 1980, pp. 17–25. Univ. of South Florida. (Also in reprint collection *Let's Talk: The Art of One-to-One Communication*, 1981)

Let's Talk: The Art of One-to-One Communication. Edward L. Levine. 1981, 79 pp. Univ. of South Florida. (A collection of reprints from SM)

Let's Talk: Tools for Spotting and Correcting Communication Problems. Edward L. Levine. SM, July 1980, pp. 25–37. Univ. of South Florida. (Also in HSM March 1981 and reprint collections *Effective Communication on the Job* (third ed.), 1981; *Let's Talk: The Art of One-to-One Communication*, 1981)

Let's Talk: Understanding One-to-One Communication. Edward L. Levine. SM, May 1980, pp. 6–12. Univ. of South Florida. (Also in reprint collections *Let's Talk: The Art of One-to-One Communication*, 1981, and *Leadership on the Job: Guides to Good Supervision* (third ed.), 1981)

Listen and Be Listened To. George R. Bell, 1981. (Extension Institute Cassette Program) By purchase only.

Listening Made Easy: How to Improve Listening on the Job, at Home, and in the Community. Robert L. Montgomery. 1981, 134 pp. R. L. Montgomery & Associates

Listening: The Quiet Side of Communicating. ES, April 1980, 16 pp.

Listening to Help the Hostile Employee. Jon T. Powell. SM, Nov. 1981, pp. 2–5. Northern Illinois Univ.

Management Guidelines: Being a Good Communicator. George Miller. SM, April 1981, pp. 20–26. George Miller Associates

Managing Authority: How to Give Directions. Beverly A. Potter. *Turning Around: The Behavioral Approach to Managing People*, 1980, pp. 143–159.

Mastering the Techniques of Two-Way Communication. Philip Lesly. SM, Nov. 1979, pp. 2–6. The Philip Lesly Co. (Also in HSM Oct. 1980 and reprint collection *Effective Communication on the Job* (third ed.), 1981)

On-the-Job Communication: Why Isn't It Easier? Leonard Sayles. *Leadership on the Job: Guides to Good Supervision* (third ed.), 1981, pp. 73–80. Columbia Univ.

Open Communication: The Key to Self-Actualization and Success. J. F. Ponthieu. July 1977, pp. 8–9. Texas Tech Univ.

Opening the Channels of Upward Communication. Russel W. Driver. SM, March 1980, pp. 24–29. Univ. of Oklahoma. (Also in reprint collection *Effective Communication on the Job* (third ed.), 1981)

Postscript: The Basics of Effective Communication. Prepared by the staff of AMA Executive Communications Course. *Effective Communication on the Job* (third ed.), 1981, pp. 315–318.

Recognizing—and Overcoming—Defensive Communication. Robert F. DeGise. SM, March 1977, pp. 31–38.

Surviving and Succeeding in the 'Political' Organization: Communication Skills are Critical. Alan Jay Weiss. SM, June 1978, pp. 16–24. Kepner-Tregoe, Inc. (Also in reprint collections *Surviving and Succeeding in the 'Political' Organization*, 1978, and *Effective Communication on the Job* (third ed.), 1981)

Synergistic Management: Creating the Climate for Superior Performance. Michael Doctoroff. 1977, 159 pp. Balzer's High Vacuum Corp.

Using Employee Communications to Support Corporate Objectives. Gerard Tavernier. MRev., Nov. 1980, pp. 8–13.

The Way We Word. Paul R. Timm. SM, May 1978, pp. 20–26. Univ. of North Carolina. (Also in reprint collection *Effective Communication on the Job* (third ed.), 1981)

When Productivity Lags, Check at the Top: Are Key Managers Really Communicating? Steward L. Tubbs, Robin N. Widgery. MRev., Nov. 1978, pp. 20–26. General Motors Institute.

Why Don't They Understand? Philip Lesly. *Effective Communication on the Job* (third ed.), 1981, pp. 11–18. Philip Lesly Co. (From *How We Discommunicate*, 1979)

COMMUNICATIONS—GRAVEVINE
Cut Those Rumors Down to Size. Keith Davis. *Leadership on the Job: Guides to Good Supervision* (third ed.), 1982, pp. 95–100. Arizona State Univ.
Rumor Must Be Reckoned With. Juliet M. Halford. *Effective Communication on the Job (third ed.)*, 1981, pp. 131–138.

COMMUNICATIONS—SPEAKING SKILLS
The Business of Speaking. Allen Weiss. *Write What You Mean*, 1977, pp. 160–168.
Corporate Speech Making: It's Not Like Selling Soap. Norman Wasserman. MRev., Nov. 1979, pp. 25–28. Ruder & Finn, Inc. (Also in reprint collection *Effective Communication on the Job* (third ed.), 1981)
Developing an Effective Voice. Ken Cooper. *Nonverbal Communication for Business Success*, 1979, pp. 162–178. KCA Associates.
Face-to-Face Communication: Breaking Down the Barriers. Robert Schachat, Joel Anastasi. SM, April 1979, pp. 8–14. Schachat/Anastasi Associates, Inc./Organization Renewal, The Gordon Lippitt Consulting Group. (Also in reprint collection *Effective Communication on the Job* (third ed.), 1981)
How to Be a Successful Public Speaker. Kathryn Cason, Shirley Cunningham. 1980. (Extension Institute Cassette Program) By purchase only.
How to Minimize Stage Fright and Make a Better Impression. W. James Hermann. MRev., March 1978, p. 35. Memorial Hospital Assn. of Stanislaus County, California.
Making Successful Presentations. George T. Vardaman. 1981, 271 pp. Univ. of Denver.
Seven Steps to Clear Instructions. William Lefsky. HSM, May 1981, pp. 9–10. Abraham & Straus.
Speaking of Speaking. James L. Hayes. MRev., Sept. 1981, pp. 2–3.
Speaking with Authority: How to Give Directions. Beverly A. Potter. SM, March 1980, pp. 2–11. (Also in reprint collection *Leadership on the Job: Guides to Good Supervision* (third ed.), 1981)
Speech for the Speechless. John Connelian. HSM, Feb. 1981, pp. 7–10. The Executive Technique.
Unaccustomed as You Are . . . Granville B. Jacobs. *Leadership on be Job: Guides to Good Supervision* (third ed.), 1981, pp. 88–94.
When the Planner Speaks, Does Management Really Listen? Arnold Brown. MRev., Nov. 1978, pp. 58–61. Weiner-Edrich-Brown, Inc.

COMMUNICATIONS—TELECOMMUNICATIONS
Communications in the 21st Century: In Defense of Media Events. Elihu Katz, Daniel Dayan, Pierre Motyl. OD, Autumn 1981, pp. 68–80. Hebrew Univ.
Communications in the 21st Century: Telecommunications and Business Policy. Peter G. W. Keen. OD, Autumn 1981, pp. 54–67. M.I.T.
Energy Crisis in the Executive Suite. R. Alec Mackenzie, Gary Richards. SM, Oct. 1978, pp. 17–26. R. Alec Mackenzie & Associates.
How to Survive in the Age of "Telecommuting." Norman Macrae. MRev., Nov. 1978, pp. 14–19. The Economist.
On Television! A Survival Guide for Media Interviews. Jack Hilton, Mary Knoblauch. 1980, 185 pp. Jack Hilton, Inc., Chicago Tribune.
Telephone Know-How. Elizabeth Marting. 1980. (AMACOM audio cassette) By purchase only.
The Telephone: The Most Misused Tool in American Business. Judith Hoy. SM, Aug. 1981, pp. 30–34.
The Use and Abuse of the Telephone. SS, Aug. 1981, 24 pp.
You're on Camera. Philip Lesly. *How We Discommunicate*, 1979, pp. 157–166. Philip Lesly Co.

COMMUNICATIONS—TRANSACTIONAL ANALYSIS

How to Change a Leadership Pattern. Heinz Weihrich. MRev., April 1979, pp. 26–28, 37–40. Arizona State Univ. (Also in reprint collection *Leadership on the Job: Guides to Good Supervision* (third ed.), 1981)

How to Use TA on the Job. ES, August 1979, 16 pp.

Nonverbal Communication. Michael Doctoroff. *Synergistic Management: Creating the Climate for Superior Performance*, 1977, pp. 137–154. Balzers High Vacuum Corp.

Nonverbal Communication and Business. Ken Cooper. *Effective Communication on the Job* (third ed.), 1981, pp. 141–149. KCA Associates. (From *Nonverbal Communication for Business Success*, 1979)

Successful Team Building Through TA. Dudley Bennet. 1980, 260 pp. MCM Consultants, Inc.

The TA Approach to Employee Development. Laird W. Mealiea. SM, Aug. 1977, pp. 11–19. Dalhousie Univ.

The TA Way to Stay on Top of Time. Maurice F. Villere, Michael Leboeuf. SM, Feb. 1977, pp. 9–15. Univ. of New Orleans.

Time Structuring and the Games People Play. ES, Feb. 1981, 16 pp.

Transactional Analysis Aids Administrators. Rita E. Numerof. HSM, Oct. 1977, pp. 8–10.

Using TA for Better Staff-Patient Relations. Beth Wells. HSM, June 1979, pp. 8–9. Bellevue Hospital.

Using TA in Career Planning: How Not to Fall into the Parent-Child Trap. Arthur M. Cohen. SM, Feb. 1979, pp. 2–9. Institute for Organization Development.

COMMUNICATIONS—WRITING

Abraham Lincoln: The Writer. Clifford D. Owsley. *Making Successful Presentations*, 1981, pp. 221–226. The U.S. Forest Service.

The Believable House Organ. Roger M. D'Aprix. MRev., Feb. 1979, pp. 23–28. Xerox Corp.

Better Business Writing: The Audience Comes First. Allen Weiss. SM, April 1977, pp. 2–11. (Also in reprint collection *Write What You Mean: Practical Guidelines for Better Business Writing*, 1978)

Better Business Writing: What's Your Communications "IQ"? Robert R. Max. SM, April 1977, pp. 12–15.

Beyond Mastery and Style. Allen Weiss. SM, Jan. 1978, pp. 29–34. (Also in reprint collection *Write What You Mean: Practical Guidelines for Better Business Writing*, 1978)

The Blank Page: Don't Let It Keep You from Sharing Your Good Ideas. William Repp. SM, Oct. 1978, pp. 28–33. National Technical Institute for the Deaf.

Breaking the Memo-Writing Habit. Arthur G. Sharp. AMJ, Summer 1977, pp. 48–51. Travelers Insurance Co.

Business Writing Quick & Easy. Laura Brill. 1981, 185 pp.

Choosing the Best Medium for the Message. Allen Weiss. SM, May 1977, pp. 16–24. (Also in reprint collection *Write What You Mean: Practical Guidelines for Better Business Writing*, 1978)

Collecting and Organizing Research Materials. Allen Weiss. SM, June 1977, pp. 18–27. (Also in reprint collection *Write What You Mean: Practical Guidelines for Better Business Writing*, 1978)

A Communications Manual for Nonprofit Organizations. Lucille A. Maddalena. 1981, 222 pp. Fairleigh Dickinson Univ.

Controlling Written Communications. George T. Vardaman. *Making Successful Presentations*, 1981, pp. 249–256. Univ. of Denver.

Debt Collection Letters in Ten Languages: With Notes on Terminology, Practice and Methods of Payment in Different Countries. John Butterworth. 1978, unpaged.

Developing a Meeting Memo. Tom Adams. SM, July 1980, pp. 39–42. Health & Welfare Agency, State of California. (Also in reprint collection *Effective Communication on the Job* (third ed.), 1981)

Developing Your Topic with Sentence and Paragraph. Allen Weiss. SM, Sept. 1977, pp. 25–32. (Also in reprint collection *Write What You Mean: Practical Guidelines for Better Business Writing*, 1978)

Fear of the Blank Page . . . And How to Overcome It. Allen Weiss. AMJ, Autumn 1978, pp. 22–29. Montclair Business Writing Consultants. (Also in reprint collection *Effective Communication on the Job* (third ed.), 1981)

Fighting Business Gobbledygook: How to Say It in Plain English. Alan Siegel. MRev., Nov. 1979, pp. 14–19. Siegel & Gale, Inc. (Also in reprint collection *Effective Communication on the Job* (third ed.), 1981)

Follow the Rules—Most of the Time. Allen Weiss. SM, Nov. 1977, pp. 22–29. (Also in reprint collection *Write What You Mean: Practical Guidelines for Better Business Writing*, 1978)

Helping Someone Else Write More Effectively. Judith Stein, Marya Holcombe. SM, Nov. 1980, pp. 2–9. Yale School of Organization & Management.

How to Get Published in Business/Professional Journals. Joel J. Shulman. 1980, 258 pp. Paperboard Packaging Magazine.

How to Say What You Mean. 1977. (Self-contained programmed instruction homestudy course) By purchase only.

How to Write a Better Memo. George T. Tade. HSM, Oct. 1981, pp. 9–10. Texas Christian Univ.

How to Write Better Letters. James Menzies Black. *Effective Communication on the Job* (third ed.), 1981, pp. 256–263. National Metal Trades Assn.

How to Write Letters and Memos That Get Results. ES, Oct. 1978, 16 pp.

How to Write Reports. ES, Feb. 1979, 16 pp.

How to Write Technical Reports. Thomas L. Warren. 1981. (Extension Institute Course) By purchase only.

How to Write Winning Reports. Leo P. Hardwick. 1981. (Extension Institute Course) By purchase only.

How We Discommunicate. Philip Lesly. 1979, 227 pp. The Philip Lesly Co.

Johnny, the Grad You Hired Last Week, Can't Write. Joseph A. Rice. *Effective Communication on the Job* (third ed.), 1981, pp. 207–216. Univ. of Houston.

Making Successful Presentations. George T. Vardaman. 1981, 271 pp. Univ. of Denver.

Memos That Get Things Moving. Harold K. Mintz. *Effective Communication on the Job* (third ed.), 1981, pp. 264–272. Honeywell Information Systems.

More About Paragraphs: The Orchestration of Elements. Allen Weiss. SM, Oct. 1977, pp. 22–28. (Also in reprint collection *Write What You Mean: Practical Guidelines for Better Business Writing*, 1978)

Outlining: An Indispensable Tool for the Business Writer. Allen Weiss. SM, July 1977, pp. 18–25. (Also in reprint collection *Write What You Mean: Practical Guidelines for Better Business Writing*, 1978)

Playing a Solo on a House Organ. Roger M. D'Aprix. *The Believable Corporation*, 1977, pp. 94–124.

The Proposal Game. Herman Holtz. *The $100 Billion Market: How to Do Business with the Government*, 1980, pp. 130–178.

Sentence Control: Solving an Old Problem. Paul Richards. SM, May 1980, pp. 37–43. (Also in reprint collection *Effective Communication on the Job* (third ed.), 1981)

A Systems Approach to Business Writing. Robert F. DeGise. SM, Oct. 1979, pp. 24–28. Caterpillar Tractor Co. (Also in reprint collection *Effective Communication on the Job* (third ed.), 1981)

Targeting Your Vocabulary. Allen Weiss. SM, Dec. 1977, pp. 22–30. (Also in reprint collection *Write What You Mean: Practical Guidelines for Better Business Writing*, 1978, and *Effective Communication on the Job* (third ed.), 1981)

Transitions: The Gates and Bridges of a Writer's Journey. Allen Weiss. SM, Aug. 1977, pp. 20–27. (Also in reprint collection *Write What You Mean: Practical Guidelines for Better Business Writing*, 1978)

Wanted: Effective Communicators. Lawrence A. Dysart. *Making Successful Presentations*, 1981, pp. 162–163. Richfield Oil Corp.

Write Clear Reports: A "Readability" Index. Dan H. Swenson. SM, Sept. 1980, pp. 27–33. Western Michigan Univ. (Also in reprint collection *Effective Communication on the Job* (third ed.), 1981)

Write to Be Seen. Norma Mortimer. SM, March 1979, pp. 19–22. Blue Cross of New Jersey.

Write What You Mean: A Handbook of Business Communication. Allen Weiss. 1977, 179 pp.

Write What You Mean: Practical Guidelines for Better Business Writing. Allen Weiss. 1978, 88 pp. (A collection of reprints from SM)

Writing: Don't Let the Mechanics Obscure the Message. Robert F. DeGise. *Effective Communication on the Job* (third ed.), 1981, pp. 251–255. Caterpillar Tractor Co.

Writing for Management Success (sec. ed.). Daphne Jameson. 1981. (Extension Institute Course) By purchase only.

The Writing Process: Step by Step. Susan Z. Diamond. *Preparing Administrative Manuals*, 1981, pp. 57–71. Diamond Associates.

Writing Reports that Work (rev. ed.) (PRIME 100). 1980. (An AMACOM Skill Series home-study course) By purchase only.

Writing Sense. Allen Weiss. 1980. (AMACOM audio cassette) By purchase only.

COMMUNITY RELATIONS. See also Social Responsibilities

Community Relations. Gerald J. Voros, Paul Alvarez (editors). *What Happens in Public Relations*, 1981, pp. 111–122. Ketchum MacLeod & Grove.

Holistic Care for the 60+: Volunteers and a Community Make It Happen. Patricia A. Winans. HSM, Jan. 1981, pp. 5–6, 11. St. Lawrence Hospital.

A Strategy for Corporate Giving and Community Involvement. Frank Koch. MRev., Dec. 1977, pp. 7–13. Syntex Corp.

COMPANY IMAGE

Corporate Communications—A Comprehensive View. Marvin L. Krasnansky. *Investor Relations That Work*, 1980, pp. 179–193. Becton Dickinson & Co.

Corporate Identity and Graphics. Gerald J. Voros, Paul Alvarez (editors). *What Happens in Public Relations*, 1981, pp. 210–215. Ketchum MacLeod & Grove.

Corporate Image and the P/E Ratio: They Often Go Hand in Hand. Walter P. Margulies. MRev., Oct. 1979, pp. 16–19. Lippincott & Margulies, Inc.

IC Industries, Inc. Frank J. Allston. *Investor Relations That Work*, 1980, pp. 135–178. IC Industries, Inc.

Image and Identity Research. Jeffrey L. Pope. *Practical Marketing Research*, 1981, pp. 164–175. Custom Research Inc.

Image Components. Sidney J. Levy. *Marketplace Behavior—Its Meaning for Management*, 1978, pp. 178–212. Northwestern Univ.

Life Styled Marketing: How to Position Products for Premium Profits (rev. ed.). Mack Hanan. 1980, 159 pp. Wellspring Group.

Remedy for a Poor Organizational Image. Michael L. McManus. AMJ, Summer 1979, pp. 31–40. Ithaca College.

What a Corporate Identity Program Can—and Cannot—Do for You? Walter P. Margulies. MRev., Aug. 1977, pp. 14–17. Lippincott & Margulies, Inc.

COMPENSATION. See also Data Processing—Applications, Job Evaluation, Motivation, Wage Incentives

Administering Pay Programs ... An Interview with Edward E. Lawler, III. CR, First Quarter 1977, pp. 8–16.

Administering Salaries and Short-Term Incentives. Bruce R. Ellig. CR, Second Quarter 1977, pp. 15–30. Pfizer.

Area Pay Differentials. Ernest C. Miller. Pers., Nov.–Dec. 1979, pp. 4–11.

Book-Value Stock as an Employee Stock Ownership and Incentive Device. Frederic W. Cook. CR, Third Quarter 1977, pp. 11–19. Frederick W. Cook & Co., Inc.

Bringing Salary Administration out of the Closet. William Wagel. Pers., July–Aug. 1978, pp. 4–10.

Calculating the Expense of COLA Clauses. Frederick L. Sullivan. MRev., July 1980, pp. 31–32.

Clearing Up Fuzziness in Salary Survey Analysis. Edward Perlin, Irwin Bobby Kaplan, John M. Curcia. CR, Second Quarter 1979, pp. 12–25. The Management Performance Group, Equitable Life Assurance Society.

Compensation (rev. ed.). Robert E. Sibson. 1981, 312 pp. The Sibson Group.

Compensation as a Management Tool. Edwin S. Mruk, Edward J. Giblin. MRev., May 1977, pp. 50–58.

Compensation Management: Its Past and Its Future. Bruce Ellig. Pers., May–June 1977, pp. 30–40. Pfizer.

Conversion from Piece-Rate to Time-Rate Pay for Production Workers. Lynn H. Bentley. CR, Fourth Quarter 1979, pp. 31–35. Warner-Lambert Co.

The Correct Way to Calculate Roll-Up. Mary Zippo. Pers., Sept.–Oct. 1980, pp. 44–45.

Designing Master, or "Ideal," Pay-Performance Matrices. Thomas A. Basnight. CR, Fourth Quarter 1980, pp. 44–50. Frank B. Manley & Co.

Designing Reward Systems for New Organizations. Edward E. Lawler, III, Raymond N. Olsen. Pers., Sept.–Oct. 1977, pp. 48–60. Univ. of Michigan, TRW.

Determinants of Organizational Pay Policy. Kenneth E. Foster, Jill Kanin-Lovers. CR, Third Quarter 1977, pp. 35–41.

Devising Pay Strategies for Diversified Companies. James Salscheider. CR, Second Quarter 1981, pp. 15–24.

Ensuring the Effectiveness of Compensation Programs. Thomas M. Hestwood. CR, First Quarter 1979, pp. 11–21. Northwestern Bank of Minneapolis.

An EPA Exceptions Model—Cracking the Sex-Based Wage Differential. Kevin W. Mossholder, Michael E. Gordon, Aaron J. Nurick, N. Norman Pryor. CR, First Quarter 1979, pp. 42–51. Auburn Univ., Univ. of Tennessee, Ford Motor Co.

Executive's Guide to Wage and Salary Administration. Robert E. Sibson. 1980. (Extension Institute Course) By purchase only.

Factoring Living-Cost Differentials into Salary Levels. Rufus E. Runzheimer, Jr. Pers., Jan.–Feb. 1979, pp. 68–78. Runzheimer and Co., Inc.

Federal Pay Policy: Impact on the Private Sector. Bruce R. Ellig. MRev., April 1980, pp. 8–13. Pfizer, Inc.

How Long Until Employees Average $100,000? Joseph A. Lavely. Pers., March–April 1977, pp. 57–61.

'I Deserve More' Talking Pay Policy. SS, July 1980, 24 pp.

Lump Sum Increases—A Creditable Change Strategy. Charles A. Smith. Pers., July–Aug. 1979, pp. 59–63. Clark Equipment Co.

Managing Pay in Emerging Companies. P. Thomas Anderson. CR, First Quarter 1977, pp. 24–31. Olanie, Hurst & Hemrich.

A Market-Oriented Approach to Salary Administration. Ted R. Gambill. AMJ, Summer 1979, pp. 41–46. Meridian Insurance Co.

A Model for Estimating Payroll Expenses. Thomas Plumberg. CR, First Quarter 1981, pp. 23–29. Lawrence-Leiter & Co.

The Mysteries of Employee Pricing Solved. Bruce Ellig. SM, Jan. 1981, pp. 16–22. Pfizer, Inc.

One Answer to Rising Costs: Objective Pay Programs. Harris Odell, Jr. HSM, Sept. 1978, pp. 4–5. Memorial Medical Center.

Open Salary Administration the Polaroid Way. Mary Zippo. Pers., May–June 1981, pp. 45–47.

Opening Up Salary Communications. Philip Springer. Pers., July–Aug. 1978, pp. 41–44.

Pay and Performance. David W. Belcher. CR, Third Quarter 1980, pp. 14–20. San Diego State Univ.

Pay Equity or Pay Fairness. David W. Belcher. CR, Second Quarter 1979, pp. 31–37. San Diego State Univ.

The Pay-for-Performance Dilemma. Frederick S. Hills. Pers., Sept.–Oct. 1979, pp. 23–31. Virginia Polytechnic Institute.

Pay Inequities: How Many Exist Within Your Organization? Bruce R. Ellig. CR, Third Quarter 1980, pp. 34–46. Pfizer. Inc.

Pay Strategies During Inflationary Times. Bruce R. Ellig. MRev., Sept. 1981, pp. 23–28, 37. Pfizer Inc.

A Problem with the "COLA Craze." Robert J. Thornton. CR, Second Quarter 1977, pp. 42–44.

Profit Center Incentives: Stimulants or Depressants? Herbert F. Floyd. MRev., April 1979, pp. 50–52. George Mason Univ.

The Revenue Act of 1978 and Employee Compensation. Frederic W. Cook. CR, First Quarter 1979, pp. 22–30. Frederic W. Cook & Co., Inc.

A Salary Administration Program for Today's Economy. James F. Carey. AMJ, Summer 1980, pp. 4–11. Carey Associates, Inc.

Salary Administration Simplified. Allan K. Worrell. MRev., March 1979, pp. 42–45. ICI Americas, Inc.

Salary Budgeting: How to Control Your Payroll. Stanley B. Henrici. SM, Oct. 1980, pp. 18–24. Heinz Corp.

Salary Management for the Nonspecialist. Stanley B. Henrici. 1980, 247 pp. Heinz, U.S.A.

A Statistical Approach to Assessing Minority/White Pay Equity. George W. Bohlander. CR, Fourth Quarter 1980, pp. 15–24. Arizona State Univ.

Talking Pay Policy Pays Off. Donald J. Petrie. SM, May 1979, pp. 2–13. United States Trust Co. (Also reprinted in HSM, Aug. 1980)

A Tool for Salary Administrators: Standard Salary Accounting. Stanley B. Henrici. Pers., Sept.–Oct. 1980, pp. 14–23.

Toward an Indemnity Model in Computing Hazard Pay. Robert Hershey. CR, First Quarter 1978, pp. 25–31. U.S. Merchant Marine Academy.

Unmentioned Problems of Salary Administration. David J. Thomsen. CR, Fourth Quarter 1977, pp. 11–21.

U.S. Urban Area Living-Cost Data for Compensation Planning. Rufus E. Runzheimer, Jr. CR, Third Quarter 1977, pp. 29–34. Runzheimer & Co., Inc.

Wage and Salary Administration. John G. Kilgour. *Preventive Labor Relations*, 1981, pp. 132–148. California State Univ.

Wage-and-Salary Administration. Linda A. Roxe. *Personnel Management for the Smaller Company*, 1979, pp. 48–69. Rox Associates.

Which Pay Delivery System Is Best for Your Organization? Robert J. Greene. Pers., May–June 1981, pp. 51–58. A. S. Hansen.

COMPENSATION—EXECUTIVES

Administering Top- and Middle-Management Base Salary and Incentive Bonus Plans. Ernest C. Miller (editor). 1977, 80 pp. (A collection of reprints from CR)

An Alternative to Stock Options: Long-Term Incentive-Retention Plans. David J. Thomsen. CR, Second Quarter 1978, pp. 12–23.

AMA's Latest Executive Compensation Service Survey Reveals Significant Increase in Pay and Bonuses for Top Management. Richard K. Lord. MRev., Nov. 1977, p. 33.

The Annual Executive Bonus. Graef S. Crystal. *Executive Compensation: Motivation and Imagination*, 1978, pp. 69–116. Towers, Perrin, Forster & Crosby.

Appraising Restricted Stock. P. Thomas Anderson. CR, Second Quarter 1980, pp. 26–32. The Wyatt Co.

Base Salary and Incentive Compensation Practices in Not-for-Profit Organizations. Henry Hellwig. CR, Fourth Quarter 1978, pp. 34–38.

Compensating a Company's Board and Top Management—An Interview with Courtney C. Brown, Corporate Director. *Administering Top- and Middle-Management Base Salary and Incentive Bonus Plans*, 1977, pp. 34–38.

Compensating Key Executives in the Smaller Company. Theodore Cohn, Roy A. Lindberg. 1979, 224 pp.

Compensating Transferred Employees. Eugene F. Finkin. Pers., Nov.–Dec. 1978, pp. 43–52. DEVCO.

Compensation. Dorothy Baum. *National Account Marketing Handbook*, 1981, pp. 187–193.

The Compensation Director and the Board's Compensation Committee. Frederic W. Cook. CR, Second Quarter 1981, pp. 37–41. Frederic W. Cook & Co., Inc.

Compensation Elements: Market Phase Determines the Mix. Bruce R. Ellig. CR, Third Quarter 1981, pp. 30–38. Pfizer Inc.

Deferred Cash Compensation—The Other Side of the Coin. James J. Sullivan. CR, Second Quarter 1979, pp. 38–42. Cresap, McCormick & Paget, Inc.

Deferred Compensation. Graef S. Crystal. *Executive Compensation: Money, Motivation and Imagination*, 1978, pp. 117–136. Towers, Perrin, Forster & Crosby.

Determinants of Equity of Rewards for Managers. Henry A. Tombari. CR, Second Quarter 1979, pp. 26–30. California State Univ.

A Different Perspective on Executive Compensation. Kenneth E. Foster. CR, Third Quarter 1980, pp. 47–54. Towers, Perrin, Forster & Crosby.

Emerging Problems in Administering Management Compensation Programs: A Compensation Review Symposium. CR, Second Quarter 1977, pp. 45–59. (Also in reprint collection *Administering Top- and Middle-Management Base Salary and Incentive Bonus Plans*, 1977)

Executive Compensation: A Look at the Shape of Things to Come. Fred W. Meuter, Jr. Pers., Jan.–Feb. 1977, pp. 65–70.

Executive Compensation: Climbing Higher. Ernest C. Miller, William H. Wagel. Pers., Jan.–Feb. 1978, pp. 44–46.

Executive Compensation in the 1980s: Conservative Strategies to Emphasize Retention. Edwin S. Mruk. MRev., Dec. 1978, pp. 29–32. Arthur Young & Co.

Executive Compensation: Money, Motivation and Imagination. Graef S. Crystal. 1978, 206 pp. Towers, Perrin, Forster & Crosby.

Executive Compensation: Planning for New Directions. Pearl Meyer. MRev., Aug. 1980, pp. 45–49. Handy Associates, Inc.

Gauging Executive Salaries: How Much, To Whom, For What? David R. Meredith. MRev., Oct. 1978, pp. 47–48.

How Companies Set the Base Salary and Incentive Bonus Opportunity for Chief Executive and Chief Operating Officers . . . A Compensation Review Symposium. *Administering Top- and Middle-Management Base Salary and Incentive Bonus Plans*, 1977, pp. 39–52.

How Companies Set Top- and Middle-Management Salaries . . . A Compensation Review Symposium. CR, First Quarter 1977, pp. 32–46. (Also in reprint collection *Administering Top- and Middle-Management Base Salary and Incentive Bonus Plans*, 1977)

How to Feather Your Nest When It's Time to Talk Turkey. Robert Jameson Gerberg. AMJ, Winter 1979, pp. 15–20. Performance Dynamics Intl. (Also reprinted in *Making Successful Presentations*, 1981)

Impact of the Anti-Inflation Program on Executive Compensation. William L. White. Pers., July–Aug. 1979, pp. 12–27. Wyatt Co.

Incentive Compensation for Staff Managers. Robert J. Greene. CR, First Quarter 1978, pp. 20–24.

An Incentive Plan for Middle Management: A New Approach at International Harvester Co. William H. Hrabak. CR, Fourth Quarter 1978, pp. 26–33. International Harvester Co.

Individual Performance in Incentive Compensation. F. Dean Hildebrandt, Jr. CR, Third Quarter 1978, pp. 28–33. American Insurance Associates.

Long-Term Incentives Based on Market Price. Graef S. Crystal. *Executive Compensation: Money, Motivation and Imagination*, 1978, pp. 137–164. Towers, Perrin, Forster, & Crosby.

Long-Term Incentives for Management, Part I: An Overview. Frederic W. Cook. CR, Second Quarter 1980, pp. 15–25. Frederic W. Cook & Co., Inc.

Long-Term Incentives for Management, Part 7: Combination Market-Based and Performance-Based Grants. Dawn B. H. Sullivan, CR, Fourth Quarter 1981, pp. 34–42. Frederic W. Cook & Co., Inc.

Long-Term Incentives for Management, Part 3: Executive Stock Purchase Plans. Richard J. Kimball. CR, Fourth Quarter 1980, pp. 25–33. Frederic W. Cook & Co., Inc.

Long-Term Incentives for Management, Part 5: Formula Value Incentive Plans. Robert J. Lerner. CR, Second Quarter, 1981, pp. 42–50. Frederic W. Cook & Co., Inc.

Long-Term Incentives for Management, Part 6: Performance Attainment Plans. Lawrence C. Bickford. CR, Third Quarter 1981, pp. 14–29. Frederic W. Cook & Co., Inc.

Long-Term Incentives for Management, Part 4: Restricted Stock. Carol Meyers Edelstein. CR, First Quarter 1981, pp. 30–40. Frederic W. Cook & Co., Inc.

Long-Term Incentives for Management, Part 2: What's New in Stock Option and Appreciation Right Plans. Wendy Jay. CR, Third Quarter 1980, pp. 21–33. Frederic W. Cook & Co., Inc.

Management Compensation. Robert E. Sibson. *Compensation* (rev. ed.), 1981, pp. 232–261. The Sibson Group.

Middle Management Compensation in Regulated and Nonregulated Firms: A Comparison. David R. Kamerschen. CR, First Quarter 1981, pp. 14–22. Univ. of Georgia.

Myth Vs. Reality: The Relationship Between Top Executive Pay and Corporate Performance. Edward T. Redling. CR, Fourth Quarter 1981, pp. 16–24. The Wyatt Co.

Perquisites: The Intrinsic Form of Pay. Bruce R. Ellig. Pers., Jan.–Feb. 1981, pp. 23–31. Pfizer Inc.

Reinforcing Corporate Strategy Through Executive Compensation. David J. McLaughlin. MRev., Oct. 1981, pp. 9–15. Hay Group.

Salary Negotiation: Don't Undersell Yourself. Robert Jameson Gerberg. MRev., Nov. 1978, pp. 30–31. Performance Dynamics International.

Setting Supervisor's Pay and Pay Differentials. Ernest C. Miller. CR, Third Quarter 1978, pp. 13–27.

Stock Appreciation Rights—Hefty Price to Pay for a Little Convenience? Why Not Make Them Twice as Good? Frederick A. Teague. CR, First Quarter 1977, pp. 17–23.

Supervisory Overtime, Incentive, and Bonus Practices. Ernest Miller. CR, Fourth Quarter 1978, pp. 12–25.

Surging Executive Pay: Where Is It Going? David J. McLaughlin. MRev., Jan. 1978, pp. 8–16.

The Tax Reform Act of 1976 and Executive Stock Compensation Plans. James E. McKinney. Pers., May–June 1977, pp. 50–56.

Top- and Middle-Management Compensation. Ernest C. Miller. Part 1. Determining Base Salary. Part 2. Incentive Bonus and Merit Increase Plans. *Administering Top- and Middle-Management Base Salary and Incentive Bonus Plans*, 1977, pp. 4–33.

Trends in Executive Benefits and Deferred Compensation. Thomas H. Paine. CR, Fourth Quarter 1979, pp. 9–21. Hewitt Associates

Voluntary Deferred Compensation—Off Again, on Again. Edward Redling. Pers., May–June 1979, pp. 64–67. The Wyatt Co.

Whither Voluntary Deferred Compensation Plans? Anthony M. Pasquale. Pers., July–Aug. 1978, pp. 75–78. A. M. Pasquale & Co.

Working with the Board on Management Compensation . . . A Compensation Review Symposium. CR, First Quarter 1978, pp. 12–19. (Also in reprint collection *The Human Resources Function: Its Emergence and Character*, 1978)

COMPENSATION—MERIT PAY

Another Look at Merit Pay Programs. Myles H. Goldberg. CR, Third Quarter 1977, pp. 20–28.

Consentient Merit Rating: A Critical Incident Approach. William M. Fox. Pers., July–Aug. 1981, pp. 72–78. Univ. of Florida.

Developmental Pay: Forerunner to Merit Pay in the Federal Government. Buddy Robert Stephen Silverman. CR, Second Quarter 1981, pp. 25–36. U.S. Office of Personnel Management.

Merit Pay Fact or Fiction? Edward E. Lawler. MRev., April 1981, pp. 50–53. Univ. of Southern California.

Merit Pay for College Faculty? James J. Johnston. AMJ, Spring 1978, pp. 44–47. Univ. of Wisconsin.

Merit Pay: Viable? Richard C. Farmer. Pers., Sept.–Oct. 1978, pp. 57–63.

A New Mathematical Approach to Merit-Based Compensation Systems. Douglas M. Stokes. CR, Fourth Quarter 1981, pp. 43–55. The Sullivan Group, Inc.

COMPENSATION—PROFESSIONAL (INCLUDING SALES) EMPLOYEES

College Recruiting Pay Practices. Ernest C. Miller. CR, First Quarter 1979, pp. 31–41.

Compensation for HMO Physicians: Pay Policies for Staff Retention and Motivation. Henry J. Adolfi. HSM, March 1980, pp. 8–9. Cape Ann Medical Center.

Compensation for HMO Physicians: What Program Is Best for Them and Their Patients? Henry J. Adolfi. HSM, Feb. 1980, pp. 5–7. Cape Ann Medical Center.

Compensation of Professional Personnel. Robert E. Sibson. *Compensation* (rev. ed.), 1981, pp. 189–207. The Sibson Group.

Designing an Effective Sales Compensation Program. John K. Moynahan. 1980, 214 pp. Towers, Perrin, Forster & Crosby, Inc.

How to Compensate the Technical Professional. William A. Cohen. *Principles of Technical Management*, 1980, pp. 83–99. California State Univ.

The Impact of Free Agency on Baseball Salaries. Paul D. Staudohar, Edward B. Smith. CR, Third Quarter 1981, pp. 46–55. California State Univ., United States Air Force.

Incentives for Salesmen: Designing a Plan That Works. William White. MRev., Feb. 1977, pp. 27–36.

Putting Incentive in Physicians' Pay. Gary W. Eiland. HSM, Feb. 1981, pp. 13–14. Wood, Lucksinger & Epstein.

Sales Compensation. Robert E. Sibson. *Compensation* (rev. ed.), 1981, pp. 170–188. The Sibson Group.

COMPENSATION—SURVEYS AND SPECIAL REPORTS

Banking Compensation Report. Executive Compensation Service. By purchase only.

Benefits and Employment Contracts. Executive Compensation Service. By purchase only.

A Compensation Survey, Appendix II. Theodore Cohn, Roy A. Lindberg. *Compensating Key Executives in the Smaller Company*, 1979, pp. 211–214.

Corporate Directorship Report. Executive Compensation Service. By purchase only.

Current and Deferred Incentive Compensation. Executive Compensation Service. By purchase only.

Hospital and Health Care Report. Executive Compensation Service. By purchase only.

Middle Management Report. Executive Compensation Service. By purchase only.

Office Personnel Report. Executive Compensation Service. By purchase only.

Professional and Scientific Report. Executive Compensation Service. By purchase only.

Puerto Rico Report. Executive Compensation Service. By purchase only.

Salary Administration and Control. Executive Compensation Service. By purchase only.

Sales Personnel Report. Executive Compensation Service. By purchase only.

Statistical Supplement to the Middle Management Report. Executive Compensation Service. By purchase only.

Statistical Supplement to the Top Management Report. Executive Compensation Service. By purchase only.

Stock Purchase Plans. Executive Compensation Service. By purchase only.

Supervisory Management Report. Executive Compensation Service. By purchase only.

Technician Report. Executive Compensation Service. By purchase only.

Top Management Report. Executive Compensation Service. By purchase only.

COMPETITIVE INTELLIGENCE

Competitive Intelligence for the Smaller Company. Robert Hershey. MRev., Jan. 1977, pp. 18–22. New York Univ.

Competitor Analysis—A Prize Centered Approach. Alred R. Oxenfeldt, William L. Moore. MRev., May 1981, pp. 23–28, 37. Columbia Univ.

Competitor Analysis: The Missing Link in Strategy. William E. Rothschild. MRev., July 1979, pp. 22–28, 37–39. General Electric.

Rival-Related Decisions. Alfred R. Oxenfeldt. *Cost-Benefit Analysis for Executive Decision Making*, 1979, pp. 373–416. Columbia Univ.

COMPUTERS. See Data Processing

CONSULTANTS

Building a Successful Professional Practice with Advertising. Irwin Braun. 1981, 289 pp. Braun Advertising, Inc.

The Consulting Business. Herman R. Holtz. *Profit from your Money-Making Ideas: How to Build a New Business or Expand an Existing One*, 1980, pp. 256–268.

Getting the Most of an Executive Search Firm. Mary Zippo. Pers., Sept.–Oct. 1980, pp. 47–48.

Hiring a Consultant? Establish a Collaborative Approach. John J. Sherwood. Pers., Nov.–Dec. 1981, pp. 44–49. Organizational Consultants Inc.

Hiring a Consultant? First Do Your Homework. Larry L. Axline. Pers., Nov.–Dec. 1981, pp. 39–43. Management Action Planning.

Internal Consultants: Captive Problem Solvers. Michael A. Tita. MRev., June 1981, pp. 27–28, 37–38. 3M.

The Use of Public Relations Counseling. Gerald J. Voros, Paul Alvarez (editors). *What Happens in Public Relations*, 1981, pp. 216–226. Ketchum MacLeod & Grove.

Why Management Consultants? Peter F. Drucker. *The Evolving Science of Management*, 1979, pp. 475–478. Claremont Univ.

CONTRACTS

Contracting with the Federal Government. Grant E. Mayberry. 1978. (Extension Institute Course) By purchase only.

Contracts: The Move to Plain Language. Paul H. Till, Albert F. Gargiulo. 1979, 56 pp. MB.

Do's and Don'ts in Subcontract Management. George Sammet, Jr., Clifton G. Kelley. 1980, 40 pp. Martin Marietta Aerospace. MB.

A General Service Contract? Three Checklists Worth Considering. Roger Drue. HSM, May 1981, pp. 1–3. Mills Memorial Hospital.

How to Negotiate a Successful Hospital-HMO Contract. James J. O'Keefe III. HSM, June 1981, pp. 12–14. Laventhol & Horwath.

The $100 Billion Market: How to Do Business with the Government. Herman Holtz. 1980, 272 pp.

Purchasing Computers: A Practical Guide for Buyers of Computers and Computing Equipment. Edward R. Sambridge. 1979, 139 pp. Central Electricity Generating Board.

Remuneration and Contracts. Roman L. Yanda, M.D. *Doctors as Managers of Health Teams: A Career Guide for Hospital-Based Physicians*, 1977, pp. 159–190. Univ. of Southern California.

Subcontract Management Handbook. George Sammet, Jr., Clifton G. Kelley. 1981, 246 pp. Martin Marietta Corp.

Systems Contracting: A New Look. Ralph A. Bolton. 1979, 45 pp. MB.

COOPERATION, COORDINATION AND CONFLICT RESOLUTION. See also Line-Staff, Team Management

Accounting for the Conflict Between Line Management and the Controller's Office. John R. Simon, Curt Norton, Neil J. Lonergan. AMJ, Winter 1979, pp. 4–14. Northern Illinois Univ.

Affirmative Action, Conflict Resolution, and the Case of Rudolph, The Red-Nosed

Reindeer. Fred L. Fry, Frank A. Wiebe. MRev., Dec. 1978, pp. 40–43. Bradley Univ., Univ. of Mississippi.

At the End of the Chute. James L. Hayes. MRev., July 1979, pp. 2–3.

Conflict in the Organization. Michael Doctoroff. *Synergistic Management: Creating the Climate for Superior Performance*, 1977, pp. 7–35. Balzers High Vacuum Corp.

Conflicts and Power in the Nurse Role. Rita E. Numerof. HSM ,June 1978, pp. 7–8.

Confrontation—Shoot-Out in the Executive Suite. Auren Uris. SM, Nov. 1978, pp. 11–16. Research Institute of America.

Consensus-Building: A Creative Approach to Resolving Conflicts. Andrew K. Hoh. MRev., March 1981, pp. 52–54. Creighton Univ.

The Constructive Approach to Confrontation. Roy Trueblood. SM, Sept. 1980, pp. 39–40. Atlanta Consulting Group.

Control, Change, and Coordination. William C. Waddell. *Overcoming Murphy's Law*, 1981, pp. 237–257. California State Univ., Los Angeles.

Cooperation: An Alternative Management Strategy. Steven H. Appelbaum. PA #64, 1977, 36 pp. St. Peter's College. By purchase only.

Creative Conflict Management. Paul Preston, Brian L. Hawkins. SM, Nov. 1979, pp. 7–11. Preston Associates, Univ. of Texas.

Effective Coordination in Organizations. Derek Pugh. AMJ, Winter 1979, pp. 28–35. London Graduate School of Business Studies.

Finding Answers to School Problems. Gaye Vandermyn, H. Dean Smith. *Managing Nonprofit Organizations*, 1977, pp. 220–228. Project Interaction.

Getting Computer People and Users to Understand Each Other. Ronald S. Kintisch, Marvin R. Weisbord. AMJ, Spring 1977, pp. 4–14. Executive Services, Inc., Block Petrella Associates.

How to Keep Managerial Mistakes from Turning into Organizational Failures. Harold J. Novick. MRev., Nov. 1981, pp. 55–61. Novick & Associates.

How to Make Conflict Work for You. Brian H. Kleiner. SM, Sept. 1978, pp. 2–6.

The Likerts on Managing Conflict. Rensis Likert, Janet Likert. 1977. (AMACOM audio cassette) By purchase only.

Managing Conflict. Donald H. Weiss. 1981. (Extension Institute Cassette Program) By purchase only.

Managing Conflict: Do You Solve or Resolve Friction? James J. Cribbin. *Leadership: Strategies for Organizational Effectiveness*, 1981, pp. 206–222. St. John's Univ.

Managing Conflict—The Art of Gaining Commitment. John R. Drake. *Corporate Planning Techniques and Applications*, 1979, pp. 370–373. Drake Beam & Associates.

Managing Conflicts. Beverly A. Potter. *Turning Around: The Behavioral Approach to Managing People*, 1980, pp. 187–219.

The Positive No: A Manager's Guide to Dealing with Superiors, Peers, and Subordinates. Auren Uris. 1980. (AMACOM audio cassette) By purchase only.

Problems: Part IV. James L. Kammert. *International Commercial Banking Management*, 1981, pp. 281–352. Equibank.

Resolving Conflict: A Guide for the Industrial Relations Manager. Jeffrey Gandz. Pers., Nov.–Dec. 1979, pp. 22–32. Univ. of Western Ontario.

Rules of the Road: Doing Something Simple About Conflict in the Organization. Donald G. Livingston. Pers., Jan.–Feb. 1977, pp. 23–29. Electronic Associates.

Three Cheers for Conflict! Dennis King. Pers., Jan.–Feb. 1981, pp. 13–22. Procter & Gamble Manufacturing Co.

Tools and Techniques of National Account Marketing. V. B. Chamberlain III. *National Account Marketing Handbook*, 1981, pp. 126–157. The Stanley Works.

When and How to Argue. W. A. Delaney. SM, Dec. 1979, pp. 16–21. Analysis & Computer Systems, Inc. (Also in reprint collection *Effective Communication on the Job* (third ed.), 1981)

Working Effectively with Others. Lois Borland Hart. *Moving Up: Women and Leadership*, 1980, pp. 60–86. Mountain States Employers Council, Inc.

CORPORATE GIVING. See Community Relations, Public Relations

COST ACCOUNTING. See Accounting, Financial Management

COST CONTROL. See also Management Controls

A Basic Approach to Cutting Costs. Harold E. Levenson. SM, April 1977, pp. 16–20. City Univ. of N.Y.

Before the Economy Dips: Planning Protective Action. Eugene H. Fram, Herbert J. Mossien. PA #66, 1977, 29 pp. Rochester Institute of Technology. By purchase only.

Controlling Costs. Herman R. Holtz. *Profit-Line Management: Managing a Growing Business Successfully*, 1981, pp. 128–146.

Controlling the Costs of Retirement Income and Medical Care Plans. Philip M. Alden, Jr. 1980, 78 pp. Towers, Perrin, Forster & Crosby. MB.

Cost Analysis Form. (Appendix D). William R. Tracey. *Human Resource Development Standards*, 1981, pp. 587–590. U.S. Army Intelligence Training School.

Cost-Benefit Analysis for Executive Decision Making. Alfred R. Oxenfeldt. 1979, 432 pp. Columbia Univ.

Creative Cost Reduction: A Participative Route to Profit Improvement. Louis E. Tagliaferri. MRev., June 1979, pp. 49–54. Management Resource Center, Inc.

How to Calculate the Manufacturer's Costs in Collective Bargaining. Frederick L. Sullivan. 1980, 68 pp. Sullivan & Hayes. MB.

How to Improve Packaging Costs. Edmund A. Leonard. 1981, 67 pp. General Foods Corp.

Leaks. Herman R. Holtz. *Profit-Line Management: Managing a Growing Business Successfully*, 1981, pp. 23–40.

Scrap and Rework: A Systematic Approach to Reducing Bottom-line Costs. Alfred Segar. MRev., Oct. 1981, pp. 69–73. IBM.

Simplified Business Procedures: Deactivating Those Cost Generators. Clair F. Vough, Bernard Asbell. *Productivity, A Practical Program for Improving Efficiency* (rev. ed.— former title: *Tapping the Human Resource: A Strategy for Productivity*), 1979, pp. 143–149. Productivity Research International, Inc.

Take an Entrepreneurial Look ... Finding New Opportunities for Profitability in Manufacturing Cost. Ward C. Smith. MRev., March 1980, pp. 60–62. Corning Glass Works.

COST CONTROL—NON-MANUFACTURING COSTS. See also Sales Management, Systems Analysis

Combine Methods to Contain Costs, Maintain Quality, Satisfy Employees. Fred F. Fifield. HSM, April 1977, pp. 1–5. Mercy Hospital.

Containing Health-Care Costs: How Ford Fights Medical Inflation. Jack K. Shelton. MRev., July 1978, pp. 29–31. Ford Motor Co.

Controlling the Costs of Health Care Where it Counts—from Within the System. Harry L. Sutton. MRev., Sept. 1981, pp. 48–55. Towers, Perrin, Forster & Crosby.

The Cost-Effectiveness of Industrial Health Programs. Joseph F. Follmann, Jr. *The Economics of Industrial Health: History, Theory, and Practice*, 1978, pp. 368–396. New York Univ.

Curbing Costs? Consult Your Computer. Stephen Karas, Jr. HSM, Jan. 1981, pp. 1–2. Tri-City Hospital.

Fight the High Cost of Healthcare: The Staff Shows How. Patricia O. Mebane. HSM, June 1981, pp. 6, 11. St. Joseph's Hospital.

Hard Times? Manage Results, Not Just Resources. Darwin Gillett, Ronald N. Ashkenas. AMJ, Autumn 1981, pp. 4–12. Gillett Associates, Robert Schaffer & Associates.

How to Control Runaway Travel Costs. Harold L. Seligman. MRev., Jan. 1981, pp. 53–55. Management Alternatives.

Making Doctors Cost-Conscious. George C. Owen. HSM, Dec. 1980, pp. 6, 11. Columbia Hospital.

The Positive Side of Recessions: Bringing Accountability Back. Jerry Kinard, Joe Iverstine, Donald Wilson, Mary Blalock, John Davis, Merle Peper, John Yeargain, Dick Sillavan, Peter Wright. SM, Feb. 1981, pp. 13–16. Southeastern Louisiana Univ.

Postage Goes Higher: But You Can Still Cut Costs in the Mailroom. Harry J. Brown. MRev., Dec. 1981, pp. 41–45. Pitney Bowes.

Rochester Area Hospitals Launch Major Cost-Containment Program. James A. Block, Donna J. Regenstreif, Jan Baker Pass. HSM, Feb. 1981, pp. 1–3, 11–12. Rochester Area Hospitals' Corp.

Tough Talk About Health Care and Its Costs—from a Corporate Chairman Who also Serves as a Hospital Trustee. David M. Roderick. MRev., Sept. 1981, pp. 52–53. U.S. Steel Corp.

Turnover Costs. Edward Roseman. *Managing Employee Turnover: A Positive Approach,* 1981, pp. 65–74. Answers & Insights, Inc.

CREATIVITY

The Case for Disorderly Conduct: How to Get the Most Out of Managerial Manpower. Dudley Lynch. MRev., Feb. 1980, pp. 15–19. The Idea Counselors.

Creating Profitable New Products and Markets. Richard H. Corbin, R. Donald Gamache. 1980, 53 pp. Innotech. MB.

Creativity and Synergy. Michael Doctoroff. *Synergistic Management: Creating the Climate for Superior Performance,* 1977, pp. 51–70. Balzers High Vacuum Corp.

Creativity in Business, Part I. Frederick D. Buggie. *New Product Development Strategies,* 1981, pp. 3–54. Strategic Innovations.

Creativity in Decision Making. Alfred R. Oxenfeldt, David W. Miller, Roger A. Dickinson. *A Basic Approach to Executive Decision Making,* 1978, pp. 152–176. Columbia Univ., Univ. of Texas.

Creativity Techniques: Yesterday, Today, and Tomorrow. F. D. Barrett. AMJ, Winter 1978, pp. 23–35. Management Concepts Ltd.

Creativity: The Supervisor's Secret Weapon. Ronald Hermone. SM, June 1979, pp. 24–28.

Creativity Training: B. F. Goodrich's New Approach. MRev., March 1980, pp. 29–30.

Don't Just Sit There Thinking. Do Something! Frederick D. Buggie. MRev., May 1981, p. 33. Strategic Innovations, Inc.

Groupthink: When Too Many Heads Spoil the Decision. Clarence W. Von Bergen, Jr., Raymond J. Kirk. MRev., March 1978, pp. 44–49 Kellogg Co., Army Research Institute.

How Management Can Develop and Sustain a Creative Environment. Maurice I. Zeldman. AMJ, Winter 1980, pp. 23–27.

How to Develop Innovation in Yourself and in Your Subordinates. ES, Jan. 1980, 16 pp.

How to Nourish the Creative Employee. Donald W. Myers. SM, Feb. 1981, pp. 31–35. Winthrop College. (Also in reprint collection *Leadership on the Job: Guides to Good Supervision* (third ed.), 1981)

Idea Management: How to Motivate Creativity and Innovation. Charles H. Clark. 1980, 56 pp. Yankee Ingenuity Programs. MB.

Increasing Your Creativity: Do You Get Good Ideas or Profitable Ideas? James J. Cribbin. *Leadership: Strategies for Organizational Effectiveness,* 1981, pp. 223–240. St. John's Univ.

Innovation and the Economic Long Wave. Jay W. Forrester. MRev., June 1979, pp. 16–24. Massachusetts Institute of Technology.

Innovation Management: The Missing Link in Productivity. C. Joshua Abend. MRev., June 1979, pp. 25–28, 38. The Abend Group.

Managerial Breakthroughs: Action Techniques for Strategic Change. James R. Emshoff. 1980, 211 pp. Campbell Soup Co.

Managing R&D Creatively ... B. F. Goodrich's Approach. Bart A. Diliddo, Paul C. James, Harry J. Dietrick. MRev., July 1981, pp. 37–41. B. F. Goodrich.

Managing Workplace Innovations: A Framework and a New Approach. William E. Zierden. MRev., June 1981, pp. 57–61. Univ. of Virginia.

The Marketing Manager's Guide to New Product Invention. Alfred Gruber. 1977, 31 pp. Brand, Gruber & Co. MB.

Profit from Your Money-Making Ideas: How to Build a New Business or Expand an Existing One. Herman R. Holtz. 1980, 370 pp.

Releasing Creativity within Groups. Robert R. Blake, Jane Srygley Mouton. *Productivity: the Human Side*, 1981, pp. 108–117. Scientific Methods Inc.

Toward a More Creative You: Creating the Ideal Organization. Harold R. McAlindon. SM, Jan. 1980, pp. 26–32. The Institute of Financial Education. (Also in reprint collection *Getting the Most Out of Your Job and Your Organization*, 1980)

Toward a More Creative You: Stretching Your Mind. Harold R. McAlindon. SM, Feb. 1980, pp. 29–34. Institute of Financial Education. (Also in reprint collection *Getting the Most Out of Your Job and Your Organization*, 1980)

Toward a More Creative You: Unlocking Human Potential. Harold R. McAlindon. SM, Oct. 1979, pp. 2–8. The Institute of Financial Education. (Also in reprint collection *Getting the Most Out of Your Job and Your Organization*, 1980)

Wanted: A Sense of Mission. James L. Hayes. MRev., Oct. 1980, pp. 2–3.

CREDIT MANAGEMENT

Credit. William R. Osgood. *Basics of Successful Business Management*, 1981, pp. 156–169.

Debt Collection Letters in Ten Languages: With Notes on Terminology, Practice and Methods of Payment in Different Countries. John Butterworth. 1978, unpaged.

Managing Credit for Profit (sec. ed.). George H. Troughton. 1981. (Extension Institute Course) By purchase only.

When Customers Are Delinquent . . . Who Really Pays the Bills? John Gordana. MRev., April 1980, pp. 32–33. Equitable Adjustment Service.

DATA PROCESSING. See also Management Information Systems

Beyond the Computer Age. George E. Mueller. MRev., May 1977, pp. 45–49. System Development Corp.

Computer Basics for Management (rev. ed.). L. Daniel Massey. 1977. (Extension Institute Course) Revised by Richard W. Lott. By purchase only.

Computer Fundamentals for Managers (sec. ed.). L. Daniel Massey, Richard W. Lott. 1979. (Extension Institute Cassette Program) By purchase only.

Computer Fundamentals for Nonspecialists. Joseph M. Vles. 1981, 180 pp.

Computer Systems in Business: More Evolution Than Revolution. Victor A. Vyssotsky. MRev., Feb. 1979, pp. 15–22. Bell Laboratories.

Data Base Systems; Design, Implementation, and Management. Ronald G. Ross. 1978, 229 pp. Performance Development Corp.

Distributed Processing Systems: End of the Mainframe Era? Judson Breslin, C. Bradly Tashenberg. 1978, 228 pp. Schlegel Corp.

EDP Contingency Planning: How to Survive a Disaster. Leonard I. Krauss. MRev., June 1980, pp. 19–26. Ernst & Whitney.

A Manager's Guide to Profitable Computers. Norman Sanders. 1979, 216 pp.

Minicomputers and How Your Company Can Use Them. ES, Jan. 1981, 16 pp.

Minicomputers: Low-Cost Computer Power for Management (rev. ed.). Donald P. Kenney. 1978, 269 pp. Metropolitan Life Insurance Co.

Using Small Computers as Management Tools. Jack R. Buchanan, Garrett L. Sheldon. 1980. (Extension Institute Course) By purchase only.

DATA PROCESSING—APPLICATIONS

The Affordable Computer: The Microcomputer for Business and Industry. Claire Summer, Walter A. Levy (editors). 1979, 179 pp. Edgewood Computer Associates Inc.

Basic Principles of Automated Accounting. Carl Warren. *The Affordable Computer: The Microcomputer for Business and Industry*, 1979, pp. 19–30. Interface Age Magazine.

Building a Data Base Defense Against Product Liability. L. H. Berul. MRev., Nov. 1977, pp. 18–20. Aspen Systems Corp.

Case Studies in Selecting Minicomputer Systems. Donald P. Kenney. *Minicomputers: Low-Cost Computer Power for Management* (rev. ed.), 1978, pp. 178–202. Metropolitan Life Insurance Co.

Claudius: A Microcomputer Order Processing System. Walter A. Levy. *The Affordable Computer: The Microcomputer for Business and Industry*, 1979, pp. 31–38, Edgewood Computer Associates Inc.

Computer Simulation of Financial Factors. D. Bruce Merrifield. *Strategic Analysis, Selection, and Management of R&D Projects*, 1977, pp. 21–27. Continental Group Inc. MB.

Computer-Based Collection Effort Increases Income by 9 Percent. Courtney E. Howe, Sr. HSM, Sept. 1980, pp. 2–3. Jordan Howe Associates.

Computerizing Patients' Histories Cuts Cost Plus Improves Quality of Care. Stanley N. Allen. HSM, Sept. 1980, pp. 1–2. Lovelace Medical Center.

Computers: Luxury or Necessity? Specialty or Commodity? Michael J. Samek. MRev., Sept. 1977, pp. 31–33. Celanese Corp.

Corporate Cash Management (Including Electronic Funds Transfer). Alfred L. Hunt. 1978, 232 pp.

Curbing Costs? Consult Your Computer. Stephen Karas, Jr. HSM, Jan. 1981, pp. 1–2. Tri-City Hospital.

Developing Computer-Based Accounts Receivable Systems. Norbert J. Kubilus. 1981. (Extension Institute Course) By purchase only.

Developing Computer-Based General Ledger Systems. Richard W. Lott. 1978. (Extension Institute Course) By purchase only.

EDP and Accounting. Alvin A. Clay. 1979. (Extension Institute Course) By purchase only.

How to Evaluate a Prepackaged Personnel System. Alfred J. Walker. Pers., May–June 1979, pp. 31–40. AT&T.

An Introduction to Electronic Funds Transfer Systems. Claude R. Martin, Jr. 1978, 40 pp. Univ. of Michigan. MB.

Medical Costs Contained Through Computerized Appointments Scheduling. Wayne Given. HSM, Sept. 1980, p. 3–5. Carbondale Clinic.

The Microcomputer in Action: Support of Loan Collection. Randall Rustin. *The Affordable Computer: The Microcomputer for Business and Industry*, 1979, pp. 53–63.

Microcomputers Provide Accounting Benefits to Small Businesses. Claire Summer, Walter A. Levy (editors). *The Affordable Computer: The Microcomputer for Business and Industry*, 1979, pp. 78–112. Edgewood Computer Associates.

The Most Current—The Least Expensive. Claire Summer, Walter A. Levy (editors). *The Affordable Computer: The Microcomputer for Business and Industry*, 1979, pp. 64–77. Edgewood Computer Associates.

A Small Business Installs a Microprocessor System. Joe Hamilton. *The Affordable Computer: The Microcomputer for Business and Industry*, 1979, pp. 39–52. Microprocessor Applications.

Toss: AN Aerospace System That's Go for Manpower Planning. Robert A. Sylvia. Pers., Jan.–Feb. 1977, pp. 56–64. Martin Marietta Aerospace.

Using Computers in Direct Cost Systems. William E. Arnstein, Frank Gilabert. *Direct Costing*, 1980, pp. 236–249. Main Hurdman & Cranstoun.

Using the Computer as a Marketing Tool. Leonard J. Parsons, Ellen Day. 1979. (Extension Institute Course) By purchase only.

DATA PROCESSING—EVALUATION AND COSTS

Auditing the Data Processing Function. Richard W. Lott. 1980, 214 pp. Bentley College.

The Big Impact of Small Computers: Low-Cost Fast-Handling of Data. George H. Ritterbach, Victor Goldberg. MRev., March 1978, pp. 31–33. Peat, Marwick, Mitchell & Co.

Case Studies in Selecting Minicomputer Systems. Donald P. Kenney. *Minicomputers:*

Low-Cost Computer Power for Management (rev. ed.), 1978, pp. 178–202. Metropolitan Life Insurance Co.

Computers & Communications: Their Management and Integration. John Diebold, James L. Hayes. 1981. (AMACOM audio cassette) By purchase only.

The EDP Feasibility Study (sec. ed.). Michael A. Tow. 1979. (Extension Institute Course) By purchase only.

Watch Out: Those Built-in Computers Will Get You. Robert A. Lowry. MRev., Jan. 1977, pp. 12–17. Technology Marketing, Inc.

DATA PROCESSING—MANAGEMENT

Achieving Computer Security. Henry L. Parsons. 1980. (Extension Institute Cassette Program) By purchase only.

Assessing Computer Center Effectiveness. Frank Greenwood, Lee A. Gagnon. 1977, 38 pp. Univ. of New Haven, Peat, Marwick, Mitchell & Co. MB.

Data Base Systems: Design, Implementation, and Management. Ronald G. Ross. 1978, 229 pp. Performance Development Corp.

Data Dictionaries and Data Administration: Concepts and Practices for Data Resources Management. Ronald G. Ross. 1981, 454 pp. Performance Development Corp.

The Effective EDP Manager. Michael R. Frank. 1980, 197 pp. The Taubman Co., Inc.

How to Make the Computer Work for You (PRIME 1000). 1978. (An AMACOM Skill Series home-study course) By purchase only.

How to Make the EDP Function More Effective. William B. Miller. MRev., April 1977, pp. 18–27. Touche, Ross & Co.

How to Manage a Data Processing Department. John B. Campbell. 1981. (Extension Institute Course) By purchase only.

How to Organize the EDP Department. Michael R. Frank. 1980, 47 pp. MB.

In-House Versus Service Bureau: An Economic Analysis. Robert Dettman. HSM, Sept. 1980, p. 5. Medical Computer Systems.

Planning for the "Electronic Office" of the Future. Harvey L. Poppel. MRev., June 1978, pp. 29–31. Booz, Allen & Hamilton Inc.

Purchasing Computers: A Practical Guide for Buyers of Computers and Computing Equipment. Edward R. Sambridge. 1979, 139 pp. Central Electricity Generating Board.

Security Safeguards for the Computer. Charles F. Hemphill, Jr., Robert D. Hemphill. 1979, 38 pp. Ernst & Ernst. MB.

Tightening Up Security in Information Systems. C. S. Guynes. Pers., Nov.–Dec. 1979, pp. 60–66. North Texas State Univ.

Xerox's EDP Architecture: A Systematic Approach to Software Compatibility. Alan V. Purcell. MRev., April 1981, pp. 21–22. Xerox.

DATA PROCESSING—STAFFING AND HUMAN EFFECTS

Behavioral Issues and the Computer. Edward A. Tomeski, George Stephenson, B. Man Yoon. Pers., July–Aug. 1978, pp. 66–74. Fordham Univ.

Getting Computer People and Users to Understand Each Other. Ronald S. Kintisch, Marvin R. Weisbord. AMJ, Spring 1977, pp. 4–14. Executive Services, Inc., Block Petrella Associates, Inc.

How to Avoid Hassles and Headaches When Systems People and Users Meet. Hilliard McLamore. AMJ, Summer 1979, pp. 4–13. Boeing Computer Services.

DECENTRALIZATION

The Bureaucratic Paradox: The Efficient Organization Centralizes in Order to Decentralize. Charles Perrow. OD, Spring 1977, pp. 2–14. State Univ. of New York.

Centralization or Decentralization? In Patient Care, Both Can Work Together. P. J. Whalen. HSM, May 1981, pp. 4–5. Baptist Memorial Hospital.

Centralization versus Decentralization Controversy. Donald P. Kenney. *Minicomputers: Low-Cost Computer Power for Management* (rev. ed.), 1978, pp. 77–78. Metropolitan Life Insurance Co.

Changing Patterns in Organization Planning. Willys H. Monroe. MRev., Oct. 1977, pp. 29–30. Booz-Allen & Hamilton, Inc.

Conversation: An Interview with Edward Carlson. OD, Spring 1979, pp. 49–62.

Distributed Processing and Organization Design. Judson Breslin, C. Bradley Tashenberg. *Distributed Processing Systems: End of the Mainframe Era?* 1978, pp. 103–121. Schlegel Corp.

Organizing for Decentralization of Responsibilities. Harold Smiddy. *The Evolving Science of Management*, 1979, pp. 132–148.

Riding the Organizational Pendulum . . . Is It Time to (De)Centralize? Barry A. Liebling. MRev., Sept. 1981, pp. 14–20. Liebling Associates.

DECISION MAKING. See also Management Science and Statistics

Accounting Information for Operating Decisions. Jacob Birnberg. *Management Principles for Nonprofit Agencies and Organizations*, 1979, pp. 477–522. Univ. of Pittsburgh.

The Administration of Professors as Decision Makers. Martha A. Brown. *Managing Nonprofit Organizations*, 1977, pp. 303–312. Stephen F. Austin State Univ.

The Art of Decision Making. John D. Arnold. 1981. (AMACOM audio cassette book) By purchase only.

A Basic Approach to Executive Decision Making. Alfred R. Oxenfeldt, David W. Miller, Roger A. Dickinson. 1978, 229 pp. Columbia Univ., Univ. of Texas.

Better Business Decisions Through Use of Current Value Information. Pieter Bakker, Edward G. Pringle. *Current Value Accounting*, 1977, pp. 15–26. Coopers & Lybrand.

Bridging the Gap Between Analysts and Decision Makers. Raymond M. Wilmotte, G. Gail Crotts. MRev., Jan. 1979, pp. 24–26. Federal Communications Commission.

Building Financial Decision Making Models: An Introduction to Principles and Procedures. Donald Moscato. 1980, 150 pp. Iona College.

Capitalizing on Group Decision-Making. James R. Emshoff. *Managerial Breakthroughs: Action Techniques for Strategies Change*, 1980, pp. 106–129. Campbell Soup Co.

Cost-Benefit Analysis for Executive Decision Making. Alfred R. Oxenfeldt. 1979, 432 pp. Columbia Univ.

Creative Problem Solving. Robert A. Moskowitz. 1978. (Extension Institute Cassette Program) By purchase only.

Decision Analysis: How to Cope with Increasing Complexity. Ralph L. Keeney. MRev., Sept. 1979, pp. 24–28, 37–40. Woodward-Clyde Consultants.

Decision Making. Paul W. Cummings. *Open Management: Guides to Successful Practice*, 1980, pp. 51–75.

Decision Making. Herman R. Holtz. *Profit-Line Management: Managing a Growing Business Successfully*, 1981, pp. 113–127.

Decision Making. Lawrence B. Sawyer. *The Manager and the Modern Internal Auditor: A Problem-Solving Partnership*, 1979, pp. 129–159.

Decision Making and the Forces of Change. Ronna Klingenberg. MRev., Dec. 1979, pp. 13–16. American Council of Life Insurance.

Decision Making in the Purchasing Process: A Report. Phillip D. White. 1978, 54 pp. Univ. of Colorado. MB.

Decision Packages. L. Allan Austin, Logan M. Cheek. *Zero-Base Budgeting: A Decision Package Manual*, 1979, pp. 49–177. Xerox Corp.

Decision Styles—in Theory, in Practice. Phillip L. Hunsaker, Johanna S. Hunsaker. OD, Autumn 1981, pp. 23–36. Univ. of San Diego.

Delving into Decisions. Lois Borland Hart. *Moving Up: Women and Leadership*, 1980, pp. 143–170. Mountain States Employers Council, Inc.

The Discipline for Problem Solving. Fred W. Latham, George S. Sanders. *Urwick, Orr on Management*, 1980, pp. 175–186. Urwick, Orr & Partners.

Group Decision Making: What Strategies Should You Use? J. Keith Murnighan. MRev., Feb. 1981, pp. 55–62. Univ. of Illinois.

Groups Can Make the Best Decisions, If You Lead the Way. Ethel C. Glenn, Elliott Pood. SM, Dec. 1978, pp. 2–6. Univ. of North Carolina.

How to Be an Effective Worrier. Marvin M. Klein. SM, Sept. 1981, pp. 40–43.

How to Improve Your Problem-Solving Capability. Mark A. Frohman. MRev., Nov. 1980, pp. 59–61. Keithley Instruments, Inc.

How to Make a Better Decision. Don Caruth, Bill Middlebrook. SM, July 1981, pp. 12–17. Caruth Management Consultants, Inc.

How to Make a Business Decision: An Analysis of Theory and Practice. Earnest R. Archer. MRev., Feb. 1980, pp. 54–61. Winthrop College.

How to Make the Different Kinds of Decisions. Peter G. Kirby. SM, Feb. 1977, pp. 2–8. Red Lobster Inns of America, Inc. (Also reprinted in HSM Oct. 1981)

Individual Versus Group Approaches to Decision Making. John J. Sherwood, Florence M. Hoylman. SM, April 1978, pp. 2–9. Purdue Univ., Organizational Consultants, Inc. (Also in reprint collection *Leadership on the Job: Guides to Good Supervision* (third ed.), 1981)

Make Up Your Mind: The 7 Building Blocks to Better Decisions. John D. Arnold. 1978, 210 pp. Executrak Systems.

Making Decisions That Count. James L. Hayes. MRev., Dec. 1981, pp. 2–3.

Management Decision Making. Jerome D. Braverman. 1980, 241 pp. Rider College.

The Management of Ambiguity. Michael B. McCaskey. OD, Spring 1979, pp. 31–48. Harvard Univ.

Managing Risk and Uncertainty. James E. Kristy. MRev., Sept. 1978, pp. 15–22.

A New Approach to Problem Solving. Lothar A. Kreck. AMJ, Summer 1981, pp. 19–22. Washington State Univ.

Problem Management: A Behavioral Science Approach. Ralph H. Kilmann. *Management Principles for Nonprofit Agencies and Organizations*, 1979, pp. 213–255. Univ. of Pittsburgh.

Problem Solving and Decision Making. Dean P. Peskin. *The Corporate Casino*, 1978, pp. 133–155. Joseph George Distributors.

Problem-Solving Techniques That Always Cause Problems. Frederick Haas. SM, Sept. 1979, pp. 16–19. Virginia Commonwealth Univ.

A Realistic Look at Decision Making. Robard Y. Hughes. SM, Jan. 1980, pp. 2–8. California State Univ.

Sample Forms, Decision Packages, and Ranking Summaries, Appendix B. Logan M. Cheek. *Zero-Base Budgeting Comes of Age*, 1977, pp. 193–251. Xerox Corp.

Simon Says . . . Decision Making Is a 'Satisfying' Experience. John M. Roach. MRev., Jan. 1979, pp. 8–17.

Social Character and Group Decision Making. Gene E. Burton. AMJ, Summer 1978, pp. 12–20.

Styles of Decision Making. Andrew K. Hoh. SM, May 1981, pp. 19–23. Creighton Univ.

The Supervisor's Survival Guide: Involving Your Staff in the Decision-Making Process. Ken Thompson, Robert E. Pitts. SM, April 1979, pp. 31–38. Univ. of Notre Dame. (Also in reprint collection *The Supervisor's Survival Guide*, 1979)

Time to Redesign the Decision-making Process. Charles H. Ford. MRev., July 1978, pp. 50–53. Duval Corp.

Why Managers Fail to Solve Problems Quickly. William J. Altier. MRev., Sept. 1981, p. 36. Princeton Associates.

Zero-Base Budgeting: Organizational Impact and Effects. L. Allan Austin. 1977, 33 pp. Austin & Lindberg, Ltd. SR.

DELEGATION

Delegation. Paul W. Cummings. *Open Management: Guides to Successful Practice,* 1980, pp. 77–92.

Delegation and Co-ordination. Fred W. Latham, George S. Sanders. *Urwick, Orr on Management*, 1980, pp. 39–49. Urwick, Orr & Partners.

Delegation and the "Dirty Hands" Syndrome. Earnest R. Archer. SM, Nov. 1977, pp. 31–34. Winthrop College. (Also reprinted in HSM, Jan. 1981)

Delegation: There's More to It Than Letting Someone Else Do It. Marion E. Haynes. SM, Jan. 1980, pp. 9–15. Shell Oil Co. (Also in reprint collection *Leadership on the Job: Guides to Good Supervision*, 1981)

Effective Delegation of Responsibility. Ray A. Killian. *Managers Must Lead!* (rev. ed.), 1979, pp. 194–201. Belk Stores.

Guidelines for Effective Delegation. Diane Arthur. SM, Oct. 1979, pp. 9–13. Camenae Associates.

Handing Off to Subordinates: Delegating for Gain. Edward C. Schleh. MRev., May 1978, pp. 43–47.

How to Delegate Well. ES, Jan. 1979, 16 pp.

Making Delegation Work for You. Leo F. McManus. 1981. (An AMA multimedia program) By purchase only.

No-Nonsense Delegation. Dale D. McConkey. 1981. (AMACOM audio cassette book) By purchase only.

Stepping Up Supervision: Mastering Delegation. H. Kent Baker, Stevan H. Holmberg. SM, Oct. 1981, pp. 15–21. American Univ.

Successful Delegation. Kenneth M. Lizotte. 1978. (Extension Institute Cassette Program) By purchase only.

DISCIPLINE

Constructive Discipline for Supervisors. George R. Bell. 1981. (Extension Institute Cassette Program) By purchase only.

Correction: The Supervisor's Unique Opportunity. Ray A. Killian. *Managers Must Lead!* (rev. ed.), 1979, pp. 95–108. Belk Stores.

Discipline. Paul W. Cummings. *Open Management: Guides to Successful Practice*, 1980, pp. 93–108.

Discipline in the Workplace Today. Randi Sachs. *Leadership on the Job: Guides to Good Supervision* (third ed.), 1981, pp. 214–223.

Effective Employee Discipline. Louis V. Imundo. *The Effective Supervisor's Handbook*, 1980, pp. 120–146.

Five Principles of Corrective Disciplinary Action. Richard G. Martin. SM, Jan. 1978, pp. 24–28. (Also reprinted in HSM, July 1980)

"I'd Like to See You in My Office." Elanor Reiter. *Leadership on the Job: Guides to Good Supervision* (third ed.), 1981, pp. 210–213. Allstate Insurance Co.

Laying Down the Law—Progressively. George L. Heller. SM, Aug. 1981, pp. 14–16. Daytona Beach Community College.

Team Discipline: The Supervisor as Coach. Hans Picard, Lyra Picard. SM, Nov. 1980, pp. 37–39. Picard & Associates.

What's New in Discipline: A Supportive Approach. Richard Discenza, Howard L. Smith. SM, Sept. 1978, pp. 14–19.

DISCRIMINATION. See also Affirmative Action Programs, Equal Employment Opportunity

Affirmative Action and the Woman Worker. Jennie Farley. 1979, 225 pp. Cornell Univ.

Age Discrimination in Employment. William L. Kendig. 1978, 83 pp. U.S. Dept. of the Interior. MB.

Are You Complying with EEOC's Rules on National Origin Discrimination? Oscar A. Ornati, Margaret J. Eisen. Pers., March–April 1981, pp. 12–20. New York Univ., Meredith Associates, Inc.

Avoiding Charges of Bias in Hiring. SS, Dec. 1981, 24 pp.

Benefits and the Amended ADEA. Ernest C. Miller. Pers., Sept.–Oct. 1978, pp. 4–10.

Eliminating Pay Discrimination Caused by Job Evaluation. David J. Thomsen. Pers., Sept.–Oct. 1978, pp. 11–22.

Employing the Handicapped: A Practical Compliance Manual. Arno B. Zimmer. 1981, 374 pp. Eliot-Yeats, Inc.

A Guide to Equal Employment Opportunity Requirements. Erwin S. Stanton. *Successful Personnel Recruiting and Selection*, 1977, pp. 12–32.

Has the Fair-Employment Movement Affected a Manager's Ability to Manage? Jay Gottesman, Jeffrey H. Greenhaus. AMJ, Autumn 1981, pp. 13–24. Stevens Institute of Technology, Drexel Univ.

Hiring the Handicapped. Jack R. Ellner, Henry E. Bender. 1980, 74 pp. Southern Illinois Univ. RS.

Management Techniques for Winning Employment Discrimination Claims. Camille Caiozzo. HSM, Nov. 1979, pp. 1–3. Medical Center of Tarzana.

Managing Compensation and Performance Appraisal Under the Age Act. Samuel T. Beacham. MRev., Jan. 1979, pp. 51–54. Towers, Perrin, Forster, & Crosby.

Measuring Discrimination: What Is a Relevant Labor Market? Howard R. Bloch, Robert L. Pennington. Pers., July–Aug. 1980, pp. 21–29. George Mason Univ.

On Determining Back Pay Awards. Howard Risher. CR, Fourth Quarter 1977, pp. 39–53.

Patterns of Racial Exclusion in Top Management. Philip Harris. *Making Successful Presentations*, 1981, pp. 180–186. Baruch College of the City Univ. of New York.

Pay Discrimination Lawsuits: The Problems of Expert Witnesses and the Effects of the Discovery Process. Thomas H. Patten, Jr. Pers., Nov.–Dec. 1978, pp. 27–35. Michigan State Univ.

Personnel Testing Under EEO. Jerome Siegel. 1980, 92 pp. City Univ. of New York. RS.

Religious Accommodation and the Courts: An Overview. Mary Zippo. Pers., May–June 1981, pp. 47–49.

Sexual Harassment: New Concern About an Old Problem. Robert L. Woodrum. AMJ, Winter 1981, pp. 20–26. U.S. Office of Personnel Management.

Sexual Harassment: The Employer's Legal Obligations. Patricia Linenberger, Timothy J. Keaveny. Pers., Nov.–Dec. 1981, pp. 60–68. Univ. of Wyoming.

Weber Vs. Affirmative Action? Neil D. McFeeley. Pers., Jan.–Feb. 1980, pp. 38–51. Univ. of Idaho.

DISHONESTY. See also Security

A Crime: Management's Attitude Toward Theft. Harry Augenblick. MRev., Aug. 1977, pp. 29–31. Microlab/FXR.

Let's Get the Facts! James L. Hayes. MRev., June 1977, pp. 2–3.

The Second Criminal Justice System. Richard B. Cole. AMJ, Spring 1978, pp. 17–23. Loss Prevention Diagnostics, Inc.

Sticky Fingers: A Close Look at America's Fastest Growing Crime. William W. McCullough. 1981, 146 pp. U.S. Internal Revenue Service.

DISMISSAL. See Termination

DISTRIBUTION. See also Marketing, Transportation

Developing Integrated Distribution Information Systems. Bernard J. La Londe. *Managing International Distribution*, 1979, pp. 25–33. Ohio State Univ.

Improving Warehouse Productivity. Joel C. Wolff. 1981, 58 pp. Drake Sheahan/Stewart Dougall, Inc. MB.

How to Reduce Physical Distribution Costs. Wendell M. Stewart, Gordon V. Hill. *Managing International Distribution*, 1979, pp. 51–68. A. T. Kearney Inc.

Logistics Management: Who's in Charge Here? Warren L. Serenbetz. MRev., Nov. 1978, pp. 32–33. Interpool Ltd.

Logistics: The Total Distribution Concept. Martin Christopher. *Managing International Distribution*, 1979, pp. 3–13. Cranfield School of Management.

Managing International Distribution. Felix Wentworth, Martin Christopher (editors). 1979, 274 pp. Chubb Hennessey, Cranfield School of Management.

Product Service Planning: Service-Marketing-Engineering Interactions. William H. Bleuel, Henry Bender. 1980, 84 pp. AM International. RS.

Productivity in the Warehouse: Who Needs to Automate? C. A. Wunnenberg, Jr. MRev., Oct. 1977, pp. 56–58. National Distiller Products Co.

Towards Total Logistical Management. Donald J. Bowersox. *Managing International Distribution*, 1979, pp. 14–24. Michigan State Univ.

Who's Minding the Storage? Howard Way, Jr., Edward W. Smykay. MRev., Aug. 1980, pp. 14–22. Howard Way & Associates. Rutgers Univ.

DRUG ABUSE. See also Health
> **Alcohol and Drugs: Poor Remedies for Stress.** Gene Milbourn, Jr. SM, March 1981, pp. 35–42. Univ. of Baltimore.
> **Employing the Recovered Drug Abuser—Viable?** Jan P. Wijting. Pers., May–June 1979, pp. 56–63. New York Univ.

EDUCATION. See also Management Development, Supervisory Training, Training and Development
> **Career Development and Education.** David J. Cherrington. *The Work Ethic: Working Values and Values That Work*, 1980, pp. 197–221. Brigham Young Univ.
> **The Design of a Nursing Curriculum.** Susan G. Taylor. HSM, Sept. 1977, pp. 6–7. Univ. of Missouri-Columbia.
> **Doctoral Education: A Shot in the Arm for the Nursing Profession.** Luther Christman. HSM, May 1977, pp. 6–7. Rush Univ.
> **Education Levels Mirror Practice Levels.** Susan G. Taylor. HSM, July 1977, pp. 6–7. Univ. of Missouri-Columbia.
> **External Resources.** William R. Tracey. *Human Resource Development Standards*, 1981, pp. 419–457. U.S. Army Intelligence Training School.
> **Restructuring Management Education.** H. J. Zoffer. MRev., April 1981, pp. 37–41. Univ. of Pittsburgh.
> **Successful Midlife Career Change: Self-Understanding and Strategies for Action.** Paula I. Robbins. 1978, 268 pp. Fitchburg State College.
> **Training for Business.** Henry I. Meyer. *The Face of Business*, 1980, pp. 175–201.
> **What Is Practical Business Education?** G. Van Zanten. *Management Education in the 80's*, 1979, pp. 107–109.

EDUCATION MANAGEMENT. See Public Administration and Non-profit Management and headings for individual functions

EMPLOYEE BENEFITS. See also Insurance, Older Workers and Retirement, Pensions
> **Benefits.** Linda A. Roxe. *Personnel Management for the Smaller Company*, 1979, pp. 70–96. Rox Associates.
> **Benefits Administration.** John G. Kilgour. *Preventive Labor Relations*, 1981, pp. 149–177. California State Univ.
> **Controlling the Costs of Retirement Income and Medical Care Plans.** Philip M. Alden, Jr. 1980, 78 pp. Towers, Perrin, Forster & Crosby. MB.
> **Cost-Control Considerations for Designing an ESOP.** George B. Paulin. CR, Fourth Quarter 1979, pp. 22–30. Lee and Paulin Associates.
> **Employee Benefit Plans in the 1980s.** Mary Zippo. Pers., Jan.–Feb. 1980, pp. 66–68.
> **Employee Benefits.** Robert E. Sibson. *Compensation* (rev. ed.), 1981, pp. 262–277. The Sibson Group.
> **Employee-Choice Benefits—Can Employees Handle It?** Albert S. Schlachtmeyer, Robert B. Bogart. CR, Third Quarter 1979, pp. 12–19. Hewitt Associates, American Can Co.
> **Employer-Sponsored Child Care Comes of Age.** Mary Zippo. Pers., Nov.–Dec. 1980, pp. 45–48.
> **ESOPs and How They Work.** Larry D. Blust. *ESOPs and the Smaller Employer*, 1979, pp. 8–19. Jenner & Block. MB.
> **ESOPs and the Smaller Employer.** M. Mark Lee (editor). 1979, 79 pp. Standard Research Consultants. MB.
> **ESOPs as an Employee Benefit.** John F. Tercek. *ESOPs and the Smaller Employer*, 1979, pp. 20–30. Hirschfeld, Stern, Moyer & Ross, Inc. MB.
> **Fringe Benefits.** Theodore Cohn, Roy A. Lindberg. *Compensating Key Executives in the Smaller Company*, 1979, pp. 144–162.
> **Increasing the Motivational Impact of Employee Benefits.** William L. White, James W. Becker. Pers., Jan.–Feb. 1980, pp. 32–37. The Wyatt Co.

Issue for the 80's: Cutting the Costs of Workers' Rehabilitation. Eleanor M. Ross. HSM, March 1981, pp. 3, 13–15. U.S. Department of Labor.

How Do Your Fringe Benefits Stack Up? John L. Steffens. SM, April 1981, pp. 40–42. Merrill Lynch, Pierce, Fenner & Smith Inc.

Labor-Management Relations and Employee Stock-Ownership Programs. Timothy C. Jochim. Pers., Nov.–Dec. 1978, pp. 53–65.

Managing Employee Benefits. Jay William Cox. 1980. (Extension Institute Course) By purchase only.

Master Trust: Simplifying Employee Benefits Trust Fund Administration. Michael L. Costa. 1980, 213 pp. Citibank.

Maternity Disability Benefits: Why Not Compromise? William K. Cooper. Pers., March–April 1977, pp. 34–40. Merchants Insurance Group.

Perks, Fringes, and Hard Work. James L. Hayes. MRev., Nov. 1978, pp. 2–3.

Pick and Choose . . . How American Can Manage Its Flexible Benefits Program. Gerard Tavernier. MRev., Aug. 1980, pp. 8–13.

Raises Vs. Longer Vacations: Employees Choose. Mary Zippo. Pers., May–June 1981, pp. 44–45.

Risk Analysis Guide to Insurance and Employee Benefits. A. E. Pfaffle, Sal Nicosia. 1977, 71 pp. EBASCO Risk Management. MB.

Streamline Your Paid-Days Leave Programs. Donald F. Silver. HSM, April 1978, pp. 1–4, 10. The Psychiatric Institute.

Subsidized Employee Transportation: A Three-Way Benefit. Mary Zippo. Pers., May–June 1980, pp. 40–42.

The Tax Reform Act of 1976 and Prepaid Legal Insurance. Philip M. Alden, Jr. Pers., July–Aug. 1977, pp. 59–64. Towers, Perrin, Forster & Crosby.

Time-Off-With-Pay Practices. Hermine Zagat Levine. Pers., Sept.–Oct. 1981, pp. 4–12.

What to Do About Employee Absences for Jury Duty. T. J. Halatin, Jack D. Eure. SM, May 1981, pp. 32–35. Southwest Texas State Univ.

ENERGY MANAGEMENT. See also International Management

Are We Missing the Energy Train? D. R. Beall. *The International Essays for Business Decision Makers, Vol. III*, 1978, pp. 66–75. Rockwell International Corp.

Building Conservation into Products. Donald Moffitt (editor). *The Wall Street Journal Views America Tomorrow*, 1977, pp. 138–141. The Wall Street Journal.

Can International Energy Supplies Support the United States' Energy Needs? James E. Akins. *The International Essays for Business Decision Makers, Vol. IV*, 1979, pp. 61–67. Former U.S. Ambassador to Saudi Arabia.

Energy: A Global View. John C. Sawhill. *The International Essays for Business Decision Makers, Vol. V*, 1980, pp. 79–96. Synthetic Fuels Corp.

Energy in 2000. Donald Moffitt (editor). *The Wall Street Journal Views America Tomorrow*, 1977, pp. 121–126. The Wall Street Journal.

Energy Options: Our Stake in Understanding Them. Thomas A. Vanderslice. MRev., May 1979, pp. 19–23. General Electric Co.

Evaluating Risk in Petroleum Production Facilities Construction. William E. Leonhard. *The International Essays for Business Decision Makers, Vol. V*, 1980, pp. 323–329. The Parsons Corp.

Financing the International Petroleum Industry. Norman A. White (editor). 1978, 257 pp.

Happy Tinkerers. Donald Moffitt (editor). *The Wall Street Journal Views America Tomorrow*, 1977, pp. 132–137. The Wall Street Journal.

How the Energy Crisis Impacts Packaging Materials. Donald J. Bainton. *Key Social Issues for Packaging in the 1980s*, 1980, pp. 18–26. Continental Group, Inc.

How to Conduct an Energy Audit. T. Hollen, R. Redd. 1980. (an AMACOM Evaluation Tool) By purchase only.

Liquefield Natural Gas Systems. Albert W. Angulo. *Financing the International Petroleum Industry*, 1978, pp. 125–137. International Systems and Controls Corp.

LNG—A Way to Expand World Energy Supplies. Howard Boyd. *The International Essays for Business Decision Makers, Vol. III*, 1978, pp. 76–83. El Paso Co.

LNG Needs to Be in the Energy Mix. William C. Douce. *The International Essays for Business Decision Makers, Vol. IV*, 1979, pp. 86–93. Phillips Petroleum Co.

Loosening Up the "Fixed" Costs of Employee Benefits and Energy. Candace Roney. HSM, July 1981, pp. 3–6. San Jose Health Center and San Jose Hospital.

Managing Industrial Energy Conservation. 1977, 61 pp. MB.

Many Unexploited Sources . . . Energy Problem Is One of Cost, Not Supply. William B. Murphy. MRev., Aug. 1980, pp. 29–31. Campbell Soup Co.

The Nature and Structure of the Industry. Norman A. White. *Financing the International Petroleum Industry*, 1978, pp. 2–28.

Needed: A Comprehensive National Energy Plan for the United States. John C. Sawhill. *The International Essays for Business Decision Makers, Vol. IV*, 1979, pp. 68–74. U.S. Department of Energy.

Perspectives on Nuclear Energy. Edward Teller. *The International Essays for Business Decision Makers, Vol. V*, 1980, pp. 97–105. Stanford Univ.

Pipelines and Processing Plants. George S. Miller. *Financing the International Petroleum Industry*, 1978, pp. 110–124. Morgan Grenfell and Co., Ltd.

Prospects for Coal Conversion in the United States. J. R. Bowden. *The International Essays for Business Decision Makers, Vol. IV*, 1979, pp. 75–85. Conoco Coal Development Co.

Solar Power. Donald Moffitt (editor). *The Wall Street Journal Views America Tomorrow*, 1977, pp. 127–131. The Wall Street Journal.

Tankers and Offshore Drilling Rigs. Otto R. Norland. *Financing the International Petroleum Industry*, 1978, pp. 91–109. Hambros Bank, Ltd.

Total Energy Management: GM's Approach to the Fuel Problem. Neil De Koker. MRev., May 1978, pp. 29–31. General Motors Corp.

What the Supervisor Should Know About Energy Conservation. Edward A. Myers. SM, Oct. 1977, pp. 37–41. Southern California Edison Co.

World Energy in the 1980's—On a Razor's Edge. Ulf Lantzke. *The International Essays for Business Decision Makers, Vol. IV*, 1979, pp. 53–60. International Energy Agency.

ENGINEERS

CEO Urges More Sociability Among Engineers. Donald W. Frey. MRev., July 1981, pp. 29, 34. MacDonald Motivational Research Center Inc.

Needed: Excellent Engineers, Not Mediocre Managers. Moshe Krausz, Shaul Fox. Pers., Jan.–Feb. 1981, pp. 50–58. Tel Aviv Univ., Bar Ilan Univ.

EQUAL EMPLOYMENT OPPORTUNITY. See also Affirmative Action Programs, Discrimination

Affirmative Action, Conflict Resolution, and the Case of Rudolph, The Red-Nosed Reindeer. Fred L. Fry, Frank A. Wiebe. MRev., Dec. 1978, pp. 40–43. Bradley Univ., Univ. of Mississippi.

Affirmative Action Through Hiring and Promotion: How Fast a Rate? Berwyn N. Fragner. Pers., Nov.–Dec. 1979, pp. 67–71. TRW Systems & Energy.

Complying with EEO (PRIME 1000). 1979. (An AMACOM Skill Series home-study course) By purchase only.

EEO Guidelines—No Easy Answers. Deslie Beth Lawrence, Iris D. Rosendahl. Pers., March–April 1979, pp. 58–60.

EEO Pressures Changing Transfer and Promotion Policies. Philip Springer, William H. Wagel. Pers., May–June 1978, pp. 39–40.

Equal Pay for Comparable Work. Ernest C. Miller. Pers., Sept.–Oct. 1979, pp. 4–9.

How to Audit Your EEO Compliance. J. McConnell. 1979. (An AMACOM Evaluation Tool) By purchase only.

Implications of the New EEOC Guidelines. Thomas P. Dhanens. Pers., Sept.–Oct. 1979, pp. 32–39.

A New Approach to Affirmative Action. Robert L. St. John. Pers., May–June 1979, pp. 25–30. New York Telephone.

A New Approach to Affirmative Action Programs. Grover M. Clark, Jeanette Perlman. SM, Dec. 1977, pp. 10–15.

Personnel Programs and Activities. William R. Tracey. *Human Resource Development Standards*, 1981, pp. 253–295. U.S. Army Intelligence Training School.

Test Validation and EEOC Requirements: Where We Stand. Winton H. Manning. Pers., May–June 1978, pp. 70–77. Educational Testing Service.

Using Survey Feedback to Achieve Enlightened AA/EEO. George Neely, Fred Luthans. Pers., May–June 1978, pp. 18–23. Univ. of North Carolina.

What Blacks Want from Their Jobs—and What They Get. Gene Milbourn, Richard Cuba. AMJ, Autumn 1980, pp. 50–60. Univ. of Baltimore.

ETHICS

Catch 20.5: Corporate Morality as an Organizational Phenomenon. James A. Waters. OD, Spring 1978, pp. 3–19. McGill Univ.

Character. James L. Hayes. MRev., Jan. 1978, pp. 2–3.

The Emergence of the "Contemporary Employee." Roger J. Howe. *Building Profits Through Organizational Change*, 1981, pp. 117–129. Donaldson Co., Inc.

Conscience: The Spirit of the Law. James L. Hayes. MRev., Jan. 1979, pp. 2–3.

Corporate Codes of Ethics: A Key to Economic Freedom. Clark Moeller. MRev., Sept. 1980, pp. 60–62.

Ethics and the New Ideology: Can Business Adjust? George Cabot Lodge. MRev., July 1977, pp. 10–19. Harvard Business School.

Ethics in Research. Jeffrey Pope. *Practical Marketing Research*, 1981, pp. 262–270. Custom Research, Inc.

Ethics: To See Ourselves as Others Do. James L. Hayes. MRev., Dec. 1980, pp. 2–3.

Fortitude, Patience, Courage. James L. Hayes. MRev., July 1978, pp. 2–3.

Institutionalizing Corporate Ethics: A Case History. Theodore V. Purcell, James Weber. PA #71, 1980, 32 pp. Jesuit Center for Social Studies, Georgetown Univ. By purchase only.

Linking Business Ethics to Behavior in Organizations. Archie B. Carroll. AMJ, Summer 1978, pp. 4–11. Univ. of Georgia.

Other People's Money. James L. Hayes. MRev., June 1979, pp. 2–3.

Poll of Top Managers Stresses Education and Leadership-By-Example as Strong Forces for Higher Standards. Samir P. Dagher, Peter H. Spader. MRev., March 1980, pp. 54–57. Marywood College.

Rx for Reducing the Occasion of "Corporate Sin." W. Michael Blumenthal. AMJ, Winter 1977, pp. 4–13.

Toward a More Creative You: The Actualizing Philosophy. Harold R. McAlindon. SM, Nov. 1979, pp. 12–19. The Institute of Financial Education. (Also in reprint collection *Getting the Most Out of Your Job and Your Organization,* 1980)

The Work Ethic: Working Values and Values That Work. David J. Cherrington. 1980, 288 pp. Brigham Young Univ.

Your Leadership Values: Do You Stand for Something or Fall for Anything? James J. Cribbin. *Leadership: Strategies for Organizational Effectiveness*, 1981, pp. 256–272. St. John's Univ.

EXECUTIVES. See also Management

Baring Your Managerial Soul (Philosophically Speaking). Paul B. Malone, III. SM, June 1980, pp. 31–35. George Washington Univ.

Business Heroes from Homer to Horatio to Hawley. Stanley C. Vance. *The Evolving Science of Management*, 1979, pp. 391–404. Univ. of Tennessee.

The Changing Manager. H. Igor Ansoff. *Management Education in the 80's*, 1979, pp. 29–38. European Institute for Advanced Studies in Management.

Executive Accountability: Who Needs It? John A. Patton. MRev., Dec. 1978, pp. 17–21. Patton Consultants, Inc.

Executive Profile: How Do You Stack Up? Ernest C. Miller, William H. Wagel. Pers., Jan.–Feb. 1978, pp. 43–44.

Executives Under Siege: Strategies for Survival. George S. Odiorne. MRev., April 1978, pp. 7–12. Univ. of Massachusetts.

The First Rung. Robert L. Woodruff. AMJ, Winter 1980, pp. 53–59. R. G. Barry Corp.

The Invisible Manager. De Anne Rosenberg. AMJ, Spring 1977, pp. 51–62. De Anne Rosenberg, Inc.

The Coming Management Population Explosion. Jerome M. Rosow. AMJ, Autumn 1979, pp. 4–16. Work in America Institute.

Does Your Shared-Service Organization Need an Entrepreneur or an Administrator? Ted J. Leverette. HSM, June 1981, pp. 1–2. Investment Planning Associates.

Entrepreneurship in the Large Corporation: Is It Possible? Edward E. Lawler, John A. Drexler. MRev., Feb. 1981, pp. 8–11. Univ. of Southern California, Univ. of Washington.

The Exciting Manager. James L. Hayes. MRev., Oct. 1978, pp. 2–3.

Making It to the Top: A Career Profile of the Senior Executive. John A. Sussman. MRev., July 1979, pp. 15–21. Korn/Ferry International.

Management and Modes of Thought. Patrick S. Nugent. OD, Spring 1981, pp. 45–59. Univ. of Quebec.

Managers in Action: A New Look at Their Behavior and Operating Modes. Tim R. V. Davis, Fred Luthans. OD, Summer 1980, pp. 64–80. Cleveland State Univ., Univ. of Nebraska.

Managers of Change: Why They Are in Demand. Bridgford Hunt. AMJ, Winter 1980, pp. 40–44. The Hunt Co.

The Mature Executive. James L. Hayes. 1978. (AMACOM audio cassette) By purchase only.

Portrait of the Manager as an Achiever. Jay Hall, Robert K. Glasgow. SM, Aug. 1979, pp. 10–14. Teleometrics International.

Preparing for a Move to Middle Management. Robert R. Bell, J. Bernard Keys. SM, July 1980, pp. 10–16. Tennessee Technological Univ.

Unleashing Middle Managers. Mark R. Arnold. MRev., May 1981, pp. 58–61.

EXECUTIVES—CARTOON FEATURES

Funny Business: A Tongue-in-Cheek Guide to Power and Success. E. Alfred Osborne. 1979, 110 pp.

Listening Made Easy: How to Improve Listening on the Job, at Home, and in the Community. Robert L. Montgomery. 1981, 134 pp. R. L. Montgomery & Associates.

EXECUTIVES—SKILLS AND QUALIFICATIONS. See also Management Development, Selection—Professional Personnel

Action Strategies for Managerial Achievement. Dalton E. McFarland. 1977, 198 pp. Univ. of Alabama.

The Androgynous Blend: Best of Both Worlds? Alice G. Sargent. MRev., Oct. 1978, pp. 60–65.

The Androgynous Manager. Alice G. Sargent. 1981, 238 pp.

Antidotes to Personal Obsolescence. Robert A. Moskowitz. 1977. (Extension Institute Cassette Program) By purchase only.

Are You an Effective Manager? John H. Zenger. HSM, Sept. 1981, pp. 7–9. Syntex Corp.

Becoming a Nurse Manager. Monica M. Magner. HSM, June 1979, pp. 2–3. Bronx Municipal Hospital Center.

Being a Builder. William C. Waddell. *Overcoming Murphy's Law*, 1981, pp. 60–79. California State Univ., Los Angeles.

Bridging the Promotion Gap. Thomas J. Neff. MRev., Jan. 1978, pp. 42–45. Spencer Stuart & Associates.

Can You Manage in a Fishbowl? Howard Sargent. MRev., May 1978, pp. 55–62. Howard Sargent Associates.

Conquering Fear of Figures. Stanley Kogelman. SM, Part 1. Sept. 1980, pp. 2–8. Part 2. Oct. 1980, pp. 10–16. Mind Over Math.

The Corporate Casino: How Managers Win and Lose at the Biggest Game in Town. Dean P. Peskin. 1978, 243 pp. Joseph George Distributors.

Developing Political Savvy. Vicky Kaminski. SM, Sept. 1981, pp. 36–39.

Developing the High Performance Edge. Edward J. Feeney. AMJ, Autumn 1981, pp. 29–30, 35–39. Edward J. Feeney Associates.

Directing. William R. Tracey. *Human Resource Development Standards*, 1981, pp. 116–132. U.S. Army Intelligence Training School.

Efficient Reading for Managers. J. Michael Bennet. 1981. (Extension Institute Course) By purchase only.

Executive Dissent: How to Say "No" and Win. Auren Uris. 1978, 192 pp. Research Institute of America.

The Executive Look and How to Get It. Mortimer Levitt. 1979, 76 pp. MB.

The First-Time Manager. Loren B. Belker. 1981. (AMACOM audio cassette book) By purchase only.

Form Vs. Substance: Some Guidelines for Managers. William A. Delaney. MRev., Nov. 1978, pp. 46–48. Analysis & Computer Systems, Inc.

From the Gestalt Perspective: A Tool for Increasing Individual Effectiveness. H. B. Karp. MRev., Jan. 1980, pp. 58–61.

The Gentle Use of Power. James L. Hayes. MRev., May 1978, pp. 2–3.

Getting that Promotion. Robert A. Benson. SM, Dec. 1978, pp. 7–11. Monsanto Research Corp.

Getting Work Done: Is There a Right Way? Dell Lebo. HSM, May 1977, pp. 8–9. Child Guidance Clinic.

A Guide to Personal Risk Taking. Richard E. Byrd. 1981. (AMACOM audio cassette book) By purchase only.

How to Be an Effective Executive. Kenneth M. Lizotte. 1978. (Extension Institute Cassette Program) By purchase only.

How to Be an Effective Middle Manager. Joseph F. Byrnes. 1981. (Extension Institute Cassette Program) By purchase only.

How to Build Memory Skills. David V. Lewis. 1978. (Extension Institute Course) By purchase only.

How to Develop a Better Memory. ES, May 1979, 16 pp.

How to Get to the Top . . . and Stay There. Robert J. McKain. 1981, 210 pp.

How to Identify Your Negative Behavior Characteristics. John Singleton. SM, July 1980, pp. 17–24. Maryland National Bank.

How to Improve Your Memory. George R. Bell. 1980. (Extension Institute Cassette Program) By purchase only.

How to Influence People Outside Your Control. Alan Jay Weiss. SM, Dec. 1977, pp. 2–9. Kepner-Tregoe, Inc. (Also reprinted in HSM, Nov. 1980)

How to Interview Effectively. Garry Mitchell. 1980. (Extension Institute Cassette Program) By purchase only.

How to Manage Paperwork. Brook Taliaferro. 1981. (Extension Institute Course) By purchase only.

How to Read More Efficiently. ES, July 1979, 16 pp.

Impact Management: Personal Power Strategies for Success. George J. Lumsden. 1979, 150 pp. Chrysler Corp.

Learning How to Influence Others. Marvin R. Weisbord, C. James Maselko. SM, May 1981, pp. 2–10. Block Petrella Weisbord.

Learning People Skills from the Pros. Thomas Belinoski. SM, May 1981, pp. 39–43. Educational Testing Service.

Learning to Take a Risk in Five Easy Lessons. Ralph Cox. MRev., March 1981, p. 36. Atlantic Richfield Inc.

Listen Your Way to Success. Robert L. Montgomery. 1977. (AMACOM audio cassette) By purchase only.

Making Your Way Assertively. Malcolm E. Shaw. SM, March 1981, pp. 2–11. Educational Systems and Designs, Inc.

Managerial Skills for New and Prospective Managers. David V. Lewis. 1978. (Extension Institute Cassette Program) By purchase only.

A Manager's Approach to the Paperwork Explosion. Lee Grossman. MRev., Sept. 1978, pp. 57–61. Helene Curtis Industries.

Managing Incompetence. William P. Anthony. 1981, 276 pp. The Florida State Univ.

Memory Made Easy: The Complete Book of Memory Training. Robert L. Montgomery. 1979, 111 pp. R. L. Montgomery & Associates.

Negotiating Your Way to Success. Grant E. Mayberry. 1979. (Extension Institute Course) By purchase only.

Negotiation: When and How to Use It. ES, Nov. 1980, 16 pp.

A New Look at Managerial Competence: The AMA Model of Worthy Performance. James L. Hayes. MRev., Part I. Nov. 1979, pp. 2–3. Part II: The AMA Model of Superior Performance—How Can I Do a Better Job as a Manager? Feb. 1980, pp. 2–3. Part III: The AMA Model of Superior Performance—How Competent Managers Work with People. March 1980, pp. 2–3.

Opportunities in Doubt. James L. Hayes. MRev., Aug. 1981, pp. 2–3.

Paperwork Style and Managerial Effectiveness. Craig Dreilinger. MRev., Jan. 1980, pp. 21–24. D&T Associates.

Personal Power Enhancement: A Way to Executive Success. Walter Reichman, Marguerite Levy. MRev., March 1977, pp. 28–34. City Univ. of New York, Queens College.

Power in Management: How to Understand, Acquire, and Use It. John P. Kotter. 1979, 105 pp. Harvard Business School. (Also AMACOM audio cassette book. By purchase only.)

Power, Success, and Organizational Effectiveness. John P. Kotter. OD, Winter 1978, pp. 26–40.

Profile of a Tough-Minded Manager. Joe D. Batten. *Leadership on the Job: Guides to Good Supervision* (third ed.), 1981, pp. 17–23. Batten, Batten, Hudson & Swab, Inc. (From *Tough-Minded Management*, 1978)

Reading/Plus. Gloria Hunter. 1978. (AMACOM audio cassette) By purchase only.

Risk-Taking Managers: Who Gets the Top Jobs? Ronald J. Grey, George G. Gordon. MRev., Nov. 1978, pp. 8–13. Hay Associates.

Sample Lists of Management Competencies (Appendix B). Alice G. Sargent. *The Androgynous Manager*, 1981, pp. 213–223.

The Self-Reliant Manager. John Cowan. 1977, 255 pp. Control Data Corp. (Also AMACOM audio cassette book. By purchase only.)

The Several Managerial Roles. Herman R. Holtz. *Profit-Line Management: Managing a Growing Business Successfully*, 1981, pp. 52–75.

Shirt-Sleeves Management. James F. Evered. 1981, 180 pp. Redman Industries, Inc.

The Skills of Management. A. N. Welsh. 1981, 196 pp.

The Sources, Uses, and Conservation of Managerial Power. Vandra L. Huber. Pers., July–Aug. 1981, pp. 62–71. Indiana Univ.

Strategies for Managerial Impact: The Dynamics of Individual Change. Robert A. Neiman. MRev., May 1979, pp. 52–56. Robert H. Schaffer & Associates.

Success Through Assertiveness. Diane Arthur. 1980. (Extension Institute Course) By purchase only.

Surviving and Succeeding in the 'Political' Organization. Alan Jay Weiss. 1978, 48 pp. Kepner-Tregoe, Inc. (A collection of reprints from SM)

Surviving and Succeeding in the 'Political' Organization: Controlling Your Environment. Alan Jay Weiss. SM, July 1978, pp. 21–28. Kepner-Tregoe, Inc. (Also in reprint collection *Surviving and Succeeding in the 'Political' Organization*, 1978)

Surviving the Organizational Jungle. John J. Beck. SM, July 1981, pp. 32–34. Southwest Texas State Univ.

Taking Charge of Yourself and Your Job. Lyn Taetzsch, Eileen Benson. SM, Oct. 1978, pp. 2–11.

Taking Over the New Job: Breaking Through Vs. Breaking In. Harvey A. Thomson, James A. Waters. AMJ, Spring 1979, pp. 4–16. Robert H. Schaffer & Associates, McGill Univ.

Test Your Managerial Awareness with the Alphabet of Cs. Mark B. Silber. HSM, June 1977, pp. 8–9. Hume, Mansfield, Silber, Ltd.

3 RS + 8 CS = A Successful Manager. Sigmund G. Ginsburg. SM, April 1978, pp. 22–25. Adelphi Univ.

Tough-Minded Management (rev. ed.). Joe D. Batten. 1978, 224 pp. Batten, Batten, Hudson and Swab, Inc.

Toward a More Creative You: The Actualizing Executive. Harold R. McAlindon. SM, Dec. 1979, pp. 22–29. Institute of Financial Education. (Also in reprint collection *Getting the Most Out of Your Job and Your Organization*, 1980)

Using Managerial Authority. Peter Venuto. 1980. (Extension Institute Cassette Program) By purchase only.

What Every Head Nurse Should Know About Management. Sylvia Carson. HSM, March 1981, pp. 11–12. Western Baptist Hospital.

Why Can't Johnny Manage? You May Be Promoting the Wrong People. Roger Fritz. HSM, May 1979, pp. 7–9. Organizational Development Consultants.

EXECUTIVES—WOMEN

The Ambitious Woman's Guide to a Successful Career (rev. ed.). Margaret V. Higginson, Thomas L. Quick. 1980, 276 pp. The Research Institute of America.

Becoming the Executive You'd Like to Be: A Program for Female Middle Managers. Paul L. Goldstein, Jane Sorensen. AMJ, Fall 1977, pp. 41–49. Jane Sorensen Associates.

Building Teamwork and Avoiding Backlash: Keys to Developing Managerial Women. Kristin Anundsen. MRev., Feb. 1979, pp. 55–58.

Career Development and the Woman Manager—A Social Power Perspective. Gary N. Powell. Pers., May–June 1980, pp. 22–32. Univ. of Connecticut.

Developing Women Managers: What Needs to be Done? Martha G. Burrow. 1978, 32 pp. CoMedia, Inc. MB.

How Successful Women Manage. Beverly Hyman. 1981. (Extension Institute Course) By purchase only.

Men and Women as Managers: A Significant Case of No Significant Difference. Susan M. Donnell, Jay Hall. OD, Spring 1980, pp. 60–77. Teleometrics International.

Needed: Career Counseling for Women Subordinates. Margaret V. Higginson, Thomas L. Quick. HSM, Nov. 1981, pp. 6–10. Research Institute of America.

Rite of Passage ... Women for the Inner Circle. I. Thomas Sheppard. MRev., July 1981, pp. 8–14. Univ. of Texas.

Time-Management Strategy for Women. Eleanor B. Schwartz, R. Alec Mackenzie. MRev., Sept. 1977, pp. 19–25. Cleveland State Univ., Alec Mackenzie & Associates.

Two Careers—One Marriage. William M. Jones, Ruth A. Jones. 1980, 229 pp. Univ. of Missouri.

An Uppity Woman's View of Bureaucracy. Leslie Dock. MRev., June 1978, pp. 45–49. Midsummer Press.

Will He—or Won't He—Work with a Female Manager? Alma S. Baron, Ken Abrahamsen. MRev., Nov. 1981, pp. 48–53. Univ. of Wisconsin.

Women in Management: Can It Be a Renaissance for Everybody? Lou Willet Stanek. MRev., Nov. 1980, pp. 44–48. Philip Morris, Inc.

FINANCIAL MANAGEMENT. See also Accounting, Budgeting, Cash Management, Cost Control, Credit Management, International Operations—Finance, Investor Relations, Mergers and Acquisitions, Reports, Return on Investment

Bankruptcy: Not Necessarily a Disaster. Travis D. Sullivan. MRev., Aug. 1977, pp. 44–48. Main Lafrentz & Co.

Basic Financial Management (rev. ed.). Curtis W. Symonds. 1978, 208 pp. Financial Control Associates.

Basics of Finance and Accounting. Theodore Cohn, Samuel Laibstain. 1981. (AMACOM audio cassette) By purchase only.

Basics of Successful Business Planning. William R. Osgood. 1980, 252 pp.

Building Financial Decision Making Models: An Introduction to Principles and Procedures. Donald Moscato. 1980, 150 pp. Iona College.

Business Strategy and Inflation: Finding the Real Bottom Line. Robert E. MacAvoy. MRev., Jan. 1978, pp. 17–24. William E. Hill & Co.

Business Valuation. Joseph Shaw Chalfant. BPM 17, Nov. 1981, 5 pp. Shaw International.

Capital Expenditure Decisions Under Risk and Uncertainty. Narendra C. Bhandari. AMJ, Autumn 1981, pp. 52–61. Pace Univ.

Commercial Banking (sec. ed.). Geoffrey J. Mansfield, Henry C. Barkhorn. 1979. (Extension Institute Course) By purchase only.

Commercial Financing: A Tight Money Strategy for Smaller Companies. Walter Kaye. MRev., Feb. 1981, pp. 17–20. Congress Financial Corp.

The Controller: New Game, New Rules. Lionel N. Sterling. MRev., Dec. 1978, pp. 30–31. American Can Co.

Controllership in Divisionalized Firms: Structure, Evaluation and Development. Vijay Sathe. 1978, 45 pp. MB.

The Corporate Controller: Role & Responsibilities. John E. Buckley, Kenneth M. Lizotte. 1979. (Extension Institute Cassette Program) By purchase only.

ESOPs as a Technique of Corporate Finance. M. Mark Lee. *ESOPs and the Smaller Employer*, 1979, pp. 31–45. Standard Research Consultants.

Evaluating Accounting and Finance. Robert J. Thierauf. *Management Auditing: A Questionnaire Approach*, 1980, pp. 59–81. Xavier Univ.

Evaluating Capital-Investment Proposals. James D. Suver. HSM, Aug. 1979, pp. 1–4. Univ. of Colorado.

Financial Management for Small Business. Edward N. Rausch. 1979, 184 pp. Wright State Univ.

The Financial Planner's Contribution to Effective Decision Making. Surendra S. Singhvi. MRev., June 1979, pp. 12–15. Armco Inc.

Financial Plans That Are Tempered to Bend. Surendra S. Singhvi. *Corporate Planning Techniques and Applications*, 1979, pp. 297–305. Aramco Steel Corp.

Financial Reporting Under Changing Values: An Introduction to Current Value Accounting. Morley P. Carscallen, Kenneth P. Johnson. 1979, 47 pp. Coopers and Lybrand. MB.

Financing Alternatives for Small and Medium-Sized Corporations. Lawrence J. Trautman. BPM 15, Sept. 1981, 8 pp. Donaldson, Lifkin & Jenrette.

Financing Options in Corporate Real Estate Development. Thomas Selck. MRev., Aug. 1979, pp. 51–54.

Handbook of Business Finance and Capital Sources. Dileep Rao. 1979, 480 pp.

How to Audit Finance. J. McConnell. 1979. (An AMACOM Evaluation Tool) By purchase only.

How to Interpret Financial Statements. Terry Isom, Sudhir P. Amembal. 1980. (Extension Institute Cassette Program) By purchase only.

How to Read and Interpret Balance Sheets and Income Statements. ES, Dec. 1978, 16 pp.

How to Use Banking Resources. ES, Oct. 1980, 16 pp.

The Indexed Balance Sheet: A New Focus of Management. Michael J. Kami. MRev., June 1977, pp. 29–31. Corporate Planning, Inc.

Inflation and Corporate Strategy: The Rashomon Effect. John G. Main. MRev., May 1980, pp. 23–28. Main, Jackson & Garfield, Inc.

International Commercial Banking Management. James L. Kammert. 1981, 403 pp. Equibank.

An Introduction to Electronic Funds Transfer Systems. Claude R. Martin, Jr. 1978, 40 pp. Univ. of Michigan. MB.

A Job for Creative Management . . . How to Fight the Profitability Squeeze. Anders Wall. MRev., March 1979, pp. 58–62. Beijerinvest.

The Job of the Corporate Controller. John E. Buckley. 1977. (Extension Institute Course) By purchase only.

A Manager's Guide to Financial Analysis. L. Allan Austin, William Hammink. 1981. (Extension Institute Course) By purchase only.

Money and Business. Fred W. Latham, George S. Sanders. *Urwick, Orr on Management,* 1980, pp. 136–162. Urwick, Orr & Partners.

A New Look at Money Management: How to Make More Productive Use of Working Capital. Anthony E. Cascino. MRev., May 1979, pp. 42–46. International Minerals & Chemical Corp.

Principles of Finance. Elliott L. Atamian. 1981. (Extension Institute Course) By purchase only.

Principles of Investment Management. Janet J. Johnson. 1981. (Extension Institute Course) By purchase only.

Psychology and the Stock Market: Investment Strategy Beyond Random Walk. David N. Dreman. 1977, 306 pp. Rauscher Pierce Securities Corp.

Reading and Interpreting Financial Statements. George J. Chorba. 1978. (Extension Institute Course) By purchase only.

The Real Estate Gamble. Alan Rabinowitz. 1980, 308 pp. Univ. of Washington.

Selling Capital Needs to the Corporate Parent. Stanley Adler. MRev., April 1979, pp. 53–55. Western Manufacturing Co.

Short-term Funds: Where to Find Them, How to Choose Them. ES, July 1981, 16 pp.

Using Financing and Executive Talents. William E. Rothschild. *Strategic Alternatives: Selection Development and Implementation,* 1979, pp. 146–164. General Electric.

Valuation of Common Stock in ESOP Transactions. M. Mark Lee. *ESOPs and the Smaller Employer,* 1979, pp. 69–79. Standard Research Consultants. MB.

Valuing Common Stock: The Power of Prudence. George Lasry. 1979, 239 pp. E. Lasry & Co.

Venture Capital—Information for the Entrepreneur. George M. Yaworsky, Delmar W. Karger. AMJ, Spring 1979, pp. 32–39. Rensselaer Polytechnic Institute, Univ. of West Florida.

What the Supervisor Should Know About Financial Control. Thomas G. Kress. SM, Jan. 1977, pp. 30–34.

What to Look for Before Investing in Small Companies. Moustafa Abdelsamad, Alexander T. Kindling, Thomas L. Wheelen. MRev., Nov. 1977, pp. 26–28, 37–38. Virginia Commonwealth Univ., Atomatic Manufacturing Co., The Society for Advancement of Management, Univ. of Virginia.

When and How Troubled Executives Should Ask Those Tough Questions. Abraham E. Getzler. MRev., March 1979, pp. 33–34.

FORECASTING METHODS. See also Socio-Economic Conditions

Corporate Futurists. Donald Moffitt (editor). *The Wall Street Journal Views America Tomorrow,* 1977, pp. 12–17. The Wall Street Journal.

Forecasting Exchange Rates. John Heywood. *Foreign Exchange and the Corporate Treasurer* (sec. ed.), 1979, pp. 112–128. Hambros Bank, London.

Forecasting for Planning. John C. Chambers, Satinder K. Mullick. *Corporate Planning Techniques and Applications,* 1979, pp. 324–336. Xerox Corp., Corning Glass Works.

Forecasting: Systematic Subjectivism. Alfred R. Oxenfeldt, David W. Miller, Roger A. Dickinson. *A Basic Approach to Executive Decision Making,* 1978, pp. 133–151. Columbia Univ., Univ. of Texas.

The Hatching of Public Opinion. Graham T. T. Molitor. *Corporate Planning Techniques and Applications,* 1979, pp. 53–62. Public Policy Forecasting.

How to Anticipate Public-Policy Changes. Graham T. T. Molitor. AMJ, Summer 1977, pp. 4–13. General Mills, Inc.

How to Reduce Uncertainty in Sales Forecasting. Charles L. Hubbard, Carroll N. Mohn. MRev., June 1978, pp. 14–22. Georgia State Univ., Coca Cola Co.

How to Use Trend Analysis in Determining and Quantifying Long-Range Objectives.

Edmund J. Luksus, James B. Ruby. MRev., April 1979, pp. 43–49. San Jose Police Department, San Jose State Univ.

The Inflationary Flashpoint: Key to Long-Range Economic Forecasting. Gordon B. Pye. MRev., May 1978, pp. 33–34. Irving Trust Co.

Let George Do It: A New Look at Business Forecasting. David Loye. MRev., May 1978, pp. 48–52. Univ. of California, Los Angeles.

Market Forecasting: Eleven Predictors. John C. Touhey. *Stock Market Forecasting for Alert Investors*, 1980, pp. 1–89.

Overview of Forecasting Methods. Donald R. Moscato. *Building Financial Decision Making Models: An Introduction to Principles and Procedures*, 1980, pp. 22–35. Metamation Systems.

Process Is More Important than Product. J. S. Mandell, W. Lynn Tanner. *Corporate Planning Techniques and Applications*, 1979, pp. 260–265. Florida Atlantic Univ., Univ. of Calgary.

Technology Assessment—A New Imperative in Corporate Planning. George E. Humphries. *Corporate Planning Techniques and Applications*, 1979, pp. 337–344. Advanced Technology Management Associates.

The Use of Input-Output in Industrial Planning. A. George Gols. *Corporate Planning Techniques and Applications*, 1979, pp. 271–281. Arthur D. Little Inc.

FRINGE BENEFITS. See Employee Benefits

GLOSSARIES

Appendix 8. Glossary. Herman Holtz. *The $100 Billion Market: How to Do Business with the U.S. Government*, 1980, pp. 256–262.

Data Base Glossary. Ronald G. Ross. *Data Base Systems: Design, Implementation, and Management*, 1978, pp. 206–216. Performance Development Corp.

Data Dictionaries and Data Administration: Concepts and Practices for Data Resources Management. Ronald G. Ross. 1981, 454 pp. Performance Development Corp.

Decision-Making Glossary. John D. Arnold. *Make Up Your Mind*, 1978, pp. 195–196. Executrak Systems.

A Deskbook of Business Management Terms. Leon A. Wortman. 1979, 615 pp. L. A. Wortman Associates.

Glossary. David Casey, David Pearce (editors). *More than Management Development: Action Learning at GEC*, 1977, pp. 145–146. Action Learning Projects International, GEC.

Glossary. Joseph J. Famularo. *Organization Planning Manual* (rev. ed.), 1979, pp. 362–372. McGraw-Hill, Inc.

Glossary. Albert F. Gargiulo, Raymond J. Kenard, Jr. *Leveraged Leasing: New Opportunities Under the Economic Recovery Tax Act of 1981*, pp. 45–53. Raymond J. Kenard, Jr., Inc. MB.

Glossary. Richard W. Lott. *Auditing the Data Processing Function*, 1980, pp. 193–198.

Glossary. John B. McMaster. *The Network Reports System of Analysis and Control*, 1976, pp. 31–33. John B. McMaster & Associates. MB.

Glossary. James L. Mercer, Ronald J. Philips. *Public Technology: Key to Improved Government Productivity*, 1981, pp. 257–262. Korn/Ferry International, National Aeronautics & Space Administration.

Glossary. Ronald G. Ross. *Data Dictionaries and Data Administration: Concepts and Practices for Data Resources Management*, 1981, pp. 422–437. Performance Development Corp.

Glossary. Ruth H. Stack. *HMOs from the Management Perspective*, 1979, pp. 46–48. National Assn. of Employers on Health Maintenance Organizations. MB.

Glossary. Adam Starchild. *Building Wealth: A Layman's Guide to Trust Planning*, 1981, pp. 211–215. Minerva Consulting Group Inc.

Glossary. Roy D. Thylin. *Current Value Accounting*, 1977, pp. 166–171. Coopers & Lybrand.

Glossary. Paul H. Till, Albert F. Gargiulo. *Contracts: The Move to Plain Language,* 1979, pp. 50–56. MB.

Glossary. Joseph M. Vles. *Computer Fundamentals for Nonspecialists,* 1981, pp. 161–174.

A Glossary of Computer Terms. Walter A. Levy. *The Affordable Computer: The Microcomputer for Business and Industry,* 1979, pp. 159–173. Edgewood Computer Associates Inc.

Glossary of Frequently Used Terms. Lucille A. Maddalena. *A Communications Manual for Nonprofit Organizations,* 1981, pp. 213–215. Fairleigh Dickinson Univ.

Glossary of Lease Terms, Appendix A. Robert E. Pritchard, Thomas Hindelang. *The Lease/Buy Decision,* 1980, pp. 193–202. Glassboro State Univ., Drexel Univ.

Glossary of Marketing Research Terms. Jeffrey Pope. *Practical Marketing Research,* 1981, pp. 279–284. Custom Research Inc.

Glossary (Investment). C. Colburn Hardy. *Your Money & Your Life: How to Plan Your Long-Range Financial Security,* 1979, pp. 176–181.

Glossary (Life Insurance). C. Colburn Hardy. *Your Money & Your Life: How to Plan Your Long-Range Financial Security,* 1979, pp. 219–221.

Glossary (Real Estate). C. Colburn Hardy. *Your Money & Your Life: How to Plan Your Long-Range Financial Security,* 1979, p. 134.

Glossary (Retirement). C. Colburn Hardy. *Your Money & Your Life: How to Plan Your Long-Range Financial Security,* 1979, pp. 108–109.

Glossary (Taxes). C. Colburn Hardy. *Your Money & Your Life: How to Plan Your Long-Range Financial Security,* 1979, p. 222.

Glossary Terms: Appendix II. William V. Nygren. *Business Forms Management,* 1980, pp. 161–176. 3M Co.

Glossary (Trusts). C. Colburn Hardy. *Your Money & Your Life: How to Plan Your Long-Range Financial Security,* 1979, pp. 257–258.

How to Talk to Advertising People. Irwin Braun. *Building a Successful Professional Practice with Advertising,* 1981, pp. 252–264. Braun Advertising, Inc.

GOVERNMENT AND BUSINESS. See also Employee Benefits, Legislation and Regulation, Taxation

Accountability and Power ... Whither Corporate Governance in a Free Society? Irving S. Shapiro, Harold M. Williams. MRev., Feb. 1980, pp. 29–31. Du Pont, Securities Exchange Commission.

The Business Executive in Government: Look Before You Leap. Sigmund G. Ginsburg. MRev., Feb. 1980, pp. 64–66. Univ. of Cincinnati.

A Business Guide to Political Action. Roy L. Ash. MRev., May 1977, pp. 20–23. Addressograph-Multigraph Corp.

Corporate Accountability and Corporate Power. Harold M. Williams. *Corporate Governance Review,* 1981, pp. 8–25. Securities & Exchange Commission.

Difficult Decisions: Dealing with Tomorrow's Problems Today. Willis S. White, Jr. MRev., Dec. 1977, pp. 18–19. American Electric Power Co.

The Federal Government as a National Account. Edward K. Walsh. *National Accounts Marketing Handbook,* 1981, pp. 257–266. American Can Co.

For Less Onerous Regulations: A Joint Approach. Wayne L. Horvitz. MRev., Dec. 1977, pp. 21–22. Federal Mediation & Conciliation Service.

The Future of 'Free' Enterprise. Arthur M. Johnson. MRev., Oct. 1980, pp. 9–14. Univ. of Maine.

How to Sell to the Government Market. William A. Cohen, Marshall E. Reddick. *Successful Marketing for Small Business,* 1981, 211–233 pp. California State Univ.

Implementing Expansion Plans with Federal Dollars. Anthony C. Paddock. MRev., March 1980, pp. 42–45. Standard Research Consultants.

Making Capitalism More Human and More Efficient. Edward E. Barr. MRev., Dec. 1977, pp. 19–20. Sun Chemical Corp.

The Moving Force: Preserving the Profit Motive in the American Economy. Henry I. Meyer. 1981, 323 pp.

Needed: A "Bill of Rights" for Industry. Richard L. Terrell. MRev., Dec. 1977, pp. 17–18. General Motors Corp.

The $100 Billion Market: How to Do Business with the Government. Herman Holtz. 1980, 272 pp.

Participating in Public Policy Decisions. Jeffrey Salzman. *The International Essays for Business Decision Makers, Vol. IV*, 1979, pp. 103–113. Stanford Univ.

Politics and Work: Do They Mix? Mary Zippo. Pers., May–June 1981, pp. 43–44.

Redefining the Rights and Responsibilities of Capital. Hazel Henderson. MRev., Oct. 1977, pp. 9–20. Princeton Center for Alternative Futures.

Regulatory Paperwork: A Company Assesses Its Cost in Time and Money. MRev., July 1979, pp. 46–47.

Rights and Responsibilities of Capital: A Businessman's View. Jorge Bilbao. MRev., April 1978, pp. 40–43. Squibb-Spain.

Selling to the U.S. Government. Herman R. Holtz. *Profit from your Money-Making Ideas: How to Build a New Business or Expand an Existing One*, 1980, pp. 302–324.

Serving the Public Interest: Corporate Political Action Strategies for the 1980s. S. Prakash Sethi. MRev., March 1981, pp. 8–11. Univ. of Texas.

Shredding Federal Paperwork. Warren B. Buhler. MRev., Feb. 1978, pp. 16–19. Commission on Federal Paperwork.

The State and the Market: The Changing Relationship Between Business and Government. Paul A. Samuelson. MRev., Dec. 1977, pp. 14, 16. Massachusetts Institute of Technology.

Urges More Conciliation. Charles A. Meyers. MRev., Dec. 1977, p. 22. Sloan Fellows.

Wading Through the Maze of Government Bureaucracy. Gerald J. Voros, Paul Alvarez (editors). *What Happens in Public Relations*, 1981, pp. 168–175. Ketchum MacLeod & Grove.

GRAPEVINE. See Communications—Grapevine

GRIEVANCES

Cutting Down on Complaints. Lois Kaufman, John Wolf. SM, March 1981, pp. 14–17. Cook College of Rutgers Univ., John Jay College of Criminal Justice.

The Employee's Challenge—A Right and an Obligation. John H. Goss. *Human Resources Management: The Past Is Prologue*, 1979, pp. 31–38.

Five Steps for Handling Contract Grievances. Keith B. Krinke, Jerome M. Nelson. SM, Sept. 1977, pp. 14–20.

Grievance Procedure: The Case of the Botched Opportunity. Lois Kaufman, John Wolf. SM, April 1981, pp. 9–12. Cook College of Rutgers Univ., John Jay College of Criminal Justice.

Grievance Procedures for Nonunionized Employees. Thomasine Rendero. Pers., Jan.–Feb. 1980, pp. 4–10.

Guides for Handling Complaints and Changes. Ray A. Killian. *Managers Must Lead!* (rev. ed.), 1979, pp. 109–118. Belk Stores.

"I Object!" Coming to Terms with Grievances. SS, Aug. 1980, 24 pp.

Making Dissent Constructive. Auren Uris. *Executive Dissent: How to Say "No" and Win*, 1978, pp. 131–179. Research Institute of America.

Resolving Employee Complaints. Louis V. Imundo. *The Effective Supervisor's Handbook*, 1980, pp. 166–183. Management Perspectives.

Supervisory Relations: Minding the Bag Bearers. William E. Zierden. SM, April 1980, pp. 2–8. Univ. of Virginia. (Also reprinted in *Making Successful Presentations*, 1981)

What the Supervisor Should Know About Handling Employee Complaints. Ronald L. Miller. SM, Feb. 1978, pp. 38–42.

HANDICAPPED WORKERS. See also Discrimination

Employing the Handicapped: A Practical Compliance Manual. Arno B. Zimmer. 1981, 374 pp. Eliot-Yeats, Inc.

Hiring the Handicapped. Jack R. Ellner, Henry E. Bender. 1980, 74 pp. Southern Illinois Univ. RS.

Hospitals and the Handicapped: A New Approach to Quality Care. Peggy Meyer. HSM, Nov. 1981, pp. 1–2, 14. Mainstream, Inc.

Managing the Handicapped. Mary E. Tholt. SM, Oct. 1978, pp. 36–39.

Paving the Way for Hiring the Handicapped. Donald J. Petersen. Pers., March–April 1981, pp. 43–52. Loyola Univ.

Smoothing the Way for the Handicapped Worker. A. B. Zimmer. SM, April 1981, pp. 3–8. Eliot-Yeats, Inc. (Also in reprint collection *Leadership on the Job: Guides to Good Supervision* (third ed.), 1981)

HEALTH. See also Alcoholism, Drug Abuse, Employee Benefits

Cold Shouldering the Smoker. William L. Weis, Patrick C. Fleenor. SM, Sept. 1981, pp. 31–35. Albers School of Business.

Corporate Fitness Programs—How Do They Shape Up? Richard L. Pyle. Pers., Jan.–Feb. 1979, pp. 58–67. Central New England College.

The Corporate Health-Buying Spree: Boon or Boondoggle? Robert F. Allen. AMJ, Spring 1980, pp. 4–22. Human Resources Institute.

The Economics of Industrial Health: History, Theory and Practice. Joseph F. Follmann, Jr. 1978, 482 pp.

Keeping Employees Well . . . How Company-Sponsored Fitness Programs Keep Employees on the Job. C. Wayne Higgins, Billy U. Philips. MRev., Dec. 1979, pp. 53–55. Western Kentucky Univ., Univ. of Texas.

Managerial Exercises for a Healthy Department. Claude T. Mangrum. SM, March 1979, pp. 2–8. Probation Department, County of San Bernadino, California.

Managing for a Healthier Heart. John M. Ivancevich, Michael T. Matteson. MRev., Oct. 1978, pp. 14–19.

Occupational Health Management—By Objectives. Henry M. Taylor. Pers., Jan.–Feb. 1980, pp. 58–64. REC, Inc.

Optimizing Human Resources: A Case for Preventive Health and Stress Management. John M. Ivancevich, Michael T. Matteson. OD, Autumn 1980, pp. 5–25.

Planning and Implementing a Personal Fitness Program. Fitness Systems, Inc., 1979. (Extension Institute Cassette Program) By purchase only.

Protection for Pregnant Women in the Industrial Workplace. Deslie Beth Lawrence. Pers., Jan.–Feb. 1979, pp. 40–41.

A Strategy to Improve Executive Health. John P. McCann. AMJ, Spring 1977, pp. 33–37.

Transcendental Meditation. Jay B. Marcus. SM, Part 1. June 1978, pp. 31–41. Part 2. July 1978, pp. 33–39.

HEALTH—MENTAL

Alcohol and Drugs: Poor Remedies for Stress. Gene Milbourn, Jr. SM, March 1981, pp. 35–42. Univ. of Baltimore.

The "Burned-Out" Department Head—A Hidden Hospital Cost. Mark B. Silber, John D. Proe. HSM, Jan. 1979, pp. 1–3, 8. Mark B. Silber Associates.

Burnout: A Real Threat to Human Resources Managers. Oliver L. Niehouse. Pers., Sept.–Oct. 1981, pp. 25–32. Niehouse & Associates.

Burnout: Everybody's Problem. James E. Ledbetter, Nancy S. Boulware, Jan M. Fulcher. HSM, Sept. 1981, pp. 11–14, 16. William S. Hall Psychiatric Institute.

Changing Values and Management Stress. Kurt R. Student. Pers., Jan.–Feb. 1977, pp. 48–55.

Coping with Stress. John M. Ivancevich, Michael T. Matteson. 1979. (AMACOM audio cassette) By purchase only.

Coping with Stress: Training Version. John M. Ivancevich, Michael T. Matteson. 1979. (AMACOM audio cassette) By purchase only.

Determining the Right Regimen of Managerial Exercises. Claude T. Mangrum. SM, Feb. 1981, pp. 26–30. County of San Bernardino, California.

Don't Go Away Mad . . . How an Angry Executive Can Keep His Cool. Hyler Bracey. MRev., May 1980, pp. 35–36.

Executive Stress. Ari Kiev, M.D., Vera Kohn. 1979, 58 pp. Cornell Univ. Medical College. SR.

The Executive Under Stress: A Profile. Mary Zippo. Pers., Sept.–Oct. 1980, pp. 41–43.

Finding the Causes of Job Stress and Learning to Control Them. Gene Milbourn, Jr. HSM, August 1980, pp. 6, 11–12. Univ. of Baltimore.

Healthful Health Management. Steven H. Appelbaum. HSM, Dec. 1980, pp. 1–2, 6. Concordia Univ.

Helping the ICU Nurse Cope with Stress: An Educational Program. Loucine M. D. Huckabay. HSM, Oct. 1979, pp. 6–7, 10. California State Univ.

Helping the Troubled Employee. Joseph F. Follmann, Jr. 1978, 260 pp.

How to Handle Management Tension. ES, March 1980, 16 pp.

How to Manage Change to Reduce Stress. Richard A. Morano. MRev., Nov. 1977, pp. 21–25. Xerox Corp.

How to Manage Managerial Stress. Arthur P. Brief. Pers., Sept.–Oct. 1980, pp. 25–30. New York Univ.

How to Turn Off Stress. Theodore A. Jackson. 1979. (AMACOM audio cassette book) By purchase only.

Learning to Handle Stress—A Matter of Time and Training. Dennis R. Briscoe. SM, Feb. 1980, pp. 35–38. Univ. of San Diego.

Management of Mental Health in Nonprofit Organizations. James A. Wilson. *Management Principles for Nonprofit Agencies and Organizations,* 1979, pp. 120–153. Univ. of Pittsburgh.

Managing Employee Stress: Reducing the Costs, Increasing the Benefits. Joseph Grimaldi, Bette P. Schnapper. MRev., Aug. 1981, pp. 23–28, 37. International Center for the Disabled.

Managing Stress. Jere E. Yates. 1979, 165 pp. Pepperdine Univ.

Managing Stress for Increased Productivity. Vandra L. Huber. SM, Dec. 1981, pp. 2–12. Indiana Univ.

Managing Stress, Strain, and Dis-Ease. V. Clayton Sherman. HSM, Dec. 1979, pp. 6–7. Beta Group, Ltd.

Positive Mental Attitude and Stress. Robert J. McKain. *How to Get to the Top . . . and Stay There,* 1981, pp. 37–59.

Stress—An Inevitable Part of Change. Oliver L. Niehouse, Karen B. Massoni. AMJ, Spring 1979, pp. 17–25. Oliver L. Niehouse & Associates.

Stress and Performance: Are They Always Incompatible? Bruce M. Meglino. SM, March 1977, pp. 2–12. Univ. of South Carolina.

Stress and Performance: Implications for Organizational Policies. Bruce M. Meglino. SM, April 1977, pp. 22–28. Univ. of South Carolina.

Stress & the Bottom Line: A Guide to Personal Well-Being and Corporate Health. E. M. Gherman, M.D. 1981, 348 pp. Center for Organizational Effectiveness.

Stress Management: Are You Master or Victim? James J. Cribbin. *Leadership: Strategies for Organizational Effectiveness,* 1981, pp. 241–255. St. John's Univ.

Stress: Management's Twentieth-Century Dilemma. Walter H. Gmelch. SM, Sept. 1978, pp. 30–36. General Transpac System.

Teaching Stress Management: Meeting Individual and Organization Needs. John F. Pelligrino. AMJ, Spring 1981, pp. 27–30, 35–39. Mead, Inc.

Understanding and Managing Stress. Anderson Maddocks. 1980. (Extension Institute Cassette Program) By purchase only.

Understanding Midcareer Stress. Benami Blau. MRev., Aug. 1978, pp. 57–62.

What, Me Worry? Doug Eads. SM, April 1981, pp. 36–39.
What the Doctors Say About Stress. Marc E. Miller. SM, Nov. 1981, pp. 35–39.
You Can Deal with Stress. Richard J. Walsh. *Leadership on the Job: Guides to Good Supervision* (third ed.), 1981, pp. 224–229. American Appraisal Assn., Inc.

HEALTH MAINTENANCE ORGANIZATIONS
Health Maintenance Is Not a Laughing Matter. Pers., July–Aug. 1979, pp. 49–51.
HMOs from the Management Perspective. Ruth H. Stack. 1979, 49 pp. National Assn. of Employers on Health Maintenance Organizations. MB.
Hospital-HMO Relations: The Health Alliance Experience. David J. Campbell, Douglas S. Peters. HSM, Sept. 1980, pp. 6, 11–12. Henry Ford Hospital, Metropolitan Hospital.
Marketing a Health Maintenance Organization. Kenneth W. Drummer. HSM, Aug. 1978, pp. 1–4. Frank B. Hall & Co.

HOSPITAL AND HEALTH CARE MANAGEMENT. See Public Service and Non-profit Management and headings for individual functions

HOURS—ALTERNATIVE
Alternative Work Schedules: Current Trends. William H. Wagel. Pers., Jan.–Feb. 1978, pp. 4–10.
Alternative Work Schedules—Part 1: Flexitime. Stanley D. Nollen, Virginia H. Martin. 1978, 53 pp. Georgetown Univ. SR.
Alternative Work Schedules—Part 2: Permanent Part-Time Employment; Part 3: The Compressed Workweek. Stanley D. Nollen, Virginia H. Martin. 1978, 70 pp. Georgetown Univ. SR.
Beyond the Standard Shift: Staffing Geared for Today. Bruce P. Hatfield. HSM, June 1981, pp. 3–4. Hospital Management Resources Corp.
A Flexible Approach to Working Hours. J. Carroll Swart. 1978, 278 pp. Ball State Univ.
Flextime at G.M. of Canada. Ernest C. Miller, William H. Wagel. Pers., Jan.–Feb. 1978, pp. 41–43.
Flextime in the United States: The Lessons of Experience. Donald J. Peterson. Pers., Jan.–Feb. 1980, pp. 21–31. Loyola Univ.
From the Country That Gave Us Flexitime Now Comes the Flexiyear. Bernhard Teriet. MRev., April 1981. pp. 34–35. The Federal Institute of Labor, W. Germany.
How a Part-Time Workforce Runs a Full-Time Operation. MRev., Jan. 1978, pp. 40–41.
The Impact of Alternative Workweeks. Dan Olson, Arthur P. Brief. Pers., Jan.–Feb. 1978, pp. 73–77.
Interest in Permanent Part-Time Work: On the Upswing. Mary Zippo. Pers., March–April 1980, pp. 73–74.
Moonlighting: New Look for an Old Practice. Ronald L. Crawford. SM, Aug. 1978, pp. 2–9.
Moonlighting: The Employer's Dilemma. Lawrence Stessin. Pers., Jan.–Feb. 1981, pp. 32–36. Business Research Publications.
Part-Time Employment: An Increasingly Attractive Alternative to Retirement. Mary Zippo. Pers., March–April 1981, pp. 37–39.
Weekend Workers Get Full-Time Pay and Five Days Off. MRev., Dec. 1979, p. 43.
Why Rotating Shifts Sharply Reduce Productivity. Ralph D. Fly. SM, Jan. 1980, pp. 16–21.
Work Sharing—The Answer to Stabilizing Employment?. David D. Steinbrecher. Pers., Nov.–Dec. 1979, pp. 53–55.

HOURS—OVERTIME
Is Overtime the Only Answer. SS, May 1981, 24 pp.
Minimum Wages and Overtime. Linda A. Roxe. *Personnel Management for the Smaller Company*, 1979, pp. 191–193. Rox Associates.

Effective Use of Supplemental Nurses. Cheryl M. Boyer. HSM, Nov. 1979, pp. 4–6. Pennsylvania Nurses Assn.

Supervising Temporary Employees. Carol Hannah. SM, Feb. 1980, pp. 22–28. Manpower Temporary Services.

Temporary Vs. Permanent Help: How to Assess the Costs. David Gordon, Joe L. Welch. MRev., Jan. 1980, pp. 55–57. Univ. of Dallas.

HUMAN RELATIONS

About Work Groups and Group Behavior. ES, June 1981, 16 pp.

Basic Business Psychology. Robert A. Moskowitz, 1978. (Extension Institute Cassette Program) By purchase only.

Behavioral Self-Management—The Missing Link in Managerial Effectiveness. Fred Luthans, Tim R. V. Davis. OD, Summer 1979, pp. 42–60. Univ. of Nebraska, Cleveland State Univ.

Conversation with B. F. Skinner. William Dowling (editor). *Effective Management and the Behavioral Sciences,* 1978, pp. 98–110.

Conversation: An Interview with Elliot Jaques. OD, Spring 1977, pp. 24–43.

Core Managerial Strategies Culled from Behavioral Research. George F. Truell. SM, Jan. 1977, pp. 10–17. George Truell Associates.

Do You Have an "Executive Ear"? Narendra K. Nangea. SM, Aug. 1978, pp. 36–39.

Don't Manage Outside the Office. Jeff Davidson. SM, Oct. 1981, pp. 26–29. IMR Corp.

Functioning in the New Human Climate. Philip Lesly. MRev., Dec. 1981, pp. 24–28, 37–38, The Philip Lesly Co.

Giving a Helping Hand with Personal Problems. Leo Miller. AMJ, Spring 1981, pp. 49–55. Polaroid Corp.

Hanging Together. W. E. Kent. SM, July 1981, pp. 18–21. Georgia State Univ.

The Harm in Those Late-Afternoon Assignments. Jeff Davidson. SM, May 1981, pp. 36–38.

How Do You Tell A Friend? James L. Hayes. MRev., May 1977, p. 2.

How to Give and Receive Criticism Effectively. Brian H. Kleiner. SM, March 1979, pp. 37–41. California State Univ.

Huddling: The Informal Way to Management Success. V. Dallas Merrell. 1979, 208 pp.

Human Aspects. Maurice R. Hecht. *What Happens in Management,* 1980, pp. 18–81. Helmsman Management Associates, Ltd.

Human Relations Management: Concerns for the Future. Gerry E. Morse. MRev., June 1979, pp. 47–48.

The Ik in the Office. Robert F. Allen. OD, Winter 1980, pp. 27–41. Kean College.

Interpreting Employee Needs: Assuming vs. Understanding. Andrew K. Hoh. SM, April 1980, pp. 29–34. Creighton Univ.

Keeping Your Cool. John M. Stormes. SM, Dec. 1980, pp. 16–23. National Educational Media, Inc.

Management of "Technicians" or Humanists. D. W. Kressler. *Management Education in the 80's,* 1979, pp. 125–127.

A Manager's Guide to Human Behavior. Mark S. Zivan. 1977. (Extension Institute Course) By purchase only.

The Manager's Guide to Interpersonal Relations. Donald Sanzotta. 1979, 168 pp. Cayuga County Community College.

Managing Psychological Man. John M. Roach. MRev., June 1977, pp. 27–28, 37–40.

Mutual Respect: Key to Increased Productivity. Mildred Golden Pryor, R. Wayne Mondy. SM, July 1978, pp. 10–16. East Texas State Univ.

A Plea for the Man in the Ranks. E. K. Hall. *Human Resources Management: The Past Is Prologue,* 1979, pp. 5–30.

Psychology for Managers (PRIME 1000). 1978. (An AMACOM Skill Series home-study course) By purchase only.

Research in Human Relations. Elton Mayo. *Human Resources Management: The Past Is Prologue,* 1979, pp. 39–45.

The Sexual Side of Enterprise. Jeanne Bosson Driscoll, Rosemary A. Bova. MRev., July 1980, pp. 51–54.

The Silent Virtue. James L. Hayes. MRev., Aug. 1978, pp. 2–3.

Social Science: Friend of Management. Stuart Chase. *Human Resources Management: The Past Is Prologue,* 1979, pp. 81–97.

Surviving and Succeeding in the 'Political' Organization: Overcoming Organizational Myopia. Alan Jay Weiss. SM, Sept. 1978, pp. 20–28. Kepner-Tregoe, Inc. (Also in reprint collection *Surviving and Succeeding in the 'Political' Organization,* 1978)

Temper, Temper. T. J. Halatin. SM, Sept. 1981, pp. 28–30. Southwest Texas State Univ.

There is an Alternate to "Shape up or Ship Out!" Aniko Galambos. SM, Nov. 1977. pp. 16–21.

Treat Your Employees as Customers. Sandra A. Vavra. SM, April 1978, pp. 16–21. Home Federal Savings & Loan Assn. (Also in reprint collection *Leadership on the Job: Guides to Good Supervision* (third ed.), 1981)

Whatever Happened to the American Way of Work. J. Barry Du Vall, David L. Shores. SM, Feb. 1978. pp. 11–17.

Winners and Kibitzers. James L. Hayes. MRev., March 1979, pp. 2–3.

HUMAN RESOURCES MANAGEMENT. See also Compensation, Data Processing—Applications, International Operations—Human Resources, Job Descriptions, Management Development, Performance Appraisal, Testing

Back to Basics for Improved Human Resource Management. Kurt Student. MRev., Aug. 1978, pp. 51–56. Dallis, DeYoung & Student.

Basics of Personnel Management. Edith Lynch. 1980. (AMACOM audio cassette) By purchase only.

Calculating Your Personnel Ratio. Dale Yoder. *Human Resources Management: The Past Is Prologue,* 1979, pp. 280–284.

The Challenge for Personnel Administration. Paul Pigors. *Human Resources Management: The Past Is Prologue,* 1979, pp. 201–211.

Changing Concepts of the Personnel Function. James C. Worthy. *Human Resources Management: The Past Is Prologue,* 1979, pp. 212–226.

Employee Services. William R. Tracey. *Human Resource Development Standards,* 1981, pp. 324–349. U.S. Army Intelligence Training School.

Evaluating the Personnel Department. Robert D. Gray. *Human Resources Management: The Past Is Prologue,* 1979, pp. 261–271.

Evaluating the Personnel Department's Internal Functioning. R. Bruce McAfee. Pers., May–June 1980, pp. 56–62. Old Dominion Univ.

Evaluating the Personnel Function. Robert J. Thierauf. *Management Auditing: A Questionnaire Approach,* 1980, pp. 169–188. Xavier Univ.

The Expanding Role of the Human Resources Manager. Robert L. Desatnick. 1979, 230 pp. McDonald's Corp.

Fathers of Human Resources—A Rating. Deslie Beth Lawrence, Ernest C. Miller. Pers., May–June 1979, pp. 4–8.

Fundamentals of Modern Personnel Management. Kenneth T. Winters. 1980. (Extension Institute Course) By purchase only.

The Future World of Work: The Strategic Significance of Human Resource Management in the 1980s. Lynne Hall. PA #72, 1980, 64 pp. AT & T, By purchase only.

How to Audit the Personnel Department. J. McConnell. 1977. (An AMACOM Evaluation Tool) By purchase only.

Human Resource Management. William R. Osgood. *Basics of Successful Business Management,* 1981, pp. 187–222.

Human Resources Administrators: A Profile. William H. Wage. Pers., March–April 1978, pp. 44–45.

The Human Resources Executive and Corporate Planning . . . A Personnel Symposium. Pers., Sept.–Oct. 1977, pp. 12–22. (Also in reprint collection *The Human Resources Function: Its Emergence and Character,* 1978)

The Human Resources Function: Its Emergence and Character. Ernest C. Miller (editor). 1978, 85 pp. (A collection of reprints from AMACOM periodicals)

Human Resources Management: A Strategic Perspective. Mary Ann Devanna, Charles Fombrun, Noel Tichy. OD, Winter 1981, pp. 51–67. Columbia Univ., Univ. of Michigan.

Human Resources Management: The Past Is Prologue. Ernest C. Miller (editor). 1979, 361 pp. (A collection of reprints from Pers.).

Leading the Way in Human Resource Management. Ray A. Killian. 1979. (AMACOM audio cassette) By purchase only.

Managers See a Bright Future for the Human Resources Function. Mary Zippo. Pers., March–April 1981, pp. 35–37.

Managing Human Resources. James A. Craft. *Management Principles for Nonprofit Agencies and Organizations,* 1979, pp. 71–119. Univ. of Pittsburgh.

Merging the Two Faces of Personnel: A Challenge for the 1980's. John J. Leach. Pers., Jan–Feb. 1980, pp. 52–57. Univ. of Chicago.

New Frontiers for Personnel Management. Charles A. Myers. *Human Resources Management: The Past Is Prologue,* 1979, pp. 248–256.

Organizing and Staffing the Human Resources Function . . . A Personnel Symposium. Pers., Jan.–Feb. 1978, pp. 11–20. (Also in reprint collection *The Human Resources Function: Its Emergence and Character,* 1978)

People and Business. Part 4. Fred W. Latham, George S. Sanders, *Urwick, Orr on Management,* 1980, pp. 199–245. Urwick, Orr & Partners.

Personnel Activities: Where the Dollars Went in 1979. Mary Zippo. Pers., Jan–Feb. 1980, pp. 65–66.

Personnel and Personnel Management. James L. Mercer, Susan W. Woolston, William V. Donaldson. *Managing Urban Government Services: Strategies, Tools, and Techniques for the 80's,* 1981, pp. 152–165. James Mercer & Associates, U.S. Environmental Protection Agency, Philadelphia Zoological Society.

The Personnel Director as High-Status Friend. Susan A. Goodwin. SM, Aug. 1977, pp. 2–10. Univ. of Lowell.

Personnel Management for the Smaller Company. Linda A. Roxe. 1979, 246 pp. Roxe Associates.

Quantifying the Human Resources Function. Jac Fitz-Enz, Sr. Pers., March–April 1980, pp. 41–52. Four-Phase Systems, Inc.

Rethinking People Management: A New Look at the Human Resources Function. Merritt L. Kastens. 1980, 225 pp.

The Road Ahead for the Human Resources Function. Jack W. English. Pers., March–April 1980, pp. 35–39. Mobil Corp.

Selection and Performance Criteria for a Chief Human Resources Executive . . . A Presidential Perspective. Pers., May–June 1977, pp. 11–21. (Also in reprint collection *The Human Resource Function: Its Emergence and Character,* 1978)

The Specifications of a Top Human Resources Officer . . . A Personnel Symposium. Pers., May–June 1978, pp. 24–31. (Also in reprint collection *The Human Resources Function: Its Emergence and Character,* 1978)

A Stock and Flow Model for Improved Human Resources Measurement. Thomas A. Mahoney, George T. Milkovich, Nan Weiner. Pers., May–June 1977, pp. 57–66.

Teamwork: Crucial Link Between CEO and Personnel Director. Edwin B. Gilroy. MRev., Nov. 1979, pp. 30–31. VSI Corp.

Time-Span of Discretion and Human Resources Management . . . An Interview with Elliott Jacques. Pers., July–Aug. 1977, pp. 47–58.

Upcoming Human Resources Management Problems. Ernest C. Miller. Pers., May–June 1977, pp. 4–10.

What About Personnel Relations Payroll Costs? George A. Cowee, Jr., Gordon G. Bowen. *Human Resources Management: The Past Is Prologue,* 1979, pp. 293–303.

What's Wrong with the Human Resources Approach to Management? Walter R. Nord, Douglas E. Durand. OD, Winter 1978, pp. 13–25. Washington Univ., Univ. of Missouri.

Why Line Managers Don't Listen to Their Personnel Departments. T. F. Cawsey. Pers., Jan.–Feb. 1980, pp. 11–20. Western Ontario Univ.

INSPECTION. See Quality Control

INSURANCE
Fielding Risk Responsibilities in the Hospital. Timothy G. Walters. HSM, Oct. 1979, pp. 1–2. Bethesda Hospital.
Getting the Most from Your Insurance: Measures to Take Before and After a Loss. Sidney Greenspan. MRev., Jan. 1978, pp. 33–34. National Assn. of Public Insurance Adjustors.
Insurance of Oil and Gas Operations. Peter J. Wingett. *Financing the International Petroleum Industry,* 1978, pp. 162–179. Indemnity Marine Assurance Company Ltd.
Is Self-Insurance a Viable Option? Richard O. Moore. HSM, April 1978, pp. 8–9. St. Joseph's Hospital Health Center.
Risk Analysis Guide to Insurance and Employee Benefits. A. E. Pfaffle, Sal Nicosia. 1977, 71 pp. EBASCO Risk Management. MB.
Self-Insurance: A Financial Approach. Charles T. Tagman, Jr. MRev., April 1978, pp. 33–34. George Betterley Consulting Group.
What Every Nurse Manager Should Know About Risk Management. Charles E. Baxter. HSM, August 1980, pp. 4–6. Wood, Lucksinger & Epstein.

INSURANCE—LIFE, HEALTH, ACCIDENT. See also Employee Benefits
Corporate-Owned Life Insurance: How to Separate Appearance and Reality. Frank E. Finkenberg. MRev., Nov. 1980, pp. 49–53. Buck Consultants, Inc.
Health Care Coverage and Costs: A Major Challenge for Innovative Managers. Quentin I. Smith. MRev., Dec. 1980, pp. 37–40. Towers, Perrin, Forster & Crosby.
How to Use Life Insurance in Financial Planning. C. Colburn Hardy. *Your Money & Your Life: How to Plan Your Long-Range Financial Security,* 1979, pp. 192–221.
Loosening Up the "Fixed" Costs of Employee Benefits and Energy. Candace Roney. HSM, July 1981, pp. 3–6. San Jose Health Center and San Jose Hospital.
National Health Insurance Principles. Ernest C. Miller. Pers., Sept.–Oct. 1978, pp. 50–51.

INTERNATIONAL OPERATIONS. See also Distribution, Transportation
Actors on the International Stage. James L. Hayes. MRev., Aug. 1979, pp. 2–3.
After the Multinational Corporation? Richard D. Robinson. *The International Essays for Business Decision Makers, Vol. III,* 1978, pp. 38–44. Massachusetts Institute of Technology.
Agriculture: The New Frontier. Richard O. Wheeler. *The International Essays for Business Decision Makers, Vol. III,* 1978, pp. 136–139. Winrock International.
"Area-Oriented" Management. Koji Kobayashi. *The International Essays for Business Decision Makers, Vol. V,* 1980, pp. 1–6. Nippon Electric Co., Ltd.
Can the Multinationals Survive the 1980's? Loet A. Velmans. *The International Essays for Business Decision Makers, Vol. III,* 1978, pp. 31–37. Hill and Knowlton, Inc.
The Challenge of Managing the World's Deep Seabed Resources. Elliot L. Richardson. *The International Essays for Business Decision Makers, Vol. III,* 1978, pp. 61–65. Law of the Sea Conference.
A Collision Ahead: Restriction on Transborder Data Flow. Arthur T. Downey. *The International Essays for Business Decision Makers, Vol. III,* 1978, pp. 128–135. Sutherland, Asbill & Brennan.
Coping with Structural Changes Through Strategic Management. James H. Bockhaus. *The International Essays for Business Decision Makers, Vol. V,* 1980, pp. 18–34. The LTV Corp.
Corporate Communications in a Worldwide Society. Lloyd N. Hand. MRev., March 1979, pp. 29–30. T R W, Inc.
Dealing with Governments. Harald B. Malmgren. *The International Essays for Business Decision Makers, Vol. III,* 1978, pp. 222–230. Malmgren, Inc.
Economic Growth and Government-Owned Multinationals. John B. Rhodes. MRev., Feb. 1979, pp. 31–32. Booz-Allen & Hamilton International.

The Evolution of a Complementary Structure of the World Economy. Romuald Kudlinski, Wlodzimierz Siwinski. *The International Essays for Business Decision Makers, Vol. V,* 1980, pp. 330–337. Warsaw Univ.

External Affairs and the International Corporation. Derek F. Channon with Michael Jalland. *Multinational Strategic Planning,* 1978, pp. 294–327. Manchester Business School.

Facing the Realities of Interdependence. Adlai E. Stevenson. *The International Essays for Business Decision Makers, Vol. IV,* 1979, pp. 45–52. United States Senate.

The International Essays for Business Decision Makers, Vol. III. Mark B. Winchester (editor). 1978, 270 pp. The Center for International Business.

The International Essays for Business Decision Makers, Vol. IV. Mark B. Winchester (editor). 1979, 284 pp. The Center for International Business.

The International Essays for Business Decision Makers, Vol. V. Mark B. Winchester (editor). 1980, 353 pp. The Center for International Business.

International Government Relations: A Required Management Function for International Business. William J. Barton. *The International Essays for Business Decision Makers, Vol. III,* 1978, pp. 216–221. International Business-Government Counsellors.

International Interdependence vs. Protectionism. Walter E. Hoadley. *The International Essays for Business Decision Makers, Vol. III,* 1978, pp. 13–18. Bank of America.

International Relations Options: OPEC as a Political Moderating Force. Rene G. Ortiz. *The International Essays for Business Decision Makers, Vol. V,* 1980, pp. 37–44. Organization of Petroleum Exporting Countries (OPEC)

International Trade Policy and the Free Enterprise System. Warren W. Lebeck. *The International Essays for Business Decision Makers, Vol. III,* 1978, pp. 140–146. Chicago Board of Trade.

Interpol. James P. Hendrick. *Making Successful Presentations,* 1981, pp. 187–193. Interpol.

Is Capitalism the Culprit? Chris Argyris. OD, Spring 1978, pp. 20–37. McGill Univ.

The Magic of Political Risk Analysis. Robert E. Ebel. *The International Essays for Business Decision Makers, Vol. V,* 1980, pp. 287–301. ENSERCH Corp.

The Management of Political Risk. Derek F. Channon with Michael Jalland. *Multinational Strategic Planning,* 1978, pp. 234–258. Manchester Business School.

Multinational Strategic Planning. Derek F. Channon with Michael Jalland. 1978, 344 pp. Manchester Business School.

Multinational Strategic Planning Systems. Derek F. Channon with Michael Jalland. *Multinational Strategic Planning,* 1978, pp. 51–88. Manchester Business School.

Needed—A Unified Approach to Trade Policy. Daniel Minchew. *The International Essays for Business Decision Makers, Vol. III,* 1978, pp. 19–23. U.S. International Trade Commission.

A New Social Order. John F. Kennedy. *Making Successful Presentations,* 1981, pp. 200–208.

New Tools for Inventory Control. Robert Goodell Brown. *Managing International Distribution,* 1979, pp. 69–76. Materials Management Systems, Inc.

The Obsolescing Bargain: A Key Factor in Political Risk. Raymond Vernon. *The International Essays for Business Decision Makers, Vol. V,* 1980, pp. 281–286. Harvard Univ.

Organising for International Operations. Derek F. Channon with Michael Jalland. *Multinational Strategic Planning,* 1978, pp. 22–50. Manchester Business School.

A Political Forecast of the 1980's for Business Leaders. William E. Colby. *The International Essays for Business Decision Makers, Vol. III,* 1978, pp. 123–127. Colby, Miller & Hanes.

A Positive Foreign Economic Policy. Reginald H. Jones. *The International Essays for Business Decision Makers, Vol. III,* 1978, pp. 1–12. General Electric Co.

A Psychosomatic Disorder of International Trade. Kiichi Mochizuki. *The International Essays for Business Decision Makers, Vol. III,* 1978, pp. 96–104. Nippon Steel U.S.A., Inc.

The Regeneration of World Effective Demand. Ralph Horwitz. *The International Essays* *for Business Decision Makers, Vol. III,* 1978, pp. 172–179. London Regional Management Centre.

The Role of International Business in Reducing Human Conflict. William P. Bowman, O.B.E. *The International Essays for Business Decision Makers, Vol. IV,* 1979, pp. 265–269. United Biscuits (U.K.), Ltd.

Some Guidelines for Successful International Industrial Cooperation in Defense. Thomas V. Jones. *The International Essays for Business Decision Makers, Vol. IV,* 1979, pp. 242–249. Northrop Corp.

Some Thoughts on the American International Corporate Manager's Changing Global Perception. David P. Anderson. *The International Essays for Business Decision Makers, Vol. III,* 1978, pp. 111–122. Republic National Bank of Dallas.

State Intervention and International Trade. Kiichi Mochizuki. *The International Essays for Business Decision Makers, Vol. IV,* 1979, pp. 122–131. Nippon Steel U.S.A., Inc.

Strategic Portfolio Planning Systems. Derek F. Channon with Michael Jalland. *Multinational Strategic Planning,* 1978, pp. 89–119. Manchester Business School.

Through A Glass Brightly: OPEC at Maturity. Arpad Von Lazar. *The International Essays for Business Decision Makers, Vol. V,* 1980, pp. 57–65. Tufts Univ.

The Tobago Syndrome: The Extraterritorial Application of U.S. Laws and Its Impact on International Trade. Edward R. Luter. *The International Essays for Business Decision Makers, Vol. IV,* 1979, pp. 32–44. Dresser Industries, Inc.

When All Else Fails, National Industrial Planning? R. Roger Majak. *The International Essays for Business Decision Makers, Vol. V,* 1980, pp. 7–17. Foreign Affairs Committee.

INTERNATIONAL OPERATIONS—BY REGION—ASIA

American Success Story—Coca-Cola in Japan. Ian R. Wilson. *The International Essays for Business Decision Makers, Vol. V,* 1980, pp. 119–127. The Coca-Cola Co.

China Fever: Scrambling for Shares in a $600 Million Buying Spree. Bohdan O. Szuprowicz. MRev., May 1979, pp. 9–16. 21st Century Research.

China Modernizing Business Laws to Boost Trade and Investment. Jung Y. Lowe. MRev., April 1980, pp. 31–32.

The China Trader: Interviews with Julian Sobin. 1978. (AMACOM audio cassette) By purchase only.

China's Military-Industrial Complex. Bohdan O. Szuprowicz. *The International Essays for Business Decision Makers, Vol. V,* 1980, pp. 172–181. 21st Century Research.

Doing Business with China—A Pragmatic Approach. Michael Ball. MRev., May 1979, pp. 16–18.

Doing Business with China: How Peking's New Joint Ventures Law Will Work. Liu Chu. MRev., July 1980, pp. 59–61. Chinese Foreign Investment Commission.

Elephant or Inkblot? Carl Remick. AMJ, Autumn 1981. pp. 25–28

How Japanese Business Treats Its Older Workers. Shiro Sekiguchi. MRev., Oct. 1980, pp. 15–18. Nippon Steel Corp.

Impressions of a U.S. Observer . . . Why the Japanese Are So Successful. Rolph Townshend. MRev., Oct. 1980, pp. 29, 46. Westinghouse Electric's Defense & Electronic System Center.

Japan. Felix Wentworth. *Managing International Distribution, pp. 172–181.* Chubb Hennessy.

Japanese and Western Quality: A Contrast in Methods and Results. J. M. Juran. MRev., Nov. 1978, pp. 27–28, 39–45.

Japanese Management Practices and Productivity. Nina Hatvany, Vladimir Pucik. OD, Spring 1981, pp. 5–21. Columbia Univ.

Japanese Manufacturers Facing Major Barriers to Future Growth. Yoshimichi Yamashita. MRev., Dec. 1980, pp. 29, 31. Arthur D. Little Co.

Japanese Participative Management—or How Rinji Seido Can Work for You. Robert T. Moran. AMJ, Summer 1979, pp. 14–22. American Graduate School of International Management.

Japan's Automobile Industry Faces New Challenges. Taizo Ueda. *The International*

Essays for Business Decision Makers, Vol. V, 1980, pp. 109–118. Honda Motor Co., Ltd.

Japan's Synergistic Society . . . How It Works and Its Implications for the United States. Robert R. Rehder. MRev., Oct. 1981, pp. 64–66. Univ. of New Mexico.

Organizational Paradigms: A Commentary on Japanese Management and Theory Z Organizations. William G. Ouchi. OD, Spring 1981, pp. 36–43. UCLA.

Patience in Human Relations: Key to Doing Business in Japan. Yoshio Ueda, George P. Craighead. MRev., Oct. 1978, pp. 57–59.

Rolling With the Punch. James L. Hayes. MRev., Feb. 1981, pp. 2–3.

The Sino-Soviet Aircraft Trade. Bohdan O. Szuprowicz. *The International Essays for Business Decision Makers, Vol. III,* 1978, pp. 249–255. 21st Century Research.

Trade and Defense. Kiichi Mochizuki. *The International Essays for Business Decision Makers, Vol. V,* 1980, pp. 182–194. Nippon Steel U.S.A., Inc.

Trade with China in the 1980's. Christopher H. Phillips. *The International Essays for Business Decision Makers, Vol. IV,* 1979, pp. 154–161. The National Council for United States-China Trade.

INTERNATIONAL OPERATIONS—BY REGION—EUROPE

Codetermination: West Germany's Concept of Industrial Democracy. Herbert G. Hicks. *The Evolving Science of Management,* 1979, pp. 457–474. Louisiana State Univ. College.

Conditions for Another Italian Miracle. Renato Mieli. *The International Essays for Business Decision Makers, Vol. III,* 1978, pp. 196–202. Center for Study and Research on Socio-Economic Problems, Milan, Italy.

The Entrepreneur in the Economy and in the Society of the Federal Republic of Germany. Günther Schmölders. *The International Essays for Business Decision Makers, Vol. III,* 1978, pp. 188–195.

A European Marshall Plan. Rt. Hon. Geoffrey Rippon Q.C. M.P. *The International Essays for Business Decision Makers, Vol. III,* 1978, pp. 203–208.

Germany's Obligation and World Recovery. Armin Gutowski. *The International Essays for Business Decision Makers, Vol. III,* 1978, pp. 180–187. Johann Wolfgang Goethe Univ.

MNC's and the European Community . . . The Future for Multinationals in Europe. John Robinson. MRev., Feb. 1980, pp. 39–40.

The Yugoslav Experience of Enterprise. Ljubo Sirc. *The International Essays for Business Decision Makers, Vol. III,* 1978, pp. 209–215. Univ. of Glasgow.

Western Europe. A. L. Pope. *Managing International Distribution,* 1979, pp. 96–126. Carrington Viyella Ltd.

INTERNATIONAL OPERATIONS—BY REGION—LATIN AMERICA

Cuban International Trade: A First Hand Assessment. Lawrence H. Theriot. *The International Essays for Business Decision Makers, Vol. III,* 1978, pp. 231–240. U.S. Department of Commerce.

Cuba's Interest in American Business: Lenin, "Si"—Yankee, "Si" Arthur T. Downey. *The International Essays for Business Decision Makers, Vol. III,* 1978, pp. 241–248. Sutherland, Asbill & Brennan.

Growing Demand for Diverse Products Opens New Export Markets in South America. Robert Keenan. MRev., Oct. 1979, p. 47. Foreign Credit Insurance Assn.

INTERNATIONAL OPERATIONS—BY REGION—OTHER REGIONS

Australia. Peter Gilmour. *Managing International Distribution.* 1979, pp. 143–159. Monash Univ.

America's Trade Relationships with the Less Developed World: Concentration Upon Major Export Markets When Looking into the Next Decade. Alfred C. Holden. *The International Essays for Business Decision Makers, Vol. III,* 1978, pp. 53–60. Foreign Credit Insurance Assn.

Barriers to East-West Trade. Robert D. Schmidt. *The International Essays for Business Decision Makers, Vol. IV,* 1979, pp. 147–153. Control Data Corp.

Canada and Quebec: A Role for Business in a Political Crisis. H. E. Wyatt. MRev., April 1978, pp. 46–49. Royal Bank of Canada.

Current and Emerging Future Developments in the Middle East: The Iraq-Iran War of 1980. James E. Akins. *The International Essays for Business Decision Makers, Vol. V,* 1980, pp. 66–78. Former U.S. Ambassador to Saudi Arabia.

East-West Trade—The Road Back. Armand Hammer. *The International Essays for Business Decision Makers, Vol. IV,* 1979, pp. 140–146. Occidental Petroleum Corp.

Formulating Plans for Joint Venture Companies in Saudi Arabia. C. N. Jones. *The International Essays for Business Decision Makers, Vol. IV,* 1979, pp. 162–169. Kanoo Group Ltd.

A Guide to Doing Business on the Arabian Peninsula. Quentin W. Fleming. 1981, 150 pp.

The Hidden Side of the Kuwaiti Economy: A Rapidly Growing Industrial Base. Daniel M. Searby. *The International Essays for Business Decision Makers, Vol. III,* 1978, pp. 105–110. Kearns International.

Iran—A Post Mortem for Industry. Robert E. Ebel. *The International Essays for Business Decision Makers, Vol. IV,* 1979, pp. 1–9. ENSERCH Corp.

Management Needs of the Third World. Frederick G. Harmon. MRev., Jan. 1978, pp. 29.

Managerial Staffing in the Middle East. J. Winston Porter, William D. Fletcher. MRev., Oct. 1978, pp. 25–28, 51–53.

The Middle East. K. H. H. Cook. *Managing International Distribution,* 1979, pp. 160–171. NFC (International) Ltd. Tehran.

MNC's Are Hopping on the Bandwagon to the 3rd World. Nathaniel H. Leff. MRev., March 1979, pp. 30–31. Columbia Univ.

North America. Philip B. Schary. *Managing International Distribution,* 1979, pp. 127–142. Oregon State Univ.

The United States and South Africa: Coping with Complexity. Chester A. Crocker. *The International Essays for Business Decision Makers, Vol. IV,* 1979, pp. 189–199. Georgetown Univ.

INTERNATIONAL OPERATIONS—FINANCE

Easing the Tax Squeeze on the Multinational Employee. Walter F. O'Connor, Robert K. Decelles. Pers., Sept.–Oct. 1977, pp. 28–39.

The Development of Petroleum Financing. R. Kenneth Merkey. *Financing the International Petroleum Industry,* 1978, pp. 29–38. MC International

Developments Around the World. Donald R. Chilvers. *Current Value Accounting,* 1977, pp. 113–134. Coopers & Lybrand.

The Dollar Under the Regime of Floating Exchange Rates. Edward M. Bernstein. *The International Essays for Business Decision Makers, Vol. V,* 1980, pp. 239–260. EMB (Ltd.), Research Economists.

Eurocurrency Markets. Peter M. C. Clarke. *Financing the International Petroleum Industry,* 1978, pp. 219–246. United International Bank

The European Monetary System: Opportunities and Risks. Manfred Meier-Preschany. *The International Essays for Business Decision Makers, Vol. IV,* 1979, pp. 207–212. Dresdner Bank A.G.

Export Credit Finance. Radu G. Plessia. *Financing the International Petroleum Industry,* 1978, pp. 183–202. CIAVE

Factoring: Opening New Routes in International Trade. Anthony H. Ittleson. MRev. Sept. 1978, pp. 48–53. CIT Financial Corp.

Financing the International Petroleum Industry. Norman A. White (editor) 1978, 257 pp.

Financing Under Floating Exchange Rates and Role of Banks. Hans J. Mast. *The International Essays for Business Decision Makers, Vol. IV,* 1979, pp. 213–225. Credit Suisse.

Foreign Exchange and the Corporate Treasurer (sec. ed.). John Heywood. 1979, 163 pp. Hambros Bank, London.

Foreign Exchange Exposure. John Heywood. *The International Essays for Business Decision Makers, Vol. III*, 1978, pp. 154–163. Hambros Bank Ltd.

Foreign Exchange Markets—Living with Uncertainty. Dennis A. Cullen. MRev., Jan. 1978, pp. 29–32.

Foreign Exchange Risk Management. Alan C. Shapiro. 1978, 64 pp. Univ. of Southern California. MB.

Gold in International Trade and Finance. G. W. G. Browne. *The International Essays for Business Decision Makers, Vol. III*, 1978, pp. 164–171.

How to Adapt to New Foreign Tax Patterns. Walter F. O'Connor, Samuel F. Russo. MRev., July 1979, pp. 30–32. Peat, Marwick, Mitchell & Co.

Independent Oil Companies. Peter J. G. Elwes. *Financing the International Petroleum Industry*, 1978, pp. 55–71. Kleinwort Benson Ltd.

International Banking in the 1980s: The Regulatory Challenge. Alfred F. Miossi. *The International Essays for Business Decision Makers, Vol. V*, 1980, pp. 226–232. Continental Illinois Corp.

International Cash Management and Foreign Exchange Exposure Management: Separate but Interlocking Concepts. David J. Springate. *The International Essays for Business Decision Makers, Vol. V*, 1980, pp. 233–238. IMEDE Management Development Institute.

International Commercial Banking Management. James L. Kammert. 1981, 403 pp. Equibank.

International Construction and Surety Bonding. Richard I. Purnell. *The International Essays for Business Decision Makers, Vol. IV*, 1979, pp. 226–232. Johnson & Higgins.

International Integrated Companies. Brian A. Carlisle. *Financing the International Petroleum Industry*, 1978, pp. 40–54. Home Oil UK Ltd.

International Lending to Developing Countries. Irving S. Friedman. *The International Essays for Business Decision Makers, Vol. III*, 1978, pp. 45–52. Citibank, N.A.

International Tax Planning. Derek F. Channon with Michael Jalland. *Multinational Strategic Planning*, 1978, pp. 150–174. Manchester Business School.

Investment Planning and Entry Strategies. Derek F. Channon with Michael Jalland. *Multinational Strategic Planning*, 1978, pp. 175–206. Manchester Business School.

Investment Strategies for EEC Companies in the 1980's. Nicholas Steinthal. MRev., March 1979, pp. 34–35. Arthur D. Little, Inc.

Multinational Corporate Treasury Management. Derek F. Channon with Michael Jalland. *Multinational Strategic Planning*, 1978, pp. 120–149. Manchester Business School.

The Need for International Co-ordination. Sir Henry Benson. *Current Value Accounting*, 1977, pp. 135–141. Coopers & Lybrand.

Oil and the International Monetary System. H. A. Merklein. *The International Essays for Business Decision Makers, Vol. III*, 1978, pp. 84–95. Univ. of Dallas.

The Oil Surpluses and the International Banking Community. R. G. Baird. *The International Essays for Business Decision Makers, Vol. V*, 1980, pp. 203–216. Royal Bank of Scotland.

Petrodollars and Western Technology: An Appraisal of the Partnership. David H. Sambar. *The International Essays for Business Decision Makers, Vol. V*, 1980, pp. 45–56. Sharjah Investment Co., (U.K.) Ltd.

Petroleum Production. Patrick F. Connolly. *Financing the International Petroleum Industry*, 1978, pp. 74–90. Shawmut Bank.

Planning International Mergers and Acquisitions. Derek F. Channon with Michael Jalland. *Multinational Strategic Planning*, 1978, pp. 207–233. Manchester Business School.

Private Foreign Investment in America: The Vote of Confidence That Counts. Werner Gundlach. *The International Essays for Business Decision Makers, Vol. V*, 1980, pp. 261–278.

The Stability of the Dollar and the Effect on World Trade. Geoffrey Bell. *The International Essays for Business Decision Makers, Vol. III*, 1978, pp. 147–153. Schroder International Ltd.

Stock Markets. Philip Wood. *Financing the International Petroleum Industry,* 1978, pp. 203–218. Hambros Bank Ltd.

Tax Strategy for Multinationals—Economic and Social Issues. John Chown, John Humble. 1979, 30 pp. J. F. Chown & Co., Ltd. MB.

Taxation of the Expatriate Employee After the Foreign Earned Income Act of 1978. Jerry P. Leamon, Steve A. Claus. CR, First Quarter 1980, pp. 21–31. Deloitte, Haskins & Sells, Claus & Knapp.

Taxation of U.S. Expatriates Under the Tax Reform Act of 1976. Jerome I. Shagam. CR, Second Quarter 1977, pp. 31–41.

Ten Principles of International Financing. Rainer E. Gut. *The International Essays for Business Decision Makers, Vol. V,* 1980 pp. 217–225. Credit Suisse.

The U.S. Dollar as a Reserve Currency: A Perspective from the Far East. Michael Wong Pakshong. *The International Essays for Business Decision Makers, Vol. IV,* 1979, pp. 200–206. The Monetary Authority of Singapore.

The Value Added Tax: Facts and Fancies. Norman B. Ture. MRev., Feb. 1980, pp. 8–13. Institute for Research on the Economics of Taxation.

INTERNATIONAL OPERATIONS—HUMAN RESOURCES

The Challenge of Providing Benefit and Compensation Programs for Third Country Nationals. G. W. Hallmark, Charles W. Rogers III. *The International Essays for Business Decision Makers, Vol. III,* 1978, pp. 256–263. Alexander & Alexander.

Criteria for Selecting an International Manager. Jean E. Heller. Pers., May–June 1980, pp. 47–55. American Graduate School of International Management.

Developing Overseas Managers—and Managers Overseas. Paul E. Illman. 1980, 298 pp. Management Training, Inc.

Expatriate Compensation at the Crossroads. William L. White, John J. McGowan. AMJ, Fall 1977, pp. 14–23.

Government's Role in Management Education in Less Developed Countries. Rong-I Wu. *Management Education in the 80's,* 1979, pp. 111–120.

Lilliput Revisited: A Data-Based Critique of Corporate Captivity in Connection with Kidnapping and Terrorist Threat. David G. Hubbard, M.D. *The International Essays for Business Decision Makers, Vol. IV,* 1979, pp. 19–31. Aberrant Behavior Center.

Management Education—A Conceptual Framework. Bohdan Hawrylyshyn. *Management Education in the 80's,* 1979, pp. 85–97.

Management Education in the 80's. International Association of Students of Economics and Management (editor). 1979, 127 pp.

Management Education Needs in Developing Countries. Michael O. Omolayole. *Management Education in the 80's,* 1979, pp. 17–27. Lever Brothers, Nigeria, Ltd.

The Management Education Needs of Business. Kap Cassani. *Management Education in the 80's,* 1979, pp. 39–42. IBM Europe.

Management of Pension Plan Finances for Multinational Corporations. Kenneth G. Buffin. *The International Essays for Business Decision Makers, Vol. IV,* 1979, pp. 233–241. A. S. Hansen, Inc.

Managing the Personal Side of the Personnel Move Abroad. George H. Labovitz. AMJ, Summer 1977, pp. 26–39. Boston Univ.

Needed: 1,000,000,000 Jobs: Can Multinational Managers Meet the Deadline? Frederick G. Harmon. MRev., March 1980, pp. 19–24.

Negotiating with the Demon. I. Thomas Sheppard. MRev., July 1980, pp. 14–17. Univ. of Texas.

New Directions for Labor in Europe. Jack A. Peel. MRev., Jan. 1979, pp. 57–61. Commission of the European Communities.

People: Part II. James L. Kammert. *International Commercial Banking Management.* 1981, pp. 113–220. Equibank.

Problem for Foreign Companies: Compliance with U.S. Discrimination Laws. S. Prakash Sethi, Carl L. Swanson. MRev. June 1979, pp. 32–33. Univ. of Texas.

Promises and Pitfalls: The Challenge of Filling Overseas Management Positions.

Donald L. Youngs. *The International Essays for Business Decision Makers, Vol. IV,* 1979, pp. 270–276. Spencer Stuart & Associates.

Trade Union Strategy for the Private Enterprise System in Europe. Carl Nisser, John Alan James. Pers., Sept.–Oct. 1979, pp. 10–22. Goodyear International Corp, Management Counsellor International.

Transnational Corporations and the Transfer of Management Techniques to Developing Countries. Jerzy Cieślik. *Management Education in the 80's,* 1979, pp. 99–105.

A Unique Approach to Tax Equalization for Foreign Employees. Neil B. Krupp. CR, Fourth Quarter 1980, pp. 34–43. International Harvester Co.

Worker Morale: Are There Solutions Abroad? Robert Schrank. MRev., July 1979, pp. 57–62. Ford Foundation.

Worker Participation Abroad Takes Many Forms: Middle Managers, Increasingly Bypassed, Looking More to Unions. John Humble. MRev., Aug. 1979, pp. 30–31.

Worker Participation: Lessons from the European Experience. Hem C. Jain. MRev., May 1980, pp. 46–52. Univ. of New Brunswick.

Why Volvo Abolished the Assembly Line. John M. Roach. MRev., Sept. 1977, pp. 48–52.

Work Redesign: A Results-Oriented Strategy That Works. Robert Janson. AMJ, Winter 1979, pp. 21–27. Roy Walters & Associates.

INTERNATIONAL OPERATIONS—MARKETING

Brand Marketing: Fresh Thinking Is Needed. Peter Foy, Dieter Pommerening. MRev., Nov. 1979, pp. 20–24. McKinsey & Co.

Competition from Abroad . . . Testing the Durability of Yankee Know-How. William M. Agee. MRev., July 1979, pp. 29–30. The Bendix Corp.

Elements of a Trade Policy. Reginald H. Jones. *The International Essays for Business Decision Makers, Vol. V,* 1980, pp. 302–308. General Electric Co.

An Endangered Species: The Small U.S. Exporter. T. D. Williamson, Jr. *The International Essays for Business Decision Makers, Vol. V,* 1980, pp. 338–342. T. D. Williamson, Inc.

Entry Strategies for Foreign Markets: From Domestic to International Business. Franklin R. Root. 1977, 51 pp. Univ. of Pennsylvania. MB.

How to Balance Costs and Customer Service. Michele Azzarello. *Managing International Distribution,* 1979, pp. 37–50. A. T. Kearney, Italy.

How to Sell to the International Market. William A. Cohen, Marshall E. Reddick. *Successful Marketing for Small Business,* 1981, pp. 235–250. California State Univ.

How to Succeed in Foreign Markets. William F. Andrews. MRev., Oct. 1980, p. 32. Scovill, Inc.

International Aspects of National Account Marketing. John A. Mackey. *National Accounts Marketing Handbook,* 1981, pp. 267–279. Betz International, Inc.

International Economic Policy for U.S. Agriculture—After the Multilateral Trade Negotiations. Clayton K. Yeutter. *The International Essays for Business Decision Makers, Vol. IV,* 1979, pp. 256–264. Chicago Mercantile Exchange.

International Trade: The Goal's the Same but the Rules Are Different. Donald J. Yockey. *The International Essays for Business Decision Makers, Vol. V,* 1980, pp. 128–138. Rockwell International Corp.

Living with the Shifting Sands of U.S. Export Controls. D. R. Whitson. *The International Essays for Business Decision Makers, Vol. IV,* 1979, pp. 250–255. Datotek, Inc.

The Marketing Path to Global Profits. David J. Freiman. 1979, 69 pp. Imperial Knife Associated Companies. MB.

Multinational Marketing Management. Derek F. Channon with Michael Jalland. *Multinational Strategic Planning,* 1978, pp. 259–293. Manchester Business School.

A National Export Policy: What and Why. Frank A. Weil. *The International Essays for Business Decision Makers, Vol. III,* 1978, pp. 24–30. U.S. Department of Commerce.

Needed: A New Marketing Entity for International Business. Thomas J. Ryan. *The International Essays for Business Decision Makers, Vol. IV,* 1979, pp. 114–121. Pullman Kellogg.

Price vs. Policy: A Tale of Two Markets. Walter B. Wriston. *The International Essays for Business Decision Makers, Vol. V,* 1980, pp. 195–202. Citicorp.

Strategic Materials Supercartel. Bohdan O. Szuprowicz. *The International Essays for Business Decision Makers, Vol. IV,* 1979, pp. 176–188. 21st Century Research.

Synergism Needed If U.S. Companies Are to Achieve Long-Term Export Goals in Currently Troubled Economies. Harvey J. Trilli. *The International Essays for Business Decision Makers, Vol. IV,* 1979, pp. 170–175. Pullman Swindell.

Ten Steps to Successful Exporting. R. Wayne Walvoord. 1981, 79 pp. International Trade Management Co., Inc.

The Use of Barter Trade in the 1980's. Otto J. Dax. *The International Essays for Business Decision Makers, Vol. IV,* 1979, pp. 132–139. Siemens Corp.

World Trade and Investment Freedoms: A Perspective on Military Equipment Exports. Lucy Wilson Benson. *The International Essays for Business Decision Makers, Vol. V,* 1980, pp. 163–171.

INTERNATIONAL OPERATIONS—PERSONNEL SURVEYS

Belgium Report. Executive Compensation Service. By purchase only.

Brazil Report. Executive Compensation Service. By purchase only.

Canada Executive Remuneration Report. Executive Compensation Service. By purchase only.

Canada Office Personnel Report. Executive Compensation Service. By purchase only.

Canada Professional, Scientific & Technical Report. Executive Compensation Service. By purchase only.

European Benefits Report. Executive Compensation Service. By purchase only.

European Sales and Marketing Personnel Report. Executive Compensation Service. By purchase only.

European Top Management Compensation Report. Executive Compensation Service. By purchase only.

Federal Republic of Germany Report. Executive Compensation Service. By purchase only.

Flexible Working Hours in Europe. Executive Compensation Service. By purchase only.

France Report. Executive Compensation Service. By purchase only.

Industrial Democracy Report. Executive Compensation Service. By purchase only.

International Compensation Report. Executive Compensation Service. By purchase only.

International Transfers U.S.-Europe. Executive Compensation Service. By purchase only.

Italy Report. Executive Compensation Service. By purchase only.

Labour Relations: Europe. Executive Compensation Service. By purchase only.

Mexico Report. Executive Compensation Service. By purchase only.

Netherlands Report. Executive Compensation Service. By purchase only.

Office and Administrative Personnel Remuneration—Europe. Executive Compensation Service. By purchase only.

Portugal Report. Executive Compensation Service. By purchase only.

Scandinavia Report. Executive Compensation Service. By purchase only.

Spain Report. Executive Compensation Service. By purchase only.

Switzerland Report. Executive Compensation Service. By purchase only.

Termination of Employment. Executive Compensation Service. By purchase only.

United Kingdom Report. Executive Compensation Service. By purchase only.

INTERVIEWING

Appraisal and Career Counseling Interviews: Productive Interviewing No. 3 (sec. ed.). Don Faber. 1981. (AMACOM audio cassette) By purchase only.

The Appraisal Interview Guide. Robert G. Johnson. 1979, 122 pp. Learning Technology, Inc.

The Exit Interview: Productive Interviewing No. 2 (sec. ed.). John R. Hinrichs. 1981. (AMACOM audio cassette) By purchase only.

Getting Ready for the Appraisal Interview. Dan H. Nix. SM, July 1980, pp. 2–8. Reynolds Community College. (Also in reprint collection *Leadership on the Job: Guides to Good Supervision* (third ed.), 1981)

Getting the Facts: How to Set Up a Communications Framework for Interviewing. Jay N. Nisberg, Daniel Spurr. MRev., April 1977, pp. 13–17. Jay Nisberg & Associates, St. Joseph Mercy Hospital.

How to Conduct Interviews. ES, Nov. 1978, 16 pp.

How to Interview Supervisory Candidates from the Ranks. William T. Wolz. Pers., Sept.–Oct. 1980, pp. 31–39.

The Information Interview: Productive Interviewing No. 5 (sec. ed.). John R. Hinrichs. 1981. (AMACOM audio cassette) By purchase only.

Interviewing Efficiency: Speed and Effectiveness in Employee Selection. Warren D. Robb. AMJ, Spring 1980, pp. 24–30. Univ. of Texas.

Interviewing for the Next Rung Up. Mary F. Cook. SM, Nov. 1980, pp. 27–31. Rocky Mountain Energy Co.

Job Search Tips for Your Job Interview. Iris D. Rosendahl. Pers., May–June 1979, p. 42.

A Memo to Interviewers. Larry G. McDougle. SM, May 1978, pp. 17–19. Indiana Univ. (Also in reprint collection *Effective Communication on the Job* (third ed.), 1981)

The Neglected Art of Interviewing. James G. Goodale. SM, July 1981, pp. 2–10. Philbrook, Goodale Associates.

Pre-Interview Game Plans: Making the Right Moves. Don Berliner. AMJ, Autumn 1979, pp. 52–59. General Foods Corp.

Preparing for Executive Position Interviews: Questions the Interviewer Might Ask— Or Be Asked. Sigmund G. Ginsburg. Pers., July–Aug. 1980, pp. 31–36. Univ. of Cincinnati.

The Problem Employee Interview: Productive Interviewing No. 4 (sec. ed.). Glenn A. Bassett. 1981. (AMACOM audio cassette) By purchase only.

A Search for the Derogatory. Arthur A. Witkin. AMJ, Summer 1980, pp. 39–45. Personnel Sciences Center of New York.

The Selection Interview: Productive Interviewing No. 1 (third ed.). Raymond F. Valentine. 1981. (AMACOM audio cassette) By purchase only.

Step 5—The Structured Selection Interview. Erwin S. Stanton. *Successful Personnel Recruiting and Selection,* 1977, pp. 117–143.

Tested Questions for the Structured Selection Interview (Appendix A). Erwin S. Stanton. *Successful Personnel Recruiting and Selection,* 1977, 195–198.

What Should You Ask the Company Interviewer? Howard M. Mitchell. AMJ, Winter 1977, pp. 55–61. Monsanto Co.

INVENTORY CONTROL. See also International Operations, Purchasing

The High Cost of Having Things on Hand: Some Advice to Big Spenders. Gene Jackson. MRev., Oct. 1977, pp. 30–32, 39. Main, Jackson & Garfield, Inc.

Inventories: Controlling and Keeping Track of Them. ES, May 1981, 16 pp.

Inventory Control. William R. Osgood. *Basics of Successful Business Management,* 1981, pp. 170–183.

Inventory Time—Picnic or Panic? Robert J. Shaw. MRev., March 1978, pp. 16–20. Peat, Marwick, Mitchell & Co.

Inventory Valuation Under Direct Costing. William E. Arnstein, Frank Gilabert. *Direct Costing,* 1980, pp. 60–71. Main Hurdman & Cranstoun.

Stocking Up to Beat Inflation. Louis Hohenstein. AMJ, Winter 1981. pp. 15–19. C. L. Hohenstein & Associates.

INVESTOR RELATIONS

Financial Communications. Gerald J. Voros, Paul Alvarez (editors). *What Happens in Public Relations,* 1981, pp. 95–110. Ketchum MacLeod & Grove.

Growing Pains for Investor Relations. Gerald J. Voros, Paul Alvarez (editors). *What Happens in Public Relations,* 1981, pp. 150–167. Ketchum MacLeod & Grove.

How to Build Effective Investor Relations. Arthur R. Roalman. 1980. (Extension Institute Course) By purchase only.

Investor Relations at FMC Corporation. William R. Baker. *Investor Relations That Work,* 1980, pp. 231–262. FMC Corp.

Investor Relations at Medtronic. Robert A. Gaertner. *Investor Relations That Work,* 1980, pp. 195–210. Medtronic, Inc.

Investor Relations in an Adverse Environment. Gerald A. Parsons. *Investor Relations That Work,* 1980, pp. 263–268. Evans Products Co.

Investor Relations That Work. Arthur R. Roalman (editor). 1980, 278 pp. Univ. of South Carolina.

Making Investor Relations Work for Your Company. Arthur R. Roalman. MRev., Aug. 1980, pp. 27–28, 38–39. *Investor Relations Update.*

Myth and Reality in Investor Relations. Michael Seely. *Investor Relations That Work,* 1980, pp. 1–4. Investor Access Corp.

The Next Ten Years in Investor Relations. Charles D. Kuehner. *Investor Relations That Work,* 1980, pp. 269–273. American Telephone & Telegraph Co.

Plain Talk About Talking to Wall Street (Part 3 of a Series). Theodore H. Pincus. MRev., Jan. 1977, pp. 23–31. The Financial Relations Board.

Should the Proxy Statement Be Given a New Focus? Victor Futter. *Corporate Governance Review.* 1981, pp. 36–47. Allied Chemical Corp.

Stakeholder Negotiations: Building Bridges With Corporate Constituents. Ram Charan, R. Edward Freeman. MRev., Nov. 1979, pp. 8–13. Wharton School.

What's a Castle & Cooke? N. John Douglas. *Investor Relations That Work,* 1980, pp. 211–229. Castle & Cooke, Inc.

JOB DESCRIPTIONS

The Accountability Chart—A Tool for Team Building. Neil Miller. Pers., Nov.–Dec. 1977. pp. 51–56.

Beginning at the Beginning—Job Definition. Paul E. Illman. *Developing Overseas Managers—and Managers Overseas,* 1980, pp. 149–170. Management Training, Inc.

A Framework for Evaluating Job Analysis Methods. Ronald A. Ash, Edward L. Levine. Pers., Nov.–Dec. 1980, pp. 53–59. Univ. of South Florida.

How to Master Job Descriptions (PRIME 100). 1977. (An AMACOM Skill Series home-study course) By purchase only.

How to Write a Good Job Description. James Evered. SM, April 1981, pp. 14–19. Redman Industries, Inc.

Human Resources Functionalization (Appendix I). Robert L. Desatnick. *The Expanding Role of the Human Resources Manager,* 1979, pp. 193–205. McDonald's Corp.

Job Analysis Practices. Thomasine Rendero. Pers., Jan.–Feb., 1981, pp. 4–12.

The Job Description: Setting the Standard for Employee Development. Larry G. McDougle. SM, Feb. 1979, pp. 38–40. Indiana Univ.

Job Descriptions and Performance Standards. James F. Evered. *Shirt-Sleeves Management,* 1981, pp. 50–58. Redman Industries, Inc.

Job Descriptions—Critical Documents, Versatile Tools. Richard I. Henderson. *Effective Communication on the Job* (third ed.), 1981, pp. 294–313. Georgia State Univ.

Job Descriptions in Manufacturing Industries. John D. Ulery. 1981, 161 pp. Litton Industries.

Job Specifications and Job Descriptions. John Fenton. *The A to Z of Sales Management,* 1979, pp. 53–63. Sales Augmentation International Group.

Position Description for a Board of Directors. J. Keith Louden. *Managing at the Top,* 1977, pp. 146–159. Corporate Director, Inc.

Position Descriptions. Lawrence A. Appley, Keith L. Irons. *Manager Manpower Planning: A Professional Management System,* 1981, pp. 13–18.

Sample Position Descriptions. Joseph J. Famularo. *Organization Planning Manual* (rev. ed.), 1979, pp. 197–312. McGraw-Hill, Inc.

Statement of Responsibilities of Internal Auditors (Appendix A). Lawrence B. Sawyer. *The Manager and the Modern Internal Auditor: A Problem-Solving Partnership,* 1979, pp. 429–431.

JOB DESIGN/JOB ENLARGEMENT/JOB ENRICHMENT
The Design of Work in the 1980's. Richard J. Hackman. OD, Summer 1978, pp. 3–17.

Every Employee a Manager. M. Scott Myers. *The Amazing Oversight: Total Participation for Productivity,* 1979, pp. 107–126. Center for Applied Management.

Explaining Job Enrichment. Paul J. Champagne. SM, Nov. 1979, pp. 24–34. Michigan Technological Univ.

Job Design and Productivity: A New Approach. Louis E. Davis. *Human Resources Management: The Past is Prologue,* 1979, pp. 109–125.

Job Enrichment and Job Redesign. David J. Cherrington. *The Work Ethic: Working Values and Values That Work,* 1980, pp. 222–252. Brigham Young Univ.

Job Enrichment: Long on Theory, Short on Practice. Fred Luthans, William E. Reif. *Organizational Development: Theory and Practice,* 1977, pp. 90–99. Univ. of Nebraska, Arizona State Univ.

Job Enrichment Revisited. Lyle Yorks. 1979, 68 pp. Eastern Connecticut State College. MB.

MBO + Job Enrichment: How to Have Your Cake & Eat It Too. Denis D. Umstot. MRev., Feb. 1977, pp. 21–26.

A Primer on Implementing Job Redesign. Gene Milbourn. SM, Jan. 1981, pp. 27–37. Univ. of Baltimore.

Productivity: A Practical Program for Improving Efficiency (rev. ed.—former title: *Tapping the Human Resource: A Strategy for Productivity*). Clair F. Vough, Bernard Asbell. 1979, 212 pp. Productivity Research International, Inc.

Productivity Gains Through Worklife Improvement. Edward M. Glaser. Pers., Jan.–Feb. 1980, pp. 71–77. Human Interaction Research Institute.

Progress Report on Management Aides. Edward W. Cassidy, Robert J. Edelman, Robert P. Kelly. Pers., Jan.–Feb. 1978, pp. 21–29.

Reevaluating the Assembly Line. Donald D. Deming. SM, Sept. 1977, pp. 2–7.

The Relationship of Values and Job Satisfaction: Do Birds of a Feather Work Well Together? Martha A. Brown. Pers., Nov.–Dec. 1980, pp. 66–73. Angelo State Univ.

Success Story: The Team Approach to Work Restructuring. Ernesto J. Poza, M. Lynne Markus. OD, Winter 1980, pp. 3–25. Massachusetts Institute of Technology.

Team vs. Individual Approaches to Job Enrichment Programs. Antone Alber, Melvin Blumberg. Pers., Jan.–Feb. 1981, pp. 63–75. Bradley Univ., Univ. of Wisconsin.

Ungluing the Stuck: Motivating Performance and Productivity Through Expanded Opportunity. Rosabeth Moss Kanter, Barry A. Stein. MRev., July 1981, pp. 45–49. Yale Univ., Goodmeasure, Inc.

Unlocking the Secret of Job Satisfaction. Richard A. Morano. SM, May 1979, pp. 1i–20. Xerox Corp.

When Job Enrichment Doesn't Pay. Paul J. Champagne, Curt Tausky. Pers., Jan.–Feb 1978, pp. 30–40.

Why Jobs Die and What to Do About It. Robert N. Ford. 1979, 220 pp.

JOB EVALUATION
Eliminating Pay Discrimination Caused by Job Evaluation. David J. Thomsen. Pers., Sept.–Oct. 1978, pp. 11–22.

Equitable Job Evaluation and Classification with the Position Analysis Question-naire. P. R. Jeanneret. CR, First Quarter 1980, pp. 32–42. LWFW Inc.

Evalucomp: The Complete Job Evaluation Program. Executive Compensation Service. By purchase only.

Executive Position Evaluation. Graef S. Crystal. *Executive Compensation: Money, Motivation, and Imagination,* 1978, pp. 27–56. Towers, Perrin, Forster & Crosby.

Job Analysis: Methods and Applications. Ernest J. McCormick. 1979. 371 pp. PAQ Services Inc.

Job Evaluation. Stanley B. Henrici. *Salary Management for the Nonspecialist,* 1980, pp. 30–63. Heinz, U.S.A.

Job Evaluation. Robert E. Sibson. *Compensation* (rev. ed.), 1981, pp. 76–95. The Sibson Group.

Job Evaluation: Mystical or Statistical. Howard Risher. Pers., Sept.–Oct. 1978, pp. 23–36.

A Job Evaluation Program (Appendix I). Theodore Cohn, Roy A. Lindberg. *Compensating Key Executives in the Smaller Company,* 1979, pp. 203–210.

Job Evaluation—the Mexican Encounter. Robert J. Neubauer. Pers., Sept.–Oct. 1978, pp. 52–56.

Participative Job Evaluation. James F. Carey. CR, Fourth Quarter 1977, pp. 29–38.

The Scaling Method of Job Evaluation. Dov Elizur. CR, Third Quarter 1978, pp. 34–46. Bar Ilan Univ., The Israel Institute of Applied Social Research.

Take the Fat Out of Job Evaluation. Louis C. Curston. HSM, April 1981, pp. 7–10.

To Every Job a Pay Slot. Bruce R. Ellig. SM, Dec. 1980, pp. 24–31. Pfizer Inc.

LABOR-MANAGEMENT RELATIONS. See also Arbitration, Collective Bargaining

Developing Healthy Management Attitudes for Dealing with a Union. Madison Philips. Pers., Sept.–Oct. 1977, pp. 68–71.

Employee, Labor, and Public Relations. William R. Tracey. *Human Resource Development Standards.* 1981 pp. 296–323. U.S. Army Intelligence Training School.

How "Good Employee Relations" Can Prevent and Win Labor Disputes. Raymond Fleishman. HSM, June 1980, pp. 1–3. Maimonides Hospital.

How to Establish A Good Industrial Relations Climate. James M. Miles. MRev., Aug. 1980, pp. 42–44. Haynesworth, Baldwin & Miles.

Labor-Management Communications. Gerald J. Voros, Paul Alvarez (editors). *What Happens in Public Relations,* 1981, pp. 123–137. Ketchum MacLeod & Grove.

Managing Labor Relations. David B. Whittier. 1977. (Extension Institute Cassette Program) By purchase only.

New Directions for Labor-Management Cooperation. Donald N. Scobel. MRev., Feb. 1977, pp. 12–20. (Also in reprint collection *Leadership on the Job: Guides to Good Supervision* (third ed.), 1981)

Preventive Labor Relations. John G. Kilgour. 1981, 338 pp. California State Univ.

Union-Management Cooperation: A Psychological Analysis. Irving Knickerbocker, Douglas McGregor. *Human Resources Management: The Past Is Prologue,* 1979, pp. 46–67.

Walking the Supervisory Tightrope Between Management and Labor. Michael S. Golding. SM, Dec. 1979, pp. 30–35. Michael Associates. (Also in reprint collection *Leadership on the Job: Guides to Good Supervision* (third ed.), 1981)

Winning Union-Management Cooperation on Quality of Worklife Projects. Edward E. Lawler, Lee M. Ozley. MRev., March 1979, pp. 19–24. Univ. of California, Los Angeles, Responsive Organizations, Inc.

LEADERSHIP. See also Executives—Skills and Qualifications, Management

A Case for the Relational Manager. Harold J. Leavitt, Jean Lipman-Blumen. OD, Summer 1980, pp. 27–41. Stanford Univ., Univ. of Connecticut.

Can Leaders Learn to Lead? Victor H. Vroom. *Leadership: Fiedler, Vroom, and Argyris,* 1977, pp. 20–31. Yale Univ.

Choosing a Leadership Style. Vincent S. Flowers, Charles L. Hughes. Pers., Jan.–Feb. 1978, pp. 48–59. Center for Values Research.

Conversation with Rensis Likert. William Dowling (editor). Effective Management and the Behavioral Sciences. 1978, pp. 52–74.

Establishing Leadership: How to Analyze and Deal with the Basic Issues. Alan L. Frohman, Steven P. Ober. MRev., April 1980, pp. 46–50.

An Exemplary Performance in Management. James L. Hayes. MRev., Jan. 1981, pp. 2–3.

Getting Along with the Informal Leader. John Hodge. SM, Oct. 1980, pp. 41–43. Seidman College.

How to Assess Your Managerial Style. Charles Margerison. 1980, 151 pp. Cranfield School of Management, England.

How to Choose a Productive Leadership Pattern. ES, Oct. 1979, 16 pp.

How to Improve Your Management Style. Robert R. Blake, Jane Srygley Mouton. 1978. (AMACOM audio cassette) By purchase only.

How to Take a Position of Leadership. William C. Waddell. *Overcoming Murphy's Law,* 1981, pp. 31–59. California State Univ., Los Angeles.

Incompetents and Other Bunglers. Donald T. Dalena, Richard I. Henderson. HSM, June 1981, pp. 7–10. United Steel Workers of America, Georgia State Univ.

Introduction: Leadership Symposium. Lyman W. Porter. *Leadership: Fiedler, Vroom, and Argyris,* 1977, pp. 5–8. Univ. of California, Irvine.

Job Engineering for Effective Leadership: A New Approach. Fred E. Fiedler. MRev., Sept. 1977, pp. 29–31. Univ. of Washington. (Also in reprint collection *Leadership on the Job: Guides to Good Supervision* (third ed.), 1981)

Leader-Follower Behavior in 3D. Robert W. Johnston. Pers., Part 1. July–Aug. 1981, pp. 32–42. Part 2. Sept.–Oct. 1981, pp. 50–61. Western Gear Corp.

Leaders and Followers. Wesley J. Johnston, Thomas V. Bonoma. *Management Principles for Nonprofit Agencies and Organizations,* 1979, pp. 38–70. Ohio State Univ., Univ. of Pittsburgh.

Leadership: Fiedler, Vroom, and Argyris. 1977, 48 pp. (A collection of reprints from OD)

The Leadership Game: Matching the Man to the Situation. Fred E. Fiedler. *Leadership: Fiedler, Vroom, and Argyris,* 1977, pp. 9–19. Univ. of Washington.

Leadership in an Organization. Lois Borland Hart. *Moving Up: Women and Leadership,* 1980, pp. 16–22. Mountain States Employers Council, Inc.

Leadership: Is There One Best Approach? W. Warner Burke. MRev., Nov. 1980. pp. 54–56. Columbia Univ.

Leadership, Learning, and Changing the Status Quo. Chris Argyris. *Leadership: Fiedler, Vroom, and Argyris,* 1977, pp. 33–47. Harvard Univ.

Leadership on the Job: Guides to Good Supervision (third ed.). William K. Fallon (editor). 1981, 344 pp. (A collection of reprints from AMACOM publications)

Leadership Skills for Executives. James J. Cribbin. 1977. (Extension Institute Course) By purchase only.

Leadership: Strategies for Organizational Effectiveness. James J. Cribbin. 1981, 296 pp. St. John's Univ.

Leadership Style and Managerial Effectiveness: An Exercise in Self-Analysis. Joseph C. Latona. SM, Dec. 1978, pp. 18–24. Univ. of Akron.

Leadership Style: Democratic Here, Autocratic There. Ernest B. Jaski, Elizabeth Riser. HSM, Jan. 1977, pp. 6–7. Southwest College, Little Co. of Mary.

A Leading Combination. James L. Hayes. MRev., Dec. 1978, pp. 2–3.

Leading the Way to Success. Sidney P. Johnson. SM, Sept. 1979, pp. 2–11. Johnson Associates.

Leading Through the Follower's Point of View. William E. Zierden. OD, Spring 1980, pp. 27–46. Univ. of Virginia.

Leading Vs. Managing: A Guide to Some Crucial Distinctions. Roger J. Plachy. MRev., Sept. 1981, pp. 58–61. Plachy Associates.

Management Styles and the Human Component. Rensis Likert. MRev., Oct. 1977, pp. 23–28, 43–45. (Also in reprint collection *Leadership on the Job: Guides to Good Supervision* (third ed.), 1981)

Managers Must Lead! (rev. ed.). Ray A. Killian. 1979, 254 pp. Belk Stores.

Managing for the Sport of It. James L. Hayes. MRev., April 1980, pp. 2–3.

Managing in Style. Malcolm E. Shaw. SM, Sept. 1979, pp. 20–28. Educational Systems & Designs, Inc.

Managing With Style and Making It Work for You. Henry O. Golightly. 1977, 159 pp. Golightly & Co.

A Matter of Management Style. Edward C. Schleh. MRev., August 1977, pp. 8–13. Schleh Associates, Inc.

The Nonleaders: Incompetents and Other Bunglers. Donald T. Dalena, Richard I.

Henderson. *Leadership on the Job: Guides to Good Supervision* (third ed.), 1981, pp. 40–47. United Steelworkers of America, Georgia State Univ.

On Management and Managers. Clair F. Vough, Bernard Asbell. *Productivity, A Practical Program for Improving Efficiency* (rev. ed.—former title: *Tapping the Human Resource: A Strategy for Productivity*), 1979, pp. 172–187. Productivity Research International, Inc.

The Practice of Leadership. Ray A. Killian. *Leadership on the Job: Guides to Good Supervision* (third ed.), 1981, pp. 11–16. Belk Store Services, Inc. (From *Managers Must Lead!* 1979)

Prescription for Leadership. David D. Steinbrecher. Pers., Nov.–Dec. 1979, pp. 58–59.

The Price of Leadership? James L. Hayes. MRev., March 1981, pp. 2–3.

The Right Perspective. James F. Evered. *Shirt-Sleeves Management,* 1981, pp. 8–28. Redman Industries, Inc.

Situational Leadership: How Xerox Managers Fine-Tune Managerial Styles to Employee Maturity and Task Needs. Raymond Gumpert, Ronald K. Hambleton. MRev., Dec. 1979, pp. 8–12. Xerox Corp., Univ. of Massachusetts.

Surviving and Succeeding in the 'Political' Organization: Becoming a Leader. Alan Jay Weiss. SM, Aug. 1978, pp. 27–35. Kepner-Tregoe, Inc. (Also in reprint collection *Surviving and Succeeding in the 'Political' Organization,* 1978)

Two Heads Are Better Than One: The Case for Dual Leadership. James I. Mashburn, Bobby C. Vaught. MRev., Dec. 1980, pp. 53–56. Ozark Railway Supplies, Southwest Missouri State Univ.

Understanding Leadership and Creating an Effective Leadership Style. Louis V. Imundo. *The Effective Supervisor's Handbook,* 1980, pp. 94–119. Management Perspectives.

What Can Managers Learn from Leadership Theories? Terence W. Austin. SM, July 1981, pp. 22–31. JHK & Associates.

What It Takes to Be a Leader. Louis Imundo. *Leadership on the Job: Guides to Good Supervision* (third ed.). 1981, pp. 3–10. Management Perspectives. (From *The Effective Supervisor's Handbook,* 1980)

What Sets an Executive Apart from His Peers? Roger Birkman. AMJ, Summer 1978, pp. 58–62. Birkman & Associates.

Working on Your Leadership Skills. V. Dallas Merrell. SM, June 1981, pp. 38–41.

You and I Have Simply Got to Stop Meeting This Way. Part 5: Changes Leaders Can Make. Richard J. Dunsing. SM, Jan. 1977, pp. 18–29. Univ. of Richmond. (Also in reprint collection *You and I Have Simply Got to Stop Meeting This Way,* 1977 and expanded book, same title, 1978)

LEASING

How to Evaluate Leases. Robert E. Pritchard, Thomas J. Hindelang. *The Strategic Evaluation and Management of Capital Expenditures,* 1981, pp. 158–182. Glassboro State College, Drexel Univ.

The Lease/Buy Decision. Robert E. Pritchard, Thomas Hindelang. 1980, 276 pp. Glassboro State Univ., Drexel Univ.

Leasing for Profit. Terry A. Isom, Sudhir P. Amembal, 1980. (Extension Institute Course) By purchase only.

Leveraged Leasing: New Opportunities Under the Economic Recovery Tax Act of 1981. Albert F. Gargiulo, Raymond J. Kenard, Jr., 1981, 53 pp. Raymond J. Kenard, Jr., Inc. MB.

LEGISLATION AND REGULATION

Age Discrimination in Employment. William L. Kendig. 1978, 83 pp. U.S. Dept. of the Interior. MB.

Anachronistic Legislation. James L. Hayes. MRev., May 1977 p. 14.

Benefits and the Amended ADEA. Ernest C. Miller. Pers., Sept.–Oct. 1978, pp. 4–10.

Benefitting From Prospective Rate Setting. Ned Borgstrom. HSM, July 1979, pp. 1–4, 9. Arthur Andersen & Co.

Bottom-Line Accountability. S. John Byington. MRev., May 1977, p. 19. U.S. Consumer Product Safety Commission.

Can Cost/Benefit Really Work? R. David Pittle. MRev., May 1977, p. 17. U.S. Consumer Product Safety Commission.

Conflict! Equal Employment Versus Occupational Health. Nina G. Stillman. AMJ, Spring 1981, pp. 16–23. Vedder, Price, Kaufman & Kammholz.

Contracts: The Move to Plain Language. Paul H. Till, Albert F. Gargiulo. 1979, 56 pp. MB.

Controlling Paperwork—Yours and the Government's. Warren B. Buhler. 1979, 61 pp. Management Design, Inc. MB.

Corporations and the First Amendment. Herbert Schmertz. 1978, 40 pp. Mobil Oil Corp. MB.

Effect on Capital Growth. John B. Ricker, Jr. MRev., May 1977, p. 19. The Continental Corp.

The Effects of Extending the Mandatory Retirement Age. Henry M. Wallfesh. 1978, 41 pp. Retirement Advisors, Inc. MB.

Emphasize Productivity. E. S. Donnell. MRev., May 1977, p. 15. Montgomery Ward & Co.

Employee Rights—A Matter for Sensitivity. SS, Oct. 1980, 24 pp.

Employing the Handicapped: A Practical Compliance Manual. Arno B. Zimmer. 1981, 374 pp. Eliot-Yeats, Inc.

The Executive's Guide to Commercial Law. Charles L. Babcock, Richard F. Collier, Jr., 1978. (Extension Institute Course) By purchase only.

Fair Information Practices for Managers and Employees. Jack Lester Osborn. 1980, 23 pp. TRW Credit Data. SR.

The Foreign Corrupt Practices Act: New Developments and Future Challenges. Joseph E. Connor. *Corporate Governance Review,* 1981, pp. 26–35. Price, Waterhouse & Co.

Foreign Corrupt Practices Act Update. Elliot M. Schnitzer. BPM 14, April 1981, 6 pp. Gardner, Carton & Douglas.

"Free the Fortune 500"—An Economist's Response to Big Business Day. Murray L. Weidenbaum. *Productivity Improvement: Case Studies of Proven Practice,* 1981, pp. 218–229. President Reagan's Council of Economic Advisers.

The Future of Business Regulation: Private Action & Public Demand. Murray L. Weidenbaum. 1979, 183 pp.

Government Legislation and Regulation. Ned Merkle. *Do's and Don'ts of Pension Fund Management,* 1981, pp. 15–21. E. A. Merkle & Associates, Inc. MB.

How to Survive in the Regulatory Jungle. Raymond M. Momboisse. MRev., Sept. 1977, pp. 43–47. Pacific Legal Foundation.

The Impact of Legislation on the Personnel Function. Bruce R. Ellig. Pers., Sept.–Oct. 1980, pp. 49–53. Pfizer, Inc.

In the Public Interest: How to Regulate the Regulators. MRev., May 1977, pp. 13–19.

Law Day. Robert F. Kennedy. *Making Successful Presentations,* 1981, pp. 209–216.

Legal and Contractual Implications of a Current Value System. Harris J. Amhowitz, David R. Sinclair. *Current Value Accounting,* 1977, pp. 86–92. Coopers & Lybrand

Legal Aspects of National Account Marketing. Michael Malena. *National Accounts Marketing Handbook,* 1981, pp. 229–255. Kaye, Scholer, Fierman, Hayes and Handler.

Legal Aspects of R&D Management. Philip H. Francis. *Principles of R&D Management,* 1977, pp. 175–214. Southwest Research Institute.

Legal Handbook for Nonprofit Organizations. Marc J. Lane. 1980, 294 pp. Medico-Legal Institutes, Inc.

Legal Handbook for Small Business. Marc J. Lane. 1977, 181 pp.

Legal Planning Constraints on New Capital Expenditures. Ivan Wood, Jr. HSM, April 1979, pp. 4–5. Wood, Lucksinger & Epstein.

Legal Problems of ESOPs. Larry D. Blust. *ESOPs and the Smaller Employer,* 1979, pp. 56–68. Jenner & Block. MB.

74

The Legal Requirements. Jack R. Ellner, Henry E. Bender. *Hiring the Handicapped,* 1980, pp. 12–29. Southern Illinois Univ. RS.

Legislation. Linda A. Roxe. *Personnel Management for the Smaller Company.* 1979, pp. 190–214. Rox Associates.

Legislation Relevant to Alternative Work Schedules, Appendix B. Stanley D. Nollen, Virginia H. Martin. *Alternative Work Schedules—Part I: Flexitime,* 1978, pp. 48–51.

Let Public Interest Be the Guide. Robert D. Lilley. MRev., May 1977, p. 15.

Liabilities of Directors Under State Law. Michael D. Goldman. BPM 7, April 1980, 6 pp. Potter, Anderson & Corroon.

A Manager's Guide to the Antitrust Laws. Edward A. Matto. 1980, 195 pp. Borden, Inc.

Marketing and the Law—Developing a Positive Practical Program of Antitrust Compliance. Earl M. Wunderli. MRev., Feb. 1978, pp. 32, 37–38. IBM Corp.

More Business Responsibility. Senator Edmund S. Muskie. MRev., May 1977, p. 15.

Needed: Activist Managers. James L. Hayes. MRev., April 1978, pp. 2–3.

1979 Legislative Outlook. John E. Curtis, Jr. *ESOPs and the Smaller Employer,* 1979, pp. 46–55. MB.

No Sermon on the Mount But . . . Recent Developments Involving Questionable Payments. Richard S. Kraut. MRev., April 1978, pp. 29–31. Securities & Exchange Commission.

Nursing Laws and Holistic Medicine. Rita E. Numerof. HSM, July 1978, pp. 6–8.

Personal Information: Privacy at the Workplace. Jack L. Osborn. 1978, 52 pp. Purdue Univ. MB.

Personnel Testing Under EEO. Jerome Siegel. 1980, 92 pp. City Univ. of New York. RS.

Privacy of Employee Records. Hermine Levine. Pers., May–June 1981, pp. 4–11.

Protecting Charitable Donations: The Donor-Restricted Endowment Fund. Edward J. Hopkins, Keith D. Kirschbraun. HSM, Oct. 1981, pp. 5–6. Wood, Lucksinger & Epstein.

PSRO Problems? Group Action Works Best. James M. Savage. HSM, July 1980, pp. 4–6, 11–12. Edward W. Sparrow Hospital.

The Real Issue: Too Much Regulation (for everybody). James C. Miller III. MRev., May 1977, p. 16–17. Council on Wage and Price Stability.

Regulatory Reform—A Need Whose Time Has Come. Cornell C. Maier. MRev., May 1977, p. 14. Kaiser Aluminum & Chemical Corp.

Responsibility and Liability in the Age of ERISA. Daniel C. Knickerbocker, Jr. PA #68, 1978, 48 pp. John Hancock Mutual Life Insurance Co. By purchase only.

Should Corporate Ethics Be Regulated? Fred T. Allen. MRev., May 1977, p. 16. Pitney-Bowes, Inc.

A Three-Way Joint Effort. George S. Dominguez. MRev., May 1977, p. 15. CIBA/Geigy Corp.

Too Much Methodology. Harry Holiday. MRev., May 1977, p. 18. Armco Steel Corp.

Unpleasant Surprises in the Foreign Corrupt Practices Act. Norman E. Auerbach. MRev., Nov. 1978, pp. 29–31. Coopers & Lybrand.

What Rights of Privacy Should Job Applicants Have? Laurence Lipsett. SM, Oct. 1977, pp. 30–36. Empire State College.

What the Supervisor Should Know About the Fair Labor Standard Act. Brent E. Zepke. SM, Feb. 1977, pp. 30–36.

Whither Labor Standards? Some Guidelines for Management. John C. Read. MRev., Jan. 1978, pp. 25–28, 37–39. Cummings Engine Co.

Work for a "Taxpayers" Agency. J. Kevin Murphy. MRev., May 1977, p. 18. KMA Industries.

LIBRARIES

The Second Kind of Knowledge: Corporate Libraries. Irving H. Neufeld. MRev., Dec. 1978, pp. 44–47. United Technologies.

Technology Transfer from the Corporate Library. Linda M. B. McKinnon. MRev., May 1979, pp. 47–49. Sanders Associates.

LINE-STAFF

The Behavioral Dimensions of "Span of Management" Theory. James C. Worthy. *The Evolving Science of Management,* 1979, pp. 405–414. Northwestern Univ.

How to Deal with the Personnel Office. James G. Stockard. *Rethinking People Management: A New Look at the Human Resources Function,* 1980, pp. 195–214.

Idea Managers: A New Look at Staff Vs. Line Jobs. William G. Sharwell. MRev., Aug. 1978, pp. 24–25. Columbia Univ.

On the Line with Staff. James L. Hayes. MRev., June 1981, pp. 2–3.

Personnel Ratios: 1978 Food-For-Thought Figures. Deslie Beth Lawrence. Pers., Jan.–Feb. 1979, pp. 4–10.

Personnel Staff and the Line Organization. Louis A. Allen. *Human Resources Management: The Past Is Prologue,* 1979, pp. 240–247.

The Practical Application of Completed Staff Work. James W. Hill. SM, June 1980, pp. 37–41. Pennsylvania State Univ.

Putting the Specialist into Perspective. Edward C. Schleh. AMJ, Autumn 1980, pp. 35–40. Schleh Associates.

Smoothing the Way to Staff Acceptance of Management Engineering. Harris Odell, Jr. HSM, June 1979, pp. 1, 10. Memorial Medical Center.

Specialists Vs. Generalists: Who Runs the Company? F. Ross Johnson. MRev., Jan. 1980, pp. 43–45. Standard Brands, Inc.

Staff Functions. Henry I. Meyer. *The Face of Business,* 1980, pp. 125–147.

Why Line Managers Don't Listen to Their Personnel Departments. T. F. Cawsey. Pers., Jan.–Feb. 1980, pp. 11–20. Western Ontario Univ.

LINEAR PROGRAMMING. See Management Science and Statistics

MAINTENANCE

How to Manage Maintenance. Joseph J. Johnstone, Kenneth G. Ward. 1981. (Extension Institute Course) By purchase only.

Managing Maintenance: How to Control Runaway Costs. Edward J. Rand. MRev., June 1978, pp. 59–61. ORU Group, Inc.

Reliability, Maintenance and Safety. Joseph F. Engelberger. *Robotics in Practice: Management and Applications of Industrial Robots,* 1980, pp. 75–99. Unimation Inc.

MANAGEMENT. See also Cooperation, Coordination and Conflict Resolution, Executives—Skills and Qualifications, Leadership, Supervision and headings for individual functions

Basics of Management. Roy A. Lindberg. 1980. (AMACOM audio cassette) By purchase only.

Basics of Successful Business Management. William R. Osgood. 1981, 259 pp.

Challenge of Viewpoint. Erwin H. Schell. *The Amazing Oversight: Total Participation for Productivity,* 1979, pp. 5–16.

Commentary: Do American Theories Apply Abroad? Leonard D. Goodstein, John W. Hunt. OD, Summer 1981, pp. 49–62. University Associates, Inc. Univ. of London.

Conversation: An Interview with Joshua Lederberg. OD, Winter 1980, pp. 42–60.

Conversation with Sir Adrian Cadbury. William Dowling (editor). OD, Winter 1979, pp. 39–58.

Conversation with Peter F. Drucker. William Dowling (editor). *Effective Management and the Behavioral Sciences,* 1978, pp. 221–245.

Conversation with George C. Homans. William Dowling (editor). *Effective Management and the Behavioral Sciences,* 1978, pp. 111–136.

Conversation with Richard D. Wood. OD, June 1981, pp. 22–35. Eli Lilly Co.

The Corporate Casino: How Managers Win and Lose at the Biggest Game in Town. Dean P. Peskin. 1978, 243 pp. Joseph George Distributors.

Do American Theories Apply Abroad? A Reply to Goodstein and Hunt. Geert Hofstede. OD, Summer 1981, pp. 63–68. Fasson Europe.

Epilogue. Lyndall F. Urwick. *The Evolving Science of Management,* 1979, pp. 479–481. Urwick, Orr, & Partners Limited.

The Evolving Science of Management. Melvin Zimet, Ronald G. Greenwood (editors). 1979, 496 pp. Manhattan College, Univ. of Wisconsin.

The Excitement of Management. James L. Hayes. MRev., Oct. 1981, pp. 2–3.

External Integration of the Firm. William H. Newman. *The Evolving Science of Management,* 1979, pp. 438–449. Columbia Univ.

The Face of Business. Henry I. Meyer. 1980, 268 pp.

Fast-Growth Management: How to Improve Profits with Entrepreneural Strategies. Mack Hanan. 1979, 145 pp. The Wellspring Group.

The First Time Manager: A Practical Guide to the Management of People. Loren B. Belker. 1978, 165 pp. Bankers Life Insurance Co.

Formula for Success. Lawrence A. Appley. 1981. (AMACOM audio cassette book) By purchase only.

Growth Strategies in Service Businesses. Charles H. Granger. MRev., April 1977, pp. 5–12. William E. Hill & Co.

How to Audit General Management. J. McConnell. 1979. (An AMACOM Evaluation Tool) By purchase only.

The "How To" Drucker. Peter F. Drucker. 1977. (AMACOM audio cassette) By purchase only.

How U.S. Managers Can Become Competitive Again. Charles R. Ferguson, Roger Dickinson. DM, Nov. 1980, pp. 1–5. Univ. of Texas, LWFW, Inc.

Improvement Must Be Managed. Herbert F. Goodwin. *The Amazing Oversight: Total Participation for Productivity,* 1979, pp. 65–83. MIT.

Introduction. Ronald G. Greenwood. *The Evolving Science of Management,* 1979, pp. 3–8. Univ. of Wisconsin.

Introduction. Melvin Zimet. *The Evolving Science of Management,* 1979, pp. 269–272. Manhattan College.

Invitation to Achievement: Your Career in Management (rev. ed.). Elizabeth Marting. 1981, 52 pp.

Leading Vs. Managing: A Guide to Some Crucial Distinctions. Roger J. Plachy. MRev., Sept. 1981, pp. 58–61. Plachy Associates.

Looking into the Future: Management in the Twenty-first Century. Roger Talpaert. MRev., March 1981, pp. 21–25. European Institute for Advanced Studies in Management.

Making a 'Professional' Manager. James L. Hayes. MRev., Nov. 1980. pp. 2–3.

Manage Your Plant for Profit and Your Promotion. Richard W. Ogden. 1978, 194 pp. Seminole Manufacturing Co.

Management for the 1980's (rev. ed.—former title: *The Achieving Enterprise).* William F. Christopher. 1980, 295 pp.

Management, Governance & Leadership: A Guide for College and University Administrators. John D. Millett, 1980, 208 pp. Academy for Educational Development.

Management Guidelines: The Right Perspective. George Miller. SM, March 1981, pp. 22–28. George Miller Associates. (Also reprinted in HSM, Dec. 1981).

Management Science Fiction. Carl Remick. AMJ, Spring 1981, pp. 24–26.

Management Systems: The Language of Organizational Character and Competence. Thomas J. Peters. OD, Summer 1980, pp. 3–26. McKinsey & Co.

Management Theory: Its Application to the Job. Dan Pike. SM, Dec. 1978, pp. 26–30. Communications Properties, Inc.

Management's Place in the World Today. Lillian M. Gilbreth. *The Amazing Oversight: Total Participation for Productivity,* 1979, pp. 21–29.

Managerial Agendas—Reactive or Proactive? Rosemary Stewart. OD, Autumn 1979, pp. 34–47. Oxford Univ.

The Managerial Functions. Harold Smiddy. *The Evolving Science of Management,* 1979, pp. 63–67.

Managers in the Future: How Will They Be Judged? Peter Spooner, Michael Johnson. MRev., Dec. 1980, pp. 8–17.

Miles's Six Other Maxims of Management. Rufus E. Miles, Jr. OD, Summer 1979, pp. 27–40. Princeton Univ.

Modern Management—Links with Modern Internal Auditing. Lawrence B. Sawyer. *The Manager and the Modern Internal Auditor: A Problem-Solving Partnership,* 1979, pp. 35–60.

Muddling Through. Robert A. Golde. 1981. (AMACOM audio cassette book) By purchase only.

The Need for a Unified Discipline of Management. Philip W. Shay. 1977, 30 pp. Assn. of Consulting Management Engineers. MB.

New Directions for Management. Lawrence A. Appley. SM, Feb. 1981, pp. 9–12.

Notes on the Nature of Organizations. Harold Smiddy. *The Evolving Science of Management,* 1979, pp. 48–62.

Open Management: Guides to Successful Practice. Paul W. Cummings. 1980, 225 pp.

Optimal Task Accomplishment. John D. Proe. HSM, Aug. 1979, pp. 6–7. Mark Silber Associates.

Organizational Paradigms: A Commentary on Japanese Management and Theory Z Organizations. William G. Ouchi. OD, Spring 1981, pp. 36–43. UCLA.

Overcoming Murphy's Law. William C. Waddell. 1981, 296 pp. California State Univ., Los Angeles.

Peter Drucker on Management: Concentrate on 1. Liquidity 2. Productivity 3. Growth Strategy. Peter Drucker. MRev., Dec. 1979, pp. 40–41.

The Practical Manager's Guide to Excellence in Management. Ronald Brown. 1979, 120 pp. Tremco Co. and Tremco Ltd.

A Professional Method of Management. Lawrence A. Appley, Keith L. Irons. *Manager Manpower Planning: A Professional Management System,* 1981, pp. 1–8.

Professional Organizations Need Professional Management. Edward J. Giblin. OD, Winter 1978, pp. 41–57.

Reality Is. James L. Hayes. MRev., Sept. 1977, pp. 2–3.

Redefining the Manager's Job: The Proactive Manager in a Reactive World. Merritt L. Kastens. 1980, 283 pp.

Shirt-Sleeves Management. James F. Evered. 1981, 180 pp. Redman Industries, Inc. (Also AMACOM audio cassette book. By purchase only)

Small Business: Developing the Winning Management Team. George W. Rimler, Neil J. Humphreys. 1980, 180 pp. Virginia Commonwealth Univ.

Start-Up: The Care and Feeding of Infant Systems. Roger Harrison. OD, Summer 1981, 5–29. Harrison Kouzes Associates.

Successful Management the Experts' Way. 1979. (AMACOM audio cassette) By purchase only.

Symbols, Patterns, and Settings: An Optimistic Case for Getting Things Done. Thomas J. Peters. OD, Autumn 1978. McKinsey & Co.

Tough-Minded Management (third ed.). Joe D. Batten, 1978, 224 pp. Batten, Batten, Hudson and Swab, Inc.

Toward a Useful Operational Theory of Management. Harold Koontz. *The Evolving Science of Management,* 1979, pp. 327–347. Univ. of California, Los Angeles.

Understanding Management Policy & Making It Work. Victor Z. Brink. 1978, 312 pp. Columbia Univ.

Urwick, Orr on Management. Fred W. Latham, George S. Sanders. 1980, 255 pp. Urwick, Orr & Partners.

What Happens in Management. Maurice R. Hecht. 1980, 212 pp. Helmsman Management Associates.

What Managers Do (sec. ed.). Donald R. Burke. 1978. (Extension Institute Course) By purchase only.

What's Ahead in Managing? Harold Smiddy. *The Evolving Science of Management,* 1979, pp. 247–266.

MANAGEMENT BY OBJECTIVES

Applying Management by Objectives to Nonprofit Organizations. Dale D. McConkey. *Managing Nonprofit Organizations,* 1977, pp. 141–154. Univ. of Wisconsin.

Bringing MBO Back to Basics. Henry H. Beam. SM, July 1979, pp. 25–30. Western Michigan Univ.

Bringing the Upper Echelons Into MBO. Dale D. McConkey. HSM, July 1980, pp. 13–14. Univ. of Wisconsin.

Business Objectives: A Powerful Decision-Making Tool. Alfred R. Oxenfeldt. *Cost-Benefit Analysis for Executive Decision Making,* 1979, 176–219. Columbia Univ.

Computing Who Deserves the Gold Stars. William F. Christopher. *Corporate Planning Techniques and Applications,* 1979, pp. 306–311. Hooker Chemicals & Plastics Corp.

The Focused Web—Goal Setting in the MBO Process. Gary J. Salton. MRev., Jan. 1978, pp. 46–50. Chrysler Corp.

The Future: Its Challenge and Its Promise. Dale D. McConkey. *Managing Nonprofit Organizations,* 1977, pp. 199–206. Univ. of Wisconsin.

Goal Setting. Charles L. Hughes. 1981. (AMACOM audio cassette book) By purchase only.

Goal Setting—A Motivational Technique That Works. Gary P. Latham, Edwin A. Locke. OD, Autumn 1979, pp. 68–80. Univ. of Washington, Univ. of Maryland.

Goal Setting By the OK MBO Boss. Heinz Weihrich. AMJ, Fall 1977, pp. 4–13.

Goal Setting: The Tenneco Approach to Personnel Development and Management Effectiveness. John M. Ivancevich, J. Timothy McMahon, J. William Streidl, Andrew D. Szilagyi, Jr. OD, Winter 1978, pp. 58–80.

Goalstorming. Roscoe H. Adams. AMJ, Summer 1979, pp. 55–61. IBM.

Job Objectives. Joseph J. Famularo. *Organization Planning Manual* (rev. ed.), 1979, pp. 9–15. McGraw-Hill, Inc.

Making MBO Work: Matching Management Style to MBO Program. William R. Fannin. SM, Sept. 1981, pp. 20–27. Univ. of Maine.

Management by Objectives for Schools. Thorne Hacker. *Managing Nonprofit Organizations,* 1977, pp. 155–163. Univ. of Chicago.

Managing for Results in the Federal Government. Frederic V. Malek. *Managing Nonprofit Organizations,* 1977, pp. 48–56. Marriott Corp.

Managing Vs. Management By Results. John P. Singleton. SM, May 1979, pp. 31–37. Maryland National Bank.

MBGO: Putting Some Team Spirit into MBO. Rensis Likert, M. Scott Fisher. Pers., Jan.–Feb. 1977, pp. 40–47.

An MBO Checklist: Are Conditions Right for Implementation? Richard Babcock, Peter F. Sorensen. MRev., June 1979, pp. 59–62. San Francisco Univ, George Williams College.

MBO for the Public Agency. Stuart J. Savage, 1978, (Extension Institute Course) By purchase only.

MBO in Church Organizations. Dale D. McConkey. *Managing Nonprofit Organizations,* 1977, pp. 164–175. Univ. of Wisconsin.

MBO in the Hospital Business Office. Linda Neese. HSM, June 1978, pp. 3–5, 10. Kearny County Hospital.

MBO in the 1980's: Will It Survive? George S. Odiorne. MRev., July 1977, pp. 39–42. Univ. of Massachusetts.

An MBO Program for All Levels: One Company's Success Story. G. Robert Lea. AMJ, Spring 1977, pp. 24–32. The Paul Revere Life Insurance Co.

MBO: Seven Strategies for Success. Robert C. Ford, Robert R. Bell. AMJ, Winter 1977, pp. 14–24. Univ. of Northern Florida, Tennessee Technology Univ.

MBO—Today and Tomorrow. Raymond J. Pack, William Vicars. Pers., May–June 1979, pp. 68–77. Southern Illinois Univ.

Measuring Performance. James E. Gardner. *Training the New Supervisor,* 1980, pp. 128–148. Fieldcrest Mills, Inc.

Putting It Together with MBO. William C. Waddell. *Overcoming Murphy's Law,* 1981, pp. 258–288. California State Univ., Los Angeles.

Responsibility, Authority, and Accountability. James F. Evered. *Shirt-Sleeves Management,* 1981, pp. 64–77. Redman Industries, Inc.

A Study of Management by Objectives in a Professional Organization. Y. K. Shetty,

Howard M. Carlisle. *Managing Nonprofit Organizations,* 1977, pp. 187–198. Utah State Univ.

The Supervisor's Survival Guide: Making Quantified Evaluation Systems. Robert E. Pitts, Ken Thompson. SM, Feb. 1979, pp. 24–32. Univ. of Notre Dame. (Also in reprint collection *The Supervisor's Survival Guide,* 1979)

Tailoring MBO to Hospitals. Herbert H. Hand, A. Thomas Hollingsworth. *Managing Nonprofit Organizations,* 1977, pp. 176–186. Univ. of South Carolina.

There's a S.M.A.R.T. Way to Write Management's Goals and Objectives. George T. Doran. MRev., Nov. 1981, pp. 35–36. Management Assistance Programs.

Tough-Minded MBO—A Living System of Human Dynamics. Joe D. Batten. *Tough Minded Management* (third ed.), 1978, pp. 196–208. Batten, Batten, Hudson and Swab, Inc.

What Is MBO? ES, July 1980, 16 pp.

Why MBO Programs Don't Meet Their Goals. Jack Bologna. MRev., Dec. 1980. pp 32. George Odiorne Associates.

Will Your MBO Program Fly or Fizzle? Neil J. Horgan. SM, Dec. 1981, pp. 21–24.

MANAGEMENT CONTROLS. See also Budgeting, Cost Control, Financial Management, Inventory Control, Organizational Effectiveness, Production Planning and Control, Reports

Acknowledging the Past, Looking to the Future. James L. Hayes. MRev., Oct. 1979, pp. 2–3.

A Company Needs Vision as Well as Controls. Kenneth T. Wessner. MRev., Aug. 1981, pp. 34–36. ServiceMaster Industries, Inc.

Control: Key to Making Financial Strategy Work. Robert L. Dewelt. MRev., March 1977, pp. 18–25. Allis Chalmers Corp.

Control Systems. William R. Osgood. *Basics of Successful Business Management,* 1981, pp. 76–98.

Control: The Key to Successful Business Planning. George R. Seiler, 1981, 78 pp. Profit Planning Associates. MB.

Controlling. Victor Z. Brink. *Understanding Management Policy & Making It Work,* 1978, pp. 213–233. Columbia Univ.

Controlling. Lawrence B. Sawyer. *The Manager and the Modern Internal Auditor: A Problem-Solving Partnership,* 1979, pp. 381–427.

Controlling. William R. Tracey. *Human Resource Development Standards,* 1981 pp. 133–151. U.S. Army Intelligence Training School.

How to Improve Your Organization's Management Controls. Donald W. Murr, Harry B. Bracey, Jr., William K. Hill. MRev., Oct. 1980, pp. 56–63. Arthur Young & Co.

Internal Control: Testing Out Your System. Cyril F. Moore. HSM, May 1978, pp. 1–3. Seidman & Seidman.

Key Performance Areas That Determine Success. William F. Christopher. *Management for the 1980's* (rev. ed.—former title: *The Achieving Enterprise*), 1980, pp. 204–245.

Management Guidelines: Being in Control. George Miller. SM, June 1981, pp. 25–30. George Miller Associates.

"Measuring" as an Element of a Manager's Work of Leading. Harold Smiddy. *The Evolving Science of Management,* 1979, pp. 170–185.

Measuring Performance in Human Service Systems. James F. Budde. 1979, 207 pp. Univ. of Kansas.

Measuring the EDP Function. Michael R. Frank. *The Effective EDP Manager,* 1980, pp. 161–171. The Taubman Co., Inc.

Research: Management Control Systems: A Key Link Between Strategy, Structure, and Employee Performance. John Todd. OD, Spring 1977, pp. 65–78.

The Review Board. Lawrence A. Appley, Keith L. Irons. *Manager Manpower Planning: A Professional Management System,* 1981, pp. 61–74.

The Theory and Practice of Management Control (sec. ed.). Graham R. Briggs. 1980. (Extension Institute Course) Revised by Raymond B. Jordan. By purchase only.

MANAGEMENT DEVELOPMENT. See also Manpower Planning, Training and Development

Building a Field Manager: Training. Donald N. McCafferty. *Successful Field Service Management,* 1980, pp. 89–111. Honeywell, Inc.

Building Knowledge. William C. Waddell. *Overcoming Murphy's Law,* 1981, pp. 80–99. California State Univ., Los Angeles.

Design for Executive Growth and Development. James G. Stockard. *Career Development and Job Training,* 1977, pp. 259–279.

Developing Overseas Managers—and Managers Overseas. Paul E. Illman. 1980, 298 pp. Management Training, Inc.

Developing Women Managers: What Needs to be Done? Martha G. Burrow. 1978, 32 pp. CoMedia, Inc. MB.

Evaluating Management Development and Training Programs. William H. Wagel. Pers., July–Aug. 1977, pp. 4–10.

Evaluation of Management Development Programs ... An Innovative Approach. Ralph J. Brown, James D. Somerville. Pers., July–Aug. 1977, pp. 28–39.

Executive Development Programs: What Should They Teach? Robert E. Boynton. Pers., March–April 1981, pp. 60–70. Naval Postgraduate School.

General Electric's Philosophy on Manager Development. Harold Smiddy. *The Evolving Science of Management,* 1979, pp. 186–211.

How to Survive a Management Training Program. Jack J. Phillips. AMJ, Spring 1978, pp. 48–57. Stockham Valves & Fittings.

Human-Relations Training: Key to Successful Supervision. Robert L. Finkelmeier, Rose L. Kennedy. HSM, Sept. 1977, pp. 1–4. Univ. of Colorado Medical Center, American Society for Health Manpower Education & Training.

Improvement Programs. Lawrence A. Appley, Keith L. Irons. *Manager Manpower Planning: A Professional Management System,* 1981, pp. 41–46.

Management Development at Lenox Hill Hospital. Joan Holland. HSM, Aug. 1979, pp. 7–8. Lenox Hill Hospital.

Management Development: Needs and Practices. Lester A. Digman. Pers., July–Aug. 1980, pp. 45–57. Univ. of Nebraska.

Management Training? Don't Waste Your Money! James R. Cook. SM, Feb. 1978, pp. 30–37.

Management Training for Nurses: Will We Ever Have It? John P. Sullivan, Joan A. Sullivan. HSM, Nov. 1980, pp. 11–12, 14. Management Campus, Inc.

The Manager's Guide to Developing Subordinate Managers. Henry D. Meyer, Bruce L. Margolis, William M. Fifield. 1980, 60 pp. Jewel Companies, Inc. MB.

Managers in the Future: How Will They Be Judged? Peter Spooner, Michael Johnson. MRev., Dec., 1980, pp. 8–17.

More than Management Development: Action Learning at GEC. David Casey, David Pearce (editors). 1977, 146 pp. Action Learning Projects International, GEC.

Operation Enterprise: Business Leadership by Example. James L. Hayes. MRev., Sept. 1979, pp. 2–3.

Organization and Management Development Programs. William R. Tracey. *Human Resource Development Standards,* 1981 pp. 350–374. U.S. Army Intelligence Training School.

Preparing Future Leaders. James L. Hayes. MRev., May 1981, pp. 2–3.

Programme Outline. David Casey. *More than Management Development: Action Learning at GEC,* 1977, pp. 7–13. Action Learning Projects International.

Redesigning and Reassigning Your Way to a Better Job. Robert N. Ford. SM, Aug. 1979, pp. 2–9. A T & T.

Targets, Time, and Transfer: Key to Management Training Impact. Francis X. Mahoney. Pers., Nov.–Dec. 1980, pp. 25–34. Exxon Co.

A Training Program to Increase Self-Awareness. Murray Rimmer, Richard M. Cohen. HSM, Jan. 1977, pp. 1–4. Long Island Jewish-Hillside Medical Center.

What Makes Sense in Management Training? William G. Dyer. MRev., June 1978, pp. 50–56. Brigham Young Univ.

MANAGEMENT DEVELOPMENT—PROFESSIONAL PERSONNEL

How to Train Your Technical Staff. William A. Cohen. *Principles of Technical Management,* 1980, pp. 64–82. California State Univ.

Knowledge Worker Productivity. Ira B. Gregerman, 1981, 55 pp. Productivity Associates. MB.

Providing Career Prospects for Engineers and Technicians. MRev., Feb. 1981, pp. 29–31.

MANAGEMENT DEVELOPMENT—TECHNIQUES. See also Coaching and Counseling, Performance Appraisal

Action Learning. Reg Revans. *More than Management Development: Action Learning at GEC,* 1977, pp. 3–6. Univ. of Leeds.

Action Learning and the Company. Tony Eccles. *More than Management Development: Action Learning at GEC,* 1977, pp. 119–123. Glasgow Univ.

Action Learning: On-the-Job Training for the Top Manager of the Future. V. K. Unni. AMJ, Winter 1980, pp. 28–34.

ALP is Learning Too. Jean Lawrence. *More than Management Development: Action Learning at GEC,* 1977, pp. 91–104. Manchester Business School.

Behavior Analysis: A Productive Approach to Management Skills Development. Anthony W. Martin, Dennis A. Hawver. MRev., Aug. 1979, pp. 22–25. The RHR Institute.

Career Planning and Management in Organizations. Donald B. Miller. AMJ, Spring 1978, pp. 33–43. IBM.

Career Planning Practices. James W. Walker, Thomas G. Gutteridge. 1979, 40 pp. Arizona State Univ., State Univ. of New York. SR.

The Challenge Was Worth It. Ray Godsall. *More than Management Development: Action Learning at GEC,* 1977, pp. 73–78. Dunchurch Industrial Staff College.

Communication Is the Key to Getting Commitment. Barry Scott. *More than Management Development: Action Learning at GEC,* 1977, pp. 62–72. GEC Marconi Ltd.

Don't Call Me Teacher. Bob Garratt. *More than Management Development: Action Learning at GEC,* 1977, pp. 79–90. Architects' Journal.

Employee Assessment Methods Assessed. Barry A. Friedman, Robert W. Mann. Pers., Nov.–Dec. 1981, pp. 69–74. Xerox Corp.

Fast-Track Programs for MBAs: Do They Really Work? William D. Wooldrege. MRev., April 1979, pp. 8–13. B. F. Goodrich Co.

Gould's Corporate College: Where Hitting the Books Is Company Policy. William T. Ylvisaker. MRev., Sept. 1977, pp. 8–12.

How Assertive Are You? A Look Through the Johari Window. Rita E. Numerof. HSM, Feb. 1979, pp. 7–9. LaSalle College.

How Well-Managed Organizations Develop Their Executives. Lester A. Digman. OD, Autumn 1978, pp. 63–80. Univ. of Nebraska.

Identifying Managerial Potential: An Alternative to Assessment Centers. Donald H. Brush, Lyle F. Schoenfeldt. Pers., May–June 1980, pp. 68–76. Rensselaer Polytechnic Institute.

It Didn't Work for Me. David Carr. *More than Management Development: Action Learning at GEC,* 1977, pp. 48–57. English Electric Valve Co., Ltd.

It's Opening Our Minds. Mike Bett. *More than Management Development: Action Learning at GEC,* 1977, pp. 116–118. GEC.

Laboratory Training of Managers—Positive Results? Husain Mustafa, Robert Guhde. Pers., Nov.–Dec. 1978, pp. 66–73. Virginia Commonwealth Univ., State Univ. of New York.

Leading a Seminar: How Smart Companies Put More Life into Management Careers. Robert F. Reilly. MRev., May 1980, p. 33. Huffy Corp.

Learning How to Learn. Peter Preston. *More than Management Development: Action Learning at GEC,* 1977, pp. 40–44. Post Office Corp.

Management Education in the 80's. International Association of Students of Economics and Management (editor). 1979, 127 pp.

The Manager's Guide to Developing Subordinate Managers. Henry D. Meyer, Bruce L. Margolis, William M. Fifield. 1980, 60 pp. Jewel Companies, Inc. MB.

Managers on the Road. James L. Hayes. MRev., Aug. 1980, pp. 2–3.

The Model Manager: Management Development Through Behavior Modeling. Malcolm E. Shaw. SM, Jan. 1979, pp. 14–21. Educational Systems and Designs, Inc.

Now . . . To Run a Company. Colin Gaskell. *More than Management Development: Action Learning at GEC,* 1977, pp. 58–61. GEC Marconi Instruments.

The Offer Document (Appendix I). David Casey, David Pearce (editors). *More than Management Development: Action Learning at GEC,* 1977, pp. 131–134. Action Learning Projects International, GEC.

Postcript: GEC's Second and Third Programmes. David Casey, David Pearce (editors). *More than Management Development: Action Learning at GEC,* 1977, pp. 124–130. Action Learning Projects International, GEC.

Prescription Drugs and Placebos: A New Perspective on Management Training. James F. Guyot. Pers., May–June 1977, pp. 67–72.

Programme Development. David Pearce. *More than Management Development: Action Learning at GEC,* 1977, pp. 14–30. GEC.

The Project is Everything. Bill Prince. *More than Management Development: Action Learning at GEC,* 1977, pp. 31–39. GEC.

Protecting the Company from Bureaucratic Slowdown. Mark D. Lutchen. MRev., April 1980, pp. 41–45. Price Waterhouse & Co.

Start with Results: A Bottom-Line Strategy for Management Development. Claude G. Guay, James A. Waters. MRev., Feb. 1980, pp. 25–28, 41–42.

Supervisors Promoted From Within Require In-House Managerial Training. Gary L. Woods. HSM, Feb. 1979, pp. 4–6. Memorial Medical Center.

This Is the Way to Unlock Resources. Don Howell. *More than Management Development: Action Learning at GEC,* 1977, pp. 45–47. GEC Power Engineering Ltd.

Training the Supervisor as Systems Analyst Is Easy. Edwin S. Ross. HSM, Nov. 1980, pp. 4–5. Univ. of Texas.

Tuition-Aid Programs Aid Affirmative Action. David D. Steinbrecher. Pers., Nov.–Dec. 1979, pp. 56–57.

Upward Mobility: The GF Way of Opening Employee Advancement Opportunities. Betty Ann Duval, Roslyn S. Courtney. Pers., May–June 1978, pp. 43–53. General Foods Corp.

We'd Do It Again. Clem Jansen, Don Sinclair. *More than Management Development: Action Learning at GEC,* 1977, pp. 105–108. GEC Electrical Projects Ltd, GEC Industrial Controls Ltd.

Why Be a Mentor? T. J. Halatin. SM, Feb. 1981, pp. 36–39. Southwest Texas State Univ.

You Don't Need to Be an Expert. Glyn Trollop. *More than Management Development: Action Learning at GEC,* 1977, pp. 109–115. GEC.

MANAGEMENT DEVELOPMENT—TECHNIQUES—ASSESSMENT CENTER

Assessment Centers: For Selection or Development? Gary L. Hart, Paul H. Thompson. OD, Spring 1979, pp. 63–77. Louisiana Land & Exploration Co., Brigham Young Univ.

Using Assessment Centers for Individual and Organization Development. Louis Olivas. Pers., May–June 1980, pp. 63–67. Arizona State Univ.

MANAGEMENT INFORMATION—SOURCES

Alphabetical List of Data Bases Available on Dialog and Orbit Services (Appendix I). Donatas Tijunelis, Nancy Miles Clausen. *R & D on a Minimum Budget,* 1979, pp. 30–33. Borg-Warner Corp. MB.

Index to AMA Resources of the Seventies, 1970–76. Elizabeth Keegan. 1977, 162 pp.

Appendix. William A. Cohen, Marshall E. Reddick. *Successful Marketing for Small Business,* 1981, pp. 263–272. California State Univ.

Appendix: FEA Regional Offices and State Energy Offices. *Managing Industrial Energy Conservation,* 1977, pp. 47–56. MB.

Appendixes. Herman Holtz. *The $100 Billion Market: How to Do Business with the U.S. Government,* 1980, pp. 209–255.

Appendixes. Arno B. Zimmer. *Employing the Handicapped: A Practical Compliance Manual,* 1981, pp. 303–365. Eliot-Yeats, Inc.

A Business Information Guidebook. Oscar Figueroa, Charles Winkler. 1980, 190 pp. Rutgers Univ., Port Authority N.Y. & N.J.

Handbook of Business Finance and Capital Sources. Dileep Rao. 1979, 480 pp.

How and Where to Find Information: From Your Home—From the Field. Quentin W. Fleming. *A Guide to Doing Business on the Arabian Peninsula,* 1981, pp. 20–29.

Information: The Ultimate Management Resource: How to Find, Use, and Manage It. Morton F. Meltzer. 1981, 211 pp. Martin Marietta Corp.

Periodicals of Special Interest to HRD Specialists (Appendix B). William R. Tracey. *Human Resource Development Standards,* 1981, pp. 567–569. U.S. Army Intelligence Training School.

The Reference File. Herman R. Holtz. *Profit from Your Money-Making Ideas: How to Build a New Business or Expand an Existing One,* 1980, pp. 333–360.

Some College Programs Specifically Designed for Adults (Appendix A). Paula I. Robbins. *Successful Midlife Career Change,* 1978, pp. 213–218. Fitchburg State College.

Source List. Darryl J. Ellis, Peter P. Pekar, Jr. *Planning for Nonplanners: Planning Basics for Managers,* 1980, pp. 84–90. Resource Technology Development Corp., Michael Allen Co.

Sources of Economic and Financial Information from the Conference Board (Appendix C). Robert E. Pritchard, Thomas J. Hindelang. *The Strategic Evaluation and Management of Capital Expenditures,* 1981, pp. 285–304. Glassboro State College, Drexel Univ.

Sources of Economic and Financial Information from the Conference Board (Appendix E). Robert E. Pritchard, Thomas Hindelang. *The Lease/Buy Decision,* 1980, pp. 239–258. Glassboro State Univ., Drexel Univ.

Sources of U.S. Government-Sponsored Training (Appendix A). William R. Tracey. *Human Resource Development Standards,* 1981, p. 566. U.S. Army Intelligence Training School.

MANAGEMENT INFORMATION—SYSTEMS. See also Data Processing, Reports

Decision Support Systems: Personal Computing Services for Managers. Eric D. Carlson. MRev., Jan. 1977, pp. 4–11. IBM.

Evaluating the Information System. Robert J. Thierauf. *Management Auditing: A Questionnaire Approach,* 1980, pp. 213–235. Xavier Univ.

Information Management in the Office of the Future. George Grove. MRev., Dec. 1979, pp. 47–50. General Services Administration.

Information Resources Management. Robert M. Landau. 1980, 37 pp. The Information Group. MB.

Management Information Services: Systems and Computers. Fred W. Latham, George S. Sanders, *Urwick, Orr on Management,* 1980, pp. 187–196. Urwick, Orr & Partners.

Management Information Systems. James L. Mercer, Edwin H. Koester. *Public Management Systems: An Administrator's Guide,* 1978, pp. 85–103. Batelle Southern Operations, C. R. Drew Postgraduate Medical School.

Management Information Systems (third ed.). Henry L. Parsons. 1979. (Extension Institute Course). By purchase only.

Management Information Systems: What Are They? How Are They Set Up? ES, Oct. 1981, 16 pp.

Management Information Versus Misinformation Systems. Ian I. Mitroff, Ralph H. Kilmann, Vincent P. Barabba. *Management Principles for Nonprofit Agencies and Organizations,* 1979, pp. 401–429. Univ. of Pittsburgh, Xerox Corp.

Measuring the Effectiveness of the National Account Effort. Charles R. Beall. *National Account Marketing Handbook,* 1981, pp. 158–186. International Paper Co.

Methods and Task Analysis. Ernest J. McCormick. *Job Analysis: Methods and Applications,* 1979, pp. 71–105. PAQ Services Inc.

Model for Participation. Howard L. Sampson. *Managing Nonprofit Organizations*, 1977, pp. 109–117. Madison, Wisconsin Public Schools.

The Post-Implementation Review. Paul S. Benoit. MRev., July 1980, pp. 55–56. U.S. General Accounting Office.

Tailor Specific Data to Specific Needs—New Thrust of Information Management. Herbert R. Brinberg. MRev., Dec. 1981, pp. 8–11. Aspen Systems Corp.

MANAGEMENT SCIENCE AND STATISTICS. See also Return on Investment

Applying Managerial Economics. William F. Christopher. *Management for the 1980's* (rev. ed.—former title: *The Achieving Enterprise*), 1980, pp. 164–203.

The Evolution of a "Science of Managing" in America. Harold Smiddy, Lionel Naum. *The Evolving Science of Management*, 1979, pp. 273–312. General Electric Co., Syracuse Research Corp.

Implementation of Quantitative Techniques: A Managerial Perspective. Michael Freeman, Gary Mulkowsky. MRev., July 1979, pp. 51–54. City Univ. of New York.

Linear Programming—A Case Example. Wayne Drayer, Steve Seabury. *Corporate Planning Techniques and Applications*, 1979, pp. 291–296. Babcock and Wilcox; GTE Data Services.

Management Decision Making. Jerome D. Braverman. 1980, 241 pp. Rider College.

Managerial Economics. Bradley A. Latham. 1977. (Extension Institute Course) By purchase only.

The Ongoing Process of Strategic Management. Robert E. Pritchard, Thomas J. Hindelang. *The Strategic Evaluation and Management of Capital Expenditures*, 1981, pp. 232–252. Glassboro State College, Drexel Univ.

A Perspective on Operations Research and Synthesis. Harold Smiddy. *The Evolving Science of Management*, 1979, pp. 212–228. General Electric Co.

Quantitative Aids to Decision Making (third ed.). Grant E. Mayberry, Donald O. Robb. 1979. (Extension Institute Course) By purchase only.

Risk Analysis: The Forgotten Tool. Irwin Kabus. MRev., June 1981, pp. 42–50. EXE-CUCOM.

Risk and Capital Budgeting. Robert E. Pritchard, Thomas J. Hindelang. *The Strategic Evaluation and Management of Capital Expenditures*, 1981, pp. 136–157. Glassboro State College, Drexel Univ.

A Scientific Approach to the Executive Suite. James L. Hayes. MRev., Nov. 1981, pp. 2–3.

Scientific Methods. Lawrence B. Sawyer. *The Manager and the Modern Internal Auditor: A Problem-Solving Partnership*, 1979, pp. 209–240.

The Search for a "Science of Managing" Harold Smiddy. *The Evolving Science of Management*, 1979, pp. 9–25. General Electric Co.

Skills in Management Science. Lois Borland Hart. *Moving Up: Women and Leadership*, 1980, pp. 125–142. Mountain States Employers Council, Inc.

Using Mathematics as a Business Tool. George J. Chorba, Charissa J. Chou. 1979. (Extension Institute Course) By purchase only.

When to Use Multivariate Analytical Techniques. Jeffrey Pope. *Practical Marketing Research*, 1981, pp. 233–241. Custom Research, Inc.

MANPOWER PLANNING. See also Management Development

Containing Hospital Manpower-Turnover Costs. Howard L. Smith, Larry E. Watkins. HSM, Oct. 1978, pp. 1–3. San Diego State Univ., Northern Arizona Univ.

Deadwood—An Untapped Potential. Herbert T. Mines. MRev., Dec. 1980, pp. 33–34. Business Careers, Inc.

Developing and Using an in-House Interest Inventory. Cary B. Barad. Pers., Nov.–Dec. 1977, pp. 57–61. Office of Human Resources, Baltimore.

Developing Human Assets: How Good Are You? V. Clayton Sherman. HSM, Sept. 1979, pp. 3–6. Mark Silber Associates.

Executive Continuity Planning: An Idea Whose Time Has Come. William L. Bucknall. MRev., Feb. 1981, pp. 21–23. Otis Elevator Co.

How Mount Sinai Saved $7.5 Million in Manpower Costs. Samuel Davis, Barry Freedman. HSM, Nov. 1980, pp. 1–3, 12–13. Mount Sinai Hospital.

Human Resource Accounting: A Managerial Tool? Jacob B. Paperman, Desmond D. Martin. Pers., March–Apr. 1977, pp. 41–50. Miami Univ., Univ. of Cincinnati.

Human Resource Planning: A Four-Phased Approach. Craig B. Mackey. MRev., May 1981, pp. 17–22. Comshare, Inc.

Human Resource Planning: A Tool for People Development. Douglas Reid. Pers., March–April 1977, pp. 15–25. Xerox Corp.

Identifying the Good, the Bad, and the Indifferent. Robert E. Kushell. SM, April 1979, pp. 2–7. Dunhill Personnel System, Inc.

Looking Beyond Short-Term Manpower Needs. David K. Lindo. AMJ, Winter 1977, pp. 36–46.

Management Potential—The Gap in Your Plan. Dennis Hawver. *Corporate Planning Techniques and Applications,* 1979, pp. 317–323. RHR Institute.

Manager Manpower Planning: A Professional Management System. Lawrence A. Appley, Keith L. Irons. 1981, 112 pp.

Manpower Planning and Corporate Objectives: Two Points of View. How to Integrate People Needs with Development Strategies. Robert McAvoy. MRev., Aug. 1981, pp. 55–59. Applied Human Technologies.

Manpower Planning and Corporate Objectives: Two Points of View. Planning the Staffing of a Growing Business. Donald M. Hubsch. MRev., Aug. 1981. pp. 59–61. ITT.

Measuring the Human ROI: How the Upjohn Company Measures and Forecasts the Return on Its Investment in People. Henry L. Dahl, Jr. MRev., Jan. 1979, pp. 44–50. The Upjohn Co.

The New, More Substantive Approach to Manpower Planning. James W. Walker. MRev., July 1977. pp. 29–30. Towers, Perrin, Forster & Crosby.

Other Annual Reviews. Lawrence A. Appley, Keith L. Irons. *Manager Manpower Planning,* 1981, pp. 101–106.

Planning the Picking Order for the Company Totem Pole. Fred E. Lee. *Corporate Planning Techniques and Applications,* 1979, pp. 312–316. Southern Methodist Univ.

Stage Three in Personnel Administration: Strategic Human Resources Management. Stella M. Nkomo. Pers., July–Aug. 1980, pp. 69–77. Univ. of Massachusetts.

There's No Nurse Shortage at Saint Joseph Medical Center. Rhoda E. Weiss. James E. Sauer, Jr., Georgia Sobiech. HSM, Dec. 1981, pp. 3–6. Saint Joseph Medical Center.

Toward a Better System of Human Resource Planning. Felix M. Lopez. AMJ, Spring 1981, pp. 4–14. Felix M. Lopex & Associates, Inc.

The Uncertainty Factor in Human Resources Accounting. Anthony F. Jurkus. Pers., Nov.–Dec. 1979, pp. 72–75. Los Angeles Technology Univ.

MANUALS

Policy Statements (125) Part III. Joseph J. Famularo. *Organization Planning Manual* (rev. ed.), 1979, pp. 315–354. McGraw-Hill, Inc.

Preparing Administrative Manuals. Susan Z. Diamond. 1981, 133 pp. Diamond Associates.

MANUFACTURING. See Production Management

MARKETING MANAGEMENT. See also Advertising and Sales Promotion, International Operations—Marketing, Planning, Pricing, Product Development, Research & Development, Reports

Basics of Marketing Management. Houston Elam, Norton Paley. 1980. (AMACOM audio cassette) By purchase only.

Creative Marketing: King Cotton Fights to Regain His Throne. J. Dukes Wooters. MRev., Feb. 1978, pp. 45–49. Cotton Inc.

Customer or Competitor: Which Guideline for Marketing? Alfred R. Oxenfeldt, William L. Moore. MRev., Aug. 1978, pp. 43–48. Columbia Univ.

Dealing With the Effects of Market Discontinuities. Gordon Canning, Jr. MRev., Jan. 1981, pp. 29, 34–35. Towers, Perrin, Forster & Crosby.

Developing a Successful Distribution Strategy. William A Cohen, Marshall E. Reddick. *Successful Marketing for Small Business,* 1981, pp. 119–143. California State Univ.

Dramatic Retailing Changes In Store for Marketing Managers. Deborah M. Adamian. MRev., May 1981, pp. 35–36. Arthur D. Little Inc.

Elements of R&D Technical Marketing. Philip H. Francis. *Principles of R&D Management,* 1977, pp. 133–174. Southwest Research Institute.

Epilogue—Million-Dollar Marketing for a Small Business. William A. Cohen, Marshall E. Reddick. *Successful Marketing for Small Business,* 1981, pp. 261–262. California State Univ.

Evaluating the Marketing Function. Robert J. Thierauf. *Management Auditing: A Questionnaire Approach,* 1980, pp. 85–114. Xavier Univ.

Fundamentals of Direct Mail Marketing. Edward J. McGee, Norman A. P. Govoni, Robert J. Eng. 1980. (Extension Institute Course) By purchase only.

Fundamentals of Modern Marketing (rev. ed.). Judith Pedersen. 1978. (Extension Institute Course) By purchase only.

How to Audit Marketing and Sales. J. McConnell. 1978. (An AMACOM Evaluation Tool) By purchase only.

How to Market by Telephone. Garry Mitchell. 1981. (Extension Institute Cassette Program) By purchase only.

How to Match Marketing Strategies with Overall Corporate Planning. David W. Cravens. MRev., Dec. 1981, pp. 12–19. Texas Christian Univ.

How to Strengthen Marketing When the Going Gets Tough. John C. Faulkner. MRev., Sept. 1980, pp. 8–14. Case & Co., Inc.

How to Win the Market-Share Game? Try Changing the Rules. Roberto Buaron. MRev., Jan. 1981, pp. 8–17. McKinsey & Co.

An Introduction to Direct Marketing. Chaman L. Jain, Al Migliaro. 1978, 67 pp. St. Johns Univ., Glenwood Associates. MB.

Introduction—We Want You to Be Successful. William A. Cohen, Marshall E. Reddick. *Successful Marketing for Small Business,* 1981, pp. 1–4. California State Univ.

King Cotton Fights to Regain His Throne. J. Dukes Wooters. *Marketing in Nonprofit Organizations,* 1978, pp. 199–208. Cotton Inc.

Life-Styled Marketing: How to Position Products for Premium Profits (rev. ed.). Mack Hanan. 1980, 159 pp. Wellspring Group.

Marketing. Fred W. Latham, George S. Sanders. *Urwick, Orr on Management,* pp. 67–92. Urwick, Orr & Partners.

Marketing-Based Strategies. William E. Rothschild. *Strategic Alternatives: Selection Development and Implementation,* 1979, pp. 75–103. General Electric.

The Marketing Concept and How It Leads to Success. William A. Cohen, Marshall E. Reddick. *Successful Marketing for Small Business,* 1981, pp. 5–10. California State Univ.

Marketing for the Non-Marketing Executive. Houston G. Elam, Norton Paley. 1978, 261 pp. Montclair State College, John Wiley & Sons.

Motivating the Distributor to Market Your Product. Dennis A. Zalar. 1980, 34 pp. McGraw Edison, Inc. MB.

Omnimarketing: How the Growing Influence of 'Market Masters' Is Changing Consumer Marketing Strategy. JoAnn Friedman, Larry J. Rosenberg. MRev., Sept. 1980, pp. 15–21. Health Marketing Systems, Inc., New York Univ.

Politics and Ad Men: A Sticky Mess. Marketing Communications. *Marketing in Nonprofit Organizations,* 1978, pp. 214–223.

Position Your Products as Brands—Not Commodities. Mack Hanan. *Fast-Growth Management: How to Improve Profits with Entrepreneurial Strategies,* 1979, pp. 91–103. The Wellspring Group.

The Product-Line Audit: An Approach to Profit-Oriented Marketing. H. M. Tibbetts. MRev., March 1977, pp. 14–17. Thomas J. Lipton, Inc.

Reaching for the Epaulet Men. William S. Payson. MRev., Dec. 1977, pp. 23–25. The Commonwealth Group, Inc.

Sales to Marketing: The Crucial Transition. Cathy Nichols-Manning. MRev., July 1978, pp. 56–61. McKinsey & Co., Inc.

Shifting Shoals in Marketing Channels: The Midas Approach. Edward W. Smykay, Mary A. Higby. MRev., July 1981, pp. 15–25. Rutgers Univ., AT&T.

Smart Marketing in a Time of Economic Crisis. David J. Freiman. AMJ, Autumn 1980, pp. 21–34. Imperial Knife Associated Cos, Inc.

Strategic Segmentation: How to Carve Niches for Growth in Industrial Markets. Robert A. Garda. MRev., Aug. 1981, pp. 15–22. McKinsey & Co., Inc.

Successful Marketing for Small Business. William A. Cohen, Marshall E. Reddick. 1981, 282 pp. California State Univ.

The Supersalesman at the Census Bureau. Business Week. *Marketing in Nonprofit Organizations,* 1978, pp. 209–213.

Target Marketing. William R. Osgood. *Basics of Successful Business Management,* 1981, pp. 101–115.

Telephone Marketing Techniques. Murray Roman. 1979, 34 pp. Campaign Communications Institute of America, Inc., MB.

MARKETING MANAGEMENT—PUBLIC SERVICE AND NON-PROFIT ORGANIZATIONS

BAM Grows in Brooklyn. Brendan Gill. *Marketing in Nonprofit Organizations,* 1978, pp. 273–280. Municipal Art Society and Landmarks Conservancy of New York.

The Blood Business. Seymour Lusterman. *Marketing in Nonprofit Organizations,* 1978, pp. 74–86. National Industrial Conference Board.

Broadening the Concept of Marketing. Philip Kotler, Sidney J. Levy. *Marketing in Nonprofit Organizations,* 1978, pp. 3–15. Northwestern Univ.

Effective Marketing of a Cancer Screening Program. Evelyn Gutman. *Marketing in Nonprofit Organizations,* 1978, pp. 133–147. New York Univ. Medical Center.

Health Service Marketing: A Suggested Model. Gerald Zaltman, Alan Vertinsky. *Marketing in Nonprofit Organizations,* 1978, pp. 95–113. Univ. of Pittsburgh, Univ. of British Columbia.

Healthcare Marketing: Maximizing Your Competitive Position. Stephen L. Tucker. HSM, April 1981, pp. 3–6. Trinity Univ.

A Management Approach to the Buyer's Market. William Ihlanfeldt. *Marketing in Nonprofit Organizations,* 1978, pp. 172–186. Northwestern Univ.

Marketing for NPO's—from a Practitioner's Point of View. Paul A. Wagner.*Marketing in Nonprofit Organizations,* 1978, pp. 38–54. NPO Task Force.

Marketing for Nonprofit Organizations. Benson P. Shapiro. *Marketing in Nonprofit Organizations,* 1978, pp. 16–30. Harvard Business School.

Marketing for Profits and Nonprofits. George Wasem. *Marketing in Nonprofit Organizations,* 1978, pp. 31–37. Commercial National Management Consulting Co.

Marketing in Nonprofit Organizations. Patrick J. Montana (editor). 1978, 302 pp.

Marketing Management. Rohit Deshpande. *Management Principles for Nonprofit Agencies and Organizations,* 1979, pp. 363–400. Univ. of Texas.

The Marketing of Public Goods. Leo Bogart. *Marketing in Nonprofit Organizations,* 1978, pp. 62–73. Newspaper Advertising Bureau, Inc.

Marketing the University: Opportunity in an Era of Crisis. Leonard L. Berry, William R. George. *Marketing in Nonprofit Organizations,* 1978, pp. 159–171. Georgia State Univ., Virginia Commonwealth Univ.

Marketing Your Hospital. Richard D. O'Hallaron, Jeffrey Staples, Paul Chiampa. *Marketing in Nonprofit Organizations,* 1978, pp. 114–122. St. Mary's Hospital.

Marketing's Application to Fund Raising. William A. Mindak, H. Malcolm Bybee. *Marketing in Nonprofit Organizations,* 1978, pp. 187–198. Univ. of Texas, Kenyon & Eckhardt Advertising Inc.

A Mirror of Objectivity: One Hospital's Market Survey. Clifford J. Lorenz. HSM, July 1981, pp. 11–12. Mercy Hospital Center.

Museums Find a New Patron: The Retail Market. Business Week. *Marketing in Nonprofit Organizations,* 1978, pp. 281–284.

Need Analysis in the Healthcare Facility: A Marketing Approach to the Community. Robert E. Pitts. HSM, Feb. 1980, pp. 8–10. Univ. of Notre Dame.

New York City: A Portrait in Marketing Mania. William L. Shanklin. *Marketing in Nonprofit Organizations,* 1978, pp. 148–158.

The Pleasures of Nonprofitability. Forbes Magazine. *Marketing in Nonprofit Organizations,* 1978, pp. 87–91.

A Sales Pitch for New York. Michael Sterne. *Marketing in Nonprofit Organizations,* 1978, pp. 285–289. The New York Times.

Should Hospitals Market? Robin E. MacStravic. *Marketing in Nonprofit Organizations,* 1978, pp. 251–258. Univ. of Washington.

Understanding the Client as a Consumer. Melanie Wallendorf. *Management Principles for Nonprofit Agencies and Organizations,* 1979, pp. 256–290. Univ. of Michigan.

Using Marketing Strategies to Put Hospitals on Target. Richard C. Ireland. *Marketing in Nonprofit Organizations,* 1978, pp. 123–132. Ireland Educational Corp.

MARKETING RESEARCH. See also Forecasting Methods, Management Science and Statistics

Competitive Analysis. Alfred R. Oxenfeldt, Jonathan E. Schwartz. PA #75, 1981, 96 pp. Columbia Univ., The Sperry & Hutchinson Co. By purchase only.

Determining Results in the Generosity Business. Robert J. Dubin. *Managing Nonprofit Organizations,* 1977, pp. 270–279. J. R. Taft Corp.

Giving Marketing Research Its Due. Thomas N. Thurman. MRev., May 1979, pp. 32–33. Upjohn International, Inc.

Low-Cost Marketing Research and Test Marketing. William A. Cohen, Marshall E. Reddick. *Successful Marketing for Small Business,* 1981, pp. 45–67. California State Univ.

Making Buyer Behavior Concepts Work for You. William A. Cohen, Marshall E. Reddick. *Successful Marketing for Small Business,* 1981, pp. 69–96. California State Univ.

The Marketing Path to Global Profits. David J. Freiman. 1979, 69 pp. Imperial Knife Associated Cos., Inc. MB.

Marketplace Behavior: Its Meaning for Management. Sidney J. Levy. 1978, 257 pp. Northwestern Univ.

The Owner's and Manager's Market Analysis Workbook for Small to Moderate Retail and Service Establishments. Wayne A. Lemmon. 1980, 230 pp. Economic Research Associates.

Practical Marketing Research. Jeffrey Pope. 1981, 296 pp. Custom Research, Inc.

Researching Foreign Markets. R. Wayne Walvoord. *Ten Steps to Successful Exporting,* 1981, pp. 31–39. International Trade Management Co., Inc.

The Role of Marketing Research in Public Policy Decision Making. William L. Wilkie. David M. Gardner. *Marketing in Nonprofit Organizations,* 1978, pp. 224–243. Univ. of Florida, Univ. of Illinois.

Strategies in Marketing Research (third ed.). Frank H. Eby, Jr., 1979. (Extension Institute Course) By purchase only.

MATERIALS MANAGEMENT. See also Purchasing

Are You Ready for MRP? R. Michael Donovan, Steven King. MRev., Oct. 1977, pp. 46–50. Touche Ross & Co., Bose Corp.

How to Use Material Requirements Planning. Nancy J. Rosen, Jacob B. Paperman. MRev., Aug. 1978, pp. 17–23. Armco Steel Corp, Miami Univ.

Materials Management: Essential Planning Strategies. Hall B. Whitworth. MRev., March 1979, p. 32. Champion International Corp.

Materials Requirements Planning: How to Develop a Realistic Master Schedule. Gerald R. Gallagher. MRev., April 1980, pp. 19–25. Arthur Anderson & Co.

MATRIX MANAGEMENT

The Flexibility of Matrix Management. Joseph E. Ryan. HSM, Oct. 1981, pp. 1–3. HBO & Co.

Getting Results with Matrix Management. Grant E. Mayberry. 1980. (Extension Institute Course) By purchase only.

How One Company Adapted Matrix Management in a Crisis. Anthony E. Cascino. MRev., Nov. 1979, pp. 57–61. International Minerals & Chemicals Corp.

The Human Side of the Matrix. Paul R. Lawrence, Harvey F. Kolodny, Standley M. Davis. OD, Summer 1977, pp. 43–61.

Matrix Management. David I. Cleland. MRev., Part 1, The Cultural Ambience of the Matrix Organization. Nov. 1981, pp. 25–28, 37–39. Part 2. A Kaleidoscope of Organizational Systems. Dec. 1981, pp. 48–56. Univ. of Pittsburgh.

Matrix Management: A Primer for the Administrative Manager. Norman H. Wright, Jr. MRev., Part 1. April 1979, pp. 58–61. Part 2. Project Organization. May 1979, pp. 59–62. Part 3. Adjusting to Two Bosses. June 1979, pp. 57–58. Martin Marietta Aeroscpace.

Matrix Organization: Is It a Sensible Approach for Hospitals? Allen Y. Davis. HSM, May 1979, pp. 1–3,10. General Staff Associates.

Matrix Organizational Design as a Vehicle for Effective Delivery of Public Health Care and Social Services. J. L. Gray. *Managing Nonprofit Organizations,* 1977, pp. 209–219. Univ. of Manitoba.

The Variations of Matrix Organization. Robert F. Smith. PA #73, 1980, 31 pp. Phillips-Ramsey, Inc. By purchase only.

MEETINGS

Are Your Meetings Successful? P.S. How Do You Know? Charles Margerison. *How to Assess Your Managerial Style,* 1980, pp. 71–84. Cranfield School of Management.

A Conference and Workshop Planner's Manual. Lois B. Hart, J. Gordon Schleicher. 1979, 125 pp. Organizational Leadership, Inc., Michigan Department of Social Services.

Designing a Norm-Shifting Seminar. Robert R. Blake, Jane Srygley Mouton, *Productivity: the Human Side,* 1981, pp. 102–107. Scientific Methods, Inc.

Departmental Workshops. Clair F. Vough, Bernard Asbell. *Productivity, A Practical Program for Improving Efficiency* (rev. ed. - former title: *Tapping the Human Resource: A Strategy for Productivity*), 1979, pp. 159–171. Productivity Research International, Inc.

How to Make Meetings Meaningful. H. Kent Baker. MRev., Aug. 1979, pp. 45–47. American Univ.

How to Run Better Business Meetings. B. Y. Auger. SM, Aug. 1980, pp. 35–39. 3M Co.

How to Run Worthwhile Meetings. ES, June 1979, 16 pp.

Leadership Strategies for Successful Meetings. William Kirkwood, Janice Wilson. SM, Oct. 1981, pp. 2–8. East Tennessee Univ.

Less Talk, Better Meeting Decisions. Bruce D. Sanders. SM, Sept. 1980, pp. 34–38.

Making Meetings Effective: It's a Matter of Control. Mike Smith, Jan Wing. HSM. Oct. 1980, pp. 11–13. Research-Cottrell.

Making Your Meetings Count. Henry A. Tombari. SM, July 1979, pp. 35–39. California State Univ.

Managing Meetings. Beverly A. Potter. *Turning Around: The Behavioral Approach to Managing People,* 1980, pp. 160–186.

Mechanics of a Successful Program. Lucille A. Maddalena. *A Communications Manual for Nonprofit Organizations,* 1981, pp. 83–102. Fairleigh Dickinson Univ.

Meetings in Different Settings. Richard J. Dunsing. *You and I Have Simply Got to Stop Meeting This Way,* 1978, pp. 107–162. Univ. of Richmond.

The Power of Huddling. V. Dallas Merrell. *Effective Communication on the Job* (third ed.), 1981, pp. 126–130. (From *Huddling: The Informal Way to Management Success,* 1979.)

Running Conventions, Conferences, and Meetings. Robert W. Lord. 1981, 192 pp. Employee Benefits Journal.

You and I Have Simply Got to Stop Meeting This Way. Richard J. Dunsing. 1977, 88 pp. Univ. of Richmond. (A collection of reprints from SM)

You and I Have Simply Got to Stop Meeting This Way. Richard J. Dunsing. 1978, 164 pp. Univ. of Richmond.

What's Wrong with Meetings. Richard J. Dunsing. *Effective Communication on the Job (third ed.),* 1981, pp. 159–171. Univ. of Richmond

MERGERS AND ACQUISITIONS

Acquisitions and Mergers: A Shifting Route to Corporate Growth. James W. Bradley, Donald H. Korn. MRev., March 1979, pp. 46–51. Arthur D. Little, Inc.

Acquisitions—Is 50/50 Good Enough? Darryl J. Ellis, Peter P. Pekar. *Corporate Planning: Techniques and Applications,* 1979, pp. 240–248. General Electric, Quaker Oats.

Breaking the Synergism Barrier. Howard L. Jones. *Managing Nonprofit Organizations,* 1977, pp. 252–257. Northfield-Mount Hermon School.

The Human Side of Acquisitions. Robert H. Hayes. MRev., Nov. 1979, pp. 41–46. Robert H. Hayes & Associates.

Increasing the People-Organization Fit in Mergers and Acquisitions. Abraham K. Korman, Arthur H. Rosenbloom, Richard J. Walsh. Pers., May–June 1978, pp. 54–61. City Univ. of New York, S. R. Consultants, American Appraisal Assn.

Lessons from an Acquisitions Specialist. William B. Howell. MRev., Nov. 1979, pp. 37–40. Trans Union Corp.

The Leveraged Acquisition: A Buyer's Experience. Victor K. Kiam II. *PA #74 Mergers and Acquisitions in a Changing Environment,* 1980, pp. 32–40. Remington Products, Inc. By purchase only.

Leveraged Acquisitions in a Dynamic Environment. Peter Susser. *PA #74 Mergers and Acquisitions in a Changing Environment,* 1980, pp. 20–31. DRS, Inc. By purchase only.

Leveraged Buyout Becoming Popular Financing Method. Frederick S. Gilbert. MRev., Aug. 1981, pp. 29–31. Citicorp Industrial Credit, Inc.

Mergers and Acquisitions: A Financial Approach. James Jenkins, 1979. (Extension Institute Course) By purchase only.

Mergers and Acquisitions in a Changing Environment. M. Mark Lee (editor). PA #74, 1980, 53 pp. Standard Research Consultants. By purchase only.

Negotiating at 30 Paces. Gilbert W. Harrison, Brian H. Saffer. MRev., April 1980, pp. 51–54. Fianco, Inc.

The New Merger Game. Don Gussow. 1978, 262 pp. American Business Press.

Profit Planning Through Acquisition. Parmanand Kumar. *Corporate Planning Techniques and Applications,* 1979, pp. 233–239. Ralph M. Parsons Co.

29 Questions Directors Should Ask Before Responding to a Tender Offer. National Association of Corporate Directors (editor). 1981, 4 pp.

Understanding How Antitrust Laws Affect Hospital Mergers. Phillip A. Proger. HSM, Dec. 1979, pp. 4–5. Baker & Hostetler.

What It Means to Make a Merger. Alexander H. Williams III, Cynthia C. Tehan. HSM, Aug. 1981, pp. 1–3. The Church Charity Foundation of Long Island.

METHODS IMPROVEMENT. See Data Processing, Systems Analysis

METRICATION

Metric Conversion—A Slumbering Giant. John H. Landvater. MRev., May 1978, pp. 31–33. Landvater Associates.

Metric Conversion: Where We Are and Where We're Going. Lawrence P. Ettkin, Betty J. Thorne, Paul N. Keaton. AMJ, Spring 1980, pp. 31–38. Univ. of Tennessee, Wisconsin State Univ.

What the Supervisor Should Know About the Metric System. Malcolm O'Hagan. SM, April 1977, pp. 35–40. American National Metric Council.

MORALE. See Attitudes—Employee

MOTIVATION. See also Compensation, Sales Management, Wage Incentives

Authentic Motivation: How Psychological Touching Works. Thomas J. Von der Embse, Herbert E. Brown. SM, Feb. 1979, pp. 19–23. Wright State Univ. (Also reprinted in HSM, Sept. 1980).

Basic Concepts of Motivation. Leo F. McManus. 1980. (An AMA multimedia program) By purchase only.

The Challenge of Changing Work Values: Motivating the Contemporary Employee. Roger J. Howe, Mark G. Mindell. MRev., Sept. 1979, pp. 51–55. B. F. Goodrich Co.

Communicating for Improved Motivation and Performance. Larry E. Penley, Brian L. Hawkins. AMJ, Spring 1980, pp. 39–44. Univ. of Texas. (Also in reprint collection *Effective Communication on the Job* (third ed.), 1981)

Compensation and Motivation. Theodore Cohn, Roy A. Lindberg. *Compensating Key Executives in the Smaller Company,* 1979, pp. 43–67.

Constraints to Effective Motivation. John Nirenberg. SM, Nov. 1981, pp. 24–29. San Francisco State Univ.

Conversation with Frederick Herzberg. William Dowling (editor). *Effective Management and the Behavioral Sciences,* 1978, pp. 36–51.

Conversation with David McClelland. William Dowling (editor). *Effective Management and the Behavioral Sciences,* 1978, pp. 157–177.

Conversation with Fritz J. Roethlisberger. William Dowling (editor). *Effective Management and the Behavioral Sciences,* 1978, pp. 203–220.

Conversation with William F. Whyte. William Dowling (editor). *Effective Management and the Behavioral Sciences,* 1978, pp. 137–156.

Dealing with Nurse Dissatisfaction: A Management Tool that Works. Paula L. Stamps, Gretchen Ramirez-Sosa. HSM, Dec. 1980, pp. 3–6. Univ. of Massachusetts, Univ. of Puerto Rico.

Developing a Motivating Work Climate. Edward E. Lawler III. MRev., July 1977, pp. 25–28, 37–38.

Developing Organizations in Which the Self-Actualizing Executive Flourishes. Harold R. McAlindon. Pers., May–June 1977, pp. 22–29. Hospital Corp. of America.

An Employee Motivational System That Leads to Excellent Performance. John S. Piamonte. Pers., Sept—Oct. 1980, pp. 55–66. British Columbia Hydro & Power Authority.

Fear and Productivity: More Closely Related Than We Think? Hugo Barucco. MRev., Jan. 1981, pp. 23–28. Barucco Associates.

Found: The Key to Excellent Performance. Robert J. Benford. Pers., May–June 1981, pp. 68–77. Norwich-Eaton Pharmaceuticals.

Goal Setting—A Motivational Technique That Works. Gary P. Latham, Edwin A. Locke. OD, Autumn 1979, pp. 68–80. Univ. of Washington, Univ. of Maryland.

How NOT to Motivate. Don Spiegen. SM, Nov. 1977, pp. 11–15.

How to Motivate Employees: Clearly Define Goals, Keep Communication Lines Open. Paul Koellner. MRev., March 1980, pp. 34–35. Live Consultants.

Integrating and Motivating for Effective Performance. Harold Smiddy. *The Evolving Science of Management,* 1979, pp. 149–169.

Little Things Mean a Lot to Workers, as Ohio Company Learned the Hard Way. Edward R. Toth. MRev., Nov. 1981, pp. 32–33. RMI Co.

Making Money the Motivator. V. Alan Mode. SM, Aug. 1979, pp. 16–20.

Management and Motivation. Leo F. McManus. 1979 (An AMA multimedia program) By purchase only.

Management Guidelines: Understanding Needs. George Miller. SM, Aug, 1981, pp. 21–29. George Miller Associates.

Managing Dissatisfaction. Lloyd Baird. Pers., May–June 1981, pp. 12–21. Boston Univ.

A Model for Employee Motivation and Satisfaction. Philip C. Grant. Pers., Sept.–Oct. 1979, pp. 51–57. Husson College.

Motivating Employees. James F. Evered. *Shirt-Sleeves Management,* 1981, pp. 118–138. Redman Industries, Inc.

Motivating the Distributor to Market Your Product. Dennis A. Zalar. 1980, 34 pp. McGraw Edison, Inc. MB.

Motivating the New Breed. Lauren Hite Jackson, Mark G. Mindell. Pers., March–April 1980, pp. 53–61. B. F. Goodrich Corp. (Also in reprint collection *Leadership on the Job: Guidelines to Good Supervision* (third ed.), 1981).

Motivating the Overseas Workforce. Paul E. Illman. *Developing Overseas Managers— and Managers Overseas,* 1980, pp. 83–108. Management Training, Inc.

Motivating Workers for Increased Productivity—Hughes Aircraft. F. Cecil Hill. *Productivity Improvement: Case Studies of Proven Practice,* 1981, pp. 86–99. Hughes Aircraft Co.

Motivation. William F. Christopher. *Management for the 1980's* (rev. ed. - former title: *The Achieving Enterprise*), 1980, pp. 113–129.

Motivation. Paul W. Cummings. *Open Management: Guides to Successful Practice,* 1980, pp. 135–149.

Motivation. William R. Osgood. *Basics of Successful Business Management,* 1981, pp. 223–233.

Motivation. Linda A. Roxe. *Personnel Management for the Smaller Company,* 1979, pp. 121–146. Rox Associates.

Motivation: Are the Old Theories Still True? Charles A. Hanson, Donna K. Hanson. SM, June 1978, pp. 9–15.

Motivation as if People Matter. John Nirenberg. SM, Oct. 1981, pp. 22–25. San Francisco State Univ.

Motivation for Maximum Job Contribution. Ray A. Killian. *Managers Must Lead!* (rev. ed.), 1979, pp. 74–94. Belk Stores.

Motivation, Leadership, and Organization: Do American Theories Apply Abroad? Geert Hofstede. OD, Summer 1980, pp. 42–63. Fasson Europe.

Motivation Techniques: Does One Work Best? William B. Miller. MRev., Feb. 1981, pp. 47–52. Touche Ross & Co.

Motivational Theories and Applications for Managers. Donald Sanzotta. 1977, 184 pp. Cayuga Community College.

Organizational Approaches to Motivation: Do the Jobs Stimulate or Stifle People? James J. Cribbin. *Leadership: Strategies for Organizational Effectiveness,* 1981, pp. 124–138. St. John's Univ.

Pay Satisfaction: Money Is Not the Only Answer. Robert M. Monczka, Lawrence W. Foster, William E. Reif, John W. Newstrom, CR, Fourth Quarter 1977, pp. 22–28.

Persuading Groups to Buy Ideas. Lyle Yorks. *Corporate Planning Techniques and Applications,* 1979, pp. 351–358. Drake Beam & Associates.

The Pervasive Subject: Motivation. James E. Gardner. *Training the New Supervisor,* 1980, pp. 93–105. Fieldcrest Mills, Inc.

Putting the Motivation Back into Work. Robert N. Ford. 1978. (AMACOM audio cassette) By purchase only.

The Pygmalion Effect in Management. Ginny Van Almsick. SM, Feb. 1979, pp. 15–18. Pet Inc.

The Relationship of Money and Motivation. Gene Milbourn, Jr. CR, Second Quarter 1980, pp. 33–44. Univ. of Baltimore.

The Supervisor's Survival Guide: A Positive Approach to Motivation. Robert E. Pitts, Ken Thompson. SM, Nov. 1978, pp. 2–10. Univ. of Notre Dame. (Also in reprint collection *The Supervisor's Survival Guide,* 1979).

The Supervisor's Survival Guide: Alternatives to Monetary Rewards. Robert E. Pitts, Ken Thompson. SM, Dec. 1978, pp. 12–17. Univ. of Notre Dame. (Also in reprint collection. *The Supervisor's Survival Guide,* 1979).

Surprise: Theory Y Managers Get Higher Pay. Mary Zippo. Pers., March–April 1980, pp. 76–77.

Sustaining Motivation. James E. Gardner. *Training the New Supervisor,* 1980, pp. 149–164. Fieldcrest Mills, Inc.

Toward a More Creative You: The Actualizing Climate. Harold R. McAlindon. SM, April

1980, pp. 35–40. Institute of Financial Education. (Also in reprint collection *Getting the Most Out of Your Job and Your Organization,* 1980).

Understanding and Using Motivation. Bernard Rosenbaum. SM, Jan. 1979, pp. 9–13. Mohr Development, Inc.

What Every Worker Wants. Whiting Williams. *The Amazing Oversight: Total Participation for Productivity,* 1979, pp. 54–64.

Who's in Control Here? Howard R. Smith. MRev., Feb. 1980, pp. 43–47. Univ. of Georgia.

Why Jobs Die and What to Do About It. Robert N. Ford. 1979, 220 pp.

Why You Can't Motivate Everyone. William H. Franklin, Jr. SM, April 1980, pp. 21–28. Georgia State Univ.

Your Best Ain't Good Enough. C. W. Bergen, Jr., Patrick J. Germany. SM, May 1979, pp. 14–16. Western Co. of North America.

NEW PRODUCTS. See Product Development

OCCUPATIONAL SAFETY AND HEALTH ACT. See Safety

OFFICE LAYOUT

Building and Facilities. William R. Tracey. *Human Resource Development Standards,* 1981 pp. 173–210. U.S. Army Intelligence Training School.

Environmental Considerations in Building Construction. Stephen S. Rosen. MRev., Aug. 1978, pp. 31–34. Parsons, Brinckerhoff, Quade & Douglas, Inc.

The Executive's Guide to Office Space Planning. John Hathaway-Bates, Lawrence Lerner. 1980. (Extension Institute Course) By purchase only.

Keys to Success with Open Plan Offices. Andrew D. Szilagyi, Winford E. Holland, Christie Oliver. MRev., Aug. 1979, pp. 26–28, 38–41. Univ. of Houston, Planning Design Research Corp.

Managing the Use of Hospital Space. Frank W. Rees, Jr. HSM, Sept. 1981, pp. 3–6. Rees Associates.

Managing Without Obstacles: A Look At the Open Office. Eva Maddox. SM, April 1979, pp. 15–22. Eva Maddox Associates.

Planning and Using Office Space. ES, Dec. 1981, 16 pp.

A Rational Approach to Office Planning. M. Arthur Gensler, Jr., Peter B. Brandt. 1978, 52 pp. Gensler Associates. MB.

OFFICE MANAGEMENT. See also Cost Control—Non-Manufacturing Costs, Data Processing—Evaluation and Costs, Office Layout

Business Forms Management. William V. Nygren. 1980, 182 pp. 3M Co.

Controlling Paperwork—Yours and the Government's. Warren B. Buhler. 1979, 61 pp. Management Design, Inc. MB.

Cutting Clerical Backlogs. Peter Kazakoff. HSM, Sept. 1981, pp. 9–10. Pacific Gas and Electric Co.

Guidelines for Conducting an Office Systems Feasibility Study. George S. Smith, 1981, 59 pp. Nabisco, Inc. MB.

How to Manage Administrative Operations. Susan Z. Diamond. 1981 (Extension Institute Course) By purchase only.

Improving Productivity Through Advanced Office Controls. Robert E. Nolan, Richard T. Young, Ben C. DiSylvester. 1980, 404 pp. Robert E. Nolan Co., Inc.

Operation Snapshot: Ensuring Peak Office Performance. Robert A. Shiff. AMJ, Winter 1981, pp. 37–43. Naremco Services, Inc.

Records Management Can Stem Paper Flow. Thomas More P. Griffin. MRev., Nov. 1979, p. 35.

Sorting Through the New Office Gadgetry. Max V. Riley. AMJ, Autumn 1981. pp. 42–49. Southern California Edison.

Support Services. William R. Tracey. *Human Resource Development Standards,* 1981 pp. 211–250. U.S. Army Intelligence Training School.

Ten Ways to Aggravate Your Clerical "Demon." Fran Duschl. SM, May 1977, pp. 11–15. Great American Insurance Co.

OLDER WORKERS AND RETIREMENT. See also Employee Benefits, Pensions
Age Discrimination in Employment. William L. Kendig. 1978, 83 pp. U.S. Dept. of the Interior. MB.
The CEO Faces Retirement. Henry M. Wallfesh. PA #69, 1978, 34 pp. Cox Broadcasting Corp. By purchase only.
Compulsory Retirement: A Reevaluation. Douglas L. Bartley. Pers., March–April 1977, pp. 62–67. Pan American Univ.
Decades: Lifestyle Changes in Career Expectations. Edith M. Lynch. 1980, 144 pp. American Employers for Free Enterprise.
The Effects of Extending the Mandatory Retirement Age. Henry M. Wallfesh. 1978, 41 pp. Retirement Advisors, Inc. MB.
General Electric Asks: How Can We Use What's Best in Older People? MRev., Sept. 1980, pp. 29, 38–40.
How Japanese Business Treats Its Older Workers. Shiro Sekiguchi. MRev., Oct. 1980, pp. 15–18. Nippon Steel Corp.
The Management of Age in the Workface. Diane P. Jackson. MRev., Dec. 1978, pp. 50–56. Sunbeam Corp.
Planning for Retirement. C. Colburn Hardy. *Your Money & Your Life: How to Plan Your Long-Range Financial Security,* 1979, pp. 84–109.
The Retired Lives Reserve: Good News for Workers Facing Retirement. William Waters. SM, Oct. 1981, pp. 41–42. Merrill Lynch, Pierce, Fenner & Smith Inc.
Retirement: Creating Promise Out of Threat. Robert K. Kinzel. 1979, 131 pp.
The Retirement Decision: How American Managers View Their Prospects. Robert Jud, 1981, 45 pp. William M. Mercer, Inc. MB.
Retirement Planning: The State of the Art. Mary Zippo. Pers., Jan. Feb. 1980, pp. 68–70.
Successful Midlife Career Change: Self-Understanding and Strategies for Action. Paula I. Robbins. 1978, 268 pp. Fitchburg State College.
Why Stop at 65? James W. Walker. MRev., Sept. 1977, pp. 13–18. Towers, Perrin, Forster & Crosby.
Your Personal Management: How to Retire—Successfully. Klaus Hartmann, M.D. SM, March 1977, pp. 39–42.

OPERATIONS RESEARCH. See Management Sciences and Statistics

ORGANIZATION. See also Charts and Graphs, Committees, Decentralization, Manuals, Matrix, and headings of individual functions
Analyzing Your Organization: How Keen Is Your Insight? James J. Cribbin. *Leadership: Strategies for Organizational Effectiveness.* 1981, pp. 61–78. St. John's Univ.
Controllership in Divisionalized Firms: Structure, Evaluation and Development. Vijay Sathe. 1978, 45 pp. MB.
Conversation: An Interview with Edward Carlson. OD, Spring 1979, pp. 49–62.
The Data Administration Charter. Ronald G. Ross. *Data Dictionaries and Data Administration: Concepts and Practices for Data Resources Management,* 1981 pp. 171–218. Performance Development Corp.
EDP Organization. Michael R. Frank. *The Effective EDP Manager,* 1980, pp. 18–47. The Taubman Co., Inc.
Effective Executive Personnel Organization. W. J. Donald. *Human Resources Management: The Past Is Prologue,* 1979, pp. 179–200.
Establishing Successful Patterns for the Quality Assurance Program. Martin R. Smith. *Qualitysense: Organizational Approaches to Improving Product Quality and Service,* 1979, pp. 63–98. Capital Manufacturing Co.
An Exercise in Organization. James L. Hayes. MRev., June 1980, pp. 2–3.
The Experimenting Organization. Barry M. Staw. OD, Summer 1977, pp. 2–18.
Fighting and Beating Bureaucracy. William P. Anthony. *Managing Incompetence,* 1981, pp. 132–163. The Florida State Univ.
Formal Theory and the Flexible Organization. Russell Stout. AMJ, Winter 1981, pp. 44–52. American Univ.

Framework for Executive Action. Ewing W. Reilley. *Human Resources Management: The Past is Prologue,* 1979, pp. 231–234.

The Group Executive: Power Figure or 'Gray Marshmellow'? Allan F. Juers. MRev., March 1979. pp. 14–18. Robert H. Hayes & Associates, Inc.

The Group Executive's Job: Mission Impossible? James H. Ransom. MRev., March 1979, pp. 9–14. McKinsey & Co., Inc.

The Hospital Auxiliary's Role in the Organization. David L. Woodrum. HSM, April 1980, pp. 8–9. The Monongalia General Hospital.

The Hospital of the Future: How Will It Be Structured? Charles J. Austin. HSM, Oct. 1979, pp. 1–4. Goergia Southern College.

How Breakable Is the Chain of Command? Davis S. Brown. SM, Jan. 1981, pp. 2–8. George Washington Univ.

How to Organize for Achievement. William C. Waddell. *Overcoming Murphy's Law,* 1981, pp. 175–204. California State Univ., Los Angeles.

How to Organize the EDP Department. Michael R. Frank. 1980, 47 pp. MB.

How to Organize the Marketing Function. William A. Cohen, Marshall E. Reddick. *Successful Marketing for Small Business.* 1981, pp. 11–27. California State Univ.

Management Guidelines: Building an Effective Organization. George Miller. SM, July 1981, pp. 35–41. George Miller Associates.

The Missing Ingredient in Organization Theory. Leon Reinharth. AMJ, Winter 1978, pp. 14–24. City Univ. of New York.

National Accounts in Specific Markets. Daniel J. Murphy. *National Accounts Marketing Handbook,* 1981, pp. 213–227. Monsanto Co.

Organizing for International Operations. Derek F. Channon with Michael Jalland. *Multinational Strategic Planning,* 1978, pp. 22–50. Manchester Business School.

Organization Alternatives for Project Managers. Robert Youker. MRev., Nov. 1977, pp. 46–53. World Bank.

Organization and Manageability. Fred W. Latham, George S. Sanders. *Urwick, Orr On Management,* 1980, pp. 26–38. Urwick, Orr & Partners.

Organization Design: A Situational Perspective. Jay W. Lorsch. OD, Autumn 1977, pp. 2–14. Harvard Univ.

Organization Planning Manual (rev. ed.). Joseph J. Famularo. 1979, 373 pp. McGraw-Hill, Inc.

Organization—the Means to Carry Out Objectives. Maurice R. Hecht. *What Happens in Management,* 1980, pp. 113–148. Helmsman Management Associates.

Organizational Structure. Morton F. Meltzer. *Information: The Ultimate Management Resource: How to Find, Use and Manage It,* 1981, pp. 109–120. Martin Marietta Corp.

Organizing. William R. Tracey. *Human Resource Development Standards,* 1981 pp. 78–92. U.S. Army Intelligence Training School.

Organizing for Efficiency and Effectivenes. William A. Cohen. *Principles of Technical Management,* 1980, pp. 14–39. California State Univ.

Organizing for Future Challenges and Opportunities. Harold Smiddy. *The Evolving Science of Management,* 1979, pp. 112–131.

Organizing for Increased Profitability, Part II. Roger J. Howe. *Building Profits Through Organizational Change,* 1981, pp. 59–99. Donaldson Co., Inc.

Organizing for Innovation: Does a Product Group Structure Inhibit Technological Development. Gerald C. Werner. MRev., March 1981. pp. 47–51. Technical Communications Assistance.

Organizing for the Eighties. James L. Mercer, Susan W. Woolston, William V. Donaldson. *Managing Urban Government Services: Strategies, Tools, and Techniques for the 80's,* 1981, pp. 13–33. James Mercer & Associates, United States Environmental Protection Agency, Philadelphia Zoological Society.

Organizing to Overhaul a Mess. Kenneth L. Harris. *Managing Nonprofit Organizations,* 1977, pp. 229–243. Project Interaction.

The Parallel Organization Structure at General Motors . . . An Interview with Howard C. Carlson. Ernest C. Miller. Pers., Sept.–Oct. 1978, pp. 64–69.

Principles of Organization. Harold Smiddy. *The Evolving Science of Management,* 1979, pp. 26–47.

Product Service Planning: Service-Marketing-Engineering Interactions. William H. Bleuel, Henry Bender. 1980, 84 pp. AM International. RS.

The Right Side: An Organizational Dilemma. Roger L. Cason. MRev., April 1978, pp. 24–28, 38–39. The Du Pont Co.

Sector Executives: Management Evolution. Robert R. Frederick. MRev., Oct. 1978, pp. 29–30.

Senior Managers Losing Control Over Operations. Charles K. Rourke. MRev., Feb. 1981, pp. 29, 40. Hendrick & Co.

Structuring the National Account Department. James Day. *National Account Marketing Handbook,* 1981, pp. 72–80. Dow Chemical Co.

The Truth About Integration—Horizontal Versus Vertical. Robin E. MacStravic. HSM, Oct. 1980, pp. 5–6, 14. Univ. of Washington.

What Is the Right Organization Structure? Decision Tree Analysis Provides the Answer. Robert Duncan. OD, Winter 1979, pp. 59–80. Yale Univ.

When a Business Matures: How to Keep the Entrepreneurial Thrust. Robert Brown. MRev., April 1980, pp. 14–17. Seatrain Lines.

ORGANIZATIONAL DEVELOPMENT. See also Change, Team Management.

Behavior Management. Beverly A. Potter. *Turning Around: The Behavioral Approach to Managing People,* 1980, pp. 25–66.

Behavior Modification on the Job. Thomas Rotondi, Jr. HSM, July 1981, pp. 7–10. Marquette Univ.

Building Profits Through Organizational Change. Roger J. Howe, 1981, 264 pp. Donaldson Co., Inc.

By the Yard It's Hard, By the Inch a Cinch. John D. Proe. HSM., Oct. 1979, pp. 8–9. Mark Silber Associates.

Can Behavioral Science Help Design Organizations? Albert B. Cherns. OD, Spring 1977, pp. 44–64.

Can Organization Development Be Fine Tuned to Bureaucracies? Virginia E. Schein, Larry E. Greiner. OD, Winter 1977, pp. 48–61. Yale Univ., Univ. of Southern California. (Also in reprint collection *Organizational Development: Theory and Practice,* 1977)

Conversation with Warren Bennis. William Dowling (editor). *Effective Management and the Behavioral Sciences,* 1978, pp. 265–284.

Creating and Managing Opportunities for Employee Growth. Phillip L. Hunsaker. SM, April 1978, pp. 27–34.

Developing Organizations in Which the Self-Actualizing Executive Flourishes. Harold McAlindon. Pers., May–June 1977, pp. 22–29. Hospital Corp. of America.

Effective Management and the Behavioral Sciences. William Dowling (editor). 1978, 285 pp. (A collection of reprints from OD)

Getting the Most out of Your Job and Your Organization. Harold McAlindon. 1980, 78 pp. Institute of Financial Education. (A collection of reprints from SM)

Hierarchies, Clans, and Theory Z: A New Perspective on Organization Development. William G. Ouchi, Raymond L. Price. OD, Autumn 1978, pp. 25–44. Stanford Univ.

The Human Side of Growth. Eric H. Nielsen. OD, Summer 1978, pp. 61–80.

Improving Managerial Effectiveness Through Modeling-Based Training. Jerry I. Porras, Brad Anderson. OD, Spring 1981, pp. 60–77. Stanford Univ., Hewlett-Packard Corp.

Internal Consulting Groups: Catalysts for Organizational Change. Jay Spechler, John Wicker. MRev., Nov. 1980, pp. 24–28, 37–41. Florida Power & Light Co., Theodore Barry & Associates.

Introduction to Conversations. William Dowling (editor). *Effective Management and the Behavioral Sciences,* 1978, pp. 1–35.

Is HRD Enough? Milan Moravec. Pers., Jan.–Feb. 1979, pp. 53–57. Bechtel Corp.

Is Organization Development Catching On? . . . A Personnel Symposium. Pers., Nov.–Dec. 1977, pp. 10–22. (Also in reprint collection *The Human Resources Function: Its Emergence and Character,* 1978)

Is There a Climate for Success? George G. Gordon, Bonnie R. Goldberg. MRev., May 1977, pp. 37–44.

Let's Keep the OD People Honest. Lester A. Digman. Pers., Jan.–Feb. 1979, pp. 22–29. Univ. of Nebraska.

A Manager's Guide to Organizational Change. Brian H. Kleiner. Pers., March–April 1979, pp. 31–38. California State Univ.

Managing Organizational Culture. Edwin L. Baker. MRev., July 1980, pp. 8–13. McKinsey & Co.

Merging Personnel and OD: A Not-So-Odd Couple. Robert M. Frame, Fred Luthans. Pers., Jan.–Feb. 1977, pp. 12–22. Nielsen & Associates, Univ. of Nebraska.

Minimizing Risk in Organization Development Interventions. Bruce M. Meglino, William H. Mobley. Pers., Nov.–Dec. 1977, pp. 23–31. Univ. of South Carolina.

A Model for Diagnosing Organizational Behavior. David A. Nadler, Michael Tushman. OD, Autumn 1980, pp. 35–51. Columbia Univ.

O.B. Mod. in a Small Factory: How Behavior Modification Techniques Can Improve Total Organizational Performance. Fred Luthans, Jason Schweizer. MRev., Sept. 1979, pp. 43–50. Univ. of Nebraska, Univ. of Miami.

An OD Strategy at Parker Pen. Douglas M. Soat. Pers., March–April 1979, pp. 39–43. Sentry Insurance Co.

An OD Strategy at the IRS. Paul C. Buchanan. Pers., March–April 1979, pp. 44–52.

OD Techniques and the Bottom Line. Gene Milbourn, Richard Cuba. Pers., May–June 1981, pp. 34–42. Univ. of Baltimore.

Organization and Management Development Programs. William R. Tracey. *Human Resource Development Standards.* 1981 pp. 350–374. U.S. Army Intelligence Training School.

Organization Design: Organizations as Self-Designing Systems. Karl E. Weick. OD, Autumn 1977, pp. 30–46.

Organization Design: The Case for a Coalitional Model of Organizations. Jeffrey Pfeffer, Gerald Salancik. OD, Autumn 1977, pp. 15–29.

Organization Development: A Dynamic New Force? Ernest C. Miller. Pers., Nov.–Dec. 1977, pp. 4–9.

Organization Development Efforts in a Major Healthcare Organization. John F. Sullivan, Timothy J. Cotter. Pers., Nov.–Dec. 1977, pp. 32–41. Michigan State Univ., Sullivan & Shook, Inc.

Organization Development for Operating Managers. Michael E. McGill. 1977, 177 pp. Southern Methodist Univ.

Organizational Development: Promises, Performances, Possibilities. David G. Bowers. *Organizational Development: Theory and Practice,* 1977, pp. 4–16. Univ. of Michigan.

Organizational Development: Theory and Practice. William F. Dowling, Ernest C. Miller (editors). 1977, 125 pp. (A collection of reprints from OD)

Organizational Growth: The Implications for Human Resources. Phillip L. Hunsaker. Pers., Nov.–Dec. 1979, pp. 12–21. Univ. of San Diego.

Organizational Independence: Letting Employees Loose. Bruce D. Sanders. SM, Feb. 1981, pp. 2–8.

Organizational Paradigms: A Theory of Organizational Change. Alan Sheldon. OD, Winter 1980, pp. 61–80. Harvard Univ.

Organizational Passages—Diagnosing and Treating Lifecycle Problems of Organizations. Ichak Adizes. OD, Summer 1979, pp. 3–25. Univ. of California, Los Angeles.

Organizational Research and Organizational Change: GM's Approach. Howard C. Carlson. Pers., July–August 1978, pp. 11–22. (Also reprinted in *Human Resources Management: The Past Is Prologue,* 1979).

Organizations as Phrog Farms. Jerry B. Harvey. OD, Spring 1977, pp. 15–23.

People Can Be Like Pigeons. William M. Smith. SM, June 1981, pp. 10–14. Univ. of Miami.

People Processing: Strategies of Organizational Socialization. John Van Maanen. OD, Summer 1978, pp. 19–36.

People: The Reason and the Key. James L. Hayes. MRev., July 1977. pp. 2–3.

Positive Reinforcement. James F. Evered. *Shirt-Sleeves Management,* 1981, pp. 139–159. Redman Industries, Inc.

Problems Posed by a Changing Organizational Membership. Carl E. Pickhardt. OD, Summer 1981, pp. 69–80. Region XIII Education Service Center.

Searching for an Alternative Management Style. J. Louis Alpinieri, Don Yates. MRev., Jan. 1980, pp. 25–28, 37–39. Acurex Corp.

Self-Help Groups Provide Cost-Efficient Image Building. Saundra L. Atwood. HSM, Sept. 1981, pp. 1–3. Parkway General Hospital.

Strategic Planning for Work Climate Modification. Lee Ginsburg. Pers., Nov.–Dec. 1978, pp. 10–20. Miller, Ginsburg, & Brien.

Successful Team Building Through TA. Dudley Bennett. 1980, 260 pp. MCM Consultants, Inc.

Symbols, Patterns, and Settings: An Optimistic Case for Getting Things Done. Thomas J. Peters. OD, Autumn 1978, pp. 3–23. McKinsey & Co.

A Systematic Approach to Managing Corporate Change: Richard D. Babcock, William B. Alton. MRev., Dec. 1979, pp. 24–27. Univ. of San Francisco, Johnson & Johnson International.

Tapping into the Power of Informal Groups. H. Kent Baker. SM, Feb. 1981, pp. 18–25. The American Univ.

Time for Organization Development? Thomas H. Patten, Jr. Pers., March–April 1977, pp. 26–33. Michigan State Univ.

To Move an Organization: The Corning Approach to Organization Development. William F. Dowling. *Organizational Development: Theory and Practice,* 1977, pp. 46–64.

Tracking Down the "Aroundhereisms"—or, How to Foil Negative Orientation. George F. Truell. Pers., July–Aug. 1981, pp. 23–31. George Truell Associates.

Try a Little Positive Reinforcement! Darrel R. Brown. SM, October 1979, pp. 36–39. Virginia Commonwealth Univ.

Turning Around: The Behavioral Approach to Managing People. Beverly A. Potter. 1980, 266 pp.

Two Ways of Using Behavioral Science to Improve Management. George F. Wieland. HSM, Feb. 1980, pp. 1–4.

Whatever Happened to the American Way of Work. J. Barry DuVall, David L. Shores. SM, Feb. 1978, pp. 11–17.

Who Gets Power—And How They Hold on to It: A Strategic-Contingency Model of Power. Gerald R. Salancik, Jeffrey Pfeffer. OD, Winter 1977, pp. 2–21.

The Why, When, and How of Changing Organizational Structures. John D. Arnold. MRev., March 1981, pp. 17–20. John Arnold ExecuTrak Systems, Inc.

Witch Doctors, Messianics, Sorcerers, and OD Consultants: Parallels and Paradigms. Warner Woodworth, Reed Nelson. OD, Autumn 1979, pp. 17–33. Brigham Young Univ.

You and I Have Simply Got to Stop Meeting This Way, Part 6: Changes Participants Can Make. Richard J. Dunsing. SM, Feb. 1977, pp. 16–29. Univ. of Richmond. (Also in reprint collection *You and I Have Simply Got to Stop Meeting This Way,* 1977 and expanded book, same title, 1978.)

ORGANIZATIONAL EFFECTIVENESS. See also Management Control

Are Your Managers Really Managing? J. Spencer Ferebee, Jr. MRev., Jan. 1981, pp. 18–22, Price Waterhouse & Co.

Assessing Computer Center Effectiveness. Frank Greenwood, Lee A. Gagnon. 1977, 38 pp. Univ. of New Haven, Peat, Marwick, Mitchell & Co. MB.

The Company's Best Interests? William J. Altier. MRev., April 1981, p. 33. Princeton Associates Inc.

Conveying the Quality of Management. Mark J. Appleman. MRev., May 1978, pp. 7–10. The Corporate Shareholder.

Critical Questions in Assessing Organizational Effectiveness. Kim Cameron. OD, Autumn 1980, pp. 66–80. Univ. of Wisconsin.

Evaluation. Vijay Sathe. *Controllership in Divisionalized Firms: Structure, Evaluation and Development,* 1978, pp. 25–30. MB.

Evaluation of Organizational Activities. Rekha Agarwala-Rogers, Janet K. Alexander. *Management Principles for Nonprofit Agencies and Organizations,* 1979, pp. 535–559. Stanford Univ.

Listening to the Customer. James L. Hayes. MRev., Sept. 1980, pp. 2–3.

Performance Measurement and Control: Try Two Approaches. Peter M. Ginter, Andrew C. Rucks. HSM, Oct. 1977, pp. 1–3,5. Univ. of Arkansas, U.S. Army Concepts Analysis Agency.

Selecting Criteria for Measuring and Controlling Hospital Costs. Debra Ann Cohn, Walter Danco. HSM, April 1979, pp. 6–8. Hospital Administrative Services.

Self-Scoring Profiles of Organizational Characteristics. Dudley Bennett. *Successful Team Building Through TA,* 1980, pp. 46–82. MCM Consultants Inc.

ORIENTATION

Breaking in the New Employee. Dell Lebo. HSM, June 1978, pp. 1–2, 8. Child Guidance Clinic.

Hewlett-Packard's Supervisory Orientation Program. Mary Etta Port. Pers., July–Aug. 1977, pp. 73–77. Hewlett-Packard Co.

Keys to Enhancing System Development Productivity. William F. Zachmann. 1981, 52 pp. International Data Corp.

Launching the New Employee. SS, November 1981, 24 pp.

New Employee Orientation. James F. Evered. *Shirt-Sleeves Management,* 1981, pp. 59–63. Redman Industries, Inc.

New-Employee Orientation: How to Ease Their Way. Joan Holland. HSM, Jan. 1979, pp. 4–5. Lenox Hill Hospital.

Orientation and the Hiring Process. Arthur Sondak, Donna Bouvier. 1978. (Extension Institute Cassette Program) By purchase only.

Orientation of the New Employee. Paul E. Illman. *Developing Overseas Managers— and Managers Overseas,* 1980, pp. 189–203. Management Training, Inc.

Orientation Training. Judith J. Howe. *Training for Retail Sales and Profit,* 1981, pp. 52–81. Retail Resources, Inc.

A Socialization Process That Helps New Recruits Succeed. Daniel C. Feldman. Pers., March–April 1980, pp. 11–23. Northwestern Univ.

PACKAGING

How to Improve Packaging Costs. Edmund A. Leonard, 1981. 67 pp. General Foods Corp.

Key Social Issues for Packaging in the 1980s. David J. Freiman (editor). 1980, 36 pp. Imperial Knife Associated Cos., Inc. MB.

Managing the Packaging Side of the Business. Edmund A. Leonard. 1977, 50 pp. General Foods Corp. MB.

Packaging: Is Yours Doing the Right Job for Your Product? Robert E. Lee. MRev., Nov. 1978, pp. 51–55. Lee & Young Communications, Inc.

The Vital Signs of Effective Packaging Management. David B. Lansdale. 1978, 42 pp. Scott Paper Co. MB.

PACKAGING DESIGN AND MERCHANDISING

Graphics Development. Edmund A. Leonard. *Managing the Packaging Side of the Business,* 1977, pp. 33–39. General Foods Corp. MB.

Self-Selling Package Design. R. Overlock Howe. MRev., April 1978, pp. 31–32. Overlock Howe & Co.

PARTICIPATIVE MANAGEMENT. See also Management by Objectives

Awakening a Sleeping Giant ... Ford's Employee Involvement Program. Gerard Tavernier. MRev., June 1981, pp. 15–20.

Building a Democratic Work Group. Leland P. Bradford, Ronald Lippitt. *Human Resources Management: The Past is Prologue,* 1979, pp. 148–160.

Building a Workable Participative Management System. Philip A. Davis. MRev., March 1981 pp. 26–28, 37–39. General Electric Co.

Capitalizing on Group Decision-Making. James R. Emshoff. *Managerial Breakthroughs: Action Techniques for Strategic Change,* 1980, pp. 106–129. Campbell Soup Co.

Codetermination: West Germany's Concept of Industrial Democracy. Herbert G. Hicks. *The Evolving Science of Management,* 1979, pp. 457–474. Louisiana State Univ. College.

Consensus Management at Graphic Controls. William F. Dowling. OD, Winter 1977, pp. 22–47. (Also in reprint collection *Organizational Development: Theory and Practice,* 1977).

Consultative Supervision and Management. H. H. Carey. *Human Resources Management: The Past Is Prologue,* 1979, pp. 137–147.

Conversation with Warren Bennis. William Dowling (editor). *Effective Management and the Behavioral Sciences,* 1978, pp. 265–284.

Do Supervisors Thrive in Participative Work Systems? Richard E. Walton, Leonard Schlesinger. OD, Winter 1979, pp. 25–38. Harvard Univ.

Employee Participation Can Mean Increased Employee Satisfaction. David S. Davidson. SM, Feb. 1979, pp. 33–36. IT&T.

Giving Our Nurses the Responsibility They Want. Nicholas Parlette, Joan Bloom, Charles O'Reilly. HSM, Feb. 1981, pp. 4–5. Univ. of California.

Jingshen. James L. Hayes. MRev., March 1978, pp. 2–3.

Management By Whom? Trends in Participative Management. Kenneth A. Kovach, Ben F. Sands, William W. Brooks. AMJ, Winter 1981, pp. 4–14. George Mason Univ.

Management's Role in Fostering Industrial Participation. R. H. Pedler. *Management Education in the 80's,* 1979, pp. 121–124.

Multiple Management. Daniel H. Dudek. AMJ, Spring 1979, pp. 26–31. McCormick & Co.

Participative Management at Motorola—the Results. Walter B. Scott. MRev., July 1981, pp. 26–28.

Participative Management: What Is the Right Level? John R. Turney, Stanley L. Cohen. MRev., Oct. 1980, pp. 66–69. U.S. Office of Personnel Management.

Participative Problem Solving: How to Increase Organizational Effectiveness. Sidney P. Rubinstein. Pers., Jan.–Feb. 1977, pp. 30–39.

Participatory Management: An Alternative in Human Service Delivery Systems. Kenneth P. Fallon, Jr. *Managing Nonprofit Organizations,* 1977, pp. 244–251. Panhandle Child Development Assn.

Planning By Consensus—A Participative Approach to Planning. Jacob Naor. AMJ, Autumn 1978, pp. 40–47. Univ. of Maine.

Quality Circles: A Team Approach to Problem Solving. Frank M. Gryna, Jr. 1981, 96 pp. Bradley Univ. RS.

Searching for an Alternative Management Style. J. Louis Alpinieri, Don Yates. MRev., Jan. 1980, pp. 25–28, 37–39. Acurex Corp.

Semi-Autonomous Work Groups: An Alternative in Organizing Production Work? Panagiotis N. Fotilas. MRev., July 1981, pp. 50–54. Freie Univ. W. Berlin.

Too Much Management, Too Little Change. Leo B. Moore. *The Amazing Oversight: Total Participation for Productivity,* 1979, pp. 84–101. MIT.

What the Supervisor Should Know About Participative Management. Robert H. Keppler. SM, May 1978, pp. 34–40. PA International Management Consultants.

PENSIONS

Accounting Rules for Pension Plans: FASB Statements No. 35 and 36. Alex T. Arcady, Gary W. Burns. CR, Third Quarter 1981, pp. 39–45. Ernst & Whinney.

Controlling the Costs of Retirement Income and Medical Care Plans. Philip M. Alden, Jr. 1980, 78 pp. Towers, Perrin, Forster & Crosby. MB.

Do's and Don'ts of Pension Fund Management. Ned Merkle. 1981, 55 pp. E. A. Merkle & Associates. MB.

Help for Small Pension-Plan Sponsors. Robert Krogman. MRev., March 1980, pp. 25–28.

Master Trust: Simplifying Employee Benefits Trust Fund Administration. Michael L Costa. 1980, 213 pp. Citibank.

New Retirement Plan Lets Employees Choose Their Own Investments. Mary Zippo. Pers., Sept.–Oct. 1980, pp. 45–47.

Pensions in the Boardroom. Ernest C. Miller. Pers., Sept.–Oct. 1978, pp. 48–49.

Responsibility and Liability in the Age of ERISA. Daniel C. Knickerbocker, Jr. PA #68, 1978, 48 pp. John Hancock Mutual Life Insurance Co. By purchase only.

Should Your Pension Fund Settle for a Tie? It Probably Can Do Better. Thomas C. Noddings. MRev., Aug. 1979, pp. 34–35.

Simplified Employee Pensions: A Retirement Alternative for Small Organizations. Stephen A. Rubenfeld, Michael Byerly. CR, Fourth Quarter 1981, pp. 25–33. Univ of Minnesota, Peat, Marwick, Mitchell & Co.

The Social Security Act—Then and Now. Pers., July–Aug. 1979, pp. 45–49.

What Management Should Know About Reporting and Disclosure Under ERISA. Ronald H. Wohl, Richard T. Griffin. AMJ, Autumn 1978, pp. 30–39. R. H. Wohl & Associates, William M. Mercer, Inc.

PERFORMANCE APPRAISAL. See also Coaching and Counseling, Management Development

Apples and Oranges: Salary Review and Performance Review. M. E. Schnake. SM, Nov. 1980, pp. 32–36. Mississippi State Univ.

Appraisal and Career-Counseling Interviews: Productive Interviewing No. 3 (sec. ed.). Don Faber. 1981. (AMACOM audio cassette) By purchase only.

The Appriasal Interview Guide. Robert G. Johnson. 1979, 122 pp. Learning Technology, Inc.

The Appraisal of Managerial Performance. Arthur Meidan. 1981, 60 pp. Sheffield Univ., England.

Appraisals. Stanley B. Henrici. *Salary Management for the Nonspecialist,* 1980, pp. 141–157. Heinz, U.S.A.

Appraising Appraisal: Ten Lessons from Research for Practice. Marshall Sashkin. OD, Winter 1981. pp. 37–50. Univ. of Maryland.

Constructing Your Criticism. Bernard Weiss. SM, May 1981, pp. 12–18. Bernard Weiss & Associates.

Developing Valid Employee Appraisal Systems. Ken Thompson, Ann Marie Wesley. HSM, April 1980, pp. 5–7, 10. Univ. of Notre Dame.

A Different Use of Performance Appraisal: Evaluating the Boss. Gerald W. Bush, John W. Stinson. MRev., Nov. 1980, pp. 14–17. Gulf Oil Corp.

Documenting Employee Performance. Michael Smith. SM, Sept. 1979, pp. 30–37. Research-Cottrell.

Establishing Standards and Assessing Employee Performance. Louis V. Imundo. *The Effective Supervisor's Handbook,* 1980, pp. 184–202. Management Perspectives.

Evaluating and Improving Job Performance. Ray A. Killian. *Managers Must Lead!* (rev. ed.), 1979, pp. 173–186. Belk Stores.

Evaluating Subordinates: How Subjective Are You? Robert R. Bell. AMJ, Winter 1979, pp. 36–44. Tennessee Technological Univ. (Also in reprint collection *Leadership on the Job: Guides to Good Supervision* (third ed.), 1981)

Evaluating the Superior Employee. T. J. Halatin. SM, Dec. 1981, pp. 17–20. Southwest Texas State Univ.

Feedback Mechanism. Jack M. Hofkosh. HSM, Jan. 1979, pp. 9–10. Institute of Rehabilitation Medicine.

For Managers in New Jobs: An Accountability and Appraisal System. David Lyman, Fred Luthans, Nancy Carter. MRev., Jan. 1980, pp. 46–51. Pizza Hut, Inc., Univ. of Nebraska.

How to Appraise the Performance of your Personnel Accurately and Successfully. William A. Cohen. *Principles of Technical Management,* 1980, pp. 115–131. California State Univ.

How to Conduct a Performance Review. ES, April 1979, 16 pp.

How to Evaluate Performance and Assess Potential. Robert A. Moskowitz. 1979. (Extension Institute Cassette Program) By purchase only.

How to Make Performance Appraisals More Effective. Robert C. Ford, Kenneth M. Jennings. Pers., March–April 1977, pp. 51–56.

How to Measure Work By Professionals. David V. Mollenhoff. MRev., Nov. 1977, pp. 39–43.

The Impact of EEO Legislation on Performance Appraisals. Dena B. Schneirer. Pers., July–Aug. 1978, pp. 24–34. Montgomery Community College.

In Praise of Appraisal. James W. Steele. AMJ, Summer 1981. pp. 12–18. Personnel Systems and Development Co.

Increasing the Validity of Ability Measures. Benjamin Schneider. Pers., May–June 1978, pp. 62–69. Univ. of Maryland.

Keys to Effective Appraisal. Richard J. Mayer. MRev., June 1980, pp. 60–62. Battelle Memorial Institute.

Let's Talk: Discussing Job Performance. Edward L. Levine. SM, Oct. 1980, pp. 25–34. Univ. of South Florida. (Also in reprint collection *Let's Talk: The Art of One-to-One Communication,* 1981)

Managing Compensation and Performance Appraisal Under the Age Act. Samuel T. Beacham. MRev., Jan. 1979, pp. 51–54. Towers, Perrin, Forster, & Crosby.

MBO: Useful in Establishing a Merit Appraisal System. Richard K. Murray. HSM, Feb. 1977, pp. 1–5. Henry Ford Hospital.

Measurement and Evaluation. Lawrence B. Sawyer. *The Manager and the Modern Internal Auditor: A Problem-Solving Partnership,* 1979, pp. 187–207.

Measuring Managers. Harold Koontz, Heinz Weihrich. 1981. (AMACOM audio cassette) By purchase only.

More Bias in Performance Evaluation? Michael C. Gallagher. Pers., July–Aug. 1978, pp. 35–40. Southwest Texas State Univ.

Nonevaluative Approaches to Performance Appraisals. Les Wallace. SM, March 1978, pp. 2–9.

Our Hidden Managers ... Why Inept Bosses Are So Hard to Spot. William B. Cash, Jr. MRev., Aug. 1980, pp. 23–26. Travenol Laboratories.

Pay for Performance. Ernest C. Miller. Pers., July–Aug. 1979, pp. 4–11.

Performance Appraisal. Dudley Bennett. *Successful Team Building Through TA,* 1980, pp. 225–243. MCM Consultants Inc.

Performance Appraisal. Paul W. Cummings. *Open Management: Guides to Successful Practice,* 1980, pp. 151–171.

Performance Appraisal: A Human Resource Management System with Productivity Payoffs. Milan Moravec. MRev., June 1981, pp. 51–54. Arabian Bechtel Co. Ltd.

Performance Appraisal: Dilemmas and Possibilities. Michael Beer. OD, Winter 1981, pp. 24–36. Harvard.

Performance Appraisal: Match the Tool to the Task. John D. McMillan, Hoyt W. Doyel. Pers., July–Aug. 1980, pp. 12–20. A. S. Hansen, Inc.

Performance Appraisal Practices. Thomasine Rendero. Pers., Nov.–Dec. 1980, pp. 4–12.

Performance Appraisal: The Legal Implications of Title VII. Gary L. Lubben, Duane E. Thompson, Charles R. Klasson. Pers., May–June 1980, pp. 11–21. Target Stores, Univ. of Iowa.

The Performance Appraisal: The Most Needed and Neglected Supervisory Tool. Raymond A. Binis. SM, Oct. 1978, pp. 12–16.

The Performance Evaluation as Motivating Tool. Melvin E. Schnake. SM, July 1978, pp. 29–32. Illinois State Univ.

Performance Feedback. James F. Evered. *Shirt-Sleeves Management,* 1981, pp. 107–117. Redman Industries, Inc.

Performance Increases. Robert E. Sibson. *Compensation* (rev. ed.), 1981, pp. 111–127. The Sibson Group.

Performance Review: Confronting the Poor Performer. Robert C. McCoy. *Leadership on the Job: Guides to Good Supervision,* 1981, pp. 250–255. Eastern Michigan Univ.

Performance Review: Pitfalls and Possibilities. Peter B. Olney, Jr. *Effective Communication on the Job* (third ed.), 1981, pp. 109–119. Olney Associates.

The Poor Shall Always Be With You. William P. Anthony. *Managing Incompetence,* 1981, pp. 14–32. The Florida State Univ.

A Primer on Performance Appraisals. Denny Williamson. SM, June 1979, pp. 35–37. Seagull Enterprises.

Program for Performance Appraisal. James L. Hayes. 1980. (An AMA multimedia program) By purchase only.

Progress Reviews. Lawrence A. Appley, Keith L. Irons. *Manager Manpower Planning: A Professional Management System,* 1981, pp. 31–40.

Rethinking Present Appraisal Systems. Andrew F. Sikula, John P. Sikula. SM, March 1979, pp. 14–18. Chicago State Univ., Indiana Univ.

The Salesman's Self-Appraisal Chart. Ralph F. Hansen, AMJ, Winter 1980, pp. 16–22.

The Shape of Performance Appraisal in the Coming Decade. Ann M. Morrison, Mary Ellen Kranz. Pers., July–Aug. 1981, pp. 12–22. Center for Creative Leadership.

Something Important Is Missing . . . What We Need to Know About Appraisals. Selig M. Danzig. MRev., Feb. 1980, pp. 20–24. General Electric Co.

The Supervisor's Survival Guide: Using Job Behavior to Measure Employee Performance. Robert E. Pitts, Ken Thompson. SM, Jan. 1979, pp. 23–30. Univ. of Notre Dame. (Also in reprint collection *The Supervisor's Survival Guide,* 1979)

Tailoring Employee Evaluation Forms to Your Organization's Needs. William E. Fulmer. Pers., Jan.–Feb. 1978, pp. 65–72.

Taking the Pain out of Performance Appraisal Interviews. Randall S. Schuler. SM, Aug. 1981, pp. 8–12. Univ. of Maryland.

Thoughts on Criticism. John R. Heron. SM, April 1977, pp. 29–34.

Using Appraisals to Set Objectives. Bob Wooten. SM, Nov. 1981, pp. 30–34. Lemar Univ.

Using Process in Performance Discussions: How to Deal with Feelings and Needs. Arthur M. Cohen. SM, March 1979, pp. 32–36. Institute for Organization Development.

The Voluntary Standards: Opportunity to Sharpen Performance-Based Pay Standards. William L. White. MRev., July 1979, pp. 48–50. The Wyatt Co.

What's Wrong with Performance Evaluation Programs? Arturo A. Jacobs. SM, July 1977, pp. 10–15.

"Who Do You Think You're Talking To?" (The VSA Approach to Performance Analysis and Counseling). Vincent Flowers. SM, March 1977, pp. 14–24.

PERFORMANCE STANDARDS. See also Management by Objectives

Establishing Standards and Assessing Employee Performance. Louis V. Imundo. *The Effective Supervisor's Handbook,* 1980, pp. 184–202. Management Perspectives.

The HRD Manager. William R. Tracey. *Human Resource Development Standards,* 1981, pp. 31–45. U.S. Army Intelligence Training School.

Implementation, Evaluation, and Control. William R. Tracey. *Human Resource Development Standards,* 1981, pp. 528–565. U.S. Army Intelligence Training School.

Making Managers Accountable: Develop Objective Performance Standards. John O. Alexander. MRev., Dec. 1980, pp. 43–46. John Alexander Associates.

Measuring Performance in Human Service Systems. James F. Budde. 1979, 207 pp. Univ. of Kansas.

Performance Lies Are Hazardous to Organizational Health. Lee T. Perry, Jay B. Barney. OD, Winter 1981, pp. 68–80. UCLA.

Position Description for a Board of Directors. J. Keith Louden. *Managing at the Top,* 1977, pp. 146–159. Corporate Director, Inc.

Standards for the Professional Practice of Internal Auditing (Appendix B). Lawrence B. Sawyer. *The Manager and the Modern Internal Auditor: A Problem-Solving Partnership,* 1979, pp. 433–447.

Standards of Performance. Lawrence A. Appley, Keith L. Irons. *Manager Manpower Planning: A Professional Management System,* 1981, pp. 19–30.

Telling Subordinates What to Do and How to Do It. Jack W. English, Jay I. Gottesman. SM, July 1979, pp. 21–24. Mobil Oil Corp., Stevens Institute of Technology.

Using Performance Standards for Employee Development. Paul H. Pickering. HSM, Jan. 1980, pp. 6–7. Appalachian Regional Hospitals.

Using Results To Rate Performance. Jack W. English, Jay I. Gottesman. HSM, Oct. 1980, pp. 7–8. Mobil Oil Corp., Stevens Institute of Technology.

PERSONAL AFFAIRS. See also Career Management

The ABC's of Real Estate Investing. William Waters. SM, Nov. 1981, pp. 40–41. Merrill Lynch, Pierce, Fenner & Smith, Inc.

Building Wealth: A Layman's Guide to Trust Planning. Adam Starchild. 1981, 224 pp. Minerva Consulting Group Inc.

Estate Planning. Karl G. Pearson. MRev., Nov. 1977, pp. 34–35. Univ. of Michigan.

Estate Planning—After the 1976 Tax Reform Law. Edward E. Milam, D. Larry Crumbley. 1978, 230 pp. Univ. of Mississippi, Texas A & M Univ.

The Executive's Guide to Personal Financial Management. Frederick S. Brown, 1977. (Extension Institute Cassette Program) By purchase only.

Guide for Mail Order Shoppers. Carol O'Rourke. SM, July 1981, pp. 42–44. Merrill Lynch, Pierce, Fenner & Smith, Inc.

How to Plan and Track Your Personal Finances. H. Moore. 1980. (An AMACOM Evaluation Tool) By purchase only.

How to Succeed in Business and Marriage. Richard W. Ogden. 1978, 161 pp. Seminole Manufacturing Co.

How to Take Control of Your Personal Finances. ES, Sept. 1979, 16 pp.

Management and Marriage—Push and Shove. John W. Coumbe. AMJ, Summer 1978, pp. 32–39. Loren L. Law & Associates.

Money: How to Get It, Keep It, and Make It Grow. Michael Hayes. 1979, 214 pp. Registered Investment Adviser.

Money Sense: Solving the Financial Puzzle. John L. Steffens. SM, Jan. 1981, pp. 42–43. Merrill Lynch, Pierce, Fenner & Smith Inc.

Personal Financial Planning (third ed.). John T. Lyons, Joseph E. Finnerty. 1981. (Extension Institute Course) By purchase only.

Setting and Achieving Personal Goals. David V. Lewis. 1977. (Extension Institute Cassette Program) By purchase only.

Stock Market Forecasting for Alert Investors. John C. Touhey, 1980, 184 pp.

Tax Sales: Potential Bargains for Bidders. John L. Steffens. SM, Nov. 1979, pp. 36–38. Merrill Lynch, Pierce, Fenner & Smith Inc.

Two Careers—One Marriage. William M. Jones, Ruth A. Jones. 1980, 229 pp. Univ. of Missouri.

Your Money & Your Life: How to Plan Your Long-Range Financial Security. C. Colburn Hardy. 1979, 340 pp.

Your Personal Management: A Guide to Sound Securities Investment. S. Scott Massin. SM, March 1980. pp. 37–39. Illinois State Univ.

Your Personal Management. Is a Stutz Bearcat Your Idea of an Investment? John L. Steffens. SM, Jan. 1980, pp. 39–41. Merrill Lynch, Pierce, Fenner & Smith Inc.

PERSONNEL MANAGEMENT. See Human Resources Management

PERSONNEL TESTING. See Testing—Personnel

PLANNING. See also Budgeting, Financial Management, Forecasting Methods, Management by Objectives, Manpower Planning, Organization, Product Development, Scheduling Techniques

Action Planning. *Managing Industrial Energy Conservation,* 1977, pp. 32–45. MB.

Action Plans That Get Results. William F. Christopher. *Management for the 1980's* (rev. ed.—former title: *The Achieving Enterprise*), 1980, pp. 99–112.

An Administrator's Manual of Planning. Finn E. Jerstad. *Corporate Planning Techniques and Applications,* 1979, pp. 251–259. Bayly, Martin & Fay AS Scandinavia.

Analysis of the Business Environment. Eli Segev. MRev., Aug. 1979, pp. 58–61. Leon Recanati Graduate School, Tel Aviv.

Basics of Successful Business Planning. William R. Osgood. 1980, 252 pp.

A Case History of Strategic Planning. Milton Leontiades. *Corporate Planning Techniques and Applications,* 1979, pp. 200–210. Rutgers Univ.

The Chief Executive's Strategic Role and Responsibilities. Richard F. Neuschel. PA #65, 1977, 47 pp. McKinsey & Co., Inc. By purchase only.

Coming to Grips with Crisis. Charles G. Newton, Jr. PA #76, 1981, 47 pp. Ruder & Finn, Inc. By purchase only.

Contingency Planning. Joan Knutson, Layne Alexander. 1981. (Extension Institute Course) By purchase only.

Contingency Plans and Backup. Norman L. Enger, Paul W. Howerton. *Computer Security: A Management Audit Approach,* 1980, pp. 211–221. Applied Management Systems Inc., American Univ.

Conversation: An Interview with Patrick E. Haggerty. OD, Spring 1978, pp. 38–56.

Corporate Planning Techniques and Applications. Robert J. Allio, Malcolm W. Pennington (editors). 1979, 436 pp. Arthur D. Little; Golightly & Co.

Developing a Plan. William R. Osgood. *Basics of Successful Business Management,* 1981, pp. 13–28.

Developing the Business Plan for a Small Business. Bruce M. Bradway, Robert E. Pritchard. 1980, 50 pp. Glassboro State College. MB.

Diagramming GE's Planning for What's Watt. Michael G. Allen. *Corporate Planning Techniques and Applications,* 1979, pp. 211–220. General Electric.

Don't Fret, Look Ahead. James L. Hayes. MRev., Aug. 1977. pp. 2–3.

EDP Planning. Michael R. Frank. *The Effective EDP Manager,* 1980, pp. 143–160. Taubman Co., Inc.

EDP Planning. Michael R. Frank. *How to Organize the EDP Department,* 1980, pp. 36–47. MB.

The Entrepreneur: A Corporate Strategy for the 80's. Donald J. Taffi. 1981, 44 pp. The Donalen Group, Inc. MB.

Essentials of Mission. John D. Millett. *Management, Governance & Leadership: A Guide for College and University Administrators,* 1980, pp. 55–84. Academy for Educational Development.

Evaluating Corporate Planning. Robert J. Thierauf. *Management Auditing: A Questionnaire Approach,* 1980, pp. 35–58. Xavier Univ.

The Evolution of Management Strategy at General Electric. Reginald H. Jones. *The Evolving Science of Management,* 1979, pp. 313–326. General Electric Co.

Examination of a Strategy Failure. Melvin E. Salveson. *Corporate Planning Techniques and Applications,* 1979, pp. 193–199. Corporate Strategies Institute.

An Example of Long-Range Goal Setting. Joseph J. Famularo. *Organization Planning Manual* (rev. ed.), 1979, pp. 355–361. McGraw-Hill, Inc.

Financial Goals and Strategic Planning. Cosmo S. Trapani. 1981. (Extension Institute Course) By purchase only.

Formulating and Implementing a More Systematic Approach to Strategic Management. J. Kreiken. MRev., July 1980, pp. 24–28, 38–39. THT Univ. of Technology Twente, The Netherlands.

The Frontiers of Strategic Planning: Intuition or Formal Models. Harold W. Fox. MRev., April 1981, pp. 8–14. Ball State Univ.

The Galloping Cyberneticist. Robert J. Allio. *Corporate Planning Techniques and Applications,* 1979. pp. 377–384. Arthur D. Little, Inc.

Get Your Act Together—Growth Begins in Your Head. Mack Hanan. *Fast-Growth Management: How to Improve Profits with Entrepreneurial Strategies,* 1979, pp. 13–30. The Wellspring Group.

Getting the Power to Plan. Pamela Shea Cuming, William T. Bechard. *Corporate Planning Techniques and Applications,* 1979, pp. 345–350. Dialectics Inc.

Goal Setting. William C. Waddell. *Overcoming Murphy's Law,* 1981, pp. 122–143. California State Univ., Los Angeles.

Goals. Clair F. Vough, Bernard Asbell. *Productivity: A Practical Program for Improving Efficiency,* (rev. ed.—former title: *Tapping the Human Resource: A Strategy for Productivity*), 1979, pp. 134–142. Productivity Research International, Inc.

The "How" of Strategic Planning. George A. Steiner. 1978, (AMACOM audio cassette) By purchase only.

How to Develop a Strategy and a Plan for Your Organization. William C. Waddell. *Overcoming Murphy's Law,* 1981, pp. 144–174. California State Univ., Los Angeles.

How to Integrate New Environmental Forces into Strategic Planning. Harold E. Klein, William H. Newman. MRev., July 1980, pp. 40–48. Columbia Univ.

How to Make Marketing Plans More Effective. Daniel T. Carroll, MRev., Oct. 1979, pp. 60–62, Gould Inc.

How to Use Environmental Analysis in Strategy Making. Eli Segev. MRev., March 1977, pp. 4–13. Tel-Aviv Univ.

How to Use Planning Techniques. ES, Feb. 1980, 16 pp.

Implementation and Supportive Planning. Victor Z. Brink. *Understanding Management Policy & Making It Work,* 1978, pp. 95–111. Columbia Univ.

An Interview with George Odiorne. Frank E. Kuzmits. SM, August 1978, pp. 10–17. Atlanta Univ.

Interviewing Professor Mintzberg's "Right Brain." Robert J. Allio. *Corporate Planning Techniques and Applications,* 1979, pp. 385–392. Arthur D. Little, Inc.

Is the Annual Planning Cycle Really Necessary? William F. Christopher. MRev., Aug. 1981, pp. 38–42.

Long-Range Planning. Roy A. Lindberg. 1979. (Extension Institute Course) By purchase only.

Long-Range Planning. Harold Smiddy. *The Evolving Science of Management,* 1979, pp. 81–103.

Long-Range Planning: Key to the Future. ES, March 1981, 16 pp.

Macroeconomics and Company Planning (sec. ed.). Bradley A. Latham, 1977. (Extension Institute Course) By purchase only.

The Malaise of Strategic Planning. J. Quincy Hunsicker. MRev., March 1980, pp. 8–14. McKinsey & Co.

Management Awareness Strategies. Preston P. Le Breton. *The Evolving Science of Management,* 1979, pp. 415–437. Univ. of Washington.

Management Guidelines; The Art of Planning. George Miller. SM, May 1981, pp. 24–31. George Miller Associates.

Managerial Planning: Back to Basics. Louis A. Allen. MRev., April 1981, pp. 15–20. Louis A. Allen Associates, Inc.

Managing for the Upbeat. James L. Hayes. MRev., July 1980, pp. 2–3.

A Marketing Plan to Ensure Your Success. William A. Cohen, Marshall E. Reddick. *Successful Marketing for Small Business.* 1981, pp. 251–260. California State Univ.

Marketing Strategy: How to Beat Your Competition. William A. Cohen, Marshall E. Reddick. *Successful Marketing for Small Business,* 1981, pp. 29–44. California State Univ.

Matching Action Plans to Market Development Stage. Peter P. Pekar. *Corporate Planning Techniques and Applications,* 1979, pp. 153–159. Quaker Oats.

Measuring Performance in Human Service Systems. James F. Budde. 1979, 207 pp. Univ. of Kansas.

Mission—An Iterative Process. William F. Christopher. *Management for the 1980's* (rev. ed.—former title: *The Achieving Enterprise*), 1980, pp. 84–98.

Plan, Then Expand. John L. Ryan. HSM, Jan, 1981, pp. 12–14. Ryan Advisors, Inc.

The Planner Minding the Store. Robert M. Randall, Robert J. Allio. *Corporate Planning Techniques and Applications,* 1979, pp. 393–401. Lederle Laboratories, Arthur D. Little, Inc.

Planning. Maurice R. Hecht. *What Happens in Management,* 1980, pp. 82–112. Helmsman Management Associates Ltd.

Planning. Lawrence B. Sawyer. *The Manager and the Modern Internal Auditor: A Problem-Solving Partnership,* 1979, pp. 243–280.

Planning. William R. Tracey. *Human Resource Development Standards.* 1981 pp. 46–63. U.S. Army Intelligence Training School.

Planning: A Management Framework. William R. Osgood. *Basics of Successful Business Management,* 1981, pp. 3–12.

Planning and Budgeting: Important Tools for the Healthcare Manager. John D. Proe. HSM, Nov. 1979, pp. 8–9. Mark Silber Associates.

Planning and Control for Managers (sec. ed.). Peter B. Venuto. 1979. (Extension Institute Course) By purchase only.

Planning as a Fundamental Component of Managing. Harold Smiddy. *The Evolving Science of Management,* 1979, pp. 68–80.

Planning at the Center. Robert J. Allio. *Corporate Planning Techniques and Applications,* 1979, pp. 402–410. Arthur D. Little, Inc.

Planning: Establishing and Working Toward Dynamic Objectives. Harold Smiddy. *The Evolving Science of Management,* 1979, pp. 104–111.

Planning for Extinction. Robert Hershey. MRev., Sept. 1978, pp. 27–28, 38–40. U.S. Merchant Marine Academy.

Planning for Nonplanners: Planning Basics for Managers. Darryl J. Ellis, Perer P. Pekar, Jr. 1980, 152 pp. Resource Technology Development Corp., Michael Allen Co.

Planning for Profit. Bradley T. Gale. *Corporate Planning Techniques and Applications,* 1979, pp. 160–171. Strategic Planning Institute.

Planning: Part I. James L. Kammert. *International Commerical Banking Management,* 1981, pp. 51–112. Equibank.

Planning: The Key to Top Performance. William C. Waddell. *Overcoming Murphy's Law,* 1981, pp. 1–13. California State Univ., Los Angeles.

Preparing a Public Relations Program. Gerald J. Voros, Paul Alvarez (editors). *What Happens in Public Relations,* 1981, pp. 11–23. Ketchum MacLeod & Grove.

Putting It All Together. William E. Rothschild. 1981. (AMACOM audio cassette book) By purchase only.

A Rational Approach to Office Planning. M. Arthur Gensler, Jr., Peter B. Brandt. 1978, 52 pp. Gensler Associates. MB.

Report Card for Planners. Harold W. Henry. *Corporate Planning Techniques and Applications,* 1979, pp. 172–181. Univ. of Tennessee.

Responsibilities of Corporate Planning—A Checklist. Donald R. Schoen. MRev., March 1977, pp. 26–27. Philips Medical Systems, Inc.

Revamping Planning for This Era of Discontinuity. Michael J. Kami. *Corporate Planning Techniques and Applications,* 1979, pp. 147–152. Corporate Planning Inc.

Setting Objectives for the Future—Immediate and Long-Range. Ken Thompson. HSM, Dec. 1979, pp. 8–9. Univ. of Notre Dame.

Stepping Up to Supervision: Planning for Success. H. Kent Baker, Stevan H. Holmberg. SM, Nov. 1981, pp. 12–18. The American Univ.

Strategic Alternatives: Selection, Development and Implementation. William E. Rothschild, 1979, 242 pp. General Electric.

Strategic Planning and Sensitivity Analysis. Robert E. Pritchard, Thomas J. Hindelang. *The Strategic Evaluation and Management of Capital Expenditures,* 1981, pp. 183–210. Glassboro State College, Drexel Univ.

Strategic Planning Approach to Resource Allocation. Victor Weintraub. AMJ, Summer 1979, pp. 47–54.

Strategic Planning for Information Resource Management. Michael Ebenstein, Leonard I. Krauss. MRev., June 1981, pp. 21–26. Macmillan, Inc.; Ernst & Whinney.

Strategic Planning—Getting the Jump on Competition. Gerald R. Hildebrandt. DM, Nov. 1981, pp. 1–5. Gerald R. Hildebrandt Associates.

Strategic Planning in Nonprofit Organizations. William R. King. *Management Principles for Nonprofit Agencies and Organizations,* 1979, pp. 340–362. Univ. of Pittsburgh.

Strategic Planning in State Government. Michael J. Howlett. *Managing Nonprofit Organizations,* 1977, pp. 124–137.

Strategic Planning ... No Sure Cure for Corporate Surprises. Edward C. Schleh. MRev., March 1979, pp. 54–57. Schleh Associates.

Strategic Planning: Off-Limits for Financial Managers? Richard F. Schmidt. MRev., June 1979, pp. 7–12. Dun & Bradstreet.

Strategic Planning: The Future as a Journey, Not a Destination. William S. Cook. MRev., May 1980, pp. 29,34. Union Pacific Corp.

Strategic Plans: Made to Be Broken? John C. Faulkner. MRev., April 1979, pp. 21–25. Case & Co.

Strategic Thinking: Key to Corporate Survival. Benjamin B. Tregoe, John W. Zimmerman. MRev., Feb. 1979, pp. 8–14. Kepner-Tregoe, Inc.

Strategies. Houston G. Elam, Norton Paley. *Marketing for the Non-Marketing Executive,* 1978, pp. 153–237. Montclair (N.J.) State College, John Wiley & Sons.

Systematic Processes Applied to Health Care Planning. Owen B. Hardy. *Managing Nonprofit Organizations,* 1977, pp. 78–94. Medicus Planning, Inc.

Systems Planning Tomorrow's Hospitals Today. William G. Akula, Jay A. Vora. *Managing Nonprofit Organizations,* 1977, pp. 118–123. Univ. of Bridgeport.

Tax Strategy for Multinationals—Economic and Social Issues. John Chown, John Humble. 1979, 30 pp. J. F. Chown & Co., Ltd. MB.

There's No Room for Guesswork at IBM. Abraham Katz. *Corporate Planning Techniques and Applications,* 1979, pp. 221–230. IBM.

Time for a Turnaround? Take Comfort, Take Stock, Take Action. Carl Remick. AMJ, Autumn 1980, pp. 4–15.

Using a Team Approach to Market-Oriented Planning. Arnold Corbin. MRev., June 1977, pp. 9–15. (Reprinted in *Marketing in Nonprofit Organizations,* 1978) New York Univ.

Why Planning Has Failed and What Can You Do About It? Malcolm W. Pennington. *Corporate Planning Techniques and Applications,* 1979, pp. 266–270. The Marketing and Planning Group.

PLANT AND EQUIPMENT

How Corning Designed a "Talking" Building to Spur Productivity. David E. Leibson. MRev., Sept. 1981, pp. 8–13. Corning Glass Works.

Robots: New Faces on the Production Line. Carl Remick. MRev., May 1979, pp. 24–28, 38–39.

Robotics in Practice: Management and Applications of Industrial Robots. Joseph F. Engelberger. 1980, 291 pp. Unimation Inc.

Three Forces Changing American Industrial-Facilities Design. John G. Phelan. MRev., Aug. 1978, pp. 31–33. Fletcher-Thompson, Inc.

Three Great Dangers in Plant-Site Selection—And How to Avoid Them. Richard L Wilson. MRev., Aug. 1978, pp. 31–32. Fletcher-Thompson, Inc.

Four Ways to Stretch Your Facilities Dollars. Stephen P. Kaufman, Richard O. Galberaith. MRev., Aug. 1978, pp. 8–16.

The New Plant Revolution. Edward E. Lawler, III. OD, Winter 1978, pp. 2–12.

Optimizing Organization-Plant Design: A Complementary Structure for Technical and Social Systems. Louis E. Davis. OD, Autumn 1979, pp. 3–15. Univ. of California, Los Angeles.

POLICIES

Changing Ground Rules for the CEO. T. Mitchell Ford. AMJ, Autumn 1979, pp. 39–43. Emhart Corp.

Essentials of a Management Personnel Policy. Lawrence A. Appley. *Human Resources Management: The Past Is Prologue,* 1979, pp. 68–76.

How Far Can a Rule Bend? Charles C. Larson, Sheila D. Melville. SM, Dec. 1980, pp. 11–14. Larson Associates, Clinical Management Associates.

Make Policy—Not Decisions. Mack Hanan. *Fast-Growth Management: How to Improve Profits with Entrepreneurial Strategies,* 1979, pp. 33–50. The Wellspring Group.

Policies. William R. Tracey. *Human Resource Development Standards: A Self-Evaluation Manual for HRD Managers and Specialists,* 1981, pp. 56–57. U.S. Army Intelligence Training School.

Policy Statements (125) Part III. Joseph J. Famularo. *Organization Planning Manual* (rev. ed.), 1979, pp. 315–354. McGraw-Hill, Inc.

Public Policy Considerations. Susan W. Woolston. *Public Technology: Key to Improved Government Productivity,* 1981, pp. 8–22.

Salary Policy. Stanley B. Henrici. *Salary Management for the Nonspecialist,* 1980, pp. 9–29. Heinz, U.S.A.

Setting Up an Effective Policies and Procedures System. Roger W. Blackburn. HSM, Aug. 1979, pp. 8–10. The Toledo Hospital.

The Size Factor in Implementing Personnel Policies (Appendix II). Robert L. Desatnick. *The Expanding Role of the Human Resources Manager,* 1979, pp. 206–217, McDonald's Corp.

Understanding Management Policy & Making It Work. Victor Z. Brink. 1978, 312 pp. Columbia Univ.

POLLUTION CONTROL

Case Study 3: Development of an Improved Technology for Determining Coliform Levels in Water. G. Wade Miller, Arleigh Markham. *Public Technology: Key to Improved Government Productivity,* 1981, pp. 191–200. SMC-Martin Consulting Engineers, Public Technology, Inc.

Case Study 4. The People Equation: Solution to the Solid Waste Problem in Little Rock. James F. Lynch. *Public Technology: Key to Improved Government Productivity,* 1981, pp. 201–209, J. F. Associates.

The Environment. Glenn T. Seaborg. *Making Successful Presentations,* 1981, pp. 234–242. U.S. Atomic Energy Commission.

Managing Packaging Wastes in the 1980s. David J. Freiman. *Key Social Issues for Packaging in the 1980s,* 1980, pp. 27–36. Imperial Knife Associates Cos., Inc.

Pollution Control: Where Do We Go from Here? John E. Schork. MRev., March 1981, pp. 32–33. Research-Cottrell, Inc.

PRESIDENT'S JOB

A Better Approach: Situation-Oriented, Interchangeable CEOs. I. Robert Parket. AMJ, Summer 1977, pp. 14–25. Baruch College.

Bringing Personnel Administration Closer to the President. Ewing W. Reilley. *Human Resources Management: The Past Is Prologue,* 1979, pp. 227–239.

CEO Can Control the Corporate Environment. Henry O. Golightly. MRev., Jan. 1980, pp. 30–31. Golightly & Co.

The CEO Faces Retirement. Henry M. Wallfesh. PA #69, 1978, 34 pp. Cox Broadcasting Corp. By purchase only.

Changing Ground Rules for the CEO. T. Mitchell Ford. *Making Successful Presentations,* 1981, pp. 164–167. Emhart Corp.

The Chief Executive's Strategic Role and Responsibilities. Richard F. Neuschel. PA #65, 1977, 47 pp. McKinsey & Co., Inc. By purchase only.

Controlling the Sycophant: Policies and Techniques of Corporation Presidents. Robert P. Newman. AMJ, Autumn 1978, pp. 14–21. Univ. of Pittsburgh.

Conversation with Roy L. Ash. Ernest C. Miller. OD, Autumn 1979, pp. 48–67.

Conversation with Fletcher Byrom. OD, Summer 1978, pp. 37–60.

Euphoria to Reality: The CEO's First 100 Days. Per Berndtson. MRev., June 1979, pp. 29–30. Berndtson International.

How to Make the Presidency Manageable. Peter F. Drucker. *Managing Nonprofit Organizations,* 1977, pp. 280–288. Claremont Univ.

A Letter to Presidents-To-Be. E. Richard Derosa. AMJ, Winter 1979, pp. 58–62. Mission Insurance Group, Inc.

Managing at the Top: Roles and Responsibilities of the Chief Executive Officer. J. Keith Louden. 1977, 159 pp. Corporate Divisions, Inc.

The New Route to the Top. Henry H. Beam. AMJ, Spring 1979, pp. 55–62. Western Michigan Univ.

Pinning the Blame for Strategy Failures on the CEO. Melvin E. Salveson. *Corporate Planning Techniques and Applications,* 1979, pp. 182–192. Corporate Strategies Institute.

Planner at the Helm. Robert J. Allio, Robert M. Randall. *Corporate Planning Techniques and Applications,* 1979, pp. 411–416. Arthur D. Little, Inc., Lederle Laboratories.

The Role of the CEO: Arbitrator, Mediator, or Judge? Steven H. Appelbaum. *Cooperation: An Alternative Management Strategy,* PA #64, 1977, pp. 29–34. St. Peter's College. By purchase only.

Socialization at the Top—How CEO's and Subordinates Evolve Interpersonal Contracts. John J. Gabarro. OD, Winter 1979, pp. 3–23. Harvard Univ.

What Makes a Successful Chief Executive? Herbert T. Mines. SM, May 1978, pp. 11–16. Business Careers, Inc.

PRICING

Cost-Price Signals: A New Stage in the Business Cycle? Geoffrey H. Moore. MRev., Nov. 1977, pp. 9–10. National Bureau of Economic Resources, Inc.

Direct Costs and Product Pricing. William E. Arnstein, Frank Gilabert. *Direct Costing,* 1980, pp. 43–59. Main Hurdman & Cranstoun.

Factoring Inflation into Pricing. C. Daniel Bergfeld. *Strategic Pricing: Protecting Profit Margins from Inflation,* 1981, pp. 35–45. Case and Co.

How to Price for Maximum Profits Without Losing Customers. William A. Cohen, Marshall E. Reddick. *Successful Marketing for Small Business,* 1981, pp. 175–195. California State Univ.

The Market Specification Approach. Attilio Bisio, Lawrence Gastwirt. *Turning Research and Development into Profits,* 1979, pp. 229–251. Exxon Research and Engineering Co., Essochem Europe.

Pricing. William R. Osgood. *Basics of Successful Business Management,* 1981, pp. 137–155.

Pricing and Performance Analysis. Robert A. Peters. *ROI: Practical Theory and Innovative Applications* (rev. ed.), 1979, pp. 91–100. Owens-Illinois Corp.

Pricing Under Inflation. Curtis W. Symonds. *Basic Financial Management* (rev. ed.), 1978, pp. 188–199. Financial Control Associates.

Standardized Normative Pricing of New Products: How JPL Is Forecasting Future Energy Equipment Costs. Robert G. Chamberlain, Robert Bullemer. MRev., June 1978, pp. 23–26. Jet Propulsion Laboratory, Operations Research Society of America.

Strategic Pricing: Protecting Profit Margins from Inflation. C. Daniel Bergfeld. 1981, 48 pp. Case & Co. MB.

Systems Selling Strategies: How to Justify Premium Prices for Commodity Products. Mack Hanan, James Cribbin, Jack Donis. 1978, 193 pp. St. John's Univ.

PROCEDURES. See System Analysis

PRODUCT DEVELOPMENT. See also Budgeting, Research and Development.

Business Diversification: a Strategic Option for U.S. Investor-Owned Utilities. Terry Ferrar. MRev., Nov. 1981, pp. 13–23. Edison Electric Institute.

The Commodity-Premium Scale: A Force in the Development of Successful Strategy. Theodore A. Smith. MRev., Aug. 1979, pp. 9–17. RCA.

Creating Profitable New Products and Markets. Richard H. Corbin, R. Donald Gamache. 1980, 53 pp. Innotech. MB.

Developing a Successful Product Strategy. William A. Cohen, Marshall E. Reddick. *Successful Marketing for Small Business,* 1981, pp. 97–117. California State Univ.

The Dynamics of Product and Process Innovation. Christopher T. Hill, James M. Utterback. MRev., Jan. 1980, pp. 14–20. Massachusetts Institute of Technology.

The Elements of a Venture Analysis. Attilio Bisio, Lawrence Gastwirt. *Turning Research and Development into Profits,* 1979, pp. 134–190. Exxon Research and Engineering Co., Essochem Europe.

Extending Product Life: Time to Remanufacture? Robert T. Lund, W. Michael Denney. MRev., March 1978, pp. 21–26. MIT.

Innovation: The Glamor Strategy. William E. Rothschild. *Strategic Alternatives: Selection, Development and Implementation,* 1979, pp. 123–145. General Electric.

How 3M Develops Entrepreneurial Spirit Throughout the Organization. Lewis W. Lehr. MRev., Oct. 1980, p. 31. 3M Co.

How to Improve Your New Product Success Rate. Richard J. Adamec. MRev., Jan. 1981, pp. 38–42. Dun & Bradstreet, Inc.

Idea Management: How to Motivate Creativity and Innovation. Charles H. Clark. 1980, 56 pp. Yankee Ingenuity Programs. MB.

Key Question for Product Planners: Is It Better to ... Innovate or Imitate? Saul Sands. MRev., Dec. 1979, pp. 44–46. Hofstra Univ.

The Key to New Product Development: Improve the Search Process. Saul Sands. MRev., Feb. 1981, pp. 63–65. Hofstra Univ.

Life-Styled Marketing: How to Position Products for Premium Profits (rev. ed.). Mack Hanan. 1980, 159 pp. Wellspring Group.

The Marketing Manager's Guide to New Product Invention. Alfred Gruber. 1977, 31 pp. Brand, Gruber & Co. MB.

The Need for a Team Approach to Product Planning and Development. Richard H. Corbin. MRev., Sept. 1980, pp. 35–36. Innotech.

New Product Development Strategies. Frederick D. Buggie. 1981, 165 pp. Strategic Innovations.

Product Design and Specification. Fred W. Latham, George S. Sanders. *Urwick, Orr on Management,* 1980, pp. 105–114. Urwick, Orr & Partners.

Product Innovation, Organizational Change, and Risk: A New Perspective. Jacobus T. Severiens. AMJ, Fall 1977, pp. 24–31. Cleveland State Univ.

Product Life-Cycle Strategy: How to Stay on the Growth Curve. Ward C. Smith. MRev., Jan. 1980, pp. 8–13. Corning Medical.

Scorecard for New Products: How to Pick a Winner. E. Bryant Frech. MRev., Feb. 1977, pp. 4–11. Rexham Corp.

PRODUCT LIABILITY

Building a Data-Base Defense Against Product Liability. L. H. Berul. MRev., Nov. 1977. pp. 18–20. Aspen Systems Corp.

The Charge of Product Liability: Building a Strong Case for The Defendant. Mark C. Curran. AMJ, Spring 1978, pp. 4–16. Sidley & Austin.

How to Troubleshoot Your Company and Avoid Product Liability Suits. Richard S. Betterley. MRev., April 1979, pp. 34–35. Betterley Risk Consultants.

Product Liability: How the Courts Stand on "Manufacturers" Malpractice. Irwin Gray. MRev., June 1977, pp. 31–34.

Product Safety in the 1980s. Charles R. Goerth. *Key Social Issues for Packaging in the 1980s,* 1980, pp. 7–17. Dugan, Carey & Goerth. MB.

PRODUCTION MANAGEMENT. See also Maintenance, Materials Management, Plant and Equipment, Quality Control

Do You Have These Operational Problems? Arnold O. Putnam. MRev., Nov. 1980, pp. 18–23. Rath & Strong, Inc.

Evaluating the Manufacturing Function. Robert J. Thierauf. *Management Auditing: A Questionnaire Approach,* 1980, pp. 139–168. Xavier Univ.

How to Audit Operations. J. McConnell. 1980. (An AMACOM Evaluation Tool) By purchase only.

Job Descriptions in Manufacturing Industries. John D. Ulery. 1981, 161 pp. Litton Industries.

Manage Your Plant for Profit and Your Promotion. Richard W. Ogden. 1978, 194 pp. Seminole Manufacturing Co.

Manufacturing Management. William C. Nemitz. 1977. (Extension Institute Course) By purchase only.

Product Stewardship Managers: Constantly Looking for Trouble. MRev., Oct. 1981, pp. 29–31.

Production. Fred W. Latham. George S. Sanders. *Urwick, Orr on Management,* 1980, pp. 115–135. Urwick, Orr & Partners.

Production-Based Strategies. William E. Rothschild. *Strategic Alternatives: Selection Development and Implementation,* 1979, pp. 104–122. General Electric.

The Robot in Industry: Friend or Foe of Workers? Mary Zippo. Pers., Nov.–Dec. 1980, pp. 51–52.

What Happened to Production Management? Merritt L. Kastens. *Redefining the Manager's Job: The Proactive Manager in a Reactive World,* 1980, pp. 164–174.

PRODUCTION PLANNING AND CONTROL. See also Cost Control, Data Processing Materials Management

Downtime Need Not Be Bad—Just Try to Make the Most of It. Sidney S. Smith. MRev., Aug. 1980, pp. 32–33. National Productivity Institute.

How to Get Mass Production Benefits from Small-Lot Output. Dennis Rhodes. MRev., Oct. 1978, pp. 55–56.

Management Giving Production Planning Bigger Role in Shopfloor Operations. Eugene F. Baker. MRev., July 1980, pp. 34–35. The Austin Co.

Planning and Controlling Manufacturing Resources. R. Michael Donovan, Harrison H. Appleby. 1979, 48 pp. Peat, Marwick, Mitchell & Co., Touche Ross & Co. MB.

PRODUCTIVITY

Allowing Productivity to Happen. Frederick W. Harvey. SM, June 1980, pp. 21–25. Frederick Harvey Co.

The Amazing Oversight: Total Participation for Productivity. Ben S. Graham, Jr., Parvin S. Titus. (editors). 1979, 197 pp. Ben Graham Corp., RCA Corp.

American Can's Productivity Efforts Focused on Managers. MRev., March 1981, pp. 29,31.

Awakening a Sleeping Giant ... Ford's Employee Involvement Program. Gerard Tavernier. MRev., June 1981, pp. 15–20.

Background and Overview of Productivity Improvement Programs. John W. Kendrick. *Productivity Improvement: Case Studies of Proven Practice,* 1981, pp. 14–27. George Washington Univ.

Becoming a Textile Exporter Through Productivity—Crompton Company. William G. Lord II. *Productivity Improvement: Case Studies of Proven Practice,* 1981, pp. 79–85. American Textile Manufacturers Institute.

Behavioral Strategies to Improve Productivity. Gary P. Latham, Larry L. Cummings, Terence R. Mitchell. OD, Winter 1981. pp. 5–23. Univ. of Wisconsin, Univ. of Washington.

The Burger King Corporation Productivity Program. William W. Swart. *Productivity Improvement: Case Studies of Proven Practice,* 1981, pp. 113–120. Industrial Engineering and Operations Research.

Competing with Peers—For Fun and Productivity. Kaleel Jamison. Pers., Sept.–Oct. 1981, pp. 33–42. Kaleel Jamison Associates.

Diagnosing and Treating the Symptoms of Low Productivity. John L. Niles. SM, Aug. 1979, pp. 29–34. Rath & Strong, Inc.

Doing Something About Boosting Clerical Productivity in Hospitals. Harold W. Nance. HSM, Aug. 1981, pp. 4–5. Serge A. Birn Co.

The Dynamics of Productive Compatibility. Max M. Kostik, Robert Pearse. MRev., June 1977, pp. 48–54. Boston State College, Boston Univ.

Five Surefire Ways to Undermine Productivity. Madeleine Dreyfack. SM, Oct. 1980, pp. 35–40.

For Fullest Contribution to Output, Managers Must Look Beyond the Shopfloor. George F. Crosby. MRev., July 1981, pp. 32–33. Crosby & Associates.

A Fresh Look at Productivity Measurement: Measuring Employee Commitment. Dhan G. Mukergi. MRev., July 1981, pp. 29–30. MacDonal Motivational Research Center Inc.

Gainsharing: Involvement, Incentives, and Productivity. Carla S. O'Dell, 1981, 80 pp. American Productivity Center. MB.

Getting on the Productivity Learning Curve—Corning Glass Works. David E. Leibson. *Productivity Improvement: Case Studies of Proven Practice,* 1981, pp. 31–45. Corning Glass Works.

A Healthy Corporate Environment: Critical to Managerial Productivity. Mary Zippo. Pers., Sept.–Oct. 1981, pp. 45–48.

How PAR Can Save $100,000 Annually. Morton M. Kaplan, John W. Gifford. HSM, March 1981, pp. 4–6. Kent General Hospital, Middle Atlantic Shared Services.

How to Improve Productivity. William C. Waddell. *Overcoming Murphy's Law,* 1981, pp. 205–236. California State Univ., Los Angeles.

How to Improve the Performance and Productivity of the Knowledge Worker. Donald B. Miller. OD, Winter 1977, pp. 62–80.

Human Productivity: How Important Is It? How Can It Be Improved? ES, May 1980, 16 pp.

Improving Local Government Productivity. Lew Brown. *Public Technology: Key to Improved Government Productivity,* 1981, pp. 210–222. Management Improvement Corp.

Improving Productivity. James L. Mercer, Susan W. Woolston, William V. Donaldson. *Managing Urban Government Services: Strategies, Tools, and Techniques for the 80's,* 1981, pp. 90–112. James Mercer & Associates, United States Environmental Protection Agency, Philadelphia Zoological Society.

Improving Productivity: An Introduction. Vernon M. Buehler, Y. Krishna Shetty (editors). *Productivity Improvement: Case Studies of Proven Practice,* 1981, pp. 3–13. Utah State Univ.

Improving Productivity Through Advanced Office Controls. Robert E. Nolan, Richard T. Young, Ben C. DiSylvester. 1980, 404 pp. Robert E. Nolan Co., Inc.

Improving Productivity: Ways to Get People Started. Curtis E. Dobbs. *Leadership on the Job: Guides to Good Supervision* (third ed.), 1981, pp. 127–132. Ernst & Whinney. (Also reprinted in HSM, May 1981)

Improving Warehouse Productivity. Joel C. Wolff, 1981, 58 pp. Drake Sheahan/Stewart Dougall, Inc. MB.

In Defense of American Worker Productivity. Cass D. Alvin. *Productivity Improvement: Case Studies of Proven Practice,* 1981, pp. 209–217. United Steel Workers of America-AFL-CIO.

Increasing Productivity Through Behavorial Science. Robert R. Blake, Jane S. Mouton. Pers., May–June 1981, pp. 59–67. Scientific Methods, Inc.

Increasing U.S. Productivity—The Case for Capital Investment. Charles A. Shirk. *The International Essays for Business Decision Makers. Vol. V,* 1980, pp. 139–147. The Austin Co.

Job Design and Productivity: A New Approach. Louis E. Davis. *Human Resources Management: The Past Is Prologue,* 1979, pp. 109–125.

Keys to Enhancing System Development Productivity. William F. Zachmann. 1981, 52 pp. International Data Corp. MB.

Knowledge Worker Productivity. Ira B. Gregerman. 1981, 55 pp. Productivity Associates. MB.

A Labor Leader's Perspective on How to Improve Productivity. Robert A. Georgine. MRev., Aug. 1980, pp. 33–34. AFL-CIO.

The Light at the End of the Productivity Tunnel. Deborah Ann Carter. SM June 1979, pp. 29–34. State Automobile Mutual Insurance Co.

Macro Vs. Micro Input/Output Ratios. K. H. Militzer. MRev., June 1980, pp. 8–15. AT&T.

Making Productivity Improvement Work at The Tanner Companies. Carl C. Jacobson. *Productivity Improvement: Case Studies of Proven Practice,* 1981, pp. 151–174. The Tanner Companies.

Management Improvement. William R. Tracey. *Human Resource Development Standards,* 1981 pp. 152–170. U.S. Army Intelligence Training School.

Management Productivity . . . How to Uncover a Hidden Corporate Asset. Carlton P. McNamara. MRev., Dec. 1979, pp. 20–23. McNamara & Co.

Management Techniques for Productivity Improvement—Lincoln National. Frank J. Ruck, Jr. *Productivity Improvement: Case Studies of Proven Practice,* 1981, pp. 121–137. Chicago Title and Trust Co.

Managing for Productivity. George H. Labovitz. SM, Oct. 1979, pp. 29–32. Boston Univ.

Managing Productivity Improvement: Guidelines for Action. Y. Krishna Shetty, Vernon M. Buehler. *Productivity Improvement: Case Studies of Proven Practice,* 1981, pp. 233–243. Utah State Univ.

Managing Productivity Programs: A Labor Viewpoint. Cass D. Alvin. *Productivity Improvement: Case Studies of Proven Practice,* 1981, pp. 201–208. United Steel Workers of America-AFL-CIO.

Matching Behavioral with Management Science Techniques Improves Productivity. William B. Alton, Richard D. Babcock. AMJ, Summer 1980, pp. 26–31. Johnson & Johnson International, Univ. of San Francisco.

The Morale-Productivity Relationship: How Close? Robert H. Garin, John F. Cooper. Pers., Jan.–Feb. 1981, pp. 57–62. East Texas State Univ., Patrick Henry Community College.

Performance Management . . . Back-to-Basics to Reverse the Productivity Decline. Mark Marcussen. MRev., Dec. 1979, pp. 29–30. Theodore Barry & Associates.

Pressure on Managers for Short-term Results Causing Poor Decisions. Anthony J. Marolda. MRev., March 1981, pp. 29–30. Arthur D. Little Inc.

Productivity: A Matter of Standards. James L. Hayes. MRev., Feb. 1979, pp. 2–3.

Productivity: A Practical Program for Improving Efficiency (rev. ed.—former title: *Tapping the Human Resource: A Strategy for Productivity*). Clair F. Vough, Bernard Asbell. 1979, 212 pp. Productivity Research International, Inc.

Productivity Achievement at Kaiser. James W. Mason, Jr. *Productivity Improvement: Case Studies of Proven Practice,* 1981, pp. 51–65. Kaiser Aluminum & Chemical Corp.

Productivity and Morale Sagging? Try the Quality Circle Approach. Mary Zippo. Pers., May–June 1980, pp. 43–45.

The Productivity Crunch. Geoffrey N. Calvert. *The International Essays for Business Decision Makers, Vol. V,* 1980, pp. 148–155.

Productivity: Doing Something About It. SS, April 1981, 24 pp.

Productivity Experiences at Nucor. Wilburn G. Manuel. *Productivity Improvement: Case Studies of Proven Practice,* 1981, pp. 46–50. Nucor Corp.

Productivity Experiment at Maxwell House—Hoboken. Anthony W. Olkewicz. *Productivity Improvement: Case Studies of Proven Practice,* 1981, pp. 100–107. General Foods Corp.

Productivity: Getting Employees to Care. Frank G. Goble. (AMACOM audio cassettee) By purchase only.

Productivity: Identifying Trouble Spots. SS, March 1981, 24 pp.

Productivity Improvement: Case Studies of Proven Practice. Vernon M. Buehler, Y. Krishna Shetty (editors). 1981, 273 pp. Utah State Univ.

Productivity Improvement Strategy: Make Success the Building Block. Robert H. Shaffer. MRev., Aug. 1981, pp. 46–52. Robert H. Schaffer & Associates.

A Productivity Profile: Guidelines to Productive Management. Robert M. Ranftl. MRev., Nov. 1979, pp. 49–54. Hughes Aircraft Co.

Productivity: the Human Side. Robert R. Blake, Jane Srygley Mouton. 1981, 133 pp. Scientific Methods, Inc.

Promotion for Productivity—Only for Productivity. Clair F. Vough, Bernard Asbell. *Productivity, A Practical Program for Improving Efficiency.* (rev. ed.—former title: *Tapping the Human Resource: A Strategy for Productivity*), 1979, pp. 26–41. Productivity Research International, Inc.

Providing the Right Climate for Productivity. Claude T. Mangrum. SM, Oct. 1981, pp. 34–40. County of San Bernardino.

Reversing the Decline in U.S. Productivity Growth. Donald J. Donahue. *Productivity Improvement: Case Studies of Proven Practice,* 1981, pp. 108–112.

Satisfaction and Productivity. David J. Cherrington. *The Work Ethic: Working Values and Values That Work,* 1980, pp. 92–118. Brigham Young Univ.

Setting Up a Company Productivity Program. Joseph Wise. MRev., June 1980, pp. 15–18. Micromedia, Inc.

Solving the Human Equation in the Productivity Puzzle. Jerome M. Rosow. MRev., Aug. 1977, pp. 40–43. Work in America Institute.

Starting Productivity Programs in a Diversified Firm—Beatrice Foods Company. Ted Olson, Jerry Jensen. *Productivity Improvement: Case Studies of Proven Practice,* 1981, pp. 66–78. Beatrice Foods Co.

Stimulating Greater Employee Commitment—Detroit Edison. Arnold J. Benes. *Productivity Improvement: Case Studies of Proven Practice,* 1981, pp. 138–150. Detroit Edison.

The Supervisor's Guide to Boosting Productivity. Donald P. Hendricks. 1981. (Extension Institute Cassette Program) By purchase only.

The Texas Pool of Big Ideas. Karl L. Shaner. HSM, April 1981, pp. 12–13. Texas Hospital Associates.

Want to Boost Managerial Productivity and Cut Costs? Try Automation. Mary Zippo. Pers., March–April 1981, pp. 39–40.

When Workers Won't Work, and Managers Won't Manage. R. Joseph Monsen, Borje O. Saxberg. MRev., Aug. 1977, pp. 26–28, 37–39. Univ. of Washington.

Where Productivity Begins. Robert D. Harris. HSM, June 1981, pp. 4–5. Rockford Memorial Hospital.

PROJECT MANAGEMENT. See also Scheduling Techniques

Help Fight CPD: Plan Your Report with Your Project—and Optimize the Quality of Each. James W. Hill. SM, Dec. 1979, pp. 8–14. Pennsylvania State Univ.

How to Be a Successful Project Manager. Joan Ryan Knutson. 1980. (Extension Institute Course) By purchase only.

How to Select Successful R & D Projects. D. Bruce Merrifield. MRev., Dec. 1978, pp. 25–28, 37–39. The Continental Group, Inc.

Keeping Technical Projects on Target. Maurice Zeldman. 1978, 44 pp. EMZEE Associates. MB.

Postinvestment Reviews Can Help Avoid Standard International Project Traps. Michael Feinstein. MRev., Feb. 1980, p. 38. Chase Manhattan Bank.

Project Financing—Imaginative Approaches to Strategic Planning in Asset Acquisition. Robert E. Pritchard, Thomas J. Hindelang. *The Strategic Evaluation and Management of Capital Expenditures.* 1981, pp. 211–231. Glassboro State College, Drexel Univ.

See-Saw Project Management. W. A. Delaney. AMJ, Summer 1980, pp. 12–17. Analysis & Computer Systems, Inc.

Step By Step Through a Research Project. Jeffrey Pope. *Practical Marketing Research,* 1981, pp. 43–100. Custom Research, Inc.

Task Forces: Reap Big Rewards At Small Costs. David Goff. HSM, May 1980, pp. 1–2. University Hospital of Jacksonville.

Tools of Systems Management. Michael R. Frank. *The Effective EDP Manager,* 1980, pp. 65–86. The Taubman Co., Inc.

PUBLIC ADMINISTRATION. See Public Service and Non-profit Management and headings for individual functions

PUBLIC RELATIONS. See also Community Relations, Company Image, Investor Relations

The Advantages of Making Corporate Goals Public. Eddy G. Nicholson. MRev., May 1979, pp. 29–30. Congoleum Corp.

Bridging the Public Relations Gap Between Hospital Provider and Consumer. Lee F. Block, M. Elliott Taylor. *Marketing in Nonprofit Organizations*, 1978, pp. 224–250. Lee F. Block & Partners, Inc., Greenville Hospital System.

The Business-Media Relationship: Countering Misconceptions and Distrust. David Finn. 1981, 92 pp. Ruder & Finn, Inc. RS.

Coming to Grips with Crisis. Charles G. Newton, Jr. PA #76, 1981, 47 pp. Ruder & Finn, Inc. By purchase only.

Communication: Top Executive Priority. Robert J. Wood. MRev., May 1979, pp. 49–51. Carl Byoir & Associates, Inc.

A Communications Manual for Nonprofit Organizations. Lucille A. Maddalena. 1981, 222 pp. Fairleigh Dickinson Univ.

Corporations and the First Amendment. Herbert Schmertz. 1978, 40 pp. Mobil Oil Corp. MB.

The Future Public Opinion of Business. Eric A. Weiss. MRev., March 1978, pp. 8–15. Sun Co., Inc.

Getting Fair Treatment from the News Media. Lewis W. Foy. MRev., Jan. 1979, pp. 29. Bethlehem Steel Corp.

How Business Can Reconcile the Needs of Its Many Publics. James K. LaFleur. MRev., Nov. 1979, pp. 34–35. GTI Corp.

Investor Relations That Work. Arthur R. Roalman (editor). 1980, 278 pp. Univ. of South Carolina.

On Television! A Survival Guide for Media Interviews. Jack Hilton, Mary Knoblauch. 1980, 185 pp. Jack Hilton, Inc., Chicago Tribune.

Public Relations: A Valuable Management Tool. Gerard P. Boe. HSM, Feb. 1978, pp. 1–3, 5. U.S. Army Medical Service Corps.

Public Relations, Communications, and Special Events. George A. Brakeley, Jr. *Tested Ways to Successful Fund Raising*, 1980, pp. 70–79. Brakeley, John Price Jones, Inc.

Some Things That Worry Me About Public Relations. Robert Van Riper. *Making Successful Presentations*, 1981, pp. 248–249. N.Y. Ayer & Son, Inc.

Special Demands on Nonprofit PR. Don Bates. *Marketing in Nonprofit Organizations*, 1978, pp. 55–61. National Communication Council for Human Services, Inc.

What Happens In Public Relations. Gerald J. Voros, Paul Alvarez (editors). 1981, 232 pp. Ketchum MacLeod & Grove.

PUBLIC SERVICE AND NON-PROFIT MANAGEMENT. See also headings for individual functions

The Academic Role of the Vice President for Health Science: Can a Walrus Become a Unicorn? Edmund D. Pellegrino, M. D. *Managing Nonprofit Organizations*, 1977, pp. 38–47. Yale-New Haven Medical Center, Inc.

At Last—Innovation in the Federal Judicial System. Warren E. Burger. *Managing Nonprofit Organizations*, pp. 313–318. U.S. Supreme Court.

Base Salary and Incentive Compensation Practices in Not-for-Profit Organizations. Henry Hellwig. CR, Fourth Quarter 1978, pp. 34–48.

The Business Executive in Government: Look Before You Leap. Sigmund G. Ginsburg. MRev., Feb. 1980, pp. 64–66. Univ. of Cincinnati.

Can a Scientific/Technical Executive from Industry Find Happiness in a Government Agency. Robert M. Schaffner. *Managing Nonprofit Organizations*, 1977, pp. 32–37. Food and Drug Administration.

Can Nonprofit Organizations Be Well Managed? Robert N. Anthony. *Managing Nonprofit Organizations*, 1977, pp. 7–15. Harvard Univ.

A Communications Manual for Nonprofit Organizations. Lucille A. Maddalena. 1981, 222 pp. Fairleigh Dickinson Univ.

Civil Service Reform: Authority with Accountability. Jule M. Sugarman. MRev., April 1979, pp. 29–31. U.S. Office of Personnel.

Coping With the Nursing Shortage. Harris Odell, Jr., Gary L. Woods. HSM, April 1980, p. 4. Memorial Medical Center.

Counselling the Public Employee. Charles D. Little. SM, June 1981, pp. 16–18.

Design for Executive Growth and Development (Appendix I). James G. Stockard. *Career Development and Job Training.* 1977, pp. 385–401.

Doctors as Managers of Health Teams: A Career Guide for Hospital-Based Physicians. Roman L. Yanda, M.D. 1977, 271 pp. Univ. of Southern California.

The Economics of Industrial Health: History, Theory and Practice. Joseph F. Follmann, Jr. 1978, 482 pp.

Eulogy to John F. Kennedy. Lyndon B. Johnson. *Making Successful Presentations,* 1981, p. 194.

Extending the Healthcare Mission: Hospital-Based Wellness Centers. James R. Van Vorst. HSM, July 1981, pp. 1–2. St. Vincent Wellness Center.

Hospital Philanthropy: The Need Is Greater than Ever. Harold P. Kurtz. HSM, May 1981, pp. 12–14. United Hospitals.

How Carter Reorganized the EOP. Donald L. Maggin. MRev., May 1978, pp. 11–17. Train, Smith Counsel, Inc.

Legal Handbook for Nonprofit Organizations. Marc J. Lane. 1980, 294 pp. Medico-Legal Institutes, Inc.

Management: A Hospital's Number Two Priority. Steven F. Ashcraft. HSM, April 1979, pp. 1–3. The Toledo Hospital.

Management, Governance & Leadership: A Guide for College and University Administrators. John D. Millett. 1980, 208 pp. Academy for Educational Development.

Management in the Health Field. Samuel P. Martin, Robert E. Mittelstaedt, Jr. HSM, Part 1. The Challenge. Nov. 1977, pp. 1–4. Part 2. More Carrot, Less Stock. Dec. 1977, pp. 1–4. National Health Care Management Center.

Management in the Public Sector: It Really Is Harder. Donald A. Curtis. MRev., Oct. 1980, pp. 70–74. Touche Ross & Co.

The Management of Congress. Richard Bolling. *Managing Nonprofit Organizations,* 1977, pp. 102–108. U.S. House of Representatives.

Management Principles for Nonprofit Agencies and Organizations. Gerald Zaltman (editor). 1979, 584 pp. Univ. of Pittsburgh.

Management Problems Enter the Picture at Art Museums. Walter McQuade. *Managing Nonprofit Organizations,* 1977, pp. 261–269. Fortune.

Managing in the Public and Private Sectors: Similarities and Differences. David Rogers. MRev., May 1981, pp. 48–54. New York Univ.

Managing in the Public Sector: Some Lessons for Business. J. Spencer Ferebee, Jr. MRev., Aug. 1978, pp. 26–28, 37–40. Price Waterhouse & Co.

Managing Nonprofit Organizations. Diane Borst, Patrick J. Montana (editors). 1977, 328 pp. New York Medical Center.

Managing the Public Service Institution. Peter F. Drucker. *Managing Nonprofit Organizations,* 1977, pp. 16–31. Claremont Univ.

Managing Urban Government Services: Strategies, Tools, and Techniques for the 80's. James L. Mercer, Susan W. Woolston, William V. Donaldson. 1981, 242 pp. James Mercer & Associates, United States Environmental Protection Agency, Philadelphia Zoological Society.

Marketing in Nonprofit Organizations. Patrick J. Montana (editor). 1978, 302 pp. (A collection of articles from AMA and other publications)

The Naval Shore Establishment and Parkinson's Laws. Donald A. Morton. *Managing Nonprofit Organizations,* 1977, pp. 289–302. U.S. Navy.

New Directions for Community Hospitals: Occupational and Preventive Healthcare. John H. Baker, M.D. HSM, Dec. 1981, pp. 1–3. St. Joseph Hospital and Health Care Center.

New Tools and Techniques in University Administration. Daniel H. Perlman. *Managing Nonprofit Organizations,* 1977, pp. 59–70. Roosevelt Univ.

A Partnership for Rural Healthcare. Evelyn Trotzky. HSM, August 1980, pp. 1–3. St. Joseph Hospital.

Policy in Motion. Raymond T. Bedwell, Jr. HSM, April 1977, p. 10. St. Joseph's Hospital.

Profit-Minded Management in the Nonprofit World. Paul B. Firstenberg. MRev., July 1979, pp. 8–13. Children's Television Workshop.

Public Management Systems: An Administrator's Guide. James L. Mercer, Edwin H. Koester. 1978, 309 pp. Battelle Southern Operations, C. R. Drew Postgraduate Medical School.

Public Technology: Key to Improved Government Productivity. James L. Mercer, Ronald J. Philips (editors). 1981, 271 pp. Korn/Ferry International, National Aeronautics & Space Administration.

Staffing and Scheduling: Numbers Game or Nursing Management? James M. Ganong, Warren L. Ganong. HSM, Dec. 1978, pp. 6–7. W. L. Ganong Co.

Successful Time Management for Hospital Administrators. Merrill E. Douglass, Phillip H. Goodwin. 1980, 143 pp. Time Management Center, Hillcrest Medical Center.

Tested Ways to Successful Fund Raising. George A. Brakeley, Jr. 1980, 171 pp. Brakeley, John Price Jones, Inc.

Today's Challenge in Education. Max Rafferty. *Making Successful Presentations,* 1981, pp. 231–233. California Superintendant of Public Instruction.

Why Are Hospital Costs So High? William J. Watt. HSM, Sept. 1977, pp. 7–8. St. Joseph's Hospital Health Center.

PURCHASING. See also Materials Management

Analyzing the Supplier: Reversing the Marketing Process. David W. Cravens, Lowell M. Hoffman. MRev., July 1977, pp. 47–54.

A Brief Case Study. Terry A. Mort. *Systematic Selling: How to Influence the Decision Process,* 1977, pp. 26–44. Terry A. Mort Co., Inc.

Chase Bank Declares War on Rising Purchasing Costs. H. Henry Sinason. MRev., Sept. 1981, pp. 29–31. Chase Manhattan Bank, N.A.

A Corporate Purchasing View of National Account Selling. Andrew F. Storer, Jack V. Hartung. *National Account Marketing Handbook,* 1981, pp. 27–36. St. Regis Paper Co.

The Crisis in Critical Metals. Harry J. Gray. *The International Essays for Business Decision Makers, Vol. V,* 1980, pp. 156–162. United Technologies.

Dealing with the Vendor. Donald R. Moscato. *Building Financial Decision-Making Models,* 1980, pp. 103–113. Metamation Systems.

Decision Making in the Purchasing Process: A Report. Phillip D. White. 1978, 54 pp. Univ. of Colorado. MB.

Do's and Don'ts in Subcontract Management. George Sammet, Jr., Clifton G. Kelley. 1980, 40 pp. Martin Marietta Aerospace. MB.

How to Audit the Purchasing Function. J. McConnell. 1981. (An AMACOM Evaluation Tool) By purchase only.

Measuring Purchasing Performance. Robert M. Monczka, Phillip L. Carter. MRev., June 1978, pp. 27–28, 38–42. Michigan State Univ.

Product Standardization—Or How to Save Nearly $500,000. John Rettig. HSM, Nov. 1980, p. 6. Stanford Univ. Medical Center.

Purchasing Computers: A Practical Guide for Buyers of Computers and Computing Equipment. Edward R. Sambridge. 1979, 139 pp. Central Electricity Generating Board.

The Purchasing Role: A View from the Top. Charles F. Carpenter. 1977, 31 pp. Black and Deckar Mfg. Co. MB.

Purchasing Management. C. Wayne Barlow. 1977. (Extension Institute Course) By purchase only.

Reduce Costs Through Effective Purchasing. Paul B. Powell. HSM, Feb. 1977, pp. 9–10. American Medicrop. Inc.

Robotics in Practice: Management and Applications of Industrial Robots. Joseph F. Engelberger, 1980, 291 pp. Unimation Inc.

Systematic Selling: How to Influence the Buying Decision Process. Terry A. Mort. 1977, 190 pp. Terry A. Mort & Co.

Systems Contracting: A New Look. Ralph A. Bolton. 1979, 45 pp. MB.

The Thinking Man's Inventory of Natural Resources. James R. Collier. *Corporate Planning Techniques and Applications,* 1979, pp. 102–111. Marcona Corp.

QUALITY CIRCLES

The Far Side of Quality Circles. Arnold Kanarick. MRev., Oct. 1981, pp. 16–17. Honeywell Inc.

Implementing Quality Circles: A Hard Look at Some of the Realities. Gerald D. Klein. Pers., Nov–Dec. 1981, pp. 11–20. Rider College.

Learning from the Japanese: Prospects and Pitfalls. Robert E. Cole. MRev., Sept. 1980, pp. 22–28, 38–42. Univ. of Michigan.

Productivity and Morale Sagging? Try the Quality Circle Approach. Mary Zippo. Pers., May–June 1980, pp. 43–45.

Quality Circles: A Team Approach to Problem Solving. Frank M. Gryna, Jr. 1981, 96 pp. Bradley Univ. RS.

Quality Circles in the Service Sector. Kenneth M. Jenkins, Justin Shimada. SM, Aug. 1981, pp. 3–7. Portland State Univ.

QUALITY CONTROL. See also Cost Control

Bringing Quality Assurance to the Pharmacy. David P. Vogel. HSM, Oct. 1981, pp. 11–13. Univ. of Illinois Medical Center.

Creating a "Quality" Quality Control Program at SPP. Richard I. Henderson. SM, March 1977, pp. 25–30. Georgia State Univ.

As International Competition Grows, So Must Quality Control. J. M. Juran. MRev., Nov. 1979, pp. 29–31.

Product Quality: A Prescription for the West. J. M. Juran. MRev., Part 1. Training and Improvement Programs. June 1981, pp. 9–14. Part 2. Upper-Management Leadership and Employee Relations. July 1981, pp. 57–61.

A Product Recall Plan: Save Costs and Stay Competitive. Lawrence E. Hicks. MRev., Nov. 1977, pp. 29–31. Thomas J. Lipton, Inc.

Quality and Productivity: Mutually Exclusive or Interdependent in Service Organizations? John C. Shaw, Ram Capoor. MRev., March 1979, pp. 25–28, 37–39. Touche Ross & Co.

Quality Control: A Communications Function. Harry E. Williams. AMJ, Winter 1979, pp. 45–51. (Also in reprint collection *Effective Communication on the Job* (third ed.) 1981.

Quality Control in the Service Industries. Roger G. Langevin. 1977, 38 pp. Chase Manhattan Bank. MB.

Quality Control: Meeting the New Competition. Roger W. Berger. 1981. (Extension Institute Course) By purchase only.

Quality Decisions Start with Good Questions. Peter G. Kirby. SM, Aug. 1980, pp. 2–7. D. R. Lund Associates.

Qualitysense. Martin R. Smith. 1979, 194 pp. Capital Manufacturing Co.

Reliability, Maintenance and Safety. Joseph F. Engelberger. *Robotics in Practice: Management and Applications of Industrial Robots,* 1980, pp. 75–99. Unimation Inc.

The Risky Business of Quality Care. Anne O'Hara-Tumilty. HSM, Nov. 1981, pp. 5–6. Henry Mayo Newhall Memorial Hospital.

Training for Quality. Clair F. Vough, Bernard Asbell. *Productivity, A Practical Program for Improving Efficiency* (rev. ed.—former title: *Tapping the Human Resource: A Strategy for Productivity*), 1979, pp. 64–79. Productivity Research International, Inc.

Visibility Centers—A Management Approach to Quality. Jay W. Leek. MRev., Feb. 1979, pp. 42–46. Northrop Corp.

QUALITY OF WORK LIFE. See also Job Design/Job Enrichment/Job Enlargement

Collective Bargaining and the Quality of Work Life. David Lewin. OD, Autumn 1981, pp. 37–53. Columbia Univ.

Dynamic Systems and the Quality of Work Life. John F. Runcie. Pers., Nov.–Dec. 1980, pp. 13–24. Public Systems Evaluation, Inc.

Efficiency and the Quality of Worklife: The Technology of Reconciliation. Tom Lupton. *Organizational Development: Theory and Practice,* 1977, pp. 32–44. Univ. of Manchester.

Employee Values in a Changing Society. Mark G. Mindell, William I. Gorden. 1981, 72 pp. Abbott Laboratories, Kent State Univ. MB.

Evaluating the Work Environment and the Human Element. Robert J. Thierauf. *Management Auditing: A Questionnaire Approach,* 1980, pp. 191–211. Xavier Univ.

The Future of the World of Work. Ian H. Wilson. AMJ, Autumn 1978, pp. 4–13. General Electric Co.

The Future World of Work: The Strategic Significance of Human Resource Management in the 1980s. Lynne Hall. PA #72, 1980, 64 pp. AT&T. By purchase only.

GM's Quality of Work Life Efforts . . . An Interview with Howard C. Carlson. Pers., July–Aug. 1978, pp. 11–23.

How Graphic Controls Assesses the Human Side of the Corporation. Edward E. Lawler, Philip H. Mervis, William M. H. Clarkson. MRev., Oct. 1981, pp. 54–63. Graphic Controls Corp.

How to Become the Organization of the Future. Stephen H. Fuller. MRev., Feb. 1980, pp. 50–53. General Motors Corp.

Implementing Quality-of-Worklife Programs. Irving Bluestone. MRev., July 1977, pp. 43–46. United Automobile Workers.

Job Enrichment Revisited. Lyle Yorks. 1979, 68 pp. Eastern Connecticut State College. MB.

Measuring the Quality of Work Life in General Motors . . . An Interview with Howard C. Carlson. Ernest C. Miller. Pers., Nov.–Dec. 1978, pp. 21–26.

The Quality of Working Life—Some Answers and Additional Questions. J. Carroll Swart. *A Flexible Approach to Working Hours,* 1978, pp. 9–28. Ball State Univ.

QUANTITATIVE METHODS. See Management Science and Statistics

RECRUITMENT

The Employee Talent Search: Where Do Organizations Turn? Mary Zippo. Pers., March–April 1980, pp. 74–75.

Job Information Network at Fireman's Fund—More Than Posting. Deslie Beth Lawrence, Iris D. Rosendahl. Pers., March–April 1979, p. 56.

Job-Posting Practices. Thomasine Rendero. Pers., Sept.–Oct. 1980, pp. 4–13.

Recruitment and Training. Le Grand L. Thurber. *National Account Marketing Handbook,* 1981, pp. 194–205. IBM Corp.

Successful Personnel Recruiting and Selection. Erwin S. Stanton. 1977, 214 pp. E.S. Stanton & Associates.

RECRUITMENT—COLLEGE. See also Young Adults

College Recruiting Practices. Thomasine Rendero. Pers., May–June 1980, pp. 4–10.

College Recruiting Salaries. Frieda S. Brendler. Pers., March–April 1979, pp. 4–12.

How Other Companies Assess MBA Recruitment: Some Make It Big, Others Stumble. Andrew S. Edson. MRev., April 1979, pp. 13–14. Padilla & Speer, Inc.

Industry-Trained Graduates—Yes or No? Jack J. Phillips. Pers., March–April 1979, pp. 74–78. Stockham Valves & Fittings.

Managers on Campus Hunting Trips Bring Home High-Quality Recruits. Kenneth Moss. MRev., Dec. 1979, pp. 31–32. American Hospital Supply Corp.

The Value of an MBA. Robert M. Donnelly. AMJ, Spring 1981, pp. 59–63. Baurs-Krey Associates.

RECRUITMENT—MANAGERIAL, PROFESSIONAL AND TECHNICAL

Are You Hiring Obsolete Managers? Earnest G. Campbell. AMJ, Autumn 1979, pp. 33–38. Kensington Management Consultants.

The Case of the Harrowing Head-Hunt. Harold E. Lane. Pers., March–April 1978, pp. 65–78. Michigan State Univ.

Corporate Executive Participation in High-Level Recruitment. O. William Battalia. MRev., May 1978, p. 35. Battalia, Lotz & Associates.

How to Staff and Recruit for your Technical Organization. William A. Cohen. *Principles of Technical Management,* 1980, pp. 40–63. California State Univ.

Managerial Misfits . . . How to Avoid Costly Job Mismatches. Arthur F. Miller, James A. Cunningham. MRev., Nov. 1981, pp. 29,31, 36. People Management Inc.

The Perils of Looking for Number Two. Mary Zippo. Pers., Jan.–Feb. 1980, p. 70.

Recruiting and Hiring the Local Manager. Paul E. Illman. *Developing Overseas Managers—and Managers Overseas,* 1980, pp. 171–188. Management Training, Inc.

Recruiting Technical Staff: A Marketing Approach Is Needed. Arnold R. Deutsch. MRev., April 1981, pp. 29–31. Deutsch, Shea & Evans Inc.

Reducing the Risk in Hiring Senior Managers. Robert H. Schaffer. MRev., Dec. 1978, pp. 12–16. Robert H. Schaffer & Associates.

Selection and Performance Criteria for a Chief Human Resources Executive . . . A Presidential Perspective. Pers., May–June 1977, pp. 11–12.

Systematic Leadership Selection. Leo Plaszcznski, HSM, Jan. 1980, pp. 1–2. Candler General Hospital.

What to Do When the Executive Recruiter Calls. Edmund R. Hergenrather. AMJ, Autumn 1980, pp. 41–49. Hergenrather & Co.

RECRUITMENT—MINORITY EMPLOYEES

Affirmative Action for the Handicapped. Larry Steinhauser, Louis Vieceli. SM, Oct. 1978, pp. 34–36.

Employing the Handicapped. William H. Wagel. Pers., Sept.–Oct. 1977, pp. 45–47.

Lending a Hand to the Handicapped: A Primer for Business. Henry A. Tombari. AMJ, Autumn 1979, pp. 44–51.

Recruitment: Casting a Wide Net. Jennie Farley. *Affirmative Action and the Woman Worker.* 1979, pp. 36–55. Cornell Univ.

An Unmentionable Personnel Problem of the 1980s. Mark Lipton. Pers., Sept.–Oct. 1979, pp. 58–65. Univ. of Massachusetts.

RELIABILITY. See Quality Control

RELOCATION

Compensating Transferred Employees. Eugene F. Finkin. Pers., Nov.–Dec. 1978, pp. 43–52. Allegheny Ludlum Industries.

Corporate Moves—Who Pays The Psychic Costs? Lawrence W. Foster, Marilyn L. Liebrenz. Pers., Nov.–Dec. 1977, pp. 67–75.

Easing Relocations with Temporary Workers. Robert W. Stover. MRev., Sept. 1978, pp. 32, 34–35. Western Temporary Services, Inc.

Employee Relocation: Expanded Responsibilities for the Personnel Department. John M. Moore. Pers., Sept.–Oct. 1981, pp. 62–69. Merrill Lynch Relocation Management Inc.

Employee Relocation: It's a Whole New Ballgame. Mary Zippo. Pers., March–April 1980, pp. 70–73.

The High Cost and Stress of Relocation. Gerard Tavernier. MRev., July 1980, pp. 18–23.

How to Avoid People Problems in Plant Relocation: Making an Industrial Move . . . Frederick T. Thompson. MRev., Sept. 1978, pp. 32–34. Sprague Electric Co.

How to Survive a Manufacturing Move. James H. Knight. MRev., July 1981, pp. 31–32. Ultraspherics, Inc.

New York State's Relocation Policy. Mary Zippo. Pers., March–April 1981, pp. 40–42.

Office Relocations in the 1980's. Keith Wheelock. Pers., Sept.–Oct. 1979, pp. 72–77. Fantus Co.

Relocating? Keep Costs Down and Efficiency High. Helen Yates. HSM, March 1981, pp. 1–3. Abbott-Northwestern Hospital Corp.

Relocation: When Employees Say No. Ernest C. Miller. Pers., Sept.–Oct. 1978, pp. 43–45.

Relocating Women Managers: Can Your Company Meet Their Needs? R. Darlene Firestone. AMJ, Spring 1981, pp. 40–46. Merrill Lynch Relocation Management Inc.

REPORTS. See also Charts and Graphs, Communications—Writing, Management Information—Systems

Achievement Reporting—A New Management System. William F. Christopher. *Management for the 1980's* (rev. ed.—former title: *The Achieving Enterprise),* 1980, pp. 246–275.

The Annual Report as a Marketing Tool. Joseph J. Graves, Jr. MRev., April 1979, pp. 33–34. Trans Union Corp.

The Annual Report: Marketing the Corporation. George L. Beiswinger. MRev., Oct. 1979, pp. 62–68. Acme Markets, Inc.

Control: The Key to Successful Business Planning. George R. Seiler, 1981, 78 pp. Profit Planning Associates. MB.

Corporate Report Cards. Henry I. Meyer. *The Face of Business,* 1980, pp. 32–52.

Director Information Systems. Donald R. Jackson. CDSR X, 1979, 24 pp. The Barlow Corp.

Guidelines for Information Flow to Directors. Richard S. Maurer. BPM 6, March 1980, 9 pp. Delta Air Lines.

How to Analyze Accounting Reports. ES, Nov. 1979, 16 pp.

How to Excel with an Annual Report. William P. Dunk. *Investor Relations That Work,* 1980, pp. 95–133. Corpcom Services, Inc.

How to Manage Your Annual Report. Richard A. Lewis. MRev., Sept. 1979, pp. 15–19. Corporate Annual Reports, Inc.

How to Read and Interpret Balance Sheets and Income Statements. ES, Dec. 1978, 16 pp.

Improve Your Report Writing. Marshall Smith. *Effective Communication on the Job* (third ed.), 1981, pp. 277–286. The Zia Co.

Investor Relations: The Need to Disclose. Terry Wilson. *Investor Relations That Work,* 1980, pp. 5–94. Borg-Warner Corp.

The Network Reports System of Analysis and Control. John B. McMaster. 1976, 56 pp. John B. McMaster & Associates. MB.

Reporting Techniques. Robert E. Nolan, Richard T. Young, Ben C. DiSylvester. *Improving Productivity Through Advanced Office Controls,* 1980, pp. 260–283. Robert E. Nolan Co., Inc.

Subcontract Management Reports and Control Forms. George Sammet Jr., Clifton G. Kelley. *Subcontract Management Handbook,* 1981, pp. 203–224. Martin Marietta Corp.

Understanding What Those Numbers Mean. SS, June 1981, 24 pp.

RESEARCH AND DEVELOPMENT. See also Compensation, Creativity, Product Development

The Bendix Approach to Corporate R&D. Domenic Bitondo. AMJ, Fall 1977, pp. 32–40. Bendix Corp.

Conversation: An Interview with Joshua Lederberg. OD, Winter 1980, pp. 42–60.

The Effect of Continuing Technological Change on Corporate Organization and Management. Harold Smiddy. *The Evolving Science of Management,* 1979, pp. 229–246.

Evaluating Research & Development and Engineering. Robert J. Thierauf. *Management Auditing: A Questionnaire Approach,* 1980, pp. 115–136. Xavier Univ.

Federal/Intergovernmental Programs and Initiatives. Alfonso B. Linhares. *Public Tech-*

nology: Key to Improved Government Productivity, 1981, pp. 46–74. U.S. Department of Transportation.

Getting the User Involved. Lawrence P. O'Keefe. *Public Technology: Key to Improved Government Productivity,* 1981, pp. 232–238. Battelle Center for Urban Technology.

Managing Technology: Top Management Must Regain the Initiative. William P. Sommers. *The International Essays for Business Decision Makers, Vol. IV,* 1979, pp. 10–18. Booz, Allen & Hamilton, Inc.

Not-for-Profit R & D Institutes. James L. Mercer, Jules J. Duga. *Public Technology: Key to Improved Government Productivity,* 1981, pp. 75–84. Korn/Ferry International, Battelle Columbus Laboratories.

Politics of Public Technology. Ronald J. Philips. *Public Technology: Key to Improved Government Productivity,* 1981, pp. 23–34. National Aeronautics & Space Administration.

Principles of R&D Management. Philip H. Francis. 1977, 228 pp. Southwest Research Institute.

Principles of Technical Management. William A. Cohen. 1980, 222 pp. California State Univ.

Public Technology and the City-University Relationship. Richard E. Thomas. *Public Technology: Key to Improved Government Productivity,* 1981, pp. 85–106. Texas A&M Univ.

The Public Technology Transfer Process. Ronald J. Philips, Stanley R. Goldberg. *Public Technology: Key to Improved Government Productivity,* 1981, pp. 35–45. National Aeronautics & Space Administration.

The Question of Replication. Dale F. Helsel. *Public Technology: Key to Improved Government Productivity,* 1981, pp. 223–231. City of Middletown, Ohio.

Regional Science and Technology Networks. O. James Linenberger. *Public Technology: Key to Improved Government Productivity,* 1981, pp. 158–174. Southwest Innovation Group.

Research and Development. Fred W. Latham, George S. Sanders. *Urwick, Orr on Management,* pp. 93–104. Urwick, Orr & Partners.

Science and Technology Networks. James L. Mercer, Susan W. Woolston. *Public Technology: Key to Government Productivity,* 1981, pp. 239–255. Korn/Ferry International.

Selling R&D to the World's Toughest Customer. Edson W. Spencer. MRev., Aug. 1977, pp. 20–25. Honeywell, Inc.

Staffing for R&D: Assembling the Resources to Innovate. Frederick D. Buggie. MRev., Aug. 1977, pp. 31–32. INOMATION, INC.

Strategic Analysis, Selection, and Management of R&D Projects. D. Bruce Merrifield. 1977, 54 pp. Continental Group, Inc. MB.

The Strategic Integration of Corporate Research and Development. William H. Gruber, 1981, 65 pp. Research & Planning, Inc. MB.

Technology Sharing for Smaller Communities. Theodore J. Maher. *Public Technology: Key to Government Productivity,* 1981, pp. 148–157. Public Technology, Inc.

Turning Research and Development into Profits. Attilio Bisio, Lawrence Gastwirt. 1979, 275 pp. Exxon Research and Engineering Co., Essochem Europe.

The Urban Consortium for Technology Initiatives. James R. Favour, Susan W. Woolston. *Public Technology: Key to Improved Government Productivity,* 1981, pp. 107–117. City of Dallas, Texas.

The Urban Technology System. Stanley R. Goldberg. *Public Technology: Key to Improved Government Productibity,* 1981, pp. 118–147. National Aeronautics & Space Administration.

RESEARCH AND DEVELOPMENT—EVALUATION AND COSTS

Evaluation of Research and Development Proposals. Clark E. Beck. *Making Successful Presentations,* 1981, pp. 153–161. Wright-Patterson Air Force Base.

How to Budget and Control Costs. William A. Cohen. *Principles of Technical Management,* 1980, pp. 132–159. California State Univ.

R&D on a Minimum Budget. Donatas Tijunelis, Nancy Miles Clausen. 1979, 37 pp. Borg-Warner Corp. MB.

R&D: What Link to Profits? J. J. Gilman, R. H. Miller. MRev., Sept. 1978, pp. 23–26. Allied Chemical Corp.

Research and Development Can Pay Its Own Way. Louis Soltanoff. MRev., Feb. 1979, pp. 29–30. Cambridge Research and Development Group.

Technology and Society. Cornelius E. Gallagher. *Making Successful Presentations,* 1981, pp. 168–173. U.S. House of Representatives.

RETIREMENT. See Older Workers and Retirement, Pensions

RETURN ON INVESTMENT

Capital-Intensive Technology Vs. ROI: Strategic Assessment. Sidney Schoeffler. MRev., Sept. 1978, pp. 8–14. Strategic Planning Institute.

Control: The Key to Successful Business Planning. George R. Seiler. 1981, 78 pp. Profit Planning Associates.

Cost-Benefit Approach to Capital Expenditure. Prem Prakash. *Management Principles for Nonprofit Agencies and Organizations,* 1979, pp. 291–339. Univ. of Pittsburgh.

The Discounted Cash Flow Method of Economic Analysis. Attilio Bisio, Lawrence Gastwirt. *Turning Research and Development into Profits,* 1979, pp. 99–133. Exxon Research and Engineering Co., Essochem Europe.

How Customers Plan and Evaluate Capital Expenditures for Systems (Appendix 3). Mack Hanan, James Cribbin, Jack Donis. *Systems Selling Strategies.* 1978, pp. 152–184. The Greenhouse Group.

How to Invest for Maximum Total Returns. C. Colburn Hardy. *Your Money & Your Life: How to Plan Your Long-Range Financial Security,* 1979, pp, 135–181.

How We Can Keep Score. Merritt L. Kastens. *Redefining the Manager's Job: The Proactive Manager in a Reactive World,* 1980, pp. 141–163.

Life-Cycle Costing: A Business and Societal Instrument. Robert T. Lund. MRev., April 1978, pp. 17–23. Massachusetts Institute of Technology.

The Measurement of Return on Capital. Curtis W. Symonds. *Basic Financial Management* (rev. ed.), 1978, pp. 45–60. Financial Control Associates.

Real Estate Investment Strategies. Alan Rabinowitz. *The Real Estate Gamble.* 1980, pp. 260–295. Univ. of Washington.

Return on Investment (sec. ed.). Richard W. Lott. 1980. (Extension Institute Course) By purchase only.

Robot Economics. Joseph F. Engelberger. *Robotics in Practice: Management and Applications of Industrial Robots,* 1980, pp. 101–110. Unimation Inc.

ROI Basics for Nonfinancial Executives. Allen Sweeney. 1979, 115 pp. International Standard Brands.

ROI: Practical Theory and Innovative Applications (rev. ed.). Robert A. Peters. 1979, 173 pp. Ownes-Illinois Corp.

The Role of Real Estate in Financial Planning. C. Colburn Hardy. *Your Money & Your Life: How to Plan Your Long-Range Financial Security,* 1979, pp. 110–134.

The Strategic Evaluation and Management of Capital Expenditures. Robert E. Pritchard, Thomas J. Hindelang. 1981, 326 pp., Glassboro State College, Drexel Univ.

Valuing Common Stock: The Power of Prudence. George Lasry. 1979, 239 pp. E. Lasry & Co.

SAFETY. See also Government and Business, Health

Are You Running a "Fire Department?" Karl Albrecht. SM, June 1977, pp. 2–8.

Case Study 1: Development of an Automated Flow-Control System for the Fire Service. Warren D. Siemens. *Public Technology: Key to Improved Government Productivity,* 1981, pp. 176–184. Martin Marietta Laboratories.

Case Study 2: Development of a Firefighters' Breathing System. Warren D. Siemens, Tom Smith. *Public Technology: Key to Improved Government Productivity,* 1981, pp. 185–190. Martin Marietta Laboratories, Public Technology, Inc.

Controlling the Human Factor in Industrial Fires. Bruce P. Matoon. SM, June 1978, pp. 2–8. Training-Resource Center Factory Mutual Engineering.

Effective Loss-Control Management. John L. Pickens. MRev., Dec. 1977, pp. 40–43.

Effective Safety Management: Focus on the Human Element. D. Keith Denton. MRev., Dec. 1980, pp. 47–50. Southern Illinois Univ.

Electric Utilities "Light Into" Job Hazards. SM, Aug. 1977, pp. 29–34.

FSES Cuts Fire-Safety Costs in Half. Megan Carroll. HSM, Feb. 1981, p. 6. U.S. Fire Administration.

How to Prepare for a Visit from OSHA. SS, Dec. 1980, 24 pp.

The Management of Safety. Robert R. Blake, Jane Srygley Mouton. *Productivity: the Human Side,* 1981, pp. 81–87. Scientific Methods, Inc.

Off-the-Job Safety Saves Workers Pain, Company Money. Marie Scotti. MRev., Jan. 1979, pp. 32–33. General Foods Corp.

Open to OSHA? Ernest C. Miller. Pers., Nov.–Dec. 1978, pp. 4–9.

Reliability, Maintenance and Safety. Jospeh F. Engelberger. *Robotics in Practice: Management and Applications of Industrial Robots,* 1980, pp. 75–99. Unimation Inc.

Safety on the Job. SS, Sept. 1980, 24 pp.

The Supervisor's Role in Accident Prevention. Edward F. Konczel. SM, July 1979, pp. 31–34. AT&T Long Lines Co.

SALES FORECASTING. See Forecasting Methods

SALES MANAGEMENT. See also Management Information—Systems, Marketing Management, Selection—Managerial and Professional Personnel.

The A to Z of Sales Management. John Fenton. 1979, 141 pp. Sales Augmentation International Group.

Characteristics of the National Account. William R. Lindstrom. *National Account Marketing Handbook,* 1981, pp. 16–26. Purex Corp.

Defining a National Account. James C. Elf. *National Account Marketing Handbook,* 1981, pp. 1–15. Grow Chemical Corp.

How to Make the Most of Sales Information. ES, Nov. 1981, 16 pp.

Implementing National Account Operations. Thomas T. Marxer. *National Account Marketing Handbook,* 1981, pp. 81–94. Angelica Uniform Group, Inc.

Improving Consumer Relations Pays Off. David S. Davison. AMJ, Autumn 1979, pp. 17–24. ITT Corp.

Making the National Account Marketing Decision. J. Paul Ekberg. *National Account Marketing Handbook,* 1981, pp. 37–65. Tenneco Chemicals, Inc.

Marketing in Terms of Shortages. William A. Barrett. *National Account Marketing Handbook,* 1981, pp. 206–212. Diamond Crystal Salt Co.

The National Account Department in Operation. Richard H. Lang. *National Account Marketing Handbook,* 1981, pp. 95–125. Masonite Corp.

National Account Marketing Handbook. Robert S. Rogers, V. B. Chamberlain, III (editors). 1981, 292 pp. National Account Marketing Assn., Stanley Works.

Planning the National Account Program. James J. Patterson. *National Account Marketing Handbook,* 1981, pp. 66–71. Union-Camp Corp.

Related Management Processes. John K. Moynahan. *Designing an Effective Sales Compensation Program,* 1980, pp. 169–183. Towers, Perrin, Forster & Crosby, Inc.

Sales Supervisor: Coach or Adversary? James F. Carey. AMJ, Spring 1979, pp. 40–43. Carey Associates.

SALES TRAINING

The Skills of Selling. Roger W. Seng. 1977, 253 pp. Selling Power Services.

Training for Retail Sales and Profit. Judith J. Howe. 1981, 237 pp. Retail Resources, Inc.

Training Salespeople to Close. Sal T. Massimino. *The Complete Book of Closing Sales,* 1981, pp. 77–97. International Group.

SALESPEOPLE AND SALES TECHNIQUES. See also Compensation—Professional Personnel, Selection—Managerial and Professional (including Sales) Personnel

Advanced Industrial Selling. David A. Stumm. 1981, 221 pp. Barnes McHugh Co.

The Complete Book of Closing Sales. Sal T. Massimino. 1981, 154 pp. International Group.

How to Get Started as a Manufacturers' Representative. William H. Krause. 1980, 207 pp. Momentum Metals.

How to Sell Effectively. Vern Goldsmith. 1980. (Extension Institute Course) By purchase only.

How to Sell to the Government Market. William A. Cohen, Marshall E. Reddick. *Successful Marketing for Small Business,* 1981, pp. 211–234. California State Univ.

How to Sell to the Industrial Market. William A. Cohen, Marshall E. Reddick. *Successful Marketing for Small Business,* 1981, pp. 197–210. California State Univ.

Investing Sales Time for Maximum Return: Developing Key Account Sales Strategies. T. D. Daniels. MRev., Oct. 1977, pp. 39–41. General Electric Co.

Making Successful Presentations. George T. Vardaman. 1981, 271 pp. Univ. of Denver.

The Management of Personal Selling (third ed.). Wade Rothwell. 1979. (Extension Institute Course) By purchase only.

Managing Sales Time. Merrill E. Douglass, Donna N. Douglass. *Manage Your Time, Manage Your Work, Manage Yourself,* 1980, pp. 209–223. Time Management Center.

Personality Styles: The Key to Closing Sales. Leo F. McManus. 1979. (An AMA multimedia program) By purchase only.

Sales Negotiation Strategies: Building the Win/Win Customer Relationship. Mack Hanan, James Cribbin, Howard Berrian. 1977, 160 pp. St. John's Univ.

Selling . . . New Style. Robert Montgomery. 1980. (AMACOM audio cassette book) By purchase only.

Shut Up and Sell! Tested Techniques for Closing the Sale. Don Sheehan. 1981, 163 pp.

The Skills of Selling. Roger W. Seng. 1977, 253 pp. Selling Power Services.

Strategies for Successful Selling. Robert A. Weber. 1981. (An AMA multimedia program) By purchase only.

Systematic Selling. Terry A. Mort. 1981. (AMACOM audio cassette book) By purchase only.

Systematic Selling: How to Influence the Buying Decision Process. Terry A. Mort, 1977, 190 pp. Terry A. Mort Co., Inc.

Time and Territorial Management. 1979. (An AMACOM Skill Series home-study course) By purchase only.

SCHEDULING TECHNIQUES. See also Production Planning and Control

Accountability for Professional Functions. Robert E. Nolan, Richard T. Young, Ben C. DiSylvester. *Improving Productivity Through Advanced Office Controls,* 1980 pp. 300–318. Robert E. Nolan Co., Inc.

The "Deadline" Syndrome. Arthur G. Sharp. SM, Oct. 1979, pp. 14–17.

Keeping Technical Projects on Target. Maurice Zeldman. 1978, 44 pp. EMZEE Associates. MB.

SECRETARIES. See also Word Processing

Developing Your Secretary. Arlene Yerys, Beverly Hyman. SM, Feb. 1979, pp. 10–14. Effective Training System.

The Office Revolt of the "Stepford Wives." Laurel B. Giblin, Edward J. Giblin. SM, Jan. 1977, pp. 2–9. American Express, Arthur Young & Co.

Secretarial Salaries Advance. Ernest C. Miller. Pers., Sept.– Oct. 1978, pp. 47–48.

The Successful Secretary: You, Your Boss, and the Job. Loren B. Belker. 1981, 214 pp.

Successful Teamwork: How Managers & Secretaries Achieve It. Patrick J. Montana, Elizabeth Marting, Diane Borst. 1979. (AMACOM audio cassette) By purchase only.

What Your Secretary Wants to Tell You.. Vera J. Hilliard. SM, July 1978, pp. 2–9.

SECURITY

Computer Security: A Management Audit Approach. Norman L. Enger, Paul W. Howerton. 1980, 264 pp. Applied Management Systems Inc., American Univ.

Investigative Guidelines for Private Industrial Security Officers. Daniel T. Clancy. MRev., March 1978, pp. 29–30. Case Western Reserve Univ.

Safe: Security Audit & Field Evaluation for Computer Facilities and Information Systems (rev. ed.). Leonard I. Krauss. 1980, 308 pp.

Security Safeguards for the Computer. Charles F. Hemphill, Jr., Robert D. Hemphill. 1979, 38 pp. Ernst & Ernst. MB.

SELECTION. See also Equal Employment Opportunity, Recruitment

Are Employment Agencies Jeopardizing Your Selection Process? Stephen Rubenfield, Michael Crino. Pers., Sept.–Oct. 1981, pp. 70–77. Univ. of Minnesota.

Beneath the Tip of the Iceberg: How to Handle the Employee Selection Decision. Lance A. Berger. Pers., Sept.–Oct. 1977, pp. 61–67. CPC International, Inc.

Decisions, Decision: How to Make Good Ones on Employee Selection. Thomas A. Petit, Terry W. Mullins. Pers., March–April 1981, pp. 71–77. Univ. of North Carolina.

Employee Selection. John G. Kilgour. *Preventive Labor Relations,* 1981, pp. 89–110. California State Univ.

The Employment Process. Linda A. Roxe. *Personnel Management for the Smaller Company,* 1979, pp. 16–47. Rox Associates.

"Hire in Haste, Repent at Leisure"—The Team Selection Process at Graphic Controls. Ernest C. Miller. OD, Spring 1980, pp.3–26.

Hiring the Handicapped. Jack R. Ellner, Henry E. Bender. 1980, 74 pp. Southern Illinois Univ. RS.

How to Pick the Best People Under EEO. Jack W. English. AMJ, Summer 1979, pp. 23–30. Mobil Oil Corp.

Let Your Employees Choose Their Co-Workers. Robert H. Smith. AMJ, Winter 1981, pp. 27–30, 35–36. Smith-Helm Psychological Consultants.

Managing Personnel Selection. Beverly A. Potter. *Turning Around: The Behavioral Approach to Managing People,* 1980, pp. 116–142.

Paving the Way for the Nontraditional Job Seeker. Mary Zippo. Pers., May–June 1981, pp. 49–50.

Personnel Selection in the Presence of Uncertainty. Edward M. Miller. Pers., Sept.–Oct. 1980, pp. 67–76. American Productivity Center.

Recruiting and Selecting Employees. James F. Evered. *Shirt-Sleeves Management,* 1981, pp. 29–49. Redman Industries, Inc.

Reference Auditing—The New Way In. Deslie Beth Lawrence, Iris D. Rosendahl. Pers., March–April 1979, pp. 57–58.

Selecting, Orienting, and Training Employees. Louis V. Imundo. *The Effective Supervisor's Handbook,* 1980, pp. 48–71. Management Perspectives.

Selection: Choosing the Best. Jennie Farley. *Affirmative Action and the Woman Worker,* 1979, pp. 56–73. Cornell Univ.

The Selection Interview: Productive Interviewing No. 1 (third ed.). Raymond F. Valentine. 1981. (AMACOM audio cassette) By purchase only.

Staffing. William R. Tracey. *Human Resource Development Standards,* 1981 pp. 93–115. U.S. Army Intelligence Training School.

Successful Personnel Recruiting and Selection. Erwin S. Stanton. 1977, 214 pp. E.S. Stanton & Associates.

Try Before You Hire: Business Internship Programs. Sigmund G. Ginsburg. MRev., Jan. 1981, pp. 59–61. Univ. of Cincinnati.

Writing Letters of Reference That Get Results. T. J. Halatin. SM, Dec. 1980, pp. 32–34. Southwest Texas State Univ.

SELECTION—MANAGERIAL AND PROFESSIONAL PERSONNEL

The Clonal Effect in Organizations. Natasha Josefowitz. MRev., Sept. 1979, pp. 20–23. Univ. of New Hampshire.

Preparing for Executive Position Interviews. Sigmund G. Ginsburg. Pers., July–Aug. 1980, pp. 31–36.

Selecting Contemporary Managers. Roger J. Howe. *Building Profits Through Organizational Change,* 1981, pp. 130–145. Donaldson Co., Inc.

A Strategy for Hiring Sales Representatives. Samuel Cleff. Pers., July–Aug. 1980, pp. 58–68. Behavior Advisors, Inc.

SELECTION—SUPERVISORS. See also Executives–Skills and Techniques, Management
A Critical Management Decision: Selecting a First-Line Supervisor. Edwin S. Ross. HSM, Dec. 1979, pp. 1–3. Univ. of Texas Medical Branch.

Foreman Selection: One Company's Approach. T. S. Turner, Jim A. Utley. Pers., May–June 1979, pp. 47–55. Alcan Smelters and Chemicals Ltd.

How to Interview Supervisory Candidates from the Ranks. William T. Wolz. Pers., Sept–Oct. 1980, pp. 31–39. Pennsylvania State Univ.

Supervisory Selection Procedures. Thomasine Rendero. Pers., March–April 1980, pp. 4–10.

SERVICING

Custom Service Businesses. Herman R. Holtz. *Profit-Line Management: Managing a Growing Business Successfully,* 1981, pp. 265–293.

General Service Businesses. Herman R. Holtz. *Profit-Line Management: Managing a Growing Business Successfully,* 1981, pp. 245–264.

A General Service Contract? Three Checklists Worth Considering. Roger Drue. HSM, May 1981, pp. 1–3. Mills Memorial Hospital.

How to Improve Customer Service. E. Patricia Bisner, Ronald D. Balsley. 1980. (Extension Institute Cassette Program) By purchase only.

How to Succeed in a Service Industry—Turn the Organization Chart Upside Down. David S. Davidson. MRev., April 1978, pp. 13–16. ITT Corp.

Measuring Performance in Human Service Systems. James F. Budde. 1979, 207 pp. Univ. of Kansas.

Product Service Planning: Service-Marketing-Engineering Interactions. William H. Bleuel, Henry Bender. 1980, 84 pp. AM International. RS.

Quality and Productivity: Mutually Exclusive or Interdependent in Service Organizations? John C. Shaw, Ram Capoor. MRev., March 1979, pp. 25–28, 37–39.

Quality Control in the Service Industries. Roger G. Langevin. 1977, 38 pp. Chase Manhattan Bank. MB.

The Service Organization: Climate Is Crucial. Benjamin Schneider. OD, Autumn 1980, pp. 52–65, Michigan State Univ.

Successful Field Service Management. Donald N. McCafferty. 1980, 181 pp. Honeywell Inc.

SIMULATION. See also Decision Making

Building Financial Decision Making Models: An Introduction to Principles and Procedures. Donald Moscato, 1980, 150 pp. Iona College.

Catastrophe Theory Analysis of Business Activity. Ward C. Smith. MRev., June 1980, pp. 27–28, 37–40. Corning Medical & Scientific.

Computer Simulation of Financial Factors. D. Bruce Merrifield. *Strategic Analysis, Selection, and Management of R&D Projects,* 1977, pp. 21–27. Continental Group Inc. MB.

Direct Costs in Budgeting, Forecasting, and Business Modeling. William E. Arnstein, Frank Gilabert. *Direct Costing,* 1980, pp. 72–91. Main Hurdman & Cranstoun.

Models. Alfred R. Oxenfeldt. *Cost-Benefit Analysis for Executive Decision Making,* 1979, pp. 55–85. Columbia Univ.

Simulation—When All Else Fails. Robert D. Smith, James G. Morris. *Corporate Planning Techniques and Applications,* 1979, pp. 282–290. Kent State Univ.

SMALL COMPANY

Basics of Successful Business Management. William R. Osgood. 1981, 259 pp.

Boardroom Evolution in the Small and Mid-Sized Company? William Chisholm. DM, June 1981, pp. 1–2 . Boardroom Consultants, Inc.

Commercial Financing: A Tight Money Strategy for Smaller Companies. Walter Kaye. MRev., Feb. 1981, pp. 17–20. Congress Financial Corp.

Compensating Key Executives in the Smaller Company. Theodore Cohn, Roy A. Lindberg. 1979, 224 pp.

Developing the Business Plan for a Small Business. Bruce M. Bradway, Robert E. Pritchard. 1980, 50 pp. Glassboro State College. MB.

The Entrepreneur: A Corporate Strategy for the 80's. Donald J. Taffi. 1981, 44 pp. The Donalen Group, Inc. MB.

Entrepreneurs, Take Note: 10 'Musts' for Rapid, Successful Growth. Harold Levine. MRev., April 1980, p. 29. Levine, Huntley, Schmidt, Plapler & Beaver, Inc.

ESOPs and the Smaller Employer. M. Mark Lee (editor). 1979, 79 pp. Standard Research Consultants. MB.

Financial Management for Small Business. Edward N. Rausch. 1979, 184 pp. Wright State Univ.

Financing Alternatives for Small and Medium-Sized Corporations. Lawrence J. Trautman. BPM 15, Sept. 1981, 8 pp. Donaldson, Lufkin & Jenrette.

14 Financial Pitfalls for Small Businesses. Moustafa H. Abdelsamad, Guy J. Degenaro, D. Robley Wood, Jr. AMJ, Spring 1977, pp. 15–23. Virginia Commonwealth Univ., Madison College.

How to Get Started as a Manufacturers' Representative. William H. Krause. 1980, 207 pp. Momentum Metals.

How to Make Strategic Planning Work for Small Businesses. Jacob Naor. AMJ, Winter, 1980, pp. 35–39. Univ. of Maine.

Legal Handbook for Small Business. Marc J. Lane. 1977, 181 pp.

Micromanagement: How to Solve the Problems of Growing Companies. William A. Delaney. 1981, 164 pp. Analysis and Computer Systems, Inc.

New Trends in Venture Investment . . . Giving a Boost to Small Business. Richard M. Pomboy. MRev., May 1980, pp. 29–30. Ventures, Inc.

The Owner's and Manager's Market Analysis Workbook for Small to Moderate Retail and Service Establishments. Wayne A. Lemmon. 1980, 230 pp. Economic Research Associates.

Personnel Management for the Smaller Company. Linda A. Roxe. 1979, 246 pp. Rox Associates.

Preventive Management in the Smaller Firm. Rudolph L. Kagerer. SM, Sept. 1979, pp. 38–41. Univ. of Georgia.

Profit from Your Money-Making Ideas: How to Build a New Business or Expand an Existing One. Herman R. Holtz. 1980, 370 pp.

Recognizing and Dealing with the Entrepreneur. John A. Welsh, Jerry F. White. AMJ, Summer 1978, pp. 21–31. Southern Methodist Univ.

Small Business: Developing the Winning Management Team. George W. Rimler, Neil J. Humphreys. 1980, 180 pp. Virginia Commonwealth Univ.

Small Business Growth: Making a Conscious Decision. Jack F. McKenna, Paul L. Oritt. AMJ, Spring 1980, pp. 45–53. California State Univ., Univ. of the Pacific.

Small Business Investment Companies. Dileep Rao. *Handbook of Business and Capital Sources.* 1979, pp. 305–333.

Small Business Works! How to Compete and Win in the Free Enterprise System. Eugene L. Gross, Adrian R. Cancel, Oscar Figueroa. 1977, 166 pp.

Small Can Be Beautiful . . . Getting New Ventures Off the Ground. Edward B. Roberts. MRev., June 1980, pp. 51–56. M.I.T.

Strengthening the Vital Majority. James L. Hayes. MRev., Jan. 1980, pp. 2–3.

Successful Marketing for Small Business. William A. Cohen, Marshall E. Reddick. 1981, 282 pp. California State Univ.

Why Small Businesses Fail. Moustafa H. Abdelsamad. AMJ, Spring 1978, pp. 24–32. Virginia Commonwealth Univ.

SOCIAL RESPONSIBILITY. See also Socio-Economic Conditions

Androgynous Management: Key to Social Responsibility? Suzanne H. Cook, Jack L. Mendleson. AMJ, Winter 1977, pp. 25–35. Arizona State Univ.

Audits Aim Social Strategy. John Thackeray. *Corporate Planning Techniques and Applications,* 1979. pp. 115–124.

Business and Art: A Creative, Practical Partnership. Peter G. Scotese. MRev., Oct. 1978, pp. 20–24.

Business and Society in Transformation. Willis W. Harman. *Corporate Planning Techniques and Applications,* 1979, pp. 43–52. SRI International.

Changing Managerial Ideologies. George A. Steiner. *The Evolving Science of Management,* 1979, pp. 348–367. Center for Research and Dialogue on Business and Society, Univ. of California Los Angeles.

Changing Values and Institutions. John F. Mee. *The Evolving Science of Management,* 1979, pp. 368–384. Indiana Univ.

Conversation: An Interview with Kenneth E. Boulding. OD, Autumn 1977, pp. 47–67.

Corporate Giving: Policy and Practice. Frank Koch. PA #67, 1978, 40 pp. Syntex Corp. By purchase only

Corporate Governance — What's Ahead? Walter P. Blass. *Corporate Planning Techniques and Applications,* 1979, pp. 125–135. New York Telephone.

The Economic, Social, Civic, and Cultural Dimensions of Management. Andrew F. Morlion. *The Evolving Science of Management,* 1979, pp. 385–390. International Univ. of Social Studies "Pro Deo," Rome

Family and the Corporation. James L. Hayes. MRev., Dec. 1979, pp. 2–3.

15 Ways Companies Can Support Nonprofit Groups Without Cash Contributions. Frank Koch. MRev., Sept. 1979, pp. 58–62. Syntex Corp.

Improving Corporate Response to Consumer Needs. Edgar H. Twine. MRev., Dec. 1977, pp. 16–17. Atlantic Richfield Co.

Managers in the Future: How Will They Be Judged? Peter Spooner, Michael Johnson. MRev., Dec. 1980, pp. 8–17.

Managing Corporate External Affairs. Seymour Morris, Jr. MRev., March 1980, pp. 48–53. McCormick & Paget, Inc.

Managing Social Issues in a Time of Change. Mary Zippo. Pers., Sept.–Oct. 1981, pp. 43–45.

A Place for Environment in the Corporate Structure. Robert Cahn. MRev., April 1979, pp. 15–20.

A Practical Approach to Social Responsibility. John Humble. MRev., May 1978, pp. 18–22.

Public Responsibility: An Answer to the Corporate Dilemma? Lee E. Preston, James E. Post. *Corporate Planning Techniques and Applications,* 1979, pp. 136–143. State Univ. of New York, Boston Univ.

The Social Audit for Management. Clark C. Abt. 1977, 278 pp. Abt Associates Inc.

Society's Right to Jobs. James L. Hayes. MRev., July 1981, pp. 2–3.

The Ten Marks of the Conservative. Gerald J. Skibbins. *Making Successful Presentations,* 1981, pp. 242–248. Opinion Research Corp.

Worker Volunteering: A New Resources for the 1980s. Kerry Kenn Allen. 1980, 31 pp. The National Center for Citizen Involvement. MB.

SOCIO-ECONOMIC CONDITIONS. See also Government and Business, Social Responsibility

Business and the North: Whose Responsibility to Stem Decline? William C. Freund. MRev., March 1978, pp. 27–28, 37–41. New York Stock Exchange.

A CEO Looks at Work: Why We Need a Second Industrial Revolution—Led by Management. Jack F. Bere. MRev., July 1978, pp. 18–22. Borg-Warner Corp.

Changing Life Ways and Corporate Planning. Arnold Mitchell. *Corporate Planning Techniques and Applications,* 1979, pp. 29–42. SRI International.

The Conserver Society. K. Valaskakis, J. G. Smith, P. S. Sindell, I. Martin. *Corporate*

Planning Techniques and Applications, 1979, pp. 82–92. Univ. of Montreal, McGill Univ., Sindell Research Inc., GAMMA.

Conversation: An Interview with Kenneth E. Boulding. OD, Autumn 1977. pp. 47–67. (Also reprinted in *Effective Management and the Behavioral Sciences,* 1978)

Conversation with Daniel Bell. William Dowling (editor). *Effective Management and the Behavioral Sciences,* 1978, pp. 246–264.

Dystopia: The Irresponsible Society. James J. O'Toole. MRev., Oct. 1979, pp. 8–15. Univ. of Southern California.

Economics and Corporate Acquisitions. M. Mark Lee. *PA #74 Mergers and Acquisitions in a Changing Environment,* 1980, pp. 6–19. Standard Research Consultants

Egalitarianism and Market Systems. Harold M. Williams. MRev., Dec. 1978, pp. 7–11, Securities & Exchange Commission.

The Entropy State. Hazel Henderson. *Corporate Planning Techniques and Applications,* 1979, pp. 75–81. Princeton Center for Alternative Futures.

Factoring Inflation into Pricing. C. Daniel Bergfeld. *Strategic Pricing: Protecting Profit Margins from Inflation,* 1981, pp. 35–45. Case and Co. MB.

The Fast Changing World Population Outlook: Impact on Global Business. Geoffrey N. Calvert. *The International Essays for Business Decision Makers, Vol. IV,* 1979, pp. 94–102. Alexander & Alexander.

Financial Reporting Under Changing Values: An Introduction to Current Value Accounting. Morley P. Carscallen, Kenneth P. Johnson. 1979, 47 pp. Coopers and Lybrand. MB.

Food and Agriculture in the Next Quarter Century. Kenneth R. Farrell. *Corporate Planning Techniques and Applications,* 1979, pp. 93–101. U.S. Dept. of Agriculture.

The Future World of Work: The Strategic Significance of Human Resource Management in the 1980s. Lynne Hall. PA #72, 1980, 64 pp. AT&T. By purchase only.

The Hospital of the Future: How Will It Be Structured? Charles J. Austin. HSM, Oct. 1979, pp. 1–4. Georgia Southern College.

How Business Can Reconcile the Needs of Its Many Publics. James K. La Fleur. MRev., Nov. 1979, pp. 34–35. GTI Corp.

How to Anticipate Public-policy Changes. Graham T. T. Molitor. AMJ, Summer 1977, pp. 4–13. General Mills, Inc.

In Defense of the Corporate System. Robert Krieble. DM, Feb. 1981, pp. 1–2. Loctite Corp.

Indexed Escalation: A Growing Factor in Commercial Rentals. Charles S. Isaacs. MRev., Sept. 1980, pp. 50–57. Kenneth D. Laub & Co.

Inflation Fighters. Ernest C. Miller. Pers., Sept–Oct 1978, p. 51.

Inflation, the Economy, and Executive Power: An Interview with John Kenneth Galbraith. Zack Russ. MRev., July 1978, pp. 8–17.

Investment Stagnation: Are We Counting the Wrong Things? Richard N. Farmer. MRev., Oct. 1978, pp. 8–13. Indiana Univ.

It's Not What It Used to Be. Leonard Nadler. MRev., May 1978, pp. 23–28, 37–40. George Washington Univ.

Management Challenges in the 21st Century. A. H. Raskin. AMJ, Autumn 1979, pp. 25–32. The National News Council.

Managers in the Future: How Will They Be Judged? Peter Spooner, Michael Johnson. MRev., Dec. 1980, pp. 8–17.

The Moving Force: Preserving the Profit Motive in the American Economy. Henry I. Meyer. 1981, 323 pp.

Planning for Extinction. Robert Hershey. MRev., Sept. 1978, pp. 27–28, 38–40. U. S. Merchant Marine Academy.

The Real Estate Gamble. Alan Rabinowitz. 1980, 308 pp. Univ. of Washington.

Shifting Gears: The American Economy in Transition. Carter Henderson. MRev., Sept. 1978, pp. 41–45.

Steel—A Lesson in Basic Economics. Raymond M. Holliday. MRev., Feb. 1978, pp. 20–22. Hughes Tool Co.

Stocking Up to Beat Inflation. Louis Hohenstein. AMJ, Winter 1981. pp. 15–19. C. L. Hohenstein & Associates.

"Supply Side" Economic Theories: An Interview with Paul Craig Roberts. BPM 16, Oct. 1981, 5 pp. Assistant Secretary of the Treasury for Economic Policy.

The Third Wave: The Corporate Identity Crisis. Alvin Toffler. MRev., May 1980, pp. 8–17.

The Threat of Inflation to Future Business Success. Claude Isbister. *Current Value Accounting,* 1977, pp. 5–15. Currie, Coopers & Lybrand, Ltd.

The Wall Street Journal Views America Tomorrow. Donald Moffitt (editor). 1977, 184 pp. The Wall Street Journal.

Why U. S. Economy Struggles in Reverse—and What to Do About it. David T. Kearns. MRev., Oct. 1981, pp. 29, 32, 45. Xerox Corp.

STAFF. See Line-Staff

STOCKHOLDERS. See Investor Relations

STRIKES

How to Enjoy Not Having a Strike. Woodruff Imberman. MRev., Sept. 1981, pp. 43–47. Imberman & DeForest.

Is There an Alternative to a Strike? Woodruff Imberman, Mario Taracena. AMJ, Winter 1978, pp. 4–13. Imberman & DeForest.

SUGGESTION SYSTEMS

Employee Suggestion Plan Still Going Strong at Kodak. Allen W. Bergerson. SM, May 1977, pp. 32–36. Eastman Kodak Co.

The Improvement Program, A Comparison of SYI with the Team Approach. Richard F. Weaver. *The Amazing Oversight: Total Participation for Productivity,* 1979, pp. 139–154. Work Factor Foundation.

Means and Meanings of Recognition. Parvin S. Titus. *The Amazing Oversight: Total Participation for Productivity,* 1979, pp. 167–176. RCA.

When the Suggestion Box Fails. Donald W. Myers, Earnest R. Archer. Pers., Sept.–Oct. 1978, pp. 37–42.

SUPERIOR-SUBORDINATE RELATIONS

Avoiding Intimidation: The Fine Art of Saying No. William P. Anthony. SM, Nov. 1981, pp. 20–23. Florida State Univ.

Bicycle Management. William A. Delaney. SM, April 1980, pp. 15–19. Analysis & Computer Systems, Inc.

Changing an Ineffective Boss into a Model Manager. W. Randolph Flynn, William E. Stratton. SM, July 1979, pp. 14–20. Idaho State Univ.

The End-Run, or Stiff-Arming Your Superior. William A. Delaney. SM, Aug. 1981, pp. 17–20. Analysis & Computer Systems, Inc.

The Gentle Art of Saying No. Kelvin Chan. SM, Dec. 1981, pp. 14–16. Northern Lights College.

Handling Problem Employees. Paul W. Cummings. *Open Management: Guide to Successful Practice,* 1980, pp. 109–134.

How to Create Responsibility for Accomplishment. William C. Waddell. *Overcoming Murphy's Law,* 1981, pp. 100–121. California State Univ., Los Angeles.

How to Deal With A Rotten Boss. Norma Mortimer. SM, Nov. 1979, pp. 20–23. New Jersey Blue Cross.

How to Manage Your Boss. Peter F. Drucker. MRev., May 1977, pp. 8–12. (Also in reprint collection *Leadership on the Job: Guides to Good Supervision* (third ed.), 1981)

The Importance of Knowing Your Employee's Needs. Arthur Sondak. SM, May 1980, pp. 13–18. (Also in reprint collection *Leadership on the Job: Guides to Good Supervision* (third ed.), 1981)

A Letter to My Supervisor. Samuel H. Steinberg. HSM, Jan. 1977, p. 4. Episcopal Hospital.

The Other Side of the Coin—Subordinateship. M. E. Schnake. SM, Aug. 1980, pp. 25–29. Mississippi State Univ.

The Problem Employee Interview: Productive Interviewing No. 4 (sec. ed.). Glenn A. Bassett. 1981. (AMACOM audio cassette) By purchase only.

The Problems of Perfect Employees. Jeff Davidson. SM, May 1980, pp. 2–5. EMAY Corp. (Also in reprint collection *Leadership on the Job: Guides to Good Supervision* (third ed.), 1981)

Survey Suggests Managers Impede Subordinates Work. MRev., May 1981, pp. 29, 31.

What Do Middle Managers Really Want from First-Line Supervisors? Thomas DeLong. SM, Sept. 1977, pp. 8–12. Purdue Univ.

Where'd You Learn to Be a Manager? Charles Magerison. SM, Feb. 1981, pp. 40–43. Cranfield School of Management.

SUPERVISION. See also Executives—Skills and Qualifications, Management

Are "Self Defenses" Keeping You from Being a Better Manager? Robin Peterson. SM, Sept. 1977, pp. 21–24. New Mexico State Univ. (Also reprinted in HSM, Jan. 1981)

"Boss You're Killing Me." Lee Bancroft. SM, March 1978, pp. 10–14.

Changing the Rules: How to Win at Supervision. William E. Zierden. SM, June 1979, pp. 12–16. Univ. of Virginia.

Developing the Art of Supervision. James G. Stockard. *Career Development and Job Training*, 1977, pp. 238–258.

Effective Supervision. Linda A. Roxe. *Personnel Management for the Smaller Company*, 1979, pp. 147–167. Rox Associates.

The Effective Supervisor's Handbook. Louis V. Imundo. 1980, 239 pp. Management Perspectives.

The Fear of Failure—The Supervisor's Greatest Enemy. James H. Corey, Jr. SM, Dec. 1979, pp. 2–7. Quick Chek Food Stores.

First-Line Management. Grant E. Mayberry. 1979. (Extension Institute Course) By purchase only.

First-Line Supervisors Say of Middle Managers: "There's Lots of Room for Improvement." Louis J. Frangipane. MRev., Oct. 1979, p. 46. E-Systems, Inc.

First-Line Supervisors: The Key to Improved Performance. Ernest A. Doud, Jr., Edward J. Miller. MRev., Dec. 1980, pp. 18–24. R. M. Wald & Associates, Tri/Valley Growers.

The First-Time Manager: A Practical Guide to the Management of People. Loren B. Belker. 1978, 165 pp. Bankers Life Ins. Co.

Five Mistakes You Can't Afford to Make. O. A. Battista. SM, Jan. 1977, pp. 36–39. Research Services Corp. (Also in reprint collection *Leadership on the Job: Guides to Good Supervision* (third ed.), 1981)

The Foreman's Job as Perceived by His Wife. Roger C. Schoenfeldt. SM, Sept. 1980, pp. 9–15. Murray State Univ.

How Good a Supervisor Are You? R. T. Drake. SM, March 1981, pp. 18–21. Hook Drugs, Inc.

How the Right Example Can Help the New Recruit Make the Team. Charles J. Teplitz. SM, May 1980, pp. 30–35. State Univ. of New York.

How to Be an Effective Supervisor. David B. Whittier. 1978. (Extension Institute Cassette Program) By purchase only.

Keeping Your Employees Turned On—Professionally. T. J. Halatin, William T. Flannery. SM, Oct. 1981, pp. 10–14. Univ. of Texas.

Leadership for Head Nurses: Developing an Integrated Approach. James A. Rodeghero, Jr. HSM, Jan. 1979, pp. 6–8. Univ. of Tennessee.

Making the Transition to Supervisor. Claude T. Mangrum. SM, Sept. 1978, pp. 7–13. County of San Bernardino, California. (Also reprinted in HSM, July 1980)

Managing Failure. John Nirenberg. SM, June 1979, pp. 17–22. Ohio Univ.

Needed: Top Management Attention to the Role of the First-Line Supervisor. William E. Zierden. AMJ, Summer 1980, pp. 18–25. Univ. of Virginia.

The Office Romance: No Bliss for the Boss. Robert E. Quinn, Noreen A. Judge. MRev., July 1978, pp. 43–49. State Univ. of New York, New York State Division of the Budget.

Paving the Rocky Road to Managerial Success. Archie B. Carroll. SM, March 1979, pp. 9–13. Univ. of Georgia.

The Power of Supervision. Ken Thompson. HSM, June 1980, pp. 8–9. Univ. of Notre Dame.

Rethinking the Supervisory Role. David S. Brown. SM, Nov. 1977, pp. 2–10. George Washington Univ.

Six Supervisors Talk About Supervision. SM, Part 1. What Makes A Good Supervisor. Jan. 1978, pp. 2–15. Part 2. The Trouble with Relationships. Feb. 1978, pp. 18–28. Part 3. The Rewards—and Regrets—of Supervision. March 1978, pp. 23–32.

Skills in Supervision. Lois Borland Hart. *Moving Up: Women and Leadership,* 1980, pp. 88–107. Mountain States Employers Council, Inc.

So You Want to Be a Supervisor. Donald G. Begosh. SM, Feb. 1978, pp. 2–10.

Stepping Up Supervision: Making the Transition. Kent H. Baker, Steven H. Holmberg. SM, Sept. 1981, pp. 10–18. American Univ.

Supervising the Troubled Employee. Leo M. Herrmann. HSM, Nov. 1978, pp. 6–8. Saint Vincent Health Center.

Supervision Can Be Easy. David K. Lindo. 1979, 272 pp.

The Supervisor's Survival Guide. Robert E. Pitts, Ken Thompson. 1979, 64 pp. Univ. of Notre Dame (A collection of reprints from SM)

The Supervisor's Survival Guide: A Positive Approach to Motivation. Robert E. Pitts, Ken Thompson. SM, Nov. 1978, pp. 2–10. Univ. of Notre Dame. (Also in reprint collection *The Supervisor's Survival Guide,* 1979)

The Supervisor's Survival Guide: Being Group Leader. Ken Thompson, Robert E. Pitts, SM, March 1979, pp. 24–31. Univ. of Notre Dame. (Also in reprint collection *The Supervisor's Survival Guide,* 1979)

The Supervisor's Survival Guide: The Great Balancing Act. Ken Thompson, Robert E. Pitts. SM, May 1979, pp. 22–30. Univ. of Notre Dame. (Also in reprint collection *The Supervisor's Survival Guide,* 1979)

Surviving and Succeeding in the 'Political' Organization: Establishing a Corporate Vantage Point. Alan Jay Weiss. SM, May 1978, pp. 2–10. Kepner-Tregoe, Inc. (Also in reprint collection *Surviving and Succeeding in the 'Political' Organization 1978)*

Tomorrow's Employee: The Supervisor's Greatest Challenge. T. Mitchell Ford. SM, June 1979, pp. 9–11. Emhart Corp.

Tradition: Is It Always the Best Way? Kenneth W. Amrhine. SM, April 1978, pp. 10–15.

Waiting for the Other Shoe to Fall. Howard R. Smith. MRev., April 1977, pp. 28–33. Univ. of Georgia.

What to Do About the Marginal Employee. SS, Jan. 1981, 24 pp.

Your Domain and Others. Dalton E. McFarland. SM, Feb. 1980, pp. 14–20. Univ. of Alabama.

SUPERVISORY TRAINING. See also Management Development, Selection, Training and Development

How to Avoid Professional Obsolescence. Jack J. Phillips. SM, Nov. 1980, pp. 10–14. Vulcan Materials Co.

Training the New Supervisor. James E. Gardner. 1980, 192 pp. Fieldcrest Mills, Inc.

SYSTEMS ANALYSIS. See also Data Processing

Basic Systems and Procedures (sec. ed.). Richard W. Beane. 1979. (Extension Institute Course) By purchase only.

Forms Analysis. William V. Nygren. *Business Forms Management,* 1980, pp. 35–45. 3M Co.

Guidelines for Conducting an Office Systems Feasibility Study. George S. Smith. 1981, 59 pp. Nabisco, Inc. MB.

How New Office Technology Promotes Changing Work Methods. Horst Morgenbrod, Heinz Schwartzel. MRev., July 1979, pp. 42–45.

Standard Procedures and Departmental Operating Instructions. James L. Mercer, Edwin H. Koester. *Public Management Systems: An Administrator's Guide,* 1978, pp. 104–122. Battelle Southern Operations, C. R. Drew Postgraduate Medical School.

System Dynamics: A Tool for Management. V. Alan Mode. MRev., May 1980, pp. 18–22.

A Systems Approach to Planning and Managing Programs for the Handicapped. Robert Elkin. *Managing Nonprofit Organizations,* 1977, pp. 71–77. Peat, Marwick, Mitchell & Co.

Systems Planning Smooths the Way for Primary Nursing in a New Facility. Lois Hybben. HSM, Jan. 1981, pp. 2–4. Mount Sinai Hospital.

What the Supervisor Should Know About Systems Theory. Dennis C. King. SM, Part 1. Nov. 1977, pp. 35–40. Part 2. Dec. 1977, pp. 31–34. Proctor & Gamble Manufacturing Co.

TAXATION. See also Compensation—Executives. International Finance

Deferred Gifts and Bequests. George A. Brakeley, Jr. *Tested Ways to Successful Fund Raising,* 1980, pp. 136–114. Brakeley, John Price Jones, Inc.

Easing the Tax Squeeze on the Multinational Employee. Walter F. O'Connor, Robert K. Decelles. Pers., Sept.–Oct. 1977, pp. 28–39. Peat, Marwick, Mitchell & Co.

ERTA Explained ... New Opportunities in Compensation and Benefits Under the 1981 Tax Act. Frederick W. Rumack, David H. Gravitz. MRev., Nov. 1981, pp. 8–12. Buck Consultants.

Estate Planning—After the 1976 Tax Reform Law. Edward E. Milam, D. Larry Crumbley. 1978, 230 pp. Univ. of Mississippi, Texas A & M Univ.

Highlights of the Tax Reform Act of 1976. Barry Hammerling. SM, Feb. 1977, pp. 38–42. The Ayco Corp.

The Impact of Inflation on Taxation. David Y. Timbrell. *Current Value Accounting,* 1977, pp. 65–85. Coopers & Lybrand.

Importance of Depreciation and Corporate Income Taxes to Capital Budgeting. Robert E. Pritchard, Thomas J. Hindelang. *The Strategic Evaluation and Management of Capital Expenditures,* 1981, pp. 39–54. Glassboro State College, Drexel Univ.

Leveraged Leasing: New Opportunities Under the Economic Recovery Tax Act of 1981. Albert F. Gargiulo, Raymond J. Kenard, Jr. 1981, 53 pp. Raymond J. Kenard, Jr., Inc. MB.

New Tax Law's Voluntary Employee Contributions Forcing Management to Make Hard, Long-term Choices. Philip M. Alden, Jr. MRev., Dec. 1981, pp. 21–23. Towers, Perrin, Forster & Crosby.

A Payroll Tax Alternative Using FICA II. Jane L. Martin. CR, Third Quarter 1979, pp. 30–38. Management Improvement Corp. of America.

The Real Estate Gamble. Alan Rabinowitz. 1980, 308 pp. Univ. of Washington.

The Social Security Burden. Ernest C. Miller. Pers., Sept.–Oct. 1978, pp. 49–50.

Tax and Accounting Considerations in Mergers and Acquisitions. Phillip R. Peller, John B. Brown. *PA #74 Mergers and Acquisitions in a Changing Environment,* 1980, pp. 41–53. Arthur Anderson & Co. By purchase only.

The Tax Reform Act of 1976 and Prepaid Legal Insurance. Philip M. Alden, Jr. Pers., July–Aug. 1977, pp. 59–64. Towers, Perrin, Forster & Crosby.

Tax Shelters: Best for the Wealthy, Good for the Wise. C. Colburn Hardy. *Your Money & Your Life: How to Plan Your Long-Range Financial Security,* 1979, pp. 239–246.

Tax Strategy for Multinationals—Economic and Social Issues. John Chown, John Humble. 1979, 30 pp. J. F. Chown & Co., Ltd. MB.

Taxation and the Petroleum Industry. Roy T. Pleasance. *Financing the International Petroleum Industry,* 1978, pp. 140–161. British Petroleum Co. Ltd.

Taxes, Nontrusts, Probate, and Tax Reforms. Adam Starchild. *Building Wealth: A Layman's Guide to Trust Planning,* 1981, pp. 175–191. Minerva Consulting Group Inc.

Unrelated Business Taxable Income. Marc J. Lane. *Legal Handbook for Nonprofit Organizations,* 1980, pp. 198–210. Medico-Legal Institutes, Inc.

TEAM MANAGEMENT. See also Change, Cooperation, Coordination and Conflict Resolution, Job Design/Job Enlargement/Job Enrichment, Organizational Development

The Accountability Chart—A Tool for Team Building. Neil Miller. Pers., Nov.–Dec. 1977, pp. 51–56. Miller/Ginsberg & Brien.

Building Winning Management Teams Begins with a Simple, Uncomplicated Approach. Chester Gadzinski. MRev., March 1980, pp. 31–32. Kearney-National, Inc.

Coping with Team Trauma. A. Thomas Hollingsworth, Bruce M. Meglino, Michael C. Shaner. MRev., Aug. 1979, pp. 48–50. Univ. of South Carolina, St. Louis Univ.

Creativity and the Group Effort. James L. Hayes. MRev., May 1979, pp. 2–3.

Developing Teamwork in Today's Environment. Roger J. Howe. *Building Profits Through Organizational Change,* 1981, pp. 174–194. Donaldson Co., Inc.

Effective Team Building. Vern Goldsmith, William B. Brown. 1980. (Extension Institute Cassette Program) By purchase only.

Exercises in Team Building . . . A Manager's Trip Through the Hall of Mirrors of the Psyche. Henry Marksbury. MRev., Oct. 1979, pp. 53–57. Arthur Young & Co.

Fine-Tuning Team Spirit. Bruce D. Sanders. SM, June 1980, pp. 26–30.

How to Muster and Master the Change to Team Nursing. John L. Ryan, David L. Woodrum. HSM, Sept. 1978, pp. 6–8. Ryan Advisors, Inc.

The Male—Female Management Team: The Dance of Death? Janet M. Hively. William S. Howell. MRev., June 1980, pp. 44–50. City of Minneapolis, Univ. of Minneapolis.

Managerial Team Building: Casting Light on What Makes Us Tick. Henry Marksbury. MRev., Sept. 1979, pp. 8–14. Arthur Young & Co.

Successful Team Building Through TA. Dudley Bennett. 1980, 260 pp. MCM Consultants, Inc.

Team Building. Thomas H. Patten, Jr. Pers., Part 1. Designing the Intervention. Jan–Feb. 1979, pp. 11–21. Part 2. Conducting the Intervention. March–April 1979, pp. 62–68. Michigan State Univ.

Team Development. Francis X. Mahoney. Pers., Part 1. What Is TD? Why Use It? Sept.–Oct. 1981, pp. 13–24. Part 2. How to Select the Appropriate TD Approach. Nov.–Dec. 1981, pp. 21–38. Exxon Co.

Teams Work. James L. Hayes. MRev., Nov. 1977, pp. 2–3.

Tough-Minded Team Building. Joe Batten, Hal Batten. 1979. (AMACOM audio cassette) By purchase only.

Toward a More Creative You: Creating the Ideal Organization. Harold R. McAlindon. SM, Jan. 1980, pp. 26–32. The Institute of Financial Education.

TERMINATION

Alternatives to Employee Layoffs: Work Sharing and Prelayoff Consultation. Nancy J. McNeff, Marvin R. McNeff, George E. O'Connell, Joan M. O'Connell. Pers., Jan.–Feb. 1978, pp. 60–64.

Clearing Corporate Deadwood: The Practical Art of Pruning Organizational Limbs. George S. Odiorne. MRev., June 1979. pp. 39–44. Univ. of Massachusetts.

Confronting Recession-bred Litigation. Frederick L. Sullivan. SM, Dec. 1980, pp. 2–10. Sullivan & Hayes.

Easing the Pain of Plant Closure: Brown & Williamson Experience. Carroll H. Teague. MRev., April 1981, pp. 23–27. Brown & Williamson Tobacco Corp.

Easing the Pain of Termination. Lawrence M. Baytos. Pers., July–Aug. 1979, pp. 64–69. The Quaker Oats Co.

Employee Termination: Proceeed with Care. Edward Mandt. MRev., Dec. 1980, pp. 25–28. Maccabees Mutual Life Insurance Co.

Executive Termination—The New Way Out. Deslie Beth Lawrence, Iris D. Rosendahl. Pers., March–April 1979, pp. 56–57.

The Exit Interview. Edward Roseman. *Managing Employee Turnover: A Positive Approach,* 1981, pp. 173–184. Answers & Insights, Inc.

The Exit Interview: Productive Interviewing No. 2 (sec. ed.). John R. Hinrichs. 1981. (AMACOM audio cassette) By purchase only.

The Exit Interview: Why Bother? Stephen B. Wehrenberg. SM, May 1980, pp. 20–25. U. S. Coast Guard.

Outplacement Practices. Pers., July–Aug. 1980, pp. 4–5.

The Right Way to Leave Your Job. William A. Delaney. SM, Aug. 1980, pp. 30–34. Analysis & Computer.

Separation Isn't Simple. J. H. Foegen. SM, Sept. 1979. pp. 12–15. Winona State Univ.

Softening the Blow of "You're Fired." Angelo M. Troisi. SM, June 1980, pp. 14–19. Troy Associates. (Also in reprint collection *Leadership on the Job: Guides to Good Supervision* (third ed.), 1981)

Termination at Will: Some Changes in the Wind. Stuart A. Youngblood, Gary L. Tidwell. Pers., May–June 1981, pp. 22–33. Univ. of South Carolina, Army Judge Advocate General's Corps.

TESTING—PERSONNEL

Can Intelligence Tests Predict Executive Competence? Charles Bahn. Pers., July–Aug. 1979, pp. 52–58. Temple Univ.

Employee Selection Tests: Upping the Odds for Success. Mary Zippo. Pers., Nov.–Dec. 1980, pp. 48–49.

Employment Tests: Fair or Unfair Discrimination? James Weitzul. MRev., Aug. 1980, pp. 50–52. RHR Institute.

Personnel Testing Under EEO. Jerome Siegel. 1980, 92 pp. City Univ. of New York. RS.

Test Validation and EEOC Requirements: Where We Stand. Winton H. Manning. Pers., May–June 1978, pp. 70–77. Educational Testing Service.

TIME MANAGEMENT

ABCs of Time Management. Edwin C. Bliss. SM, May 1978, pp. 28–33.

Add Sixty Minutes to Each Day. David K. Lindo. *Supervision Can Be Easy,* 1979, pp. 206–214.

Are You a Roadrunner? Richard A. Morano. SM, May 1980, pp. 26–29. Xerox Corp.

Are You Running a "Fire Department?" Karl Albrecht. HSM, Dec. 1980, pp. 7–10.

Budgeting Time for Better Management. Stuart J. Wallack. SM, Oct. 1977, pp. 16–21. Western Electric.

Building a Time-Management Team. H. Kent Baker. SM, March 1980, pp. 12–16. American Univ.

Clues to Executive Time Control. Henry Mintzberg. 1977. (AMACOM audio cassette) By purchase only.

Energy Crisis in the Executive Suite. R. Alec Mackenzie, Gary Richards. SM, Oct. 1978, pp. 17–26. Alec Mackenzie & Associates.

Executive Time Management. Philip Marvin. 1980, 29 pp. Univ. of Cincinnati. SR.

Executive Time Management. Part 1: Organizational Support for Better Time Management. Richard A. Morano. AMJ, Winter 1978, pp. 36–40. Xerox Corp.

Executive Time Management. Part 2: How to Budget Your Time. Bordon Coulter, George Hayo, Sr. AMJ, Winter 1978, pp. 41–48. The Emerson Consultants, Inc.

'Four-thirty Already!' Managing Your Time. SS, Sept. 1981, 24 pp.

Getting Results with Time Management (sec. ed.). David V. Lewis. 1979. (Extension Institute Course) By purchase only.

How Much Is an Hour of Your Time Really Worth? Joseph G. Mason. MRev., June 1977, pp. 16–21. National Business Aircraft Assn.

How to Conquer Procrastination. Merrill E. Douglass. AMJ, Summer 1978, pp. 40–50. Time Management Center.

How to Make Effective Use of Time. ES, March 1979, 16 pp.

Mackenzie on Time. Alec Mackenzie. 1979. (AMACOM audio cassette book) By purchase only.

Manage Your Time, Manage Your Work, Manage Yourself. Merrill E. Douglass, Donna N. Douglass. 1980, 278 pp. Time Management Center.

Management Functions: What to Do and When. Dennis P. Slevin. *Management Principles for Nonprofit Agencies and Organizations,* 1979, pp. 11–37. Univ. of Pittsburgh.

Managing Time: Positive Clock-Watching. George H. Labowitz, Lloyd Baird. AMJ, Summer 1981. pp. 44–53. Boston Univ.

Managing Time, the Scarcest Resource. Howard L. Smith, Frank H. Besnette. HSM, Jan. 1978, pp. 1–5. Northern Arizona Univ.

No Time to Spare. James L. Hayes. MRev., Sept. 1978, pp. 2–3.

The Power of Patience. James L. Hayes. MRev., April 1981, pp. 2–3.

Stepping Up to Supervision: Managing Time and Job Pressures. H. Kent Baker, Stevan Holmberg. SM, Dec. 1981, pp. 25–32. Kogod College of Business Administration, The American University.

Success in Your Own Good Time. Merrill E. Douglass, Larry D. Baker. SM, April 1981, pp. 30–35. Time Management Center, Univ. of St. Louis.

Successful Time Management for Hospital Administrators. Merrill E. Douglass, Phillip H. Goodwin. 1980, 143 pp. Time Management Center, Hillcrest Medical Center.

Time Management. Paul W. Cummings. *Open Management: Guides to Successful Practice,* 1980, pp. 199–214.

Time Management. Louis V. Imundo. *The Effective Supervisor's Handbook,* 1980, pp. 218–231. Management Perspectives.

Time Management. William R. Osgood. *Basics of Successful Business Management,* 1981, pp. 29–51.

Time Management: Making Every Minute Count. Larry G. McDougle. SM, Aug. 1979, pp. 35–40. Indiana Univ.

Time Management: Separating the Myths and the Realities. John Humble. MRev., Oct. 1980, pp. 25–28, 49–53. Accelerated Management Development, Ltd.

Time-Management Strategy for Women. Eleanor B. Schwartz, R. Alec Mackenzie. MRev., Sept. 1977, pp. 19–25. Cleveland State Univ., Alec Mackenzie & Associates

When Priorities Close In. Sydney F. Love. MRev., April 1978, pp. 50–53. Advanced Professional Development, Inc.

Where Does Your Day Go? Phillip H. Goodwin. HSM, Oct. 1980, pp. 3–4. Hillcrest Medical Center.

TRADE SECRETS. See Competitive Intelligence

TRAINING AND DEVELOPMENT. See also Coaching and Counseling, Management Development, Sales Training, Supervisory Training

Algorithm: Helping Trainees Think Like Experienced Workers. Gerard Tavernier. MRev., April 1981, pp. 45–49.

Analysis and Design. William R. Tracey. *Human Resource Development Standards,* 1981, pp. 461–494. U.S. Army Intelligence Training School.

Assertion Training. Rita E. Numerof. HSM, Part 1. Who Needs It and Why? May 1977, pp. 1–4, 10. Part 2. Learning to Be Assertive. June 1977, pp. 1–4, 10. Part 3. Evaluating the Program's Impact. July 1977, pp. 1–4.

Audiovisual Evaluation: An Essential for Effective Patient Education. Sharon Ferrance Porter. HSM, Aug. 1981, pp. 6, 11–14. Shoal Creek Hospital.

Career Development and Job Training: A Manager's Handbook. James G. Stockard. 1977, 434 pp.

Confronting Nonpromotiability: How to Manage a Stalled Career. Edward Roseman. 1977, 244 pp. Answers & Insights, Inc.

A Continuing Education Program That Insures Quality Care. John W. Clarke, W. H. Johnson. HSM, June 1980, pp. 6–7. Research Medical Center.

Developing an Effective Field Force. Donald N. McCafferty. *Successful Field Service Management,* 1980, pp. 113–139. Honeywell, Inc.

Employee Training Programs. Hermine Zagat Levine. Pers., July–Aug. 1981, pp. 4–11.

A Guide to the Evaluation of Instruction (Appendix C). William R. Tracey. *Human*

Resource Development Standards, 1981, pp. 570–586. U.S. Army Intelligence Training School.

Have the Confidence to Train Your "Replacement." Marion Farrant. SM, Aug. 1980, pp. 8–10. (Also in reprint collection *Leadership on the Job: Guides to Good Supervision* (third ed.), 1981)

The High Cost of Buying Cheap. James L. Hayes. MRev., June 1978, pp. 2–3.

Human Relations Training: The Tailored Approach. Bob Mezoff. Pers., March–April 1981, pp. 21–27. Univ. of Connecticut.

Human Resource Development: A Manager's Guide. Ray A. Killian. 1978. (Extension Institute Course) By purchase only.

Human Resource Development Standards. William R. Tracey. 1981, 598 pp. U.S. Army Intelligence Training School.

Influencing the Training of Nurses. Robert J. Grams. HSM, Nov. 1981, pp. 11–13. Arizona Hospital Assn.

The Logic of Training Evaluation. Kent J. Chabotar. Pers., July–Aug. 1977, pp. 23–27.

Needs Analysis in the Training Department. Harry Langford. SM, Aug. 1978, pp. 18–25.

Performance Improvement the Adult Way. Peter G. Kirby. Pers., Nov.–Dec. 1980, pp. 35–43. D. R. Lund Associates.

A Proven Approach to In-House Technical Training. Kathryn A. Hackett. HSM, Sept. 1980, pp. 12–14. Bio/Dynamics Inc.

The Supervisor As Teacher. Lois B. Hart. SM, Jan. 1981, pp. 38–41. Leadership Dynamics.

A System for Evaluating Training Programs. Basil S. Deming. Pers., Nov.–Dec. 1979, pp. 33–41. U.S. Office of Personnel Management.

Toward a More Creative You: Developing the Whole Person. Harold R. McAlindon. SM, March 1980, pp. 31–35. Institute of Financial Education. (Also in reprint collection *Getting the Most Out of Your Job and Your Organization,* 1980)

Training and Development. Linda A. Roxe. *Personnel Management for the Smaller Company,* 1979, pp. 168–189. Rox Associates.

Training and Developing Your Subordinates. ES, April 1981, 16 pp.

Training Employees. James F. Evered. *Shirt-Sleeves Management,* 1981, pp. 78–94. Redman Industries, Inc.

Training for Results. R. J. Benford, William E. Brooks, M. T. Tedd, S. X. Doyle. Pers., May–June 1979, pp. 17–24. Norwich-Eaton Pharmaceuticals, SXD Associates.

Training for Productivity. Beverly Hyman. 1980. (Extension Institute Course) By purchase only.

Training Programs. William R. Tracey. *Human Resource Development Standards,* 1981, pp. 375–418. U.S. Army Intelligence Training School.

Training—the Next Step. Paul E. Illman. *Developing Overseas Managers—and Managers Overseas,* 1980, pp. 204–238. Management Training, Inc.

Training Your Nurses in Five Easy Stages. Maureen E. Mullarkey. HSM, June 1979, pp. 2–4. East Orange General Hospital.

TRAINING AND DEVELOPMENT—MINORITY PERSONNEL

Improving Performance and Results Through Training. Ray A. Killian. *Managers Must Lead!* (rev. ed.), 1979, pp. 132–142. Belk Stores.

Problems of Black Managers Can't be Solved by Them Alone. Floyd Dickens, Jacqueline Dickens. MRev., June 1981, pp. 29, 36. Procter & Gamble Co.

The Training Function: Who Should Be Learning What? Jennie Farley. *Affirmative Action and the Woman Worker,* 1979, pp. 74–92. Cornell Univ.

TRANSACTIONAL ANALYSIS. See Communications—Transactional Analysis

TRANSCENDENTAL MEDITATION. See Health

TRANSPORTATION. See also Distribution Management
Aircraft Management ... How to Keep Your Feet on the Ground in the Company

Plane. Matthew C. Weisman. MRev., May 1980, pp. 53–55. Executive Air Fleet Corp.

The Benefits of Air Freight. Martin T. Slijper. *Managing International Distribution,* 1979, pp. 223–240. Rowntree Mackintosh, Ltd.

Choosing the Freighting Mode. Martin T. Slijper. *Managing International Distribution,* 1979, pp. 250–268. Rowntree Mackintosh, Ltd.

The Freight Forwarder. R. A. Tudhope. *Managing International Distribution,* 1979, pp. 241–249. Mitchell Cotts & Co. (UK) Ltd.

Fundamentals of Traffic Management. Colin Barrett. 1980. (Extension Institute Course) By purchase only.

The Future of Containerization and the Third World. Charles I. Hiltzheimer. *The International Essays for Business Decision Makers, Vol. V,* 1980, pp. 309–315. Sea-Land Industries Investments, Inc.

How to Plan Vehicle Replacement. Felix Wentworth. *Managing International Distribution,* 1979, pp. 77–92. Chubb Hennessy.

The Impact of Through Transport on Deep-Sea Shipping. Michael Graham. *Managing International Distribution,* 1979, pp. 194–222. Overseas Containers Ltd.

Plenty. Ben Housel. HSM, Oct. 1981, pp. 3–4. Plenty Ambulance Service.

Short-Sea Routeing. I. M. Churcher. *Managing International Distribution,* 1979, pp. 185–193. P & O Ferries.

TURNOVER

Employee Turnover: Every Supervisor's Problem. Gerard P. Boe. HSM, July 1978, pp. 1–2. Dwight D. Eisenhower Army Medical Center.

How to Estimate Employee Turnover Costs. Thomas E. Hall. Pers., July–Aug. 1981, pp. 43–52. Computervision.

How to Tell When a Good Employee Is Job Hunting. Jeff Davidson. SM, Oct. 1980, pp. 2–9. James H. Lowry & Associates.

Human Factors in Production. Alfred J. Marrow. *Human Resources Management: The Past Is Prologue,* 1979, pp. 126–136.

Keeping Employee Turnover Under Control. Andrew D. Szilagyi. Pers., Nov.–Dec. 1979, pp. 42–52. Univ. of Houston.

Managing Employee Turnover: A Positive Approach. Edward Roseman. 1981, 260 pp. Answers & Insights, Inc.

Predicting Employee Turnover. Gerald A. Kesselman. HSM, July 1981, pp. 12–14. Lopez Assessment Services, Inc.

The Turnover Trap. H. Kent Baker. SM, June 1979, pp. 2–8. American Univ.

Why Some Workers Say "I Quit." SS, Nov. 1981, 24 pp.

UNIONS. See also Collective Bargaining, Labor-Management Relations

How Unions Affect Hospital Administration. D. L. Bates, Jim A. Wilterding. HSM, Nov. 1977, pp. 7, 9–10. California State Univ., Boise State Univ.

Labor Unions. Linda A. Roxe. *Personnel Management for the Smaller Company,* 1979, pp. 215–235. Rox Associates.

Preventive Labor Relations. John G. Kilgour. 1981, 338 pp. California State Univ.

Why Employees Want Unions. Jeanne M. Brett. OD, Spring 1980, pp. 47–59. Northwestern Univ.

Why Unions Need More, Not Less Competition. John H. Gerstenmaier. MRev., Dec. 1977, pp. 20–21. The Goodyear Tire & Rubber Co.

UNIONS—ORGANIZATION DRIVES

How Mismanagement Can Lead to Unionization. Richard D. Adkins. HSM, Sept. 1979, pp. 8–9. Health Industry Labor Consultants, Inc.

How to Win a Decertification Election. Woodruff Imberman. MRev., Sept. 1977, pp. 26–28, 37–39.

Learning About Labor Relations. Roger Drue. HSM, Dec. 1981, pp. 11–12. Mills Memorial Hospital.

Limiting Union Organizing Activity Through Supervisors. Frederick L. Sullivan. Pers., July–Aug. 1978, pp. 55–65. Sullivan & Hayes.

Preventive Labor Relations. John G. Kilgour. 1981, 338 pp. California State Univ.

Reworking the Union—Management Relationship. Robert R. Blake, Jane Srygley Mouton. *Productivity: the Human Side,* 1981, pp. 88–94. Scientific Methods, Inc.

Union Avoidance Campaigns: You Need More Than Hocus-Pocus. Woodruff Imberman. MRev., Sept. 1980, pp. 45–49. Imberman & Deforest.

Using Closed-Circuit Television During Union Organizing Campaigns. James C. Hogue. Pers., Sept.–Oct. 1977, pp. 72–77.

What Supervisors Can Do About Union Organizing. Christopher F. Carney. SM, Jan. 1981, pp. 10–15. E. I. du Pont de Nemours & Co.

Why Do Workers Vote for Union Decertification? William E. Fulmer, Tamara A. Gilman. Pers., March–April 1981, pp. 28–35. Univ. of Alabama.

WAGE AND SALARY. See Compensation, Job Evaluation

WAGE INCENTIVES. See also Performance Standards, Work Measurement

Administering Divisional Incentive Compensation. Robert B. Pursell. CR, First Quarter 1980, pp. 15–20. Towers, Perrin, Forster & Crosby.

Alternative Financial Schemes Based on Value Added. M. S. Silver. CR, Third Quarter 1979, pp. 10–29. Univ. of Aston Management Centre.

A Contingency Approach to Incentive Program Design. Robert C. Ford, Ronald Couture. CR, Second Quarter 1978, pp. 34–42. Univ. of North Florida, Burrough's Corp.

Gainsharing: Involvement, Incentives, and Productivity. Carla S. O'Dell. 1981, 80 pp. American Productivity Center. MB.

GAO Study on Productivity—Sharing Programs. Clement F. Preiwisch. *Productivity Improvement: Case Studies of Proven Practice,* 1981, pp. 177–200. U.S. General Accounting Office-Chicago Regional Office.

Improving Employee Productivity. Roger J. Howe. *Building Profits Through Organizational Change,* 1981, pp. 195–215. Donaldson Co., Inc.

Incentive Strategies Boost Worker Productivity. David D. Steinbrecher. Pers., Nov.–Dec. 1979, pp. 57–58.

Research: How Rewards Can Be Made More Effective by Proper Structuring. Albert S. King. CR, First Quarter 1978, pp. 32–40. Northern Illinois Univ.

The Scanlon Plan: Divvy up the Gross and Double the Profits. Fred G. Lesieur. MRev., May 1977, pp. 29–31.

The Scanlon Plan Reaps Productivity Bonus for Labor and for Management. George Sherman. MRev., May 1977, pp. 31–32.

Wage Incentive Plans. Robert E. Nolan, Richard T. Young, Ben C. DiSylvester. *Improving Productivity Through Advanced Office Controls,* 1980 pp. 348–356. Robert E. Nolan Co., Inc.

Working Creatively with a Union: Lessons from the Scanlon Plan. James W. Driscoll. OD, Summer 1979, pp. 61–80. Sloan School of Management.

WAREHOUSING. See Distribution Management

WOMEN WORKERS

Clearing the Way for the Growth of Women Subordinates. DeAnne Rosenberg. *Leadership on the Job: Guides to Good Supervision,* 1981, pp. 291–295.

Decades: Lifestyle Changes in Career Expectations. Edith M. Lynch. 1980, 144 pp. American Employers for Free Enterprise.

Developing Women Managers: What Needs to be Done? Martha G. Burrow. 1978, 32 pp. CoMedia, Inc. MB.

Harmonious Results in Working with Women. Ray A. Killian. *Managers Must Lead!* (rev. ed.), 1979, pp. 150–164. Belk Stores.

How Women Can Get Out of Dead-end Jobs. Edith M. Lynch. AMJ, Spring 1980, pp. 60–63. American Employers for Free Enterprise. (Also reprinted in *Making Successful Presentations,* 1981)

How Women Compete: A Guide for Managers. Barbara Benedict Bunker, Lisa Richer Bender. MRev., Aug. 1980, pp. 55–61. State Univ. of New York, Digital Equipment Corp.

Manager's Quiz: How Would You Deal with These Women? MRev., Aug. 1980, pp. 59, 62.

Men and Women as Managers: A Significant Case of No Significant Difference. Susan M. Donnell, Jay Hall. OD, Spring 1980, pp. 60–77. Teleometrics Intl.

Moving Up: Women and Leadership. Lois Borland Hart. 1980, 229 pp. Mountain States Employers Council, Inc.

Moving Women into "Male" Jobs. MarySue Foster. SM, June 1981, pp. 2–9. Foster & Wood Associates.

Responsive Leadership: The Woman Manager's Asset or Liability? Beverly Hyman. SM, Aug. 1980, pp. 40–43. Beverly Hyman & Associates. (Also in reprint collection *Leadership on the Job: Guides to Good Supervision* (third ed.), 1981)

Sexual Harassment: An Old Issue—A New Problem. Oliver L. Niehouse, JoAnne Ross Doades. SM, April 1980, pp. 10–14. Oliver L. Niehouse & Associates. Doades & Co. (Also in reprint collection *Leadership on the Job: Guides to Good Supervision* (third ed.), 1981)

A Special Note to Women and Their Bosses. Georgette F. McGregor, Joseph A. Robinson. *The Communication Matrix: Ways of Winning with Words,* 1981, pp. 145–168. Joseph A. Robinson Associates

Why Women Need Assertiveness Training. Arlene Yerys. SM, Oct. 1977, pp. 2–7. Effective Training System.

WORD PROCESSING

Auditing Office and Word Processing Operations. Gerald L. Hershey. MRev., Feb. 1979, pp. 49–54. Univ. of North Carolina.

An Update on Administrative Support Centers. F. Stanley Phillips. MRev., Feb. 1978, pp. 29–31. Naremco Services, Inc.

WORK MEASUREMENT. See also Wage Incentives

Formal Techniques: Predetermined Time Systems. Robert E. Nolan, Richard T. Young, Ben C. DiSylvester. *Improving Productivity Through Advanced Office Control,* 1980, pp. 138–155. Robert E. Nolan Co., Inc.

Formal Techniques: Time Study. Robert E. Nolan, Richard T. Young, Ben C. DiSylvester. *Improving Productivity Through Advanced Office Controls,* 1980, pp. 129–137. Robert E. Nolan Co., Inc.

How Westinghouse Measures White Collar Productivity. David L. Rowe. MRev., Nov. 1981, pp. 42–47. Westinghouse Electric's Corporate Productivity Center.

IBM's Common Staffing System: How to Measure Productivity of the Indirect Workforce. Kenneth A. Charon, James D. Schlump. MRev., Aug. 1981, pp. 8–14. IBM.

Knowledge Worker Productivity. Ira B. Gregerman. 1981, 55 pp. Productivity Associates. MB.

Measuring the Work of a Personnel Department. Stephen J. Carroll, Jr. *Human Resources Management: The Past Is Prologue,* 1979, pp. 272–279.

Office Standard Data. Robert E. Nolan, Richard T. Young, Ben C. DiSylvester. *Improving Productivity Through Advanced Office Control,* 1980, pp. 156–170. Robert E. Nolan Co., Inc.

Work Measurement: America's Answer to the Productivity Challenge. Robert C. Kyser, Jr., James Meade. SM, Oct. 1981, pp. 30–33. Rath & Strong Systems Products.

WORK SIMPLIFICATION. See also Methods Improvement

Five Steps to Improvement. Parvin S. Titus. *The Amazing Oversight: Total Participation for Productivity,* 1979, pp. 48–53. RCA Corp.

How It All Started. Allan H. Mogensen. *The Amazing Oversight: Total Participation for Productivity,* 1979, pp. 17–20.

Paperwork Simplification. Ben S. Graham, Sr. *The Amazing Oversight: Total Partici-pation for Productivity,* 1979, pp. 30–47.

Work Simplification Training. Clair F. Vough, Bernard Asbell. *Productivity, A Practical Program for Improving Efficiency.* (rev. ed.—former title: *Tapping the Human Resource: A Strategy for Productivity*), 1979, pp. 42–45. Productivity Research International, Inc.

YOUNG ADULTS. See also Career Management

Dr. Spock's Babies Take Charge. Jeanne Binstock. *Corporate Planning Techniques and Applications,* 1979, pp. 63–72. Consumer & Management Trends Inc.

The Future of the World of Work. Ian H. Wilson. AMJ, Autumn 1978, pp. 4–13. General Electric Co.

Invitation to Achievement: Your Career in Management (rev. ed.). Elizabeth Marting. 1981, 52 pp.

Mind-to-Mind Management. Stanley Peterfreund. 1977, 34 pp. MB.

A New Generation. James L. Hayes. MRev., Oct. 1977, pp. 2–3.

Successniks in the Corporate Suite: The Self as "Hero." Michael Freeman. MRev., May 1981, pp. 38–44. Langley Porter Psychiatric Institute.

What's Different About Younger Workers? James L. Hayes. HSM, Dec. 1981, pp. 7–8.

AMA RESOURCES

In this section AMA resources are arranged by full title. The characteristics of the publications and other media are outlined below. Nearly all titles may be ordered through AMA Bookstores in New York City, Chicago and Atlanta or through the Publications Sales Department, P.O. Box 319, Trudeau Road, Saranac Lake, NY 12983—Telephone: (518) 891-1500. In addition, AMA publications are available through hundreds of retail booksellers in the U.S. and many other countries. Multi-Media In-Company Training Programs may be ordered through AMA Centers or Regional Executive Agents. The AMA Customer Relations Department in New York—telephone: (212) 586-8100—will identify the nearest Center or REA. The prices shown on the following pages are, first the list price and, second, the AMA member price. The notation O.P. means that the publication is out of print.

Reprint Collections and certain books which are comprised of selected articles include readings originally issued by AMA and other publishers prior to 1977. Therefore a limited number of citations appearing in this *Index* are also listed in *Index to AMA Resources of the Seventies 1970–1976.*

BOOKS

Books cover a variety of functionally oriented, practical and theoretical subjects presenting the best in current management practice and thought.

PERIODICALS

Advanced Management Journal, a quarterly magazine, provides original articles on a wide range of management subjects of interest to middle- and upper-level managers.

Director's Monthly examines boardroom practices across the nation and keeps directors and trustees advised on activities of Congress, government agencies, and major pertinent decisions.

Executives Skills discusses an area of interest to managers each month. A brief self test and case study are included in each issue.

Health Services Manager, a monthly publication, gives guidance on management subjects to hospital and other health facility personnel.

Management Review, a monthly magazine, covers general management topics. Distributed to members only, it features original articles, and also includes abstracts or comments on significant articles from current business and management publications, and book reviews. Published in domestic and international editions.

Organizational Dynamics, a quarterly journal, reviews organizational behavior concepts and practices for professional managers.

Personnel, a bi-monthly magazine, covers every aspect of human resources in organizations.

Supervisory Management, a monthly magazine, furnishes the supervisor with up-to-date information about the management job.

Supervisory Sense each month discusses a specific problem area faced by first-level supervisors.

Reprint Collections have been compiled of popular articles taken from AMACOM's periodicals. They provide a basic reference library for managers and supervisors and also serve as an invaluable aid for supervisory training.

REPORTS AND STUDIES

Board Practices Monographs, issued by the National Association of Corporate Directors, discuss a variety of specific boardroom situations.

Corporate Directors' Special Reports, also prepared by NACD, are written to help directors assess how boardroom trends will affect their future.

Management Briefings are concerned with day-to-day problems encountered by management in organizations of all sizes and all industrial classifications.

Presidents Association Special Studies show how successful companies are solving high-level management problems.

Research Studies examine and analyze current management techniques and practices in specific areas of interest to AMA members. They are based on interviews, questionnaires, and other original research.

Survey Reports are based on nationwide questionnaire surveys. They include charts, tables, other graphic illustrations and interviews with management personnel in business and industry, labor, government, and education.

OTHER MANAGEMENT TRAINING MATERIALS (Available by purchase only.)

Audio Books are condensed versions of popular AMACOM publications in convenient audio cassette format.

Audio Cassettes provide managers with management concepts and conversations with management leaders in soundtape form. Most cassettes are accompanied by a manual, an illustrated brochure, or a workbook.

Evaluation Tools allow managers to evaluate their own activities and departments without using outside consultants.

Executive Compensation Service Surveys provide confidential and current job information on the salary and benefit ranges of over 3000 U. S. and foreign companies. *Evalucomp* makes available a comprehensive job evaluation program for salaried employees.

Extension Institute Courses train executives through private, self-paced study at home under the guidance of a qualified AMA instructor. *Extension Institute Cassettes* are brief courses which give an overview on specific management skills or areas. A typical course consists of six cassettes, workbook, and binder. Each also includes a pre- and post-test which may be sent in for evaluation and feedback.

Multi-Media In-Company Training Programs use every modern learning technique—films, case studies, participative exercises, role plays and simulations—to help supervisors and managers learn rapidly and retain more.

Skill Series provides the basis of self-study courses which enable managers to obtain valuable information on a variety of important topics.

Other AMA publications, not included in this *Index* because of the brevity of their articles and digests, include:

Alerts, from the National Association of Corporate Directors, giving directors warning of legal and regulatory changes.

AMA Management Digest, a monthly containing digests and briefs of significant management articles from any sources.

CompFlash, a monthly newsletter presenting brief reportorial items on current compensation developments.

Current Compensation References, prepared by the staff of the Executive Compensation Service, featuring abstracts of articles of interest to the compensation manager.

The International Manager, a quarterly newsletter serving the worldwide network of Correspondent Associations of AMA.

New Developments in Management, a monthly newsletter prepared by the staff of the Research & Information Service, providing briefs on management trends and developments of particular interest to CEOs. *The President,* a monthly newsletter helping members of the Presidents Association keep up to date with PA activities and personalities.

TITLE/SERIES INDEX

AUDIO BOOKS

Advertising Pure and Simple. Hank Seiden. 1981. $15.95/14.95
The Art of Decision Making. John D. Arnold. 1981. $15.95/14.95
The First-Time Manager. Loren B. Belker. 1981. $15.95/14.95
Formula for Success. Lawrence A. Appley. 1981. $15.95/14.95
Goal Setting. Charles L. Hughes. 1981. $15.95/14.95.
A Guide to Personal Risk Taking. Richard E. Byrd. 1981. $15.95/14.95
How to Inspire Your Subordinates. Thomas L. Quick. 1981. $15.95/14.95
How to Survive and Market Yourself in Management. Andrew Pleninger. 1981. $15.95/
  14.95
How to Turn Off Stress. Theodore A. Jackson. 1979. $15.95/14.95
Mackenzie on Time. Alec Mackenzie. 1979. $15.95/14.95
Muddling Through. Robert A. Golde. 1981. $15.95/14.95
No-Nonsense Delegation. Dale D. McConkey. 1981. $15.95/14.95
Power in Management. John P. Kotter. 1981. $15.95/14.95
Putting It All Together. William E. Rothschild. 1981. $15.95/14.95
The Self-Reliant Manager. John Cowan. 1981. $15.95/14.95
Selling . . . New Style. Robert Montgomery. 1980. $15.95/14.95
Shirt-Sleeves Management. James F. Evered. 1981. $15.95/14.95
Systematic Selling. Terry A. Mort. 1981. $15.95/14.95

AUDIO CASSETTES

Appraisal and Career-Counseling Interviews: Productive Interviewing No. 3 (sec. ed.). Don
  Faber. 1981. (audio cassette and manual) $34.95/29.95
Basics of Finance and Accounting. Theodore Cohn, Samuel Laibstain. 1981. (4 audio
  cassettes and guide) $79.95/67.95
Basics of Management. Roy A. Lindberg. 1980. (3 audio cassettes and guide) $69.95/
  59.45
Basics of Marketing Management. Houston Elam, Norton Paley. 1980. (3 audio cassettes
  and guide) $69.95/59.45

Basics of Personnel Management. Edith Lynch. 1980. (4 audio cassettes and guide) $79.95/67.95

Career Success. Eugene Emerson Jennings. 1980. (3 audio cassettes and guidebook) $49.95/42.50

The China Trader: Interviews with Julian Sobin. 1978. (12 audio cassettes and brochure) $150.00/150.00

Clues to Executive Time Control. Henry Mintzberg. 1977. (4 audio cassettes and workbook) $114.95/97.95.

Computers & Communications: Their Management and Integration. John Diebold, James L. Hayes. 1981.(3 audio cassettes and brochure) $99.95/84.95.

Coping with Stress. John M. Ivancevich, Michael T. Matteson. 1979. (3 audio cassettes and brochure) $74.95/63.75

Coping with Stress: Training Version. John M. Ivancevich, Michael T. Matteson. 1979. (3 audio cassettes and brochures) $89.95/76.50

The Crisis of the American Board. Warren Bennis. 1978. (3 audio cassettes and brochure) $56.25/56.25

The Exit Interview: Productive Interviewing No. 2 (sec. ed.). John R. Hinrichs. 1981. (audio cassette and manual) $34.95/29.95

The "How" of Strategic Planning. George A. Steiner. 1978. (4 audio cassettes and manual) $129.95/110.50

The "How To" Drucker. Peter F. Drucker. 1977. (4 audio cassettes and manual) $139.95/119.00

How to Improve Your Management Style. Robert R. Blake, Jane Srygley Mouton. 1978. (3 audio cassettes) $89.95/76.50

The Information Interview: Productive Interviewing No. 5 (sec. ed.). John R. Hinrichs. 1981. (audio cassette and manual) $34.95/29.95

Leading the Way in Human Resource Management. Ray A. Killian. 1979. (4 audio cassettes and manual) $89.95/76.50

The Likerts on Managing Conflict. Rensis Likert, Janet Likert. 1977. (5 audio cassettes and manual) $139.95/119.00

Listen Your Way to Success. Robert L. Montgomery. 1977. (3 audio cassettes and workbook) OP.

Making the Job Connection: Four Steps to Career Power. Richard J. Rinella, Claire C. Robbins. 1981. (2 audio cassettes and workbook) $34.95/29.95

The Mature Executive. James L. Hayes. 1978. (3 audio cassettes and brochure) $80.00/68.00

Measuring Managers. Harold Koontz, Heinz Weihrich. (3 audio cassettes and manual) $79.95/69.95

The Positive No: A Manager's Guide to Dealing with Superiors, Peers and Subordinates. Auren Uris. 1980. (3 audio cassettes and brochure) $64.95/55.25.

The Problem-Employee Interview: Productive Interviewing No. 4 (sec. ed.). Glenn A. Bassett. 1981. (audio cassette and manual) $34.95/29.95

Productivity: Getting Employees to Care. Frank G. Goble. 1980. (4 audio cassettes and brochure) $99.95/84.95.

Putting the Motivation Back into Work. Robert N. Ford. 1978. (3 audio cassettes and brochure) $80.00/65.00

Reading/Plus. Gloria Hunter. 1978. (6 audio cassettes and workbook) $115.00/97.75

The Selection Interview: Productive Interviewing No. 1 (third ed.). Raymond F. Valentine. 1981. (audio cassette and manual) $34.95/29.95

Successful Management the Experts' Way. 1979. (5 audio cassettes and brochure) $129.95/110.50

Successful Teamwork: How Managers & Secretaries Achieve It. Patrick J. Montana, Elizabeth Marting, Diane Borst. 1979. (2 audio cassettes and brochure) $45.00/38.25.

Telephone Know-How. Elizabeth Marting. 1980. (2 audio cassettes and brochure) $44.95/38.25.

Tough-Minded Team Building. Joe Batten, Hal Batten. 1979. (3 audio cassettes and brochure) $89.95/76.50

Writing Sense. Allen Weiss. 1980. (5 audio cassettes and workbook) $99.95/84.95

BOARD PRACTICES MONOGRAPHS
BPM 1. Board Practices Monographs: Objectives and Scope. Stephen I. Cummings, April 1979, 5 pp. $5.00/4.50

BPM 2. Director Selection Considerations. Ira G. Corn, Jr., May 1979, 6 pp. $5.00/4.50

BPM 3. Eyes on the Audit Committee. Thomas W. McMahon, Jr., June 1979, 5 pp. $5.00/4.50

BPM 4. Satisfying Corporate Accountability: The Roles of the Board, the Corporate Secretary, and the SEC Disclosure Rules. Victor Futter, Dec. 1979, 10 pp. $5.00/4.50

BPM 5. A Performance Model for Boards of Directors. Bruce C. Sherony, Philipp A. Stoeberl, Jan. 1980, 7 pp. $5.00/4.50

BPM 6. Guidelines for Information Flow to Directors. Richard S. Maurer, March 1980, 9 pp. $5.00/4.50

BPM 7. Liabilities of Directors Under State Law. Michael D. Goldman, April 1980, 6 pp. $5.00/4.50

BPM 8. Keeping Directors Informed: The Role of the Corporate Secretary. John B. Megahan, May 1980, 7 pp. $5.00/4.50

BPM 9. What Every Director Should Know About Computer Security. Jack Bologna, June 1980, 6 pp. $5.00/4.50

BPM 10. Boards of Directors of Nonprofit Corporations. Glen A. Wilkinson, July 1980, 9 pp. $5.00/4.50

BPM 11. Guidelines with Respect to "Board Influences on Company Organization Structure." James W. Fisher, Aug. 1980, 11 pp. $5.00/4.50

BPM 12. Business Leadership on Nonprofit Boards. John Carver, Oct. 1980, 9 pp. $5.00/4.50

BPM 13. Role of the Audit Committee: Update and Implementation. Lawrence J. Trautman, James H. Hammond, Jr. Nov. 1980, 10 pp. $5.00/4.50

BPM 14. Foreign Corrupt Practices Act Update. Elliot M. Schnitzer, April 1981, 6 pp. $5.00/4.50

BPM 15. Financing Alternatives for Small and Medium-Sized Corporations. Lawrence J. Trautman, Sept. 1981, 8 pp. $5.00/4.50

BPM 16. "Supply Side" Economic Theories: An Interview with Paul Craig Roberts. Paul Craig Roberts, Oct. 1981, 5 pp. $5.00/4.50

BPM 17. Business Valuation. Joseph Shaw Chalfant, Nov. 1981, 5 pp. $5.00/4.50

BOOKS
The A to Z of Sales Management. John Fenton, 1979, 141 pp. $14.95/13.45

Action Strategies for Managerial Achievement. Dalton E. McFarland, 1977, 198 pp. O.P.

Advanced Industrial Selling. David A. Stumm, 1981, 221 pp. $17.95/15.26

Advertising Pure and Simple. Hank Seiden, 1977, 198 pp. $13.95/12.55; paperback $5.95/5.35

Affirmative Action and the Woman Worker. Jennie Farley, 1979, 225 pp. $15.95/13.56

The Affordable Computer: The Microcomputer for Business and Industry. Claire Summer, Walter A. Levy (editors), 1979, 179 pp. $13.95/12.55

The Amazing Oversight: Total Participation for Productivity. Ben S. Graham, Jr., Parvin S. Titus (editors), 1979, 197 pp. $13.95/12.55

The Ambitious Woman's Guide to a Successful Career (rev. ed.). Margaret V. Higginson, Thomas L. Quick, 1980, 276 pp. $14.95/13.45

The Androgynous Manager. Alice G. Sargent, 1981, 238 pp. $13.95/12.55

The Appraisal Interview Guide. Robert G. Johnson, 1979, 122 pp. $14.95/13.45

Audit Committee Interface with the Internal Auditor. National Association of Corporate Directors, Institute of Internal Auditors, 1979, 154 pp. $35.00/30.00

Audit Committee Interface with the Internal Auditor. National Association of Corporate Directors, Institute of Internal Auditors, 1980, 150 pp. $35.00/30.00

Auditing the Data Processing Function. Richard W. Lott, 1980, 214 pp. $17.95/15.26

A Basic Approach to Executive Decision Making . Alfred R. Oxenfeldt, David W. Miller, Roger A. Dickinson, 1978, 229 pp. $14.95/13.45; paperback $7.95/7.15

Basic Financial Management (rev. ed.). Curtis W. Symonds, 1978, 208 pp. $13.95/12.55; paperback $5.95/5.35

Basics of Successful Business Management. William R. Osgood, 1981, 259 pp. $19.95/16.96

Basics of Successful Business Planning. William R. Osgood, 1980, 252 pp. $21.95/18.66

The Believable Corporation. Roger M. D'Aprix, 1977, 211 pp. O.P.

Building Financial Decision Making Models: An Introduction to Principles and Procedures. Donald Moscato, 1980, 150 pp. $12.95/11.65

Building Profits Through Organizational Change. Roger J. Howe, 1981, 264 pp. $17.95/15.26

Building a Successful Professional Practice with Advertising. Irwin Braun, 1981, 289 pp. $24.95/21.21

Building Wealth: A Layman's Guide to Trust Planning. Adam Starchild, 1981, 224 pp. $15.95/13.56

Business Forms Management. William V. Nygren, 1980, 182 pp. $22.95/19.51

A Business Information Guidebook. Oscar Figueroa, Charles Winkler, 1980, 190 pp. $19.95/16.96: paperback $9.95/8.95

Business Writing Quick & Easy. Laura Brill, 1981, 185 pp. $13.95/12.55

Career Development and Job Training: A Manager's Handbook. James G. Stockard, 1977, 434 pp. $24.95/21.21

Career Life Planning for Americans: Agenda for Organizations and Individuals. Patrick J. Montana, Margaret V. Higginson, 1978, 204 pp. $17.95/15.26

Career Power. Richard J. Rinella, Claire C. Robbins, 1980, 167 pp. $14.95/13.45

Career Satisfaction and Success: How to Know and Manage Your Strengths (rev. ed.). Bernard Haldane, 1981, 210 pp. $12.95/11.65; paperback $4.95/4.45

Career Strategies: Planning for Personal Achievement. Andrew H. Souerwine, 1978, 292 pp. $15.95/13.56; paperback $7.95/7.15

The Communication Matrix: Ways of Winning with Words. Georgette F. McGregor, Joseph A. Robinson, 1981, 230 pp. $15.95/13.56

A Communications Manual for Nonprofit Organizations. Lucille A. Maddalena, 1981, 222 pp. $17.95/15.26

A Compendium of Monographs on Board Practices. National Association of Corporate Directors (editor), 1981, 86 pp. $35.00/25.00

Compensating Key Executives in the Smaller Company. Theodore Cohn, Roy A. Lindberg, 1979, 224 pp. $16.95/14.41

Compensation (rev. ed.). Robert E. Sibson, 1981, 312 pp. $18.95/16.11

The Complete Book of Closing Sales. Sal T. Massimino, 1981, 154 pp. $14.95/13.45

Computer Fundamentals for Nonspecialists. Joseph M. Vles, 1981, 180 pp. $14.95/13.45

Computer Security: A Management Audit Approach. Norman L. Enger, Paul W. Howerton, 1980, 264 pp. $21.95/18.66

A Conference and Workshop Planner's Manual. Lois B. Hart, J. Gordon Schleicher, 1979, 125 pp. $24.95/21.21; paperback $15.95/13.56

Confronting Nonpromotability: How to Manage a Stalled Career. Edward Roseman, 1977, 244 pp. $14.95/13.45; paperback $5.95/5.35

Corporate Cash Management (Including Electronic Funds Transfer). Alfred L. Hunt, 1978, 232 pp. $19.95/16.96

The Corporate Casino: How Managers Win and Lose at the Biggest Game in Town. Dean P. Peskin, 1978, 243 pp. $12.95/11.65

Corporate Confrontations: A 3-Year Retrospect. National Association of Corporate Directors (editor), 1981,147 pp. $55.00/45.00

Corporate Directors Legal Case Books (Vol. 1–4) and 1980 Update. National Association of Corporate Directors (editor), 1981. $250.00/225.00

Corporate Governance Issues and the Corporate Secretary. National Association of Corporate Directors (editor), 1981, 111 pp. $55.00/45.00

Corporate Governance Review. National Association of Corporate Directors (editor), 1981, 63 pp. $35.00/25.00

Corporate Planning Techniques and Applications. Selections from Planning Review. Robert J. Allio, Malcolm W. Pennington (editors), 1979, 436 pp. $21.95/18.66

Cost-Benefit Analysis for Executive Decision Making. Alfred R. Oxenfeldt, 1979, 432 pp. $24.95/21.21

Current Value Accounting: A Practical Guide for Business. Warren Chippindale, Philip L. Defliese (editors), 1977, 184 pp. $21.95/18.66

Data Base Systems: Design, Implementation, and Management. Ronald G. Ross, 1978, 229 pp. $21.95/18.66

Data Dictionaries and Data Administration: Concepts and Practices for Data Resources Management. Ronald G. Ross, 1981, 454 pp. $29.95/25.46

Debt Collection Letters in Ten Languages: With Notes on Terminology, Practice and Methods of Payment in Different Countries. John Butterworth, 1978, unpaged. $35.00/29.75

Decades: Lifestyle Changes in Career Expectations. Edith M. Lynch, 1980, 144 pp. $10.95/ 9.85

Designing an Effective Sales Compensation Program. John K. Moynahan, 1980, 214 pp. $16.95/14.41

A Deskbook of Business Management Terms. Leon A. Wortman, 1979, 615 pp. paperback $14.95/13.45

Developing Overseas Managers—and Managers Overseas. Paul E. Illman, 1980, 298 pp. $19.95/16.96

Direct Costing. William E. Arnstein, Frank Gilabert, 1980, 280 pp. $26.50/22.52

Distributed Processing Systems: End of the Mainframe Era? Judson Breslin, C. Bradley Tashenberg, 1978, 228 pp. $19.95/16.96

Doctors as Managers of Health Teams: A Career Guide for Hospital-Based Physicians. Roman L. Yanda, M.D., 1977, 271 pp. $15.95/13.56

The Economics of Industrial Health: History, Theory and Practice. Joseph F. Follmann, Jr., 1978, 482 pp. $27.50/23.37

Effective Communication on the Job (third ed.). William K. Fallon, 1981, 328 pp. $17.95/ 15.26

The Effective EDP Manager. Michael R. Frank, 1980, 197 pp. $17.95/15.26

Effective Management and the Behavioral Sciences. William Dowling (editor), 1978, 285 pp. $13.95/12.55; paperback $8.95/8.05

The Effective Supervisor's Handbook. Louis V. Imundo, 1980, 239 pp. $15.95/13.56

Employing the Handicapped: A Practical Compliance Manual. Arno B. Zimmer, 1981, 374 pp. $21.95/18.66

Estate Planning—After the 1976 Tax Reform Law. Edward E. Milam, D. Larry Crumbley, 1978, 230 pp. $14.95/13.45; paperback $6.95/6.25

The Evolving Science of Management. Melvin Zimet, Ronald G. Greenwood, 1979, 496 pp. $24.95/21.21

Executive Compensation: Money, Motivation and Imagination. Graef S. Crystal, 1978, 206 pp. $15.95/13.56

Executive Dissent: How to Say "No" and Win. Auren Uris, 1978, 192 pp. $12.95/11.65

The Executive's Guide to Finding a Superior Job. William Cohen, 1978, 166 pp. $14.95/ 13.45; paperback $5.95/5.35

The Expanding Role of the Human Resources Manager. Robert L. Desatnick, 1979, 230 pp. $15.95/13.56

The Face of Business. Henry I. Meyer, 1980, 268 pp. $13.95/12.55

Fast-Growth Management: How to Improve Profits with Entrepreneurial Strategies. Mack Hanan, 1979, 145 pp. $14.95/13.45

Financial Management for Small Business. Edward N. Rausch, 1979, 184 pp. $13.95/ 12.55

Financing the International Petroleum Industry. Norman A. White (editor), 1978, 257 pp. $40.00/34.00

The First-Time Manager: A Practical Guide to the Management of People. Loren B. Belker, 1978, 165 pp. $14.95/13.45

A Flexible Approach to Working Hours. J. Carroll Swart, 1978, 278 pp. $19.95/16.96

Foreign Exchange and the Corporate Treasurer (sec. ed.). John Heywood, 1979, 163 pp. $16.95/14.41

Funny Business: A Tongue-in-Cheek Guide to Power and Success. E. Alfred Osborne, 1979, 110 pp. $10.95/9.85

The Future of Business Regulation: Private Action & Public Demand. Murray L. Weidenbaum, 1979, 183 pp. paperback $5.95/5.35

A Guide to Doing Business on the Arabian Peninsula. Quentin W. Fleming, 1981, 150 pp. $29.95/25.46

Handbook of Business Finance and Capital Sources. Dileep Rao, 1979, 480 pp. O.P.

Helping the Troubled Employee. Joseph F. Follmann, Jr., 1978, 260 pp. $17.95/15.26

How to Assess Your Managerial Style. Charles Margerison, 1980, 151 pp. $13.95/12.55

How to Find a Job When Jobs Are Hard to Find. Donald R. German, Joan W. German, 1981, 242 pp. $15.95/13.56

How to Get Published in Business/Professional Journals. Joel J. Shulman, 1980, 258 pp. $16.95/14.41

How to Get Started as a Manufacturers' Representative. William H. Krause, 1980, 207 pp. $15.95/13.56; paperback $8.95/8.05

How to Get to the Top . . . and Stay There. Robert J. McKain, 1981, 210 pp. $12.95/11.65

How to Succeed in Business and Marriage. Richard W. Ogden, 1978, 161 pp. $10.95/9.85

How to Survive and Market Yourself in Management. Andrew Pleninger, 1977, 238 pp. $12.95/11.65; paperback $6.95/6.25

How We Discommunicate. Philip Lesly, 1979, 227 pp. $13.95/12.55

Huddling: The Informal Way to Management Success. V. Dallas Merrell, 1979, 208 pp. $11.95/10.75

Human Resource Development Standards. William R. Tracey, 1981, 598 pp. $39.95/33.96

Impact Management: Personal Power Strategies for Success. George J. Lumsden, 1979, 150 pp. $13.95/12.55; paperback $6.95/6.25

Improving Productivity Through Advanced Office Controls. Robert E. Nolan, Richard T. Young, Ben C. DiSylvester, 1980, 404 pp. $29.95/25.46

Index to AMA Resources of the 70s, 1970–76. Elizabeth Keegan, 1977, 162 pp. $10.00/7.50

Information: The Ultimate Management Resource: How to Find, Use, and Manage It. Morton F. Meltzer, 1981, 211 pp. $15.95/13.56

International Commercial Banking Management. James L. Kammert, 1981, 403 pp. $24.95/21.21

The International Essays for Business Decision Makers, Vol. III. Mark B. Winchester (editor), 1978, 270 pp. O.P.

The International Essays for Business Decision Makers, Vol. IV. Mark B. Winchester (editor), 1979, 284 pp. $17.95/15.26

The International Essays for Business Decision Makers, Vol. V. Mark B. Winchester (editor), 1980, 353 pp. $21.95/18.66

Investor Relations That Work. Arthur R. Roalman (editor), 1980, 278 pp. $34.95/29.71

Invitation to Achievement: Your Career in Management (rev. ed.). Elizabeth Marting, 1981, 52 pp. $.75

Job Analysis: Methods and Applications. Ernest J. McCormick, 1979, 371 pp. $25.95/22.06

Job Descriptions in Manufacturing Industries. John D. Ulery, 1981, 161 pp. $21.95/18.66

Job Search: The Complete Manual for Jobseekers. H. Lee Rust, 1979, 258 pp. $14.95/13.45; paperback $7.95/7.15

Leadership on the Job: Guides to Good Supervision (third ed.). William K. Fallon (editor), 1981, 344 pp. $17.95/15.26

Leadership: Strategies for Organizational Effectiveness. James J. Cribbin, 1981, 296 pp. $14.95/13.45

The Lease/Buy Decision. Robert E. Pritchard, Thomas Hindelang, 1980, 276 pp. O.P.

Legal Handbook for Nonprofit Organizations. Marc J. Lane, 1980, 294 pp. $17.95/15.26

Legal Handbook for Small Business. Marc J. Lane, 1977, 181 pp. $15.95/13.56

Life-Styled Marketing: How to Position Products for Premium Profits (rev. ed.). Mack Hanan, 1980, 159 pp. $17.95/15.26

Listening Made Easy: How to Improve Listening on the Job, at Home, and in the Community. Robert L. Montgomery, 1981, 134 pp. $11.95/10.75

Make Up Your Mind! The 7 Building Blocks to Better Decisions. John D. Arnold, 1978, 210 pp. $13.95/12.55

Making Successful Presentations. George T. Vardaman, 1981, 271 pp. $18.95/16.11

Manage Your Plant for Profit and Your Promotion. Richard W. Ogden, 1978, 194 pp. $14.95/13.45

Manage Your Time, Manage Your Work, Manage Yourself. Merrill E. Douglass, Donna N. Douglass, 1980, 278 pp. $15.95/13.56

Management Auditing: A Questionnaire Approach. Robert J. Thierauf, 1980, 239 pp. $19.95/16.96

Management Decision Making. Jerome D. Braverman, 1980, 241 pp. $16.95/14.41

Management Education in the 80's. International Association of Students of Economics and Management (editor), 1979, 127 pp. OP

Management for the 1980's (rev. ed.–former title: *The Achieving Enterprise*). William F. Christopher, 1980, 295 pp. $16.95/14.41

Management, Governance & Leadership: A Guide for College and University Administrators. John D. Millett, 1980, 208 pp. $15.95/13.56

Management Principles for Nonprofit Agencies and Organizations. Gerald Zaltman (editor), 1979, 584 pp. $34.95/29.71

The Manager and the Modern Internal Auditor: A Problem-Solving Partnership. Lawrence B. Sawyer, 1979, 466 pp. $24.95/21.21

Manager Manpower Planning: A Professional Management System. Lawrence A. Appley, Keith L. Irons, 1981, 112 pp. $14.95/13.45

Managerial Breakthroughs: Action Techniques for Strategic Change. James R. Emshoff, 1980, 211 pp. $15.95/13.56

The Manager's Guide to Interpersonal Relations. Donald Sanzotta, 168 pp. $12.95/11.65

A Manager's Guide to Profitable Computers. Norman Sanders, 1979, 216 pp. $14.95/13.45

A Manager's Guide to the Antitrust Laws. Edward A. Matto, 1980, 195 pp. $14.95/13.45

Managers Must Lead! (rev. ed.). Ray A. Killian, 1979, 254 pp. O.P.

Managing at the Top: Roles and Responsibilities of the Chief Executive Officer. J. Keith Louden, 1977, 159 pp. O.P.

Managing Employee Turnover: A Positive Approach. Edward Roseman, 1981, 260 pp. $17.95/15.26

Managing Incompetence. William P. Anthony, 1981, 276 pp. $17.95/15.26

Managing International Distribution. Felix Wentworth, Martin Christopher (editors), 1979, 274 pp. O.P.

Managing Nonprofit Organizations. Diane Borst, Patrick J. Montana (editors), 1977, 328 pp. $16.95/14.41; paperback $5.95/5.35

Managing Stress. Jere E. Yates, 1979, 165 pp. $12.95/11.65; paperback $5.95/5.35

Managing Urban Government Services: Strategies, Tools, and Techniques for the 80's. James L. Mercer, Susan W. Woolston, William V. Donaldson, 1981, 242 pp. $21.95/18.66

Managing With Style and Making It Work for You. Henry O. Golightly, 1977, 159 pp. O.P.

Marketing for the Non-Marketing Executive. Houston G. Elam, Norton Paley, 1978, 261 pp. $15.95/13.56

Marketing in Nonprofit Organizations. Patrick J. Montana (editor), 1978, 302 pp. $13.95/12.55

Marketplace Behavior: Its Meaning for Management. Sidney J. Levy, 1978, 257 pp. $16.95/14.41

Master Trust: Simplifying Employee Benefits Trust Fund Administration. Michael L. Costa, 1980, 213 pp. $19.95/16.96

Measuring Performance in Human Service Systems. James F. Budde, 1979, 207 pp. $14.95/13.45

Memory Made Easy: The Complete Book of Memory Training. Robert L. Montgomery, 1979, 111 pp. $11.95/10.75; paperback $5.95/5.35

Micromanagement: How to Solve the Problems of Growing Companies. William A. Delaney, 1981, 164 pp. $13.95/12.55

Minicomputers: Low-Cost Computer Power for Management (rev. ed.). Donald P. Kenney, 1978, 269 pp. $15.95/13.56; paperback $7.95/7.15

Money: How to Get It, Keep It, and Make It Grow. Michael Hayes, 1979, 214 pp. $15.95/13.56

More than Management Development: Action Learning at GEC. David Casey, David Pearce (editors), 1977, 146 pp. $12.50/11.25

Motivational Theories and Applications for Managers. Donald Sanzotta, 1977, 184 pp. $12.95/11.65

The Moving Force: Preserving the Profit Motive in the American Economy. Henry I. Meyer, 1981, 323 pp. $12.95/11.65

Moving Up: Women and Leadership. Lois Borland Hart, 1980, 229 pp. $14.95/13.45; paperback $6.95/6.25

Multinational Strategic Planning. Derek F. Channon with Michael Jalland, 1978, 344 pp. $35.00/29.75

National Account Marketing Handbook. Robert S. Rogers, V.B. Chamberlain, III. (editors), 1981, 292 pp. $24.95/21.21

The New Merger Game. Don Gussow, 1978, 262 pp. $12.50/11.25

New Product Development Strategies. Frederick D. Buggie, 1981, 165 pp. $16.95/14.41

The 1979 Proxy Season Analysis of the Newly Required Board and Director Proxy Disclosures. National Association of Corporate Directors (editor), 1979, 216 pp. $75.00/56.25

Nonverbal Communication for Business Success. Ken Cooper, 1979, 214 pp. $13.95/12.55

On Television: A Survival Guide for Media Interviews. Jack Hilton, Mary Knoblauch, 1980, 185 pp. $12.95/11.65

The $100 Billion Market: How to Do Business with the Government. Herman Holtz, 1980, 272 pp. $16.95/14.41; paperback $10.95/9.85

Open Management: Guides to Successful Practice. Paul W. Cummings, 1980, 225 pp. $14.95/13.45

Organization Development for Operating Managers. Michael E. McGill, 1977, 177 pp. paperback $5.95/5.35

Organization Planning Manual (rev. ed.). Joseph J. Famularo, 1979, 373 pp. $29.95/25.46

Overcoming Mid & Late Career Crises. Patrick J. Montana, 1978, 43 pp. $13.50/10.00

Overcoming Murphy's Law. William C. Waddell, 1981, 296 pp. $14.95/13.45; paperback $5.95/5.35

The Owner's and Manager's Market Analysis Workbook for Small to Moderate Retail and Service Establishments. Wayne A. Lemmon, 1980, 230 pp. $29.95/25.46; paperback $9.95/8.95

Personnel Management for the Smaller Company. Linda A. Roxe, 1979, 246 pp. $14.95/13.45

Planning for Change: Bank Directorship in the '80s. National Association of Corporate Directors (editor), 1981, 86 pp. $55.00/45.00

Planning for Nonplanners: Planning Basics for Managers. Darryl J. Ellis, Peter P. Pekar, Jr., 1980, 152 pp. $12.95/11.65

Power in Management: How to Understand, Acquire, and Use It. John P. Kotter, 1979, 105 pp. $11.95/10.75

The Practical Manager's Guide to Excellence in Management. Ronald Brown, 1979, 120 pp. $11.95/10.75

Practical Marketing Research. Jeffrey Pope, 1981, 296 pp. $24.95/21.21

Preparing Administrative Manuals. Susan Z. Diamond, 1981, 133 pp. $17.95/15.26

Preventive Labor Relations. John G. Kilgour, 1981, 338 pp. $24.95/21.21

Principles of R&D Management. Philip H. Francis, 1977, 228 pp. $17.95/15.26

Principles of Technical Management. William A. Cohen, 1980, 222 pp. $19.95/16.96

Productivity: A Practical Program for Improving Efficiency (rev. ed.–former title: Tapping the Human Resource: A Strategy for Productivity). Clair F. Vough, Bernard Asbell, 1979, 212 pp. $15.95/13.56

Productivity Improvement: Case Studies of Proven Practice. Vernon M. Buehler, Y. Krishna Shetty (editors), 1981, 273 pp. $19.95/16.96

Productivity: the Human Side. Robert R. Blake, Jane Srygley Mouton, 1981, 133 pp. $11.95/10.75

Profit from Your Money-Making Ideas: How to Build a New Business or Expand an Existing One. Herman R. Holtz, 1980, 370 pp. $14.95/13.45; paperback $8.95/8.05

Profit-Line Management. Managing a Growing Business Successfully. Herman R. Holtz, 1981, 337 pp. $17.95/15.26

Psychology and the Stock Market: Investment Strategy Beyond Random Walk. David N. Dreman, 1977, 306 pp. $14.95/13.45

Public Management Systems: An Administrator's Guide. James L. Mercer, Edwin H. Koester, 1978, 309 pp. $24.95/21.21

Public Technology: Key to Improved Government Productivity. James L. Mercer, Ronald J. Philips (editors), 1981, 271 pp. $24.95/21.21

Purchasing Computers: A Practical Guide for Buyers of Computers and Computing Equipment. Edward R. Sambridge, 1979, 139 pp. $14.95/13.45

Qualitysense. Martin R. Smith, 1979, 194 pp. O.P.

ROI Basics for Nonfinancial Executives. Allen Sweeny, 1979, 115 pp. $12.95/11.65

ROI: Practical Theory and Innovative Applications (rev. ed.). Robert A. Peters, 1979, 173 pp. $23.95/20.36

The Real Estate Gamble. Alan Rabinowitz, 1980, 308 pp. $17.95/15.26

Redefining the Manager's Job: The Proactive Manager in a Reactive World. Merritt L. Kastens, 1980, 283 pp. $14.95/13.45

Rethinking People Management: A New Look at the Human Resources Function. James G. Stockard, 1980, 225 pp. $14.95/13.45

Retirement: Creating Promise Out of Threat. Robert K. Kinzel, 1979, 131 pp. $12.95/11.65

Robotics in Practice: Management and Applications of Industrial Robots. Joseph F. Engelberger, 1980, 291 pp. $39.95/33.96

Running Conventions, Conferences, and Meetings. Robert W. Lord, 1981, 192 pp. $23.50/19.97

Sacked! What to Do When You Lose Your Job. Dean B. Peskin, 1979, 177 pp. $12.95/11.65

Safe: Security Audit & Field Evaluation for Computer Facilities and Information Systems (rev. ed.). Leonard I. Krauss, 1980, 308 pp. $29.95/25.46

Salary Management for the Nonspecialist. Stanley B. Henrici, 1980, 247 pp. $15.95/13.56

Sales Negotiation Strategies: Building the Win/Win Customer Relationship. Mack Hanan, James Cribbin, Howard Berrian, 1977, 160 pp. $12.95/11.65

The Self-Reliant Manager. John Cowan, 1977, 255 pp. O.P.

Shirt-Sleeves Management. James F. Evered, 1981, 180 pp. $13.95/12.55

Shut Up and Sell: Tested Techniques for Closing the Sale. Don Sheehan, 1981, 163 pp. $12.95/11.65

The Skills of Management. A.N. Welsh, 1981, 196 pp. $14.95/13.45

The Skills of Selling. Roger W. Seng, 1977, 253 pp. $14.95/13.45; paperback $7.95/7.15

Small Business: Developing the Winning Management Team. George W. Rimler, Neil J. Humphreys, 1980, 180 pp. $13.95/12.55

Small Business Works! How to Compete and Win in the Free Enterprise System. Eugene L. Gross, Adrian R. Cancel, Oscar Figueroa, 1977, 166 pp. $15.95/13.56

The Social Audit for Management. Clark C. Abt, 1977, 278 pp. O.P.

Sticky Fingers: A Close Look at America's Fastest Growing Crime. William W. McCullough, 1981, 146 pp. $11.95/10.75

Stock Market Forecasting for Alert Investors. John C. Touhey, 1980, 184 pp. O.P.

Strategic Alternatives: Selection, Development and Implementation. William E. Rothschild, 1979, 242 pp. $16.95/14.41

The Strategic Evaluation and Management of Capital Expenditures. Robert E. Pritchard, Thomas J. Hindelang, 1981, 326 pp. $24.95/21.21

Stress & the Bottom Line: A Guide to Personal Well-Being and Corporate Health. E.M. Gherman, M.D., 1981, 348 pp. $16.95/14.41

Subcontract Management Handbook. George Sammet, Jr., Clifton G. Kelley, 1981, 246 pp. $24.95/21.21

Successful Field Service Management. Donald N. McCafferty, 1980, 181 pp. $16.95/14.41

Successful Marketing for Small Business. William A. Cohen, Marshall E. Reddick, 1981, 282 pp. $17.95/15.26

Successful Midlife Career Change: Self-Understanding and Strategies for Action. Paula I. Robbins, 1978, 268 pp. $14.95/13.45; paperback $7.95/7.15

Successful Personnel Recruiting and Selection. Erwin S. Stanton, 1977, 214 pp. $15.95/13.56; paperback $8.95/8.05

The Successful Secretary: You, Your Boss, and the Job. Loren B. Belker, 1981, 214 pp. $14.95/13.45

Successful Team Building Through TA. Dudley Bennett, 1980, 260 pp. $14.95/13.45

Successful Time Management for Hospital Administrators. Merrill E. Douglass, Phillip H. Goodwin, 1980. 143 pp. $16.95/14.41

Supervision Can Be Easy. David K. Lindo, 1979, 272 pp. $14.95/13.45

Synergistic Management: Creating the Climate for Superior Performance. Michael Doctoroff, 1977, 159 pp. $13.95/12.55

Systematic Selling: How to Influence the Buying Decision Process. Terry A. Mort, 1977, 190 pp. $14.95/13.45; paperback $6.95/6.25

Systems Selling Strategies: How to Justify Premium Prices for Commodity Products. Mack Hanan, James Cribbin, Jack Donis, 1978, 193 pp. $14.95/13.45

Tested Ways to Successful Fund Raising. George A. Brakeley, Jr., 1980, 171 pp. $16.95/14.41; paperback $8.95/8.05

Tough-Minded Management (third ed.). Joe D. Batten, 1978, 224 pp. $14.95/13.45

Training for Retail Sales and Profit. Judith J. Howe, 1981, 237 pp. $14.95/13.45

Training the New Supervisor. James E. Gardner, 1980, 192 pp. $15.95/13.56

Turning Around: The Behavioral Approach to Managing People. Beverly A. Potter, 1980, 266 pp. $15.95/13.56

Turning Research and Development into Profits. Attilio Bisio, Lawrence Gastwirt, 1979, 275 pp. $27.95/23.76

The 27 Most Common Mistakes in Advertising. Alec Benn, 1978, 156 pp. $13.95/12.55; paperback $5.95/5.35

Two Careers—One Marriage. William M. Jones, Ruth A. Jones, 1980, 229 pp. $12.95/11.65

Understanding Management Policy & Making It Work. Victor Z. Brink, 1978, 312 pp. $19.95/16.96

Urwick, Orr on Management. Fred W. Latham, George S. Sanders, 1980, 255 pp. $17.95/15.26

Valuing Common Stock: The Power of Prudence. George Lasry, 1979, 239 pp. $17.95/15.26

The Wall Street Journal Views America Tomorrow. Donald Moffitt (editor), 1977, 184 pp. $11.95/10.75

Want a Job? Get Some Experience. Want Experience? Get a Job. Don Berliner, 1978, 184 pp. $12.95/11.65; paperback $5.95/5.35

What Happens in Management. Maurice R. Hecht, 1980, 212 pp. $15.95/13.56; paperback $7.95/7.15

What Happens in Public Relations. Gerald J. Voros, Paul Alvarez (editors), 1981, 232 pp. $17.95/15.26

Why Jobs Die and What To Do About It. Robert N. Ford, 1979, 220 pp. $15.95/13.56

The Work Ethic: Working Values and Values That Work. David J. Cherrington, 1980, 288 pp. $17.95/15.26

Write What You Mean: A Handbook of Business Communication. Allen Weiss, 1977, 179 pp. $12.95/11.65; paperback $5.95/5.35

You and I Have Simply Got to Stop Meeting This Way. Richard J. Dunsing, 1978, 164 pp. $10.95/9.85; paperback $5.95/5.35

Your Money & Your Life: How to Plan Your Long-Range Financial Security. C. Colburn Hardy, 1979, 340 pp. $15.95/13.56

Zero-Base Budgeting: A Decision Package Manual. L. Allan Austin, Logan M. Cheek, 1979, 207 pp. $16.95/14.41

Zero-Base Budgeting Comes of Age. Logan M. Cheek, 1977, 314 pp. $23.95/20.36; paperback $6.95/6.25

CORPORATE DIRECTORS SPECIAL REPORTS

CDSR I. Evolution in the Boardroom, 1978, 24 pp. $6.25/5.63

CDSR II. Board Functions, 1978, 24 pp. $6.25/5.63

CDSR III. Board Models, 1978, 24 pp. $6.25/5.63

CDSR IV. Inside vs. Outside Directors. Stanley C. Vance, 1978, 24 pp. $6.25/5.63

CDSR VI. The Role of the Chairman of the Board. Ira G. Corn, Jr., 1979, 23 pp. $6.25/5.63

CDSR IX. Director Qualifications and Selections. William H. Chisholm, 1980, 11 pp. $6.25/5.63

CDSR X. Director Information Systems. Donald R. Jackson, 1979, 24 pp. $6.25/5.63

29 Questions Directors Should Ask Before Responding to a Tender Offer. 4 pp. $5.00/4.50

EVALUATION TOOLS

How to Audit Finance. J. McConnell, 1979, $100.00/87.50

How to Audit General Management. J. McConnell, 1979, $100.00/87.50

How to Audit Marketing and Sales. J. McConnell, 1978, $100.00/87.50.

How to Audit Operations. J. McConnell, 1980, $135.00/122.50.

How to Audit the Personnel Department. J. McConnell, 1977, $100.00/87.50.

How to Audit the Purchasing Function. J. McConnell, 1981, $100.00/87.50.

How to Audit Your EEO Compliance. J. McConnell, 1979, $100.00/87.50.

How to Conduct an Energy Audit. T. Hollen, R. Redd, 1980, $100.00/87.50.

How to Plan and Track Your Personal Finances. H. Moore, 1980, $29.95/$24.95.

EXECUTIVE COMPENSATION SERVICE REPORTS (Survey non-participant and participant price. AMA members receive 10% discount off these prices.) Those ECS reports containing salary surveys are updated annually.

North American Service (U.S. and Canada)

Banking Compensation Report. $395.00/245.00

Benefits and Employment Contracts. $70.00/70.00

Canada Executive Remuneration Report. $550.00/275.00

Canada Office Personnel Report. $145.00/65.00

Canada Professional, Scientific & Technical Report. $325.00/175.00

Corporate Directorship Report. $175.00/85.00

Current and Deferred Incentive Compensation. $70.00/70.00

Evalucomp: The Complete Job Evaluation Program. (Prices upon request)

Hospital and Health Care Report. $350.00/170.00

Middle Management Report. $350.00/170.00

Office Personnel Report. $180.00/80.00

Professional and Scientific Report. $325.00/125.00

Puerto Rico Report. $340.00/170.00

Salary Administration and Control. $70.00/70.00

Sales Personnel Report. $250.00/90.00

Statistical Supplement to the Middle Management Report. $350.00/170.00

Statistical Supplement to the Top Management Report. $445.00/200.00

Stock Purchase Plans. $70.00/70.00

Supervisory Management Report. $250.00/90.00

Technician Report. $180.00/80.00

Termination of Employment. $250.00/250.00

Top Management Report. $445.00/200.00

International Service

Belgium Report. $340.00/170.00

Brazil Report. $340.00/170.00

European Benefits Report. $215.00/215.00

European Sales and Marketing Personnel Report. $250.00/250.00

European Top Management Compensation Report. $360.00/360.00

Federal Republic of Germany Report. $340.00/170.00

Flexible Working Hours in Europe. $190.00/190.00

France Report. $340.00/170.00

Industrial Democracy Report. $250.00/250.00

International Compensation Report. $340.00/170.00

International Transfers U.S.-Europe. $500.000/500.00

Italy Report. $340.00/170.00

Labour Relations: Europe. $370.00/370.00

Mexico Report. $340.00/170.00

Netherlands Report. $340.00/170.00

Office and Administrative Personnel Remuneration—Europe. $250.00/250.00

Portugal Report. $340.00/170.00

Scandinavia Report. $340.00/170.00

Spain Report. $340.00/170.00

Switzerland Report. $340.00/170.00

United Kingdom Report. $340.00/170.00

EXTENSION INSTITUTE CASSETTE/WORKBOOK PROGRAMS

Achieving Computer Security. Henry L. Parsons, 1980. (6 audio cassettes, workbook, pre- and post-testing) $145.00/135.00. Workbooks $18.00/16.00

Antidotes to Personal Obsolescence. Robert A. Moskowitz, 1977. (6 audio cassettes, workbook, pre- and post-testing) $145.00/135.00. Workbooks $18.00/16.00

Assertiveness for Career and Personal Success. Robert A. Moskowitz, 1977. (6 audio cassettes, workbook, pre- and post-testing) $145.00/135.00. Workbooks $18.00/16.00

Basic Business Psychology. Robert A. Moskowitz, 1978. (6 audio cassettes, workbook, pre- and post-testing) $145.00/135.00. Workbooks $18.00/16.00

Communication Skills for Secretaries. Kathleen J. Hansell, 1981. (6 audio cassettes, workbook, pre- and post-testing) $145.00/135.00. Workbooks $18.00/16.00

Computer Fundamentals for Managers (sec. ed.). L. Daniel Massey, Richard W. Lott, 1979. (6 audio cassettes, workbook, pre- and post-testing) $145.00/135.00. Workbooks $18.00/16.00

Constructive Discipline for Supervisors. George R. Bell, 1981. (6 audio cassettes, workbook, pre- and post-testing) $145.00/$135.00. Workbooks $18.00/$16.00

The Corporate Controller: Role & Responsibilities. John E. Buckley, Kenneth M. Lizotte, 1979. (6 audio cassettes, workbook, pre- and post-testing) $145.00/$135.00. Workbooks $18.00/$16.00

Creative Problem Solving. Robert A. Moskowitz, 1978. (6 audio cassettes, workbook, pre- and post-testing) $145.00/135.00. Workbooks $18.00/16.00

Effective Team Building. Vern Goldsmith, William B. Brown, 1980. (6 audio cassettes, workbook, pre- and post-testing) $145.00/135.00. Workbooks $18.00/16.00

The Executive's Guide to Personal Financial Management. Frederick S. Brown, 1977. (6 audio cassettes, workbook, pre- and post-testing) O.P.

Fundamentals of Budgeting. Kenneth M. Lizotte, 1979. (6 audio cassettes, workbook, pre- and post-testing) $145.00/135.00. Workbooks $18.00/16.00

A Guide to Operational Auditing. Archie McGhee, Mary Etzel Fleischer, 1979. (6 audio cassettes, workbook, pre- and post-testing) $145.00/135.00. Workbooks $18.00/16.00

How to Be a Successful Public Speaker. Kathryn Cason, Shirley Cunningham, 1980. (6 audio cassettes, workbook, pre- and post-testing) $145.00/135.00. Workbooks $18.00/16.00

How to Be an Effective Executive. Kenneth M. Lizotte, 1978. (6 audio cassettes, workbook, pre- and post-testing) $145.00/135.00. Workbooks $18.00/16.00

How to Be an Effective Middle Manager. Joseph F. Byrnes, 1981. (6 audio cassettes, workbook, pre- and post-testing) $145.00/135.00. Workbooks 18.00/16.00

How to Be an Effective Supervisor. David B. Whittier, 1978. (6 audio cassettes, workbook, pre- and post-testing) $145.00/135.00 Workbooks $18.00/16.00

How to Evaluate Performance and Assess Potential. Robert A. Moskowitz, 1979. (6 audio cassettes, workbook, pre- and post-testing) $145.00/135.00. Workbooks $18.00/16.00

How to Improve Customer Service. E. Patricia Bisner, Ronald D. Balsley, 1980. (6 audio cassettes, workbook, pre- and post-testing) $145.00/135.00 Workbooks $18.00/16.00

How to Improve Your Memory. George R. Bell, 1980. (6 audio cassettes, workbook, pre- and post-testing) $145.00/135.00. Workbooks $18.00/16.00

How to Interpret Financial Statements. Terry Isom, Sudhir P. Amembal, 1980. (6 audio cassettes, workbook, pre- and post-testing) $145.00/135.00. Workbooks $18.00/16.00

How to Interview Effectively. Garry Mitchell, 1980. (6 audio cassettes, workbook, pre- and post-testing) $145.00/135.00. Workbooks $18.00/16.00

How to Market by Telephone. Garry Mitchell, 1981. (6 audio cassettes, workbook, pre- and post-testing) $145.00/135.00. Workbooks $18.00/16.00

Listen and Be Listened To. George R. Bell, 1981. (6 audio cassettes, workbook, pre- and post-testing) $145.00/135.00. Workbooks $18.00/16.00

Managerial Skills for New and Prospective Managers. David V. Lewis, 1978. (6 audio cassettes, workbook, pre- and post-testing) $145.00/135.00. Workbooks $18.00/16.00.

Managing Cash Flow. Kenneth M. Lizotte, 1978. (6 audio cassettes, workbook, pre- and post-testing) $145.00/135.00. Workbooks $18.00/16.00

Managing Conflict. Donald H. Weiss, 1981. (6 audio cassettes, workbook, pre- and post-testing) $145.00/135.00. Workbooks $18.00/16.00

Managing Labor Relations. David B. Whittier, 1977. (6 audio cassettes, workbook, pre- and post-testing) $145.00/135.00 Workbooks $18.00/16.00

Orientation and the Hiring Process. Arthur Sondak, Donna Bouvier, 1978. (6 audio cassettes, workbook, pre- and post-testing) $145.00/135.00 Workbooks $18.00/16.00

Planning and Implementing a Personal Fitness Program. Fitness Systems, Inc., 1979. (6 audio cassettes, workbook, pre- and post-testing) $145.00/135.00. Workbooks $18.00/16.00

Setting and Achieving Personal Goals. David V. Lewis, 1977. (6 audio cassettes, workbook, pre- and post-testing) $145.00/135.00. Workbooks $18.00/16.00

Successful Delegation. Kenneth M. Lizotte, 1978. (6 audio cassettes, workbook, pre- and post-testing) $145.00/135.00. Workbooks $18.00/16.00

The Supervisor's Guide to Boosting Productivity. Donald P. Hendricks, 1981. (6 audio cassettes, workbook, pre- and post-testing) $145.00/135.00. Workbooks $18.00/16.00

Understanding and Managing Stress. Anderson Maddocks, 1980. (6 audio cassettes, workbook, pre- and post-testing) $145.00/135.00.00. Workbook $18.00/16.00

Using Managerial Authority. Peter Venuto, 1980. (6 audio cassettes, workbook, pre- and post-testing) $145.00/135.00. Workbooks $18.00/16.00

EXTENSION INSTITUTE COURSES

Accounting for Managers (sec. ed.). George J. Chorba, 1978. $85.00/75.00. Leader's Guide. $18.00/15.00.

Advertising: Strategy and Design (fourth ed.). Elizabeth Trotman, 1979. Revised by Gertrude Salaway. $85.00/75.00

Basic Systems and Procedures (sec. ed.). Richard W. Beane, 1979. $85.00/75.00

Budgeting by Department and Functional Area (third ed.). Wayne G. Bremser, 1981. $85.00/75.00. Leader's Guide. $18.00/15.00.

Commercial Banking (sec. ed.). Geoffrey J. Mansfield, Henry C. Barkhorn, 1979. $85.00/75.00

Communication Skills for Managers (sec. ed.). Brook Taliaferro, 1980. $85.00/75.00. Leader's Guide. $18.00/15.00.

Computer Basics for Management (rev. ed.). L. Daniel Massey, 1977. Revised by Richard W. Lott. $85.00/75.00. Leader's Guide. $18.00/15.00.

Contingency Planning. Joan Knutson, Layne Alexander, 1981. $85.00/75.00

Contracting with the Federal Government. Grant E. Mayberry, 1978. $85.00/75.00

Cost Accounting for Profit Improvement. Raymond Jordan, 1979. $85.00/75.00

Developing Computer-Based Accounts Receivable Systems. Norbert J. Kubilus, 1981. $85.00/75.00

Developing Computer-Based General Ledger Systems. Richard W. Lott, 1978. $85.00/75.00

EDP and Accounting. Alvin A. Clay, 1979. $85.00/75.00

The EDP Feasibility Study (sec. ed.). Michael A. Tow, 1979. $85.00/75.00

Efficient Reading for Managers. J. Michael Bennet, 1981. $85.00/75.00

The Executive's Guide to Commerical Law. Charles L. Babcock, Richard F. Collier, Jr., 1978. $85.00/75.00

The Executive's Guide to Office Space Planning. John Hathaway-Bates, Lawrence Lerner, 1980. $85.00/75.00

Executive's Guide to Wage and Salary Administration. Robert E. Sibson, 1980. $85.00/75.00

Financial Goals and Strategic Planning. Cosmo S. Trapani, 1981. $85.00/75.00

First-Line Management. Grant E. Mayberry, 1979. $85.00/75.00. Leader's Guide. $18.00/15.00.

Fundamentals of Direct Mail Marketing. Edward J. McGee, Norman A.P. Govoni, Robert J. Eng, 1980. $85.00/75.00

Fundamentals of Modern Marketing (rev. ed.). Judith Pedersen, 1978. $85.00/75.00

Fundamentals of Modern Personnel Management. Kenneth T. Winters, 1980. $85.00/75.00

Fundamentals of Traffic Management. Colin Barrett, 1980. $85.00/75.00

Getting Results with Matrix Management. Grant E. Mayberry, 1980. $85.00/75.00

Getting Results with Time Management (sec. ed.). David V. Lewis, 1979. $85.00/75.00. Leader's Guide. $18.00/15.00.

How Successful Women Manage. Beverly Hyman, 1981. $85.00/75.00

How to Be a Successful Project Manager. Joan Ryan Knutson, 1980. $85.00/75.00

How to Build Effective Investor Relations. Arthur R. Roalman, 1980. $85.00/75.00

How to Build Memory Skills. David V. Lewis, 1978. $85.00/75.00

How to Manage Administrative Operations. Susan Z. Diamond, 1981. $85.00/75.00

How to Manage a Data Processing Department. John B. Campbell, 1981. $85.00/75.00

How to Manage Maintenance. Joseph J. Johnstone, Kenneth G. Ward, 1981. $85.00/75.00

How to Manage Paperwork. Brook Taliaferro, 1981. $85.00/75.00

How to Sell Effectively. Vern Goldsmith, 1980. $85.00/75.00

How to Write Technical Reports. Thomas L. Warren, 1981. $85.00/75.00

How to Write Winning Reports. Leo P. Hardwick, 1981. $85.00/75.00

Human Resource Development: A Manager's Guide. Ray A. Killian, 1978. $85.00/75.00
The Job of the Corporate Controller. John E. Buckley, 1977. $85.00/75.00. Leader's Guide. $18.00/15.00.
Leadership Skills for Executives. James J. Cribbin, 1977. $85.00/75.00
Leasing for Profit. Terry A. Isom, Sudhir P. Amembal, 1980. $85.00/75.00
Long-Range Planning. Roy A. Lindberg, 1979. $85.00/75.00
Macroeconomics and Company Planning (sec. ed.). Bradley A. Latham, 1977. $85.00/75.00
Management Information Systems (third ed.). Henry L. Parsons, 1979. $85.00/75.00
The Management of Personal Selling (third ed.). Wade Rothewell, 1979. $85.00/75.00
Managerial Economics. Bradley A. Latham, 1977. $85.00/75.00
A Manager's Guide to Affirmative Action. Mary E. Fulton, 1979. $85.00/75.00
A Manager's Guide to Financial Analysis. L. Allan Austin, William Hammink, 1981. $85.00/75.00
A Manager's Guide to Human Behavior. Mark S. Zivan, 1977. $85.00/75.00. Leader's Guide. $18.00/15.00.
Managing Corporate Cash (sec. ed.). Joseph E. Finnerty, 1980. $85.00/75.00
Managing Credit for Profit (sec. ed.). George H. Troughton, 1981. $85.00/75.00
Managing Employee Benefits. Jay William Cox, 1980. $85.00/75.00
Manufacturing Management. William C. Nemitz, 1977. $85.00/75.00
MBO for the Public Agency. Stuart J. Savage, 1978. $85.00/75.00
Mergers and Acquisitions: A Financial Approach. James Jenkins, 1979. $85.00/75.00
Negotiating Your Way to Success. Grant E. Mayberry, 1979. $85.00/75.00
Performing the Operations Audit (sec. ed.). Archie McGhee, 1978. $85.00/75.00
Personal Financial Planning (third ed.). John T. Lyons, Joseph E. Finnerty, 1981. O.P.
Planning and Administering the Company Budget (sec. ed.). Reginald L. Jones, H. George Trentin, 1977. O.P.
Planning and Administering the Company Budget (third ed.). Wayne G. Bremser, 1981. $85.00/75.00. Leader's Guide. $18.00/15.00.
Planning and Control for Managers (sec. ed.). Peter B. Venuto, 1979. $85.00/75.00
Planning Cash Flow (third ed.). Leslie P. Anderson, John Heptonstall, Joseph E. Finnerty, 1980. $85.00/75.00
Principles of Finance. Elliott L. Atamian, 1981. $85.00/75.00
Principles of Investment Management. Janet J. Johnson, 1981. $85.00/75.00
Purchasing Management. C. Wayne Barlow, 1977. $85.00/75.00
Quality Control: Meeting the New Competition. Roger W. Berger, 1981. $85.00/75.00
Quantitative Aids to Decision Making (third ed.). Grant E. Mayberry, Donald O. Robb, 1979. $85.00/75.00
Reading and Interpreting Financial Statements. George J. Chorba, 1978. $85.00/75.00
Return on Investment (sec. ed.). Richard W. Lott, 1980. $85.00/75.00
The Role of the Internal Auditor. Elizabeth Trotman, 1977. $85.00/75.00
Strategies in Marketing Research (third ed.). Frank H. Eby, Jr., 1979. $85.00/75.00
Success Through Assertiveness. Diane Arthur, 1980. $85.00/75.00
The Theory and Practice of Management Control (sec. ed.). Graham R. Briggs, 1980. $85.00/75.00
Training for Productivity. Beverly Hyman, 1980. $85.00/75.00. Leader's Guide. $18.00/15.00.
Using Mathematics as a Business Tool. George J. Chorba, Charissa J. Chou, 1979. $85.00/75.00
Using Small Computers as Management Tools. Jack R. Buchanan, Garrett L. Sheldon, 1980. $85.00/75.00
Using the Computer as a Marketing Tool. Leonard J. Parsons, Ellen Day, 1979. $85.00/75.00
What Accounting Managers Do. Arthur S. O'Neill, Jr., 1980. $85.00/75.00
What Managers Do (sec. ed.). Donald R. Burke, 1978. $85.00/75.00. Leader's Guide. $18.00/15.00.

Writing for Management Success (sec. ed.). Daphne Jameson, 1981. $85.00/75.00
Zero-Base Planning & Budgeting. L. Allan Austin, Edward Ritvo, 1978. $85.00/75.00

MANAGEMENT BRIEFINGS

Age Discrimination in Employment. William L. Kendig, 1978, 83 pp. O.P.

The Appraisal of Managerial Performance. Arthur Meidan, 1981, 60 pp. $7.50/5.00

Assessing Computer Center Effectiveness. Frank Greenwood, Lee A. Gagnon, 1977, 38 pp. O.P.

Cash Management: Principles and Practices for the '80s. Paul J. Beehler, 1980, 67 pp. O.P.

Contracts: The Move to Plain Language. Paul H. Till, Albert F. Gargiulo, 1979, 56 pp. O.P.

Control: The Key to Successful Business Planning. George R. Seiler, 1981, 78 pp. $10.00/7.50

Controllership in Divisionalized Firms: Structure, Evaluation and Development. Vijay Sathe, 1978, 45 pp. O.P.

Controlling the Costs of Retirement Income and Medical Care Plans. Philip M. Alden, Jr., 1980, 78 pp. $10.00/7.50

Controlling Paperwork—Yours and the Government's. Warren B. Buhler, 1979, 61 pp. O.P.

Corporations and the First Amendment. Herbert Schmertz, 1978, 40 pp. $10.00/7.50

Creating Profitable New Products and Markets. Richard H. Corbin, R. Donald Gamache, 1980, 53 pp. $10.00/7.50

Decision Making in the Purchasing Process: A Report. Phillip D. White, 1978, 54 pp. O.P.

Developing the Business Plan for a Small Business. Bruce M. Bradway, Robert E. Pritchard, 1980, 50 pp. O.P.

Do's and Don'ts in Subcontract Management. George Sammet, Jr., Clifton G. Kelley, 1980. 40 pp. $10.00/7.50

Do's and Don'ts of Pension Fund Management. Ned Merkle, 1981, 55 pp. $10.00/7.50

ESOPs and the Smaller Employer. M. Mark Lee (editor), 1979, 79 pp. $10.00/7.50

The Effects of Extending the Mandatory Retirement Age. Henry M. Wallfesh, 1978, 41 pp. $10.00/7.50

Employee Values in a Changing Society. Mark G. Mindell, William I. Gorden, 1981, 72 pp. $10.00/7.50

The Entrepreneur: A Corporate Strategy for the 80's. Donald J. Taffi, 1981, 44 pp. $10.00/7.50

Entry Strategies for Foreign Markets: From Domestic to International Business. Franklin R. Root, 1977, 51 pp. $10.00/7.50

The Executive Look and How to Get It. Mortimer Levitt, 1979, 76 pp. O.P.

Financial Reporting Under Changing Values: An Introduction to Current Value Accounting. Morley P. Carscallen, Kenneth P. Johnson, 1979, 47 pp. O.P.

Foreign Exchange Risk Management. Alan C. Shapiro, 1978, 64 pp. $10.00/7.50

Gainsharing: Involvement, Incentives, and Productivity. Carla S. O'Dell, 1981, 80 pp. $10.00/7.50

Guidelines for Conducting an Office Systems Feasibility Study. George S. Smith, 1981, 59 pp. $10.00/7.50

HMOs from the Management Perspective. Ruth H. Stack, 1979, 49 pp. $10.00/7.50

How to Calculate the Manufacturer's Costs in Collective Bargaining. Frederick L. Sullivan, 1980, 68 pp. $10.00/7.50

How to Improve Packaging Costs. Edmund A. Leonard, 1981, 67 pp. $10.00/7.50

How to Organize the EDP Department. Michael R. Frank, 1980, 47 pp. $10.00/7.50

Idea Management: How to Motivate Creativity and Innovation. Charles H. Clark, 1980, 56 pp. $10.00/7.50

Improving Warehouse Productivity. Joel C. Wolff, 1981, 58 pp. $10.00/7.50

Information Resources Management. Robert M. Landau, 1980, 37 pp. $10.00/7.50

An Introduction to Direct Marketing. Chaman L. Jain, Al Migliaro, 1978, 67 pp. $10.00/7.50

An Introduction to Electronic Funds Transfer Systems. Claude R. Martin, Jr. 1978, 40 pp. O.P.

Job Enrichment Revisited. Lyle Yorks, 1979, 68 pp. O.P.

Keeping Technical Projects on Target. Maurice Zeldman, 1978, 44 pp. O.P.

Key Social Issues for Packaging in the 1980s. David J. Freiman (editor), 1980, 36 pp. $10.00/7.50

Keys to Enhancing System Development Productivity. William F. Zachmann, 1981, 52 pp. $10.00/7.50

Knowledge Worker Productivity. Ira B. Gregerman, 1981, 55 pp. $10.00/7.50

Leveraged Leasing: New Opportunities Under the Economic Recovery Tax Act of 1981. Albert F. Gargiulo, Raymond J. Kenard, Jr., 1981, 53 pp. $10.00/7.50

The Manager's Guide to Developing Subordinate Managers. Henry D. Meyer, Bruce L. Margolis, William M. Fifield, 1980, 60 pp. $10.00/7.50

Managing Industrial Energy Conservation. 1977, 61 pp. O.P.

Managing the Packaging Side of the Business. Edmund A. Leonard, 1977, 50 pp. $10.00/7.50

The'Marketing Manager's Guide to New Product Invention. Alfred Gruber, 1977, 31 pp. O.P.

The Marketing Path to Global Profits. David J. Freiman, 1979, 69 pp. $10.00/7.50

Mind-to-Mind Management. Stanley Peterfreund, 1977, 34 pp. O.P.

Motivating the Distributor to Market Your Product. Dennis A. Zalar, 1980, 34 pp. $10.00/7.50

The Need for a Unified Discipline of Management. Philip W. Shay, 1977, 30 pp. O.P.

The Network Reports System of Analysis and Control. John B. McMaster, 1976, 56 pp. O.P.

Personal Information: Privacy at the Workplace. Jack L. Osborn, 1978, 52 pp. O.P.

Planning and Controlling Manufacturing Resources. R. Michael Donovan, Harrison H. Appleby, 1979, 48 pp. $10.00/7.50

The Purchasing Role: A View from the Top. Charles F. Carpenter, 1977, 31 pp. O.P.

Quality Control in the Service Industries. Roger G. Langevin, 1977, 38 pp. $7.50/5.00

R & D on a Minimum Budget. Donatas Tijunelis, Nancy Miles Clausen, 1979, 37 pp. $10.00/7.50

A Rational Approach to Office Planning. M. Arthur Gensler, Jr., Peter B. Brandt, 1978, 52 pp. O.P.

Risk Analysis Guide to Insurance and Employee Benefits. A.E. Pfaffle, Sal Nicosia, 1977, 71 pp. $10.00/7.50

Security Safeguards for the Computer. Charles F. Hemphill, Jr., Robert D. Hemphill, 1979, 38 pp. $10.00/7.50

Strategic Analysis, Selection, and Management of R&D Projects. D. Bruce Merrifield, 1977, 54 pp. O.P.

The Strategic Integration of Corporate Research and Development. William H. Gruber, 1981, 65 pp. $7.50/5.00

Strategic Pricing: Protecting Profit Margins from Inflation. C. Daniel Bergfeld, 1981, 48 pp. $10.00/7.50

Systems Contracting: A New Look. Ralph A. Bolton, 1979, 45 pp. $10.00/7.50

Tax Strategy for Multinationals—Economic and Social Issues. John Chown, John Humble, 1979, 30 pp. O.P.

Telephone Marketing Techniques. Murray Roman, 1979, 34 pp. O.P.

Ten Steps to Successful Exporting. R. Wayne Walvoord, 1981, 79 pp. $10.00/7.50

The Vital Signs of Effective Packaging Management. David B. Lansdale, 1978, 42 pp. $10.00/7.50

Worker Volunteering: A New Resource for the 1980s. Kerry Kenn Allen, 1980, 31 pp. $10.00/7.50

MULTI-MEDIA IN-COMPANY TRAINING PROGRAMS (Prices upon request)
Basic Concepts of Motivation. Leo F. McManus, 1980.

Communicating for Productivity. Lawrence A. Appley, Gabriel Stillian, 1981.

How to Improve Your Managerial Communications. James L. Hayes, 1980.
Making Delegation Work for You. Leo F. McManus, 1981.
Management and Motivation. Leo F. McManus, 1979.
Personality Styles: The Key to Closing Sales. Leo F. McManus, 1979.
Program for Performance Appraisal. James L. Hayes, 1980.
Strategies for Successful Selling. Robert A. Weber, 1981.

PRESIDENTS ASSOCIATION SPECIAL STUDIES

PA 64 Cooperation: An Alternative Management Strategy. Steven H. Appelbaum, 1977, 36 pp. O.P.

PA 65 The Chief Executive's Strategic Role and Responsiblities. Richard F. Neuschel, 1977, 47 pp. O.P.

PA 66 Before the Economy Dips: Planning Protective Action. Eugene H. Fram, Herbert J. Mossien, 1977, 29 pp. O.P.

PA 67 Corporate Giving: Policy and Practice. Frank Koch, 1978, 40 pp. $20.00/10.00

PA 68 Responsibility and Liability in the Age of ERISA. Daniel C. Knickerbocker, Jr., 1978, 48 pp. O.P.

PA 69 The CEO Faces Retirement. Henry M. Wallfesh, 1978, 34 pp. O.P.

PA 70 Building and Operating an Effective Board of Directors. Milton C. Lauenstein, 1979, 64 pp. O.P.

PA 71 Institutionalizing Corporate Ethics: A Case History. Theodore V. Purcell, James Weber, 1979, 32 pp. $20.00/10.00

PA 72 The Future World of Work: The Strategic Significance of Human Resource Management in the 1980s. Lynne Hall, 1980, 64 pp. $20.00/10.00

PA 73 The Variations of Matrix Organization. Robert F. Smith, 1980, 31 pp. O.P.

PA 74 Mergers and Acquisitions in a Changing Environment. M. Mark Lee (editor), 1980, 53 pp. $20.00/10.00

PA 75 Competitive Analysis. Alfred R. Oxenfeldt, Jonathan E. Schwartz, 1981, 96 pp. O.P.

PA 76 Coming to Grips with Crisis. Charles G. Newton, Jr., 1981, 47 pp. $20.00/10.00

REPRINT COLLECTIONS

Administering Top- and Middle-Management Base Salary and Incentive Bonus Plans. Ernest C. Miller (editor), 1977, 80 pp. $8.00/6.75

Career Strategies: Planning for Personal Achievement. Andrew H. Souerwine, 1977, 63 pp. $6.95/6.25

Getting the Most out of Your Job and Your Organization. Harold McAlindon, 1980, 78 pp. $5.95/5.35

The Human Resources Function: Its Emergence and Character. Ernest C. Miller (editor), 1978, 85 pp. $8.95/7.50

Human Resources Management: The Past Is Prologue. Ernest C. Miller (editor), 1979, 361 pp. $10.50/9.45

Leadership: Fiedler, Vroom, and Argyris. 1977, 48 pp. $6.50/5.85

Let's Talk: The Art of One-to-One Communication. Edward L. Levine, 1981, 79 pp. $5.95/5.35

Organizational Development: Theory and Practice. William F. Dowling, Ernest C. Miller (editors), 1977, 125 pp. $10.50/9.45

The Supervisor's Survival Guide. Robert E. Pitts, Ken Thompson, 1979, 64 pp. $4.95/4.45

Surviving and Succeeding in the 'Political' Organization. Alan Jay Weiss, 1978, 48 pp. $3.95/3.55

Write What You Mean: Practical Guidelines for Better Business Writing. Allen Weiss, 1978, 88 pp. $4.95/4.45

You and I Have Simply Got to Stop Meeting This Way. Richard J. Dunsing, 1977, 88 pp. $3.95/3.55

RESEARCH STUDIES

The Business-Media Relationship: Countering Misconceptions and Distrust. David Finn, 1981, 92 pp. $13.50/10.00

Hiring the Handicapped. Jack R. Ellner, Henry E. Bender, 1980, 74 pp. $13.50/10.00
Personnel Testing Under EEO. Jerome Siegel, 1980, 92 pp. $13.50/10.00
Product Service Planning: Service-Marketing-Engineering Interactions. William H. Bleuel,
    Henry E. Bender, 1980, 84 pp. $13.50/10.00
Quality Circles: A Team-Approach to Problem Solving. Frank M. Gryna, Jr., 1981, 96 pp.
    $13.50/10.00

SKILL SERIES
Complying with EEO (PRIME 1000). 1979. $45.00/38.25
How to Make the Computer Work for You (PRIME 1000). 1978. $45.00/38.25
How to Master Job Descriptions (PRIME 100). 1977. $50.00/45.00
How to Say What You Mean. 1977. $25.00/21.25
Psychology for Managers (PRIME 1000). 1978. $45.00/38.25
Time and Territorial Management. 1979. $79.95/67.95
Writing Reports that Work (rev. ed.) (PRIME 100). 1980. $50.00/45.00

SURVEY REPORTS
Alternative Work Schedules–Part 1: Flexitime. Stanley D. Nollen, Virginia H. Martin. 1978,
    53 pp. $13.50/10.00
Alternative Work Schedules–Part 2: Permanent Part-Time Employment–Part 3: The Com-
    pressed Workweek. Stanley D. Nollen, Virginia H. Martin, 1978, 70 pp. $13.50/10.00
Career Planning Practices. James W. Walker, Thomas G. Gutteridge, 1979, 40 pp. $13.50/
    10.00
Developing Women Managers: What Needs to be Done? Martha G. Burrow, 1978, 32 pp.
    $13.50/10.00
Executive Stress. Ari Kiev, M.D., Vera Kohn, 1979, 58 pp. O.P.
Fair Information Practices for Managers and Employees. Jack Lester Osborn, 1980, 23
    pp. O.P.
Executive Time Management. Philip Marvin, 1980, 29 pp. $13.50/10.00
The Manager and Self-Respect: A Follow-up Survey. Preston G. McLean, M.D., Katherine
    Jillson, 1977, 28 pp. $13.50/10.00
Manager to Manager II: What Managers Think of Their Managerial Careers. Robert F.
    Pearse, 1977, 65 pp. $13.50/10.00
The Retirement Decision: How American Managers View Their Prospects. Robert Jud,
    1981, 45 pp. $10.00/7.50
Zero-Base Budgeting: Organizational Impact and Effects. L. Allan Austin, 1977, 33 pp.
    $13.50/10.00

AUTHOR INDEX

Abdelsamad, Moustafa H., 49, 130
Abend, C. Joshua, 32
Abrahamsen, Ken, 47
Abt, Clark C., 131
Adamec, Richard J., 112
Adamian, Deborah M., 87
Adams, Roscoe H., 79
Adams, Tom, 21
Adizes, Ichak, 98
Adkins, Richard D., 141
Adler, Stanley, 49
Adolfi, Henry J., 28
Agarwala-Rogers, Rekha, 100
Agee, William., 66
Akins, James E., 41, 63
Akula, William G., 109
Alber, Antone, 70
Albrecht, Karl, 125, 138
Alden, Jr., Philip M., 31, 40, 41, 102, 136
Alexander, Janet K., 100
Alexander, John O., 104
Alexander, Layne, 106
Allen, Fred T., 75
Allen, Kerry Kenn, 131
Allen, Louis A., 4, 76, 107
Allen, Michael G., 106
Allen, Robert F., 1, 53, 56
Allen, Stanley N., 34
Allio, Robert J., 106, 107, 108, 111

Allston, Frank J., 23
Almsick, Ginny Van, 93
Alpinieri, J. Louis, 99, 101
Altier, William J., 37, 99
Alton, William B., 99, 115
Alvarez, Paul, 3, 6, 9, 18, 23, 29, 52, 68, 69, 71, 117
Alvin, Cass D., 114, 115
Ameen,, Philip D., 6
Amembal, Sudhir P., 48, 73
Amhowitz, Harris J., 74
Amrhine, Kenneth W., 135
Anastasi, Joel, 20
Anderson, Brad, 97
Anderson, David P., 61
Anderson, Donald N., 9
Anderson, Leslie P., 14
Anderson, P. Thomas, 24, 25
Andrews, William F., 66
Angulo, Albert W., 41
Ansoff, H. Igor, 43
Anthony, Robert N., 117
Anthony, William P., 46, 95, 104, 133
Anundsen, Kristin, 47
Aplin, John C., 10
Appelbaum, Steven H., 30, 54, 111
Appleby, Harrison H., 113
Appleman, Mark J., 99

Appley, Lawrence A., 15, 17, 69, 77, 78, 80, 81, 86, 104, 105, 110
Arcady, Alex T., 101
Archer, Earnest R., 37, 133
Arffa, Gerald L., 15
Argyris, Chris, 60, 72
Arnold, John D., 12, 36, 37, 50, 99,
Arnold, Mark R., 44
Arnstein, William E., 2, 34, 68, 111, 129
Arthur, Diane, 38, 46
Asbell, Bernard, 31, 70, 73, 90, 107, 115, 116, 120, 144
Ash, Ronald A., 69
Ash, Roy L., 51
Ashcraft, Steven F., 118
Ashkenas, Ronald N., 31
Atamian, Elliott L., 49
Atwood, Saundra L., 99
Auerbach, Norman E., 75
Augenblick, Harry, 39
Auger, B. Y., 90
Austin, Charles J., 96, 132
Austin, L. Allan, 10, 36, 37, 49
Austin, Terence W., 73
Axline, Larry L., 29
Azzarello, Michele, 66

Babcock, Charles L., 74
Babcock, Richard D., 79, 99, 115
Baderschneider, Earl, 4
Bahn, Charles, 138
Bailyn, Lotte, 13
Bainton, Donald J., 41
Baird, Lloyd, 92, 139
Baird, R. G., 64
Baker, Edwin L., 98
Baker, Eugene F., 113
Baker, H. Kent, 38, 90, 99, 108, 138, 139, 141
Baker, John H., 118
Baker, Kent H., 15, 16, 135
Baker, Larry D., 139
Baker, William R., 69
Bakker, Pieter, 36
Ball, Michael, 61
Balsley, Ronald D., 129
Bancroft, Lee, 134
Barabba, Vincent P., 84
Barad, Cary B., 85
Barkhaus, Robert, 10
Barkhorn, Henry C., 48
Barlow, C. Wayne, 119
Barney, Jay B., 104
Baron, Alma S., 47
Barr, Edward E., 51
Barrett, Colin, 141
Barrett, F. D., 32
Barrett, William A., 126
Barry, Theodore, 7
Bartley, Douglas L., 95
Bartolome, Fernando, 5
Barton, William J., 60
Barucco, Hugo, 92
Basnight, Thomas A., 24
Bassett, Glenn A., 68, 134
Bates, Don, 117
Bates, D. L., 141
Battalia, O. William, 122
Batten, Hal, 137
Batten, Joe D., 46, 78, 80, 137
Battista, O. A., 134
Baum, Dorothy, 26
Baxter, Charles E., 59
Baytos, Lawrence M., 137
Beacham, Samuel T., 39, 103
Beall, Charles R., 84
Beall, D. R., 41
Beam, Henry H., 79, 111
Beane, Richard W., 135

Bechard, William T., 107
Beck, Clark E., 124
Beck, John J., 46
Becker, James W., 40
Bedwell, Jr., Raymond T., 119
Beehler, Paul J., 14
Beer, Michael, 103
Begosh, Donald G., 135
Beiswinger, George L., 123
Belcher, David W., 24
Belinoski, Thomas, 45
Belker, Loren B., 45, 77, 134
Bell, Geoffrey, 64
Bell, George R., 19, 38, 45
Bell, Robert R., 44, 79, 102
Bender, Henry E., 15, 39, 53, 75, 96, 128, 129
Bender, Lisa Richer, 142
Benes, Arnold J., 116
Benford, Robert J., 92, 140
Benn, Alec, 3
Bennet, Dudley, 21
Bennet, J. Michael, 45
Bennett, Dudley, 99, 100, 103, 137
Bennis, Warren, 7
Benoit, Paul S., 85
Benson, Eileen, 46
Benson, Lucy Wilson, 67
Benson, Philip G., 12
Benson, Robert A., 45
Benson, Sir Henry, 64
Bentley, Lynn H., 24
Bere, Jack F., 131
Bergen, Jr., C. W., 94
Berger, Lance A., 128
Berger, Roger W., 120
Bergerson, Allen W., 133
Bergfeld, C. Daniel, 111, 132
Bergmann, Thomas J., 14
Berliner, Don, 14, 68
Berndtson, Per, 110
Bernstein, Edward M., 63
Berrian, Howard, 127
Berry, Leonard L., 88
Berul, L. H., 34, 112
Bett, Mike, 82
Betterley, Richard S., 112
Bhandari, Narendra C., 9, 48

Bickford, Lawrence C., 27
Bilbao, Jorge, 52
Binis, Raymond A., 103
Binstock, Jeanne, 144
Birkman, Roger, 73
Birnberg, Jacob, 36
Bisio, Attilio, 111, 112, 124, 125
Bisner, E. Patricia, 129
Bitondo, Domenic, 123
Black, James Menzies, 22
Blackburn, Roger W., 110
Blake, Robert R., 33, 72, 90, 114, 116, 126, 142
Blalock, Mary, 31
Blass, Walter P., 131
Blau, Benami, 54
Bleuel, William H., 15, 39, 96, 129
Bliss, Edwin C., 138
Bloch, Howard R., 39
Block, James A., 32
Block, Lee F., 117
Bloom, Joan, 101
Bluestone, Irving, 121
Blumberg, Melvin, 70
Blumenthal, W. Michael, 43
Blust, Larry D., 74
Blust, Esq., Larry D., 40
Bockhaus, James H., 59
Boe, Gerard P., 17, 117, 141
Bogart, Leo, 88
Bogart, Robert B., 40
Bohlander, George W., 25
Bolling, Richard, 118
Bologna, Jack, 80
Bolton, Ralph A., 29, 120
Bolyard, Charles, 10
Bonoma, Thomas V., 72
Borgstrom, Ned, 73
Borst, Diane, 118
Boulware, Nancy S., 53
Bouvier, Donna, 100
Bova, Rosemary A., 57
Bowden, J. R., 42
Bowen, Gordon G., 58
Bowers, David G., 98
Bowersox, Donald J., 39
Bowman, William P., 61
Boyd, Howard, 42
Boyer, Cheryl M., 56
Boynton, Robert E., 81
Bracey, Jr., Harry B., 80

Bracey, Hyler, 54
Bradford, Leland P., 101
Bradley, James W., 91
Bradway, Bruce M., 106, 130
Brady, William F., 13
Brakeley, Jr., George A., 117, 119, 136
Brandt, Peter B., 94, 108
Braun, Irwin, 3, 29, 51
Braverman, Jerome D., 37, 85
Brendler, Frieda S., 121
Breslin, Judson, 33, 36
Brett, Jeanne M., 141
Brief, Arthur P., 54, 55
Briggs, Graham R., 80
Brill, Laura, 21
Brinberg, Herbert R., 85
Brink, Victor Z., 78, 80, 107, 110
Briscoe, Dennis R., 54
Brooks, William E., 140
Brooks, William W., 101
Brown, Arnold, 20
Brown, Darrel R., 99
Brown, David S., 96, 135
Brown, Frederick S., 105
Brown, Harry J., 32
Brown, Herbert E., 92
Brown, John B., 136
Brown, Lew, 114
Brown, Martha A., 36, 70
Brown, Ralph J., 81
Brown, Robert, 97
Brown, Robert Goodell, 60
Brown, Ronald, 78
Brown, William B., 137
Browne, G. W. G., 64
Brush, Donald H., 82
Buaron, Roberto, 87
Buchanan, Jack R., 33
Buchanan, Paul C., 98
Buckley, John E., 48, 49
Bucknall, William L., 85
Budde, James F., 80, 104, 107, 129
Buehler, Vernon M., 114, 115
Buffin, Kenneth G., 65
Buggie, Frederick D., 32, 112, 124
Buhler, Warren B., 52, 74, 94
Bullemer, Robert, 111
Bunker, Barbara Benedict, 142

Burger, Warren E., 117
Burke, Donald R., 78
Burke, W. Warner, 72
Burrow, Martha G., 47, 81, 142
Burton, Gene E., 37
Bush, Gerald W., 102
Butterworth, John, 21, 33
Bybee, H. Malcolm, 88
Byerly, Michael, 102
Byington, S. John, 74
Byrd, Richard E., 45
Byrnes, Joseph F., 45

Cahn, Robert, 131
Caiozzo, Camille, 39
Calish, Irving G., 15
Calvert, Geoffrey N., 115, 132
Cameron, Kim, 100
Cammann, Cortlandt, 5
Campbell, David J., 55
Campbell, Earnest G., 122
Campbell, John B., 35
Cancel, Adrian R., 130
Canning. Jr., Gordon, 87
Capoor, Ram, 120, 129
Carey, H. H., 101
Carey, James F., 25, 71, 126
Carlisle, Brian A., 64
Carlisle, Howard M., 80
Carlson, Eric D., 84
Carlson, Howard C., 98
Carney, Christopher F., 142
Carpenter, Charles F., 119
Carr, David, 82
Carroll, Archie B., 43, 135
Carroll, Daniel T., 107
Carroll, Megan, 126
Carroll, Jr., Stephen J., 143
Carscallen, Morley P., 2, 48, 132
Carson, Sylvia, 47
Carter, Deborah Ann, 115
Caruth, Don, 37
Carver, John, 7
Cascino, Anthony E., 49, 90
Casey, David, 50, 81, 83
Cash, William B., 103
Cason, Kathryn, 20
Cason, Roger L., 96
Cassani, Kap, 65
Cassidy, Edward W., 70

Cawsey, T. F., 58, 76
Chabotar, Kent J., 140
Chalfant, Joseph Shaw, 48
Chamberlain, Robert G., 111
Chamberlain, III, V. B., 30, 126
Chambers, John C., 49
Champagne, Paul J., 70
Channon, Derek F., 15, 60, 61, 64, 66, 96
Charan, Ram, 69
Charon, Kenneth A., 143
Chase, Stuart, 57
Chaska, Norma L., 17
Checkett, Anna L., 4
Cheek, Logan M., 10, 36, 37
Cherns, Albert B., 97
Cherrington, David J., 5, 40, 43, 70, 116
Chiampa, Paul, 88
Chilvers, Donald R., 63
Chippindale, Warren, 2
Chisholm, William H., 7, 8, 130
Chorba, George J., 2, 49, 85
Chou, Charissa J., 85
Chown, John, 65, 109, 136
Christman, Luther, 40
Christopher, Martin, 39
Christopher, William F., 14, 77, 79, 80, 85, 93, 106, 107, 123
Chu, Liu, 61
Churcher, I. M., 141
Cieślik, Jerzy, 66
Clancy, Daniel T., 128
Clark, Charles H., 32, 112
Clark, Grover M., 43
Clarke, John W., 139
Clarke, Peter M. C., 63
Clarkson, William M. H., 121
Claus, Steve A., 65
Clausen, Nancy Miles, 9, 83, 125
Clay, Alvin A., 34
Cleff, Samuel, 129
Cleland, David I., 90
Close, M. John, 14
Cohen, Arthur M., 21, 104
Cohen, Richard M., 81
Cohen, Stanley L., 101

Cohen, William A., 3, 9, 13, 28, 51, 66, 82, 83, 87, 88, 89, 96, 103, 107, 111, 112, 122, 124, 127, 130
Cohn, Debra Ann, 100
Cohn, Theodore, 25, 28, 40, 48, 71, 92, 130
Colby, John B., 17
Colby, William E., 60
Cole, Richard B., 39
Cole, Robert E., 120
Collier, James R., 120
Collier, Jr., Richard F., 74
Conarroe, Richard R., 11
Connelian, John, 20
Connolly, Patrick F., 64
Connor, Joseph E., 74
Cook, Frederic W., 16, 23, 25, 26
Cook, James R., 81
Cook, K. H. H., 63
Cook, Mary F., 68
Cook, Suzanne H., 131
Cook, William S., 109
Cooke, Robert A., 15
Cooper, John F., 115
Cooper, Ken, 20, 21
Cooper, William K., 41
Corbin, Arnold, 109
Corbin, Richard H., 32, 112
Corey, Jr., James H., 134
Corn, Jr., Ira G., 8
Costa, Michael L., 41, 102
Cotter, Timothy J., 98
Coulter, Bordon, 138
Coumbe, John W., 105
Courtney, Roslyn S., 83
Couture, Ronald, 142
Cowan, Glenn R., 15
Cowan, John, 46
Cowee, Jr., George A., 58
Cox, Jay William, 41
Cox, Ralph, 45
Craft, James A., 58
Craighead, George P., 62
Cravens, David W., 87, 119
Crawford, Ronald L., 55
Cribbin, James J., 15, 17, 30, 32, 43, 54, 72, 93, 95, 111, 125, 127
Crino, Michael, 128
Crocker, Chester A., 63
Crosby, George F., 114
Crotts, G. Gail, 36

Crumbley, D. Larry, 105, 136
Crystal, Graef S., 25,26, 70
Cuba, Richard, 43, 98
Cullen, Dennis A., 64
Cuming, Pamela Shea, 107
Cummings, Larry L., 113
Cummings, Paul W., 13, 18, 36, 37, 38, 78, 93, 103, 133, 139
Cummings, Stephen I., 7
Cunningham, Bernard, 7
Cunningham, James A., 122
Cunningham, Shirley, 20
Curcia, John M., 24
Curran, Mark C., 112
Curston, Louis C., 71
Curtis, Donald A., 118
Curtis, Jr., John E., 75

Dagher, Samir P., 43
Dahl, Jr., Henry L., 86
Dalena, Donald T., 72
Dalton, Gene W., 13
Danco, Walter, 100
Daniels, T. D., 127
Danzig, Selig M., 4, 104
D'Aprix, Roger M., 17, 21, 22
Davidson, David S., 101, 129
Davidson, Jeff, 56, 134, 141
Davis, Allen Y., 90
Davis, John, 31
Davis, Keith, 20
Davis, Louis E., 70, 109, 114
Davis, Philip A., 101
Davis, Samuel, 86
Davis, Standley M., 90
Davis, Tim R. V., 44, 56
Davison, David S., 126
Dax, Otto J., 67
Day, Ellen, 34
Day, James, 97
Dayan, Daniel, 20
Dean, Donald R., 13
Decelles, Robert K., 63, 136
Defliese, Philip L., 2
Degenaro, Guy J., 130
DeGise, Robert F., 19, 22, 23

Deitsch, Clarence R., 2
De Koker, Neil, 42
DeLong, Thomas, 134
Delaney, William A., 17, 30, 45, 116, 130, 133, 138
Deming, Basil S., 140
Deming, Donald D., 70
Denney, W. Michael, 112
Denton, D. Keith, 126
Derosa, E. Richard, 111
DeSalvia, Donald, 11
Desatnick, Robert L., 57, 69, 110
Deshpande, Rohit, 88
Dettman, Robert, 35
Deutsch, Arnold R., 122
Devanna, Mary Ann, 58
Dewelt, Robert L., 80
Dhanens, Thomas P., 42
Diamond, Susan Z., 23, 86, 94
Dickens, Floyd, 140
Dickens, Jacqueline, 140
Dickinson, Roger A., 32, 36, 49, 77
Diebold, John, 35
Dietrick, Harry J., 32
Digman, Lester A., 81, 82, 98
Diliddo, Bart A., 32
Dilts, David A., 2
Discenza, Richard, 38
DiSylvester, Ben C., 2, 94, 114, 123, 127, 142, 143
Doades, JoAnne Ross, 143
Dobbs, Curtis E., 114
Dobson, G. M., 14
Dock, Leslie, 47
Doctoroff, Michael, 19, 21, 30, 32
Dominguez, George S., 75
Donahue, Donald J., 116
Donald, W. J., 95
Donaldson, William V., 58, 96, 114, 118
Donis, Jack, 111, 125
Donnell, E. S., 74
Donnell, Susan M., 47, 143
Donnelly, Robert M., 121
Donovan, R. Michael, 89, 113
Doran, George T., 80
Douce, William C., 42

Doud, Jr., Ernest A., 134
Douglas, N. John, 69
Douglass, Donna N., 127, 139
Douglass, Merrill E., 119, 127, 138, 139
Dowling, William F., 4, 14, 56, 71, 76, 92, 97, 98, 99, 101, 132
Downey, Arthur T., 59, 62
Doyel, Hoyt W., 103
Doyle, S. X., 140
Drake, John D., 18, 30
Drake, R. T., 134
Drayer, Wayne, 85
Dreilinger, Craig, 46
Dreman, David N., 49
Drew, C. R., 136
Drexler, John A., 44
Dreyfack, Madeleine, 114
Driscoll, James W., 142
Driscoll, Jeanne Bosson, 57
Driver, Russel W., 18, 19
Drucker, Peter F., 29, 77, 78, 111, 118, 133
Drue, Roger, 29, 129, 141
Drummer, Kenneth W., 55
Dubin, Robert J., 89
Dudek, Daniel H., 101
Duga, Jules J., 124
Dulsky, Robert J., 18
Duncan, Robert, 97
Dunk, William P., 123
Dunsing, Richard J., 73, 90, 91, 99
Durand, Douglas E., 58
Duschl, Fran, 94
Duval, Betty Ann, 83
DuVall, J. Barry, 57, 99
Dyer, William G., 81
Dysart, Lawrence A., 22

Eads, Douglas H., 11, 54
Ebel, Robert E., 60, 63
Ebenstein, Michael, 108
Eby, Jr.,, Frank H., 89
Eccles, Tony, 82
Edelman, Robert J., 70
Edelstein, Carol Meyers, 27
Edson, Andrew S., 121
Eiland, Gary W., 28
Eisen, Margaret J., 38
Ekberg, J. Paul, 126
Elam, Houston G., 86, 87, 109

Elf, James C., 126
Elizur, Dov, 71
Elkin, Robert, 136
Ellig, Bruce R., 23, 24, 25, 26, 27, 71, 74
Ellis, Darryl J., 15, 84, 91, 108
Ellner, Jack R., 39, 53, 75, 128
Elwes, Peter J. G., 64
Emery, David, 18
Emshoff, James R., 32, 36, 101
Eng., Robert J., 87
Engelberger, Joseph F., 76, 109, 119, 120, 125, 126
Enger, Norman L., 106, 128
English, Jack W., 58, 105, 128
Ettkin, Lawrence P., 91
Eure, Jack D., 41
Evans, Paul A. Lee, 5
Evered, James F., 15, 46, 69, 73, 78, 79, 92, 99, 100, 104, 128, 140

Faber, Don, 67, 102
Fallon, William K., 72
Fallon, Jr., Kenneth P., 101
Famularo, Joseph J., 4, 15, 17, 50, 69, 79, 86, 96, 106, 110
Fannin, William R., 79
Farley, Jennie, 3, 38, 122, 128, 140
Farmer, C. Richard, 28
Farmer, Richard N., 132
Farrant, Marion, 140
Farrell, Kenneth R., 132
Faulkner, John C., 87, 109
Favour, James R., 124
Feeney, Edward J., 45
Feinstein, Michael, 116
Feldman, Daniel C., 100
Fenton, John, 15, 69, 126
Ferebee, Jr., J. Spencer, 99, 118
Ferguson, Charles R., 77
Ferrance, Sharon, 139
Ferrar, Terry, 111
Fiedler, Fred E., 72
Field, Andrew H., 3
Field, Carol, 3
Fifield, Fred F., 31

Fifield, William M., 81, 83
Figueroa, Oscar, 84, 130
Finkelmeier, Robert L., 81
Finkenberg, Frank E., 59
Finkin, Eugene F., 25, 122
Finkler, Steven A., 9
Finn, David, 4, 117
Finnerty, Joseph E., 14, 105
Firestone, R. Darlene, 123
Firm, C. Connie, 4
Firstenberg, Paul B., 119
Fisher, James W., 8
Fisher, M. Scott, 79
Fitz-Enz, Jac, 58
Flannery, William T., 134
Fleenor, Patrick C., 53
Fleischer, Mary Etzel, 6
Fleishman, Raymond, 71
Fleming, Quentin W., 63, 84
Fletcher, William D., 63
Flowers, Vincent S., 71, 104
Floyd, Herbert F., 25
Fly, Ralph D., 55
Flynn, W. Randolph, 133
Foegen, J. H., 2, 9, 15, 138
Follmann, Jr., Joseph F., 31, 53, 54, 118
Fombrun, Charles, 58
Ford, Charles H., 37
Ford, Robert C., 79, 103, 142
Ford, Robert N., 70, 81, 93, 94
Ford, T. Mitchell, 109, 110, 135
Forrester, Jay W., 32
Foster, Kenneth E., 24, 26
Foster, Lawrence W., 93, 122
Foster, MarySue, 143
Fotilas, Panagiotis N., 101
Fox, Harold W., 106
Fox, Shaul, 42
Fox, William M., 27
Foy, Lewis W., 117
Foy, Peter, 66
Fragner, Berwyn N., 42
Fram, Eugene H., 31
Frame, Robert M., 98
Francis, G. James, 4
Francis, Philip H., 74, 87, 124
Frangipane, Louis J., 134

171

Frank, Michael R., 15, 35, 80, 95, 96, 106, 116
Franklin, Jerome L., 5
Franklin, Jr., William H., 94
Fraser, Ronald, 15
Frech, E. Bryant, 112
Frederick, Robert R., 96
Freedman, Barry, 86
Freeman, Michael, 85, 144
Freeman, R. Edward, 69
Freiman, David J., 66, 88, 89, 100, 110
Freund, William C., 131
Frey, Donald W., 42
Friedman, Barry A., 82
Friedman, Irving S., 64
Friedman, JoAnn, 87
Fritz, Roger, 47
Frohman, Alan L., 71
Frohman, Mark A., 37
Fry, Fred L., 30, 42
Fugate, Donald L., 3
Fulcher, Jan M., 53
Fuller, Stephen H., 121
Fulmer, William E., 104, 142
Fulton, Mary E., 3
Funkhouser, Ray G., 2
Futter, Victor, 8, 69

Gabarro, John J., 111
Gadzinski, Chester, 137
Gaertner, Robert A., 69
Gaffney, Dennis J., 2
Gagnon, Lee A., 6, 35, 99
Galambos, Aniko, 57
Galberaith, Richard O., 109
Gale, Bradley T., 108
Gale, James C., 2
Gallagher, Cornelius E., 125
Gallagher, Gerald R., 89
Gallagher, Michael C., 103
Gamache, R. Donald, 15, 32, 112
Gambill, Ted R., 24
Gandz, Jeffrey, 30
Ganong, James M., 119
Garda, Robert A., 88
Gardner, James E., 79, 93, 135
Gargiulo, Albert F., 29, 50, 51, 73, 74, 136
Garin, Robert H., 115

Garratt, Bob, 82
Gaskell, Colin, 83
Gastwirt, Lawrence, 111, 112, 125
Gemmill, Gary, 11
Gensler, Jr., M. Arthur, 94, 108
George, William R., 88
Georgine, Robert A., 115
Gerberg, Robert Jameson, 11, 26, 27
German, Donald R., 13
German, Joan W., 13
Germany, Patrick J., 94
Gerstenmaier, John H., 141
Gerster, Darlene K., 10
Getzler, Abraham E., 49
Gherman, M.D., E. M., 54
Giblin, Edward J., 18, 24, 78, 127
Giblin, Laurel B., 127
Gifford, John W., 6, 114
Gilabert, Frank, 2, 9, 34, 68, 111
Gilbert, Frederick S., 91
Gilbreth, Lillian M., 77
Gill, Brendan, 88
Gillett, Darwin, 31
Gilman, J. J., 125
Gilman, Tamara A., 142
Gilmour, Peter, 62
Gilroy, Edwin B., 58
Gilsdorf, J. W., 16
Ginsburg, Lee R., 11, 99
Ginsburg, Sigmund G., 10, 47, 51, 68, 117, 128, 129
Ginter, Peter M., 100
Ginzberg, Eli, 11
Given, Wayne, 34
Glaser, Edward M., 70
Glasgow, Robert K., 44
Glenn, Ethel C., 36
Gmelch, Walter H., 54
Goble, Frank G., 115
Godsall, Ray, 82
Goerth, Charles R., 112
Goetz, Billy E., 2
Goff, David, 116
Gold, Charlotte, 4
Goldberg, Bonnie R., 98
Goldberg, Myles H., 27
Goldberg, Stanley R., 124
Goldberg, Victor, 34
Golde, Robert A., 78
Golding, Michael S., 71

Goldman, H. Henry, 10
Goldman, Michael D., 8, 75
Goldsmith, Vern, 127, 137
Goldstein, Paul L., 47
Golightly, Henry O., 72, 110
Gols, A. George, 50
Gomberg, Edith S., 4
Goodale, James G., 68
Goodstein, Leonard D., 76
Goodwin, Herbert F., 77
Goodwin, Phillip H., 119, 139
Goodwin, Susan A., 58
Gordana, John, 33
Gorden, George G., 46, 98
Gorden, Michael E., 24
Gorden, William I., 5, 121
Gordon, David, 56
Gorman, Ronald H., 15, 16
Goss, John H., 52
Gottesman, Jay I., 38, 105
Gottsdanker, Josephine S., 4
Govoni, Norman A. P., 87
Graham, Michael, 141
Graham, Jr., Ben S., 10, 113
Graham, Sr., Ben S., 144
Grams, Robert J., 140
Granger, Charles H., 77
Grant, Philip C., 92
Graves, Joseph J., 123
Gravitz, David H., 136
Gray, Harry J., 119
Gray, Irwin, 112
Gray, J. L., 90
Gray, Robert D., 57
Greenberg, Karen, 10, 12
Greene, Robert J., 25, 26
Greenhaus, Jeffrey H., 38
Greenspan, Sidney, 59
Greenwood, Frank, 6, 35, 99
Greenwood, Ronald G., 77
Gregerman, Ira B., 82, 114, 143
Greiner, Larry E., 97
Grey, Ronald J., 46
Griffin, P., 94
Griffin, Richard T., 102
Griffith, Albert R., 10

Grimaldi, Joseph, 54
Gross, Eugene L., 130
Grossman, Lee , 46
Grove, George, 84
Gruber, Alfred, 33, 112
Gruber, William H., 124
Gryna, Jr., Frank M., 101, 120
Guay, Claude G., 83
Guest, Robert H., 5
Guhde, Robert, 82
Gumpert, Raymond, 73
Gundlach, Werner, 64
Gussow, Don, 91
Gut, Rainer E., 65
Gutman, Evelyn, 88
Gutowski, Armin, 62
Gutteridge, Thomas G., 11, 82
Guynes, C. S., 35
Guyot, James F., 83

Haas, Frederick, 37
Hacker, Thorne, 79
Hackett, Kathryn A., 140
Hackman, Richard J., 70
Haire, Mason, 5
Halatin, T. J., 41, 57, 83, 102, 128, 134
Halford, Juliet M., 20
Hall, Douglas T., 10, 11, 12
Hall, E. K., 56
Hall, Francine S., 11
Hall, Jay, 44, 47
Hall, Lynne, 57, 121, 132
Hall, Thomas E., 141
Hallmark, G. W., 65
Halverson, Jr., W. Stanton, 8
Hambleton, Ronald K., 73
·Hamilton, Joe, 34
Hammer, Armand, 63
Hammerling, Barry, 136
Hammink, William, 49
Hammond, Jr., James H., 7, 17
Hamner, W. Clay, 12
Hanan, Mack, 23, 77, 87, 107, 111, 112, 125, 127
Hand, Herbert H., 80
Hand, Lloyd N., 59
Hannah, Carol, 56
Hansell, Kathleen J., 18
Hansen, Ralph F., 104
Hanson, Charles A., 93
Hanson, Donna K., 93

Hardwick, Leo P., 22
Hardy, C. Colburn, 51, 59, 95, 105, 125, 136
Hardy, Owen B., 109
Harman, Jr., J. Robert, 16
Harman, Willis W., 131
Harmon, Frederick G., 63, 65
Harris, Kenneth L., 97
Harris, Philip, 39
Harris, Robert D., 116
Harrison, Gilbert W., 91
Harrison, Roger, 78
Hart, Gary L., 83
Hart, Lois Borland, 12, 15, 16, 17, 30, 36, 72, 85, 90, 135, 140, 143
Hartmann, M.D., Klaus, 95
Hartshorn, Terry O., 7
Hartung, Jack V., 119
Harvey, Frederick W., 10, 113
Harvey, Jerry B., 98
Hatfield, Bruce P., 55
Hathaway-Bates, John, 94
Hatvany, Nina, 61
Hawkins, Brian L., 17, 30, 92
Hawrylyshyn, Bohdan, 65
Hawver, Dennis A., 82, 86
Hayes, James L., 5, 12, 18, 20, 30, 33, 35, 37, 39, 41, 43, 44, 45, 46, 56, 57, 59, 62, 71, 72, 73, 75, 76, 77, 78, 80, 81, 83, 85, 95, 99, 100, 101, 104, 106, 107, 115, 130, 131, 137, 139, 140, 144
Hayes, Michael, 105
Hayes, Robert H., 91
Haynes, Marion E., 18, 37
Hayo, Sr., George, 138
Hecht, Maurice R., 56, 78, 96, 108
Heier, William D., 4
Heller, George L., 38
Heller, Jean E., 65
Hellwig, Henry, 25, 117
Helsel, Dale F., 124
Hemphill, Jr., Charles F., 35, 128
Hemphill, Robert D., 35, 128
Henderson, Carter, 132
Henderson, Hazel, 52, 132

Henderson, Richard I., 69, 72, 73, 120
Hendrick, James P., 60
Hendricks, Donald P., 116
Henrici, Stanley B., 9, 16, 25, 71, 102, 110
Heptonstall, John, 14
Hergenrather, Edmund R., 122
Hermann, W. James, 20
Hermone, Ronald, 32
Heron, John R., 104
Herrmann, Leo M., 135
Hershey, Gerald L., 143
Hershey, Robert, 25, 29, 108, 132
Hestwood, Thomas M., 24
Heywood, John, 49, 64
Hicks, Herbert G., 62, 101
Hicks, Lawrence E., 120
Higby, Mary A., 88
Higgins, C. Wayne, 53
Higgins, Michael, 1
Higginson, Margaret V., 10, 16, 47
Hildebrandt, Jr., F. Dean, 26
Hildebrandt, Gerald R., 109
Hill, Christopher T., 112
Hill, F. Cecil, 93
Hill, Gordon V., 39
Hill, James W., 76, 116
Hill, Lawrence W., 8
Hill, William K., 80
Hilliard, Vera J., 127
Hills, Frederick S., 24
Hilton, Jack, 20, 117
Hiltzheimer, Charles I., 141
Hindelang, Thomas J., 9, 14, 51, 73, 84, 85, 108, 116, 125, 136
Hinrichs, John R., 67, 68, 138
Hively, Janet M., 137
Hoadley, Walter E., 60
Hodge, John, 71
Hoffman, Lowell M., 119
Hofkosh, Jack M., 102
Hofstede, Geert, 76, 93
Hogue, James C., 142
Hoh, Andrew K., 30, 37, 56
Hohenstein, Louis, 68, 133

Holcombe, Marya, 22
Holden, Alfred C., 62
Holiday, Harry, 75
Holland, Joan, 81, 100
Holland, Winford E., 94
Hollen, T., 6, 41
Holliday, Raymond M.,
    132
Hollingsworth, A. Thomas,
    80, 137
Holmberg, Stevan H. 38,
    108, 135, 139
Holmes, Sandra L., 5
Holtz, Herman R., 3, 22,
    29, 31, 33, 36, 46, 50,
    52, 84, 129, 130
Hoover, J. Duane, 18
Hopkins, Edward J., 75
Horgan, Neil J., 80
Horvitz, Wayne L., 51
Horwitz, Ralph, 60
Hosman, David, 3
Housel, Ben, 141
Howe, Courtney E., 34
Howe, Judith J., 100, 126
Howe, Roger J., 5, 14, 43,
    92, 96, 97, 129, 137,
    142
Howe, R. Overlock, 100
Howell, Don, 83
Howell, William B., 91
Howell, William S., 137
Howerton, Paul W., 106,
    128
Howlett, Michael J., 109
Hoy, Judith, 20
Hoylman, Florence M., 37
Hrabak, William H., 26
Hubbard, Charles L., 49
Huber, Vandra L., 46, 54
Hubsch, Donald M., 86
Huckabay, Loucine M. D.,
    54
Hughes, Charles L., 71,
    79
Hughes, Robard Y., 37
Humble, John, 65, 66,
    108, 131, 136, 139
Humphreys, Neil J., 78,
    130
Humphries, George E., 50
Hunsaker, Johanna S., 36
Hunsaker, Phillip L., 36,
    97, 98
Hunsicker, J. Quincy,
    107
Hunt, Alfred L., 14, 34

Hunt, Bridgford, 44
Hunt, John W., 76
Hunter, Gloria, 46
Hybben, Lois, 136
Hyman, Beverly, 47, 127,
    140, 143

Ihlanfeldt, William, 88
Illman, Paul E., 15, 65, 69,
    81, 93, 100, 122, 140
Imberman, Woodruff, 133,
    141, 142
Imundo, Louis V., 2, 15,
    18, 38, 52, 73, 102,
    104, 128,134, 139
Inglis, Robert, 6
Ireland, Richard C., 89
Irons, Keith L., 15, 17, 69,
    78, 80, 81, 86, 104,
    105
Isaacs, Charles S., 132
Isbister, Claude, 133
Isom, Terry A., 48, 73
Ittleson, Anthony H., 63
Ivancevich, John M., 53
Iverstine, Joe, 31

Jackson, Diane P., 95
Jackson, Donald R., 7,
    123
Jackson, Gene, 68
Jackson, Lauren Hite, 93
Jackson, Theodore A., 54
Jackson, W. C., 9
Jacobs, Arturo A., 104
Jacobs, Granville B., 20
Jacobs, Jeffrey L., 13
Jacobson, Carl C., 115
Jacques, Elliott, 58
Jain, Chaman L., 3, 87
Jain, Hem C., 66
Jalland, Michael, 15, 60,
    61, 64, 66, 96
James, John Alan, 66
James, Paul C., 32
Jamison, Kaleeleel, 113
Jansen, Clem, 83
Janson, Robert, 66
Jaski, Ernest B., 72
Jay, Wendy, 27
Jeanneret, P. R., 70
Jenkins, James, 91
Jenkins, Kenneth M., 120
Jennings, Eugene
    Emerson, 11
Jennings, Kenneth M.,
    103

Jensen, Jerry, 116
Jerstad, Finn E., 106
Jillson, Katherine, 5
Jindal, Gopi R., 14
Jochim, Timothy C., 41
Johnson, Arthur M., 51
Johnson, F. Ross, 76
Johnson, Janet J., 49
Johnson, Kenneth P., 2,
    48, 132
Johnson, Lyndon B., 118
Johnson, Michael, 77, 81,
    131, 132
Johnson, Robert G., 67,
    102
Johnson, Sidney P., 72
Johnson, W. H., 139
Johnston, James J., 28
Johnston, Robert W., 72
Johnston, Wesley J., 72
Johnstone, Joseph J., 76
Jones, C. N., 63
Jones, Howard L., 91
Jones, Reginald H., 60,
    66, 106
Jones, Ruth A., 13, 47,
    105
Jones, Thomas V., 61
Jones, William M., 13, 47,
    105
Jordan, Raymond, 2
Josefowitz, Natasha, 128
Joslin, Edward O., 10
Jud, Robert, 95
Judge, Noreen A., 135
Juers, Allan F., 96
Juran, J. M., 61, 120
Jurkus, Anthony F., 86

Kabus, Irwin, 85
Kagerer, Rudolph L., 130
Kamerschen, David R., 27
Kami, Michael J., 48, 108
Kaminski, Vicky, 45
Kammert, James L., 30,
    48, 64, 65, 108
Kanarick, Arnold, 120
Kanin-Lovers, Jill, 24
Kanter, Rosabeth Moss,
    70
Kaplan, Irwin Bobby, 24
Kaplan, Morton M., 6, 114
Karas, Jr., Stephen, 31,34
Karger, Delmar W., 49
Karp, H. B., 45
Kastens, Merritt L., 2, 58,
    78, 113, 125

Katz, Abraham, 109
Katz, Elihu, 20
Kaufman, Lois, 52
Kaufman, Stephen P., 109
Kaye, Beverly L., 13
Kaye, Walter, 48, 130
Kazakoff, Peter, 94
Kearns, David T., 133
Keaton, Paul N., 91
Keaveny, Timothy J., 39
Keegan, Elizabeth, 83
Keen, Peter G. W., 20
Keenan, Robert, 62
Keeney, Ralph L., 36
Kelley, Clifton G., 29, 119, 123
Kelly, Robert P., 70
Kenard, Jr., Raymond J., 50, 73, 136
Kendig, William L., 38, 73, 95
Kendrick, John W., 113
Kennedy, John F., 60
Kennedy, Robert F., 74
Kennedy, Rose L., 81
Kenney, Donald P., 34, 35
Kent, W. E., 56
Keppler, Robert H., 101
Kesselman, Gerald A., 141
Kets de Vries, Manfred F. R., 12
Keys, J. Bernard, 44
Kiam II, Victor K., 91
Kiev, M.D., Ari, 54
Kilgour, John G., 16, 25, 40, 71, 128, 141, 142
Killian, Ray A., 15, 38, 52, 58, 72, 73, 93, 102, 140, 142
Kilmann, Ralph H., 37, 84
Kimball, Richard J., 27
Kinard, Jerry, 31
Kindling, Alexander T., 49
King, Albert S., 142
King, Dennis C., 30, 136
King, Steven, 89
King, William R., 109
Kintisch, Ronald S., 30, 35
Kinzel, Robert K., 95
Kirby, Peter G., 37, 120, 140
Kirk, Raymond J., 32
Kirkwood, William, 90
Kirschbraun, Keith D., 75

Klasson, Charles R., 103
Klein, Gerald D., 120
Klein, Harold E., 107
Klein, Marvin M., 36
Kleiner, Brian H., 12, 30, 56, 98
Klingenberg, Ronna, 36
Knickerbocker, Jr., Daniel C., 75, 102
Knickerbocker, Irving, 71
Knight, James H., 122
Knoblauch, Mary, 20, 117
Knutson, Joan Ryan, 106, 116
Koch, Frank, 23, 131
Koellner, Paul, 92
Koester, Edwin H., 9, 84, 119
Kogelman, Stanley, 45
Kohn, Vera, 54
Kolodny, Harvey F., 90
Konczel, Edward F., 126
Koontz, Harold, 78, 103
Korman, Abraham K., 91
Kornhauser, Arthur W., 5
Kosnik, Thomas J., 13
Kostik, Max M., 114
Kotler, Philip, 88
Kotter, John P., 46
Kovach, Kenneth A., 5, 16, 101
Kranz, Mary Ellen, 104
Krasnansky, Marvin L., 23
Krause, William H., 127, 130
Krauss, Leonard I., 7, 17, 33, 108, 128
Krausz, Moshe, 42
Kraut, Richard S., 75
Kreck, Lothar A., 37
Kreiken, J., 106
Kress, Thomas G., 49
Kressler, D. W., 56
Krieble, Robert, 132
Krinke, Keith B., 52
Kristy, James E., 37
Krogman, Robert, 102
Krupp, Neil B., 66
Kubilus, Norbert J., 34
Kudlinski, Romuald, 60
Kuehner, Charles D., 69
Kumar, Parmanand, 91
Kurtz, Harold P., 118
Kushell, Robert E., 86
Kuzmits, Frank E., 1, 2, 107
Kyser, Jr., Robert C., 143

La Londe, Bernard J., 39
Labovitz, George H., 65, 115, 139
LaFleur, James K., 117, 132
Laibstain, Samuel, 48
Landau, Robert M., 84
Landvater, John H., 91
Lane, Harold E., 122
Lane, Marc J., 74, 118, 130, 137
Lang, Richard H., 126
Langevin, Roger G., 120, 129
Langford, Harry, 140
Lansdale, David B., 100
Lantzke, Ulf, 42
Larson, Charles C., 110
Lasry, George, 49, 125
Latham, Bradley A., 85, 107
Latham, Fred W., 36, 37, 49, 58, 78, 84, 87, 96, 112, 113, 124
Latham, Gary P., 79, 92, 113
Latona, Joseph C., 72
Lauenstein, Milton C., 7
Lavely, Joseph A., 24
Lawler, III, Edward E., 23, 24, 28, 44, 71, 92, 109, 121
Lawrence, Deslie Beth, 14, 16, 42, 53, 57, 76, 121, 128, 137
Lawrence, Jean, 82
Lawrence, Paul R., 90
Lazar, Arpad Von, 61
Lea, G. Robert, 79
Leach, John J., 10, 58
Leamon, Jerry P., 65
Lear, Robert W., 16
Leavitt, Harold J., 71
Lebeck, Warren W., 60
Lebo, Dell, 45, 100
Leboeuf, Michael, 21
Le Breton, Preston P., 107
Ledbetter, James E., 53
Lee, Fred E., 86
Lee, John A., 6
Lee, M. Mark, 40, 48, 49, 91, 130, 132
Lee, Nancy, 11
Lee, Robert E., 100
Leek, Jay W., 120
Leff, Nathaniel H., 63
Lefsky, William, 20

Lehr, Lewis W., 112
Leibson, David E., 109, 114
Lein, Charles D., 16
Lemmon, Wayne A., 89, 130
Leonard, Edmund A., 16, 31, 100
Leonhard, William E., 41
Leontiades, Milton, 106
Lerner, Lawrence, 94
Lerner, Robert J., 27
Lesieur, Fred G., 142
Lesly, Philip, 18, 19, 20, 22, 56
Levenson, Harold E., 31
Leverette, Ted J., 44
Levine, Edward L., 18, 19, 69, 103
Levine, Harold, 130
Levine, Hermine Zagat, 16, 41, 75, 139
Levinson, Robert E., 11, 12
Levitt, Mortimer, 11, 45
Levy, Sidney J., 23, 88, 89
Levy, Walter A., 33, 34, 51
Lewicki, Roy J., 5
Lewin, David, 121
Lewis, David V., 45, 46, 105, 138
Lewis, Lou, 9
Lewis, Richard A., 123
Liebling, Barry A., 36
Liebrenz, Marilyn L., 122
Likert, Janet, 30
Likert, Rensis, 30, 72, 79
Lilley, Robert D., 75
Lindberg, Roy A., 25, 28, 40, 71, 76, 92, 107, 130
Lindo, David K., 13, 18, 86, 135, 138
Lindstrom, William R., 126
Linenberger, O. James, 124
Linenberger, Patricia, 39
Linhares, Alfonso B., 123
Lipman-Blumen, Jean, 71
Lippitt, Ronald, 101
Lipsett, Laurence, 75
Lipton, Mark, 122
Little, Arthur D., 106
Little, Charles D., 118

Livingston, Donald G., 30
Lizotte, Kenneth M., 9, 14, 38, 45, 48
Locke, Edwin A., 79, 92
Lodge, George Cabot, 43
Lonergan, Neil J., 29
Lopez, Felix M., 86
Lord, Richard K., 25
Lord, Robert W., 90
Lord, William G. II., 113
Lorenz, Clifford J., 88
Lorey, Will, 15
Lorsch, Jay W., 96
Lott, Richard W., 6, 33, 34, 50, 125
Louden, J. Keith, 7, 17, 69, 105, 111
Love, Sydney F., 139
Lowe, Jung Y., 61
Lowry, Robert A., 35
Loye, David, 50
Lubben, Gary L., 103
Luksus, Edmund J., 9, 50
Lumsden, George J., 45
Lund, Robert T., 112, 125
Lupton, Tom, 121
Lusterman, Seymour, 88
Lutchen, Mark D., 83
Luter, Edward R., 61
Luthans, Fred, 3, 43, 44, 56, 70, 98
Lyman, David, 102
Lynch, Dudley, 32
Lynch, Edith M., 5, 11, 57, 95, 142, 143
Lynch, James F., 110
Lyons, John T., 105

Maanen, John Van, 98
MacAvoy, Robert E., 48
Mackenzie, R. Alec, 20, 47, 138, 139
Mackey, Craig B., 86
Mackey, John A., 66
Macrae, Norman, 20
MacStravic, Robin E., 89, 97
Maddalena, Lucille A., 3, 21, 51, 90, 117, 118
Maddocks, Anderson, 54
Maddox, Eva, 94
Maggin, Donald L., 118
Magner, Monica M., 44
Maher, Theodore J., 124
Mahoney, Francis X., 81, 137

Mahoney, Thomas A., 58
Maier, Cornell C., 75
Main, John G., 48
Majak, R. Roger, 61
Malek, Frederic V., 79
Malena, Michael, 74
Malmgren, Harald B., 59
Malone, III., Paul B., 43
Mandell, J. S., 50
Mandt, Edward, 137
Mangrum, Claude T., 53, 54, 116, 134
Mann, Robert W., 82
Manning, Winton H., 43, 138
Mansfield, Geoffrey J., 48
Manuel, Wilburn G., 115
Marcus, Jay B., 53
Marcussen, Mark, 115
Margerison, Charles, 5, 72, 90, 134
Margolis, Bruce L., 81, 83
Margulies, Walter P., 23
Marino, Kenneth E., 3
Markham, Arleigh, 110
Marksbury, Henry, 137
Markus, M. Lynne, 70
Marolda, Anthony J., 115
Marrow, Alfred J., 141
Martier, Alison, 10
Martin, Anthony W., 82
Martin, Jr., Claude R., 34, 48
Martin, Desmond D., 86
Martin, I., 131
Martin, Jane L., 136
Martin, Richard G., 38
Martin, Samuel P., 118
Martin, Virginia H., 55, 75
Marting, Elizabeth, 12, 20, 77, 144
Marvin, Philip, 138
Marxer, Thomas T., 126
Maselko, C. James, 45
Mashburn, James I., 73
Mason, Jr., James W., 115
Mason, Joseph G., 138
Massey, L. Daniel, 33
Massimino, Sal T., 126, 127
Massin, S. Scott, 105
Massoni, Karen B., 54
Mast, Hans J., 63
Matoon, Bruce P., 126
Matteson, Michael T., 53
Matto, Edward A., 75
Maurer, Richard S., 8, 123

Mautz, Robert K., 2
Max, Robert R., 21
Mayberry, Grant E., 29, 46, 85, 90, 134
Mayer, Richard J., 103
Mayo, Elton, 56
McAfee, R. Bruce, 6, 57
McAlindon, Harold R., 33, 43, 47, 92, 93, 97, 137, 140
McAvoy, Robert, 86
McCafferty, Donald N., 81, 129, 139
McCann, John P., 53
McCaskey, Michael B., 37
McClendon, Edward L., 13
McConkey, Dale D., 38, 78, 79
McConnell, J., 6, 42, 48, 57, 77, 87, 113, 119
McCormick, Ernest J., 70, 84
McCoy, Robert C., 104
McCubbin, Jr., Charles C., 9
McCullough, William W., 39
McDonald, J. Michael, 2
McDougle, Larry G., 68, 69, 139
McEwan, Bruce, 13
McFarland, Dalton E., 44, 135
McFeeley, Neil D., 39
McGee, Edward J., 87
McGhee, Archie, 6
McGill, Michael E., 98
McGowan, John J., 65
McGregor, Douglas, 71
McGregor, Georgette F., 17, 143
McKain, Robert J., 12, 45, 54
McKenna, Jack F., 130
McKinney, James E., 27
McKinnon, Linda M. B., 75
McLamore, Hilliard, 35
McLaughlin, David J., 27
McLean, M.D., Preston G., 5
McMahon, J. Timothy, 79
McMahon, Jr., Thomas W., 16
McManus, Leo F., 38, 92, 127
McManus, Michael L., 23
McMaster, John B., 18, 50, 123

McMillan, John D., 103
McNamara, Carlton P., 115
McNeff, Marvin R., 137
McNeff, Nancy J., 137
McQuade, Walter, 118
Meade, James, 143
Mealiea, Laird W., 14, 21
Mebane, Patricia O., 31
Mee, John F., 131
Megahan, John B., 8
Meglino, Bruce M., 54, 98, 137
Meidan, Arthur, 102
Meier-Preschany, Manfred, 63
Meltzer, Morton F., 10, 84, 96
Melville, Sheila D., 110
Mendleson, Jack L., 131
Mercer, James L., 9, 50, 58, 84, 96, 114, 118, 119, 124, 136
Meredith, David R., 26
Merkey, R. Kenneth, 63
Merkle, Ned, 74, 102
Merklein, H. A., 64
Merrell, V. Dallas, 56, 73, 90
Merrifield, D. Bruce, 34, 116, 124, 129
Mervis, Philip H., 121
Metzger, Norman, 16
Meuter, Jr., Fred W., 26
Meyer, Henry D., 81, 83
Meyer, Henry I., 40, 52, 76, 77, 123, 132
Meyer, Pearl, 26
Meyer, Peggy, 53
Meyers, Charles A., 52
Mezoff, Bob, 140
Middlebrook, Bill, 37
Mieli, Renato, 62
Migliaro, Al, 3, 87
Milam, Edward E., 105, 136
Milbourn, Jr., Gene, 4, 40, 43, 53, 54, 70, 93, 98
Miles, James M., 71
Miles, John N., 2
Miles, Jr., Rufus E., 77
Militzer, K. H., 115
Milkovich, George T., 58
Miller, Arthur F., 122

Miller, David W., 32, 36, 49
Miller, Donald B., 82, 114
Miller, Edward J., 134
Miller, Edward M., 128
Miller, Ernest C., 4, 11, 17, 23, 25, 26, 27, 28, 38, 42, 44, 55, 57, 58, 59, 73, 97, 98, 102, 103, 121, 123, 126, 127, 128, 132, 136
Miller, George, 19, 77, 80, 92, 96, 107
Miller, George S., 42
Miller, G. Wade, 110
Miller, III, James C., 75
Miller, III, J. Thomas, 17
Miller, Leo, 56
Miller, Marc E., 54
Miller, Neil, 69, 137
Miller, Ronald L., 52
Miller, R. H., 125
Miller, William B., 35, 93
Millett, John D., 15, 77, 106, 118
Minchew, Daniel, 60
Mindak, William A., 88
Mindell, Mark G., 5, 92, 93, 121
Mines, Herbert T., 85, 111
Mintz, Harold K., 22
Mintzberg, Henry, 138
Miossi, Alfred F., 64
Mirvis, Philip, 5
Mitchell, Arnold, 131
Mitchell, Garry, 45, 87
Mitchell, Howard M., 68
Mitchell, Terence R., 113
Mitroff, Ian I., 84
Mittelstaedt, Jr., Robert E., 118
Mobley, William H., 98
Mochizuki, Kiichi, 60, 61
Mode, V. Alan, 92, 136
Moeller, Clark, 43
Moffitt, Donald, 41, 42, 49, 133
Mogensen, Allan H., 143
Mohammed, Fazel, 13
Mohn, Carroll N., 49
Molitor, Graham T. T., 49, 132
Mollenhoff, David V., 103
Momboisse, Raymond M., 74
Monczka, Robert M., 93, 119

177

Mondy, R. Wayne, 5, 56
Monroe, Willys H., 36
Monsen, R. Joseph, 116
Montana, Patrick J., 10,
    12, 88, 118, 127
Montgomery, Robert L.,
    19, 44, 45, 46, 127
Moore, Cyril F., 80
Moore, Geoffrey H., 111
Moore, H., 6, 105
Moore, John M., 122
Moore, Leo B., 101
Moore, Lynda L., 11
Moore, Richard O., 59
Moore, William L., 29, 86
Moran, Robert T., 61
Morano, Richard A., 54,
    70, 138
Moravec, Milan, 97, 103
More, Thomas, 94
Morgan, Daniel C., 10
Morgan, Marilyn A., 10, 12
Morgenbrod, Horst, 136
Morlion, Andrew F., 131
Morris, James G., 129
Morris, Jr., Seymour, 131
Morrison, Ann M., 104
Morse, Gerry E., 56
Mort, Terry A., 120, 127
Mortimer, Norma, 23, 133
Morton, Donald A., 118
Moscato, Donald R., 36,
    48, 50, 119, 129
Mosely, Owen B., 9
Moser, S. Thomas, 6
Moskowitz, Robert A., 10,
    36, 44, 56, 103
Moss, Kenneth, 121
Mossholder, Kevin W., 24
Mossien, Herbert J., 31
Motyl, Pierre, 20
Mouton, Jane Srygley, 33,
    72, 90, 114, 116, 126,
    142
Moynahan, John K., 28,
    126
Mruk, Edwin S., 24, 26
Mueller, George E., 33
Mukergi, Dhan G., 114
Mulkowsky, Gary, 85
Mullarkey, Maureen E.,
    140
Mullick, Satinder K., 49
Mullins, Terry W., 128
Munchus III., George, 16
Murnighan, J. Keith, 36
Murphy, Daniel J., 96

Murphy, J. Kevin, 75
Murphy, William B., 42
Murr, Donald W., 80
Murray, Richard K., 103
Murray, William A., 10
Muskie, Senator Edmund
    S., 75
Mustafa, Husain, 82
Myers, Charles A., 58
Myers, Donald W., 32,
    133
Myers, Edward A., 42
Myers, M. Scott, 70

Nadler, David A., 5, 98
Nadler, Leonard, 132
Nance, Harold W., 114
Nangea, Narendra K., 56
Naor, Jacob, 101, 130
Naum, Lionel, 85
Neely, George, 3, 43
Neese, Linda, 79
Neff, Thomas J., 44
Neiman, Robert A., 46
Nelson, Jerome M., 52
Nelson, Reed, 99
Nemitz, William C., 113
Neubauer, Robert J., 71
Neufeld, Irving H., 75
Neuschel, Richard F., 106,
    110
Newman, Robert P., 18,
    110
Newman, William H., 77,
    107
Newstrom, John W., 93
Newton, Jr., Charles G.,
    106, 117
Nicholson, Eddy G., 117
Nichols-Manning, Cathy,
    88
Nicosia, Sal, 7, 41, 59
Niehouse, Oliver L., 53,
    54, 143
Nielsen, Eric H., 97
Niles, John L., 113
Nirenberg, John, 92, 93,
    134
Nisberg, Jay N., 68
Nisser, Carl, 66
Nix, Dan H., 68
Nkomo, Stella M., 86
Noddings, Thomas C.,
    102
Nolan, Robert E., 2, 94,
    114, 123, 127, 142,
    143

Nollen, Stanley D., 55, 75
Nonberg, Randy E., 8
Nord, Walter R., 58
Norland, Otto R., 42
Norton, Curt, 29
Novick, Harold J., 30
Nugent, Patrick S., 44
Numerof, Rita E., 21, 30,
    75, 82, 139
Nurick, Aaron J., 24
Nygren, William V., 51,
    94, 135

Ober, Steven P., 71
O'Connell, George E., 137
O'Connell, Joan M., 137
O'Connor, Walter F., 63,
    64, 136
O'Dell, Carla S., 114, 142
Odell, Jr., Harris, 1, 24,
    76, 118
Odiorne, George S., 44,
    79, 137
Ogden, Richard W., 12,
    77, 105, 113
O'Hagan, Malcolm, 91
O'Hallaron, Richard D., 88
O'Hara-Tumilty, Anne, 120
O'Keefe III., James J., 29
O'Keefe, Lawrence P.,
    124
Older, Harry J., 3
Olivas, Louis, 83
Oliver, Christie, 94
Olkewicz, Anthony W.,
    115
Olney, Jr., Peter B., 104
Olsen, Raymond N., 24
Olson, Dan, 55
Olson, Ted, 116
Omolayole, Michael O., 65
O'Neill, Jr., Arthur S., 3
O'Reilly, Charles, 101
Oritt, Paul L., 130
Ornati, Oscar A., 38
O'Rourke, Carol, 105
Ortiz, Rene G., 60
Osborn, Jack Lester, 74, 75
Osborne, E. Alfred, 44
Osgood, William R., 3, 9,
    33, 48, 57, 68, 76, 80,
    88, 93, 106, 108, 111,
    130, 139
O'Toole, James J, 132
Otten, Gerard L., 10
Ouchi, William G., 62, 78,
    97

178

Owen, George C., 31
Owsley, Clifford D., 21
Oxenfeldt, Alfred R., 29, 31, 32, 36, 49, 79, 86, 89, 129
Ozley, Lee M., 71

Pack, Raymond J., 79
Paddock, Anthony C., 51
Paine, Thomas H., 27
Pakshong, Michael Wong, 65
Paley, Norton, 86, 87, 109
Pancrazio, James J., 17
Pancrazio, Sally Bulkley, 17
Paperman, Jacob B., 86, 89
Paris, Darlene L., 14
Parket, I. Robert, 110
Parlette, Nicholas, 101
Parsons, Gerald A., 69
Parsons, Henry L., 35, 84
Parsons, Leonard J., 34
Pasquale, Anthony M., 27
Pass, Jan Baker, 32
Pati, Gopal C., 3
Patten, Jr., Thomas H., 39, 99, 137
Patterson, James J., 126
Patton, James M., 2, John A., 43
Paulin, George B., 40
Payson, William S., 88
Pearce, David, 50, 81, 83
Pearse, Robert F., 5, 12, 114
Pearson, Karl G., 105
Pedersen, Judith, 87
Pedler, R. H., 101
Peel, Jack A., 65
Pekar, Peter P., 15, 84, 107, 108
Pellegrino, Edmund D., 117
Peller, Phillip R., 136
Pelligrino, John F., 54
Penley, Larry E., 17, 92
Pennington, Malcolm W., 106, 109
Pennington, Robert L., 39
Peper, Merle, 31
Perlin, Edward, 24
Perlman, Daniel H., 119
Perlman, Jeanette, 43
Perrow, Charles, 35
Perry, Lee T., 104
Peskin, Dean B., 14

Peskin, Dean P., 11, 37, 45, 76
Peterfreund, Stanley, 5, 144
Peters, Douglas S., 55
Peters, Robert A., 111, 125
Peters, Thomas J., 77, 78, 99
Petersen, Donald J., 53, 55
Peterson, Robin, 134
Petit, Thomas A., 128
Petrie, Donald J., 25
Pfaffle, A. E., 7, 41, 59
Pfeffer, Jeffrey, 98, 99
Phelan, John G., 109
Philips, Billy U., 53
Philips, Donald A., 3
Philips, Madison, 71
Philips, Ronald J., 50, 124
Phillips, Christopher H., 62
Phillips, F. Stanley, 143
Phillips, Jack J., 81, 121, 135
Piamonte, John S., 92
Picard, Hans, 38
Picard, Lyra, 38
Pickens, John L., 126
Pickering, Paul H., 105
Pickhardt, Carl E., 99
Pigors, Paul, 57
Pike, Dan, 77
Pincus, Theodore H., 69
Pittle, R. David, 74
Pitts, Robert E., 4, 37, 80, 89, 93, 104, 135
Plachy, Roger J., 72, 77
Plaszcznski, Leo, 122
Pleasance, Roy T., 136
Pleninger, Andrew, 12
Plessia, Radu G., 63
Plumberg, Thomas, 24
Pomboy, Richard M., 130
Pomeranz, Felix, 2, 6
Pommerening, Dieter, 66
Ponthieu, J. F., 19
Pood, Elliott, 36
Pope, A. L., 62
Pope, Jeffrey L., 23, 43, 51, 85, 89, 116
Poppel, Harvey L., 35
Porras, Jerry I., 97
Port, Mary Etta, 100
Porter, J. Winston, 63
Porter, Lyman W., 5, 72
Post, James E., 131

Potter, Beverly A., 14, 19, 20, 30, 90, 97, 99, 128
Powell, Gary N., 47
Powell, Jon T., 19
Powell, Paul B., 119
Poza, Ernesto J., 70
Prakash, Prem, 125
Preiwisch, Clement F., 142
Preston, Lee E., 131
Preston, Paul, 30
Preston, Peter, 82
Price, Raymond L., 13, 97
Prince, Bill, 83
Pringle, Edward G., 36
Pritchard, Robert E., 9, 14, 51, 73, 84, 85, 106, 108, 116, 125, 130, 136
Proe, John D., 53, 78, 97, 108
Proger, Phillip A., 91
Pryor, Mildred Golden, 5, 56
Pryor, N. Norman, 24
Pucik, Vladimir, 61
Pugh, Derek, 30
Purcell, Alan V., 35
Purcell, Theodore V., 43
Purnell, Richard I., 64
Pursell, Robert B., 142
Putnam, Arnold O., 112
Pye, Gordon B., 50
Pyle, Richard L., 53

Quaglieri, Philip L., 18
Quay, John, 6
Quick, Thomas L., 16, 18, 47
Quinn, Robert E., 135

Rabinowitz, Alan, 49, 125, 132, 136
Rader, M. H., 16
Ramirez-Sosa, Gretchen, 92
Rand, Edward J., 76
Randall, Robert M., 108, 111
Ranftl, Robert M., 115
Ransom, James H., 96
Rao, Dileep, 48, 84, 130
Rappaport, Gary B., 14
Raskin, A. H., 132
Rausch, Edward N., 48, 130

Read, John C., 75
Redd, R., 6, 41
Reddick, Marshall E., 3, 66, 83, 87, 88, 89, 96, 107, 111, 112, 127, 130
Redling, Edward T., 27
Rees, Jr., Frank W., 94
Regenstreif, Donna J., 32
Rehder, Robert R., 62
Reichman, Walter, 46
Reid, Douglas, 86
Reif, Jr., Richard A., 8
Reif, William E., 70, 93
Reilley, Ewing W., 96, 110
Reilly, Robert F., 6, 82
Reinharth, Leon, 96
Reiter, Elanor, 38
Remick, Carl, 61, 77, 109
Rendero, Thomasine, 52, 69, 103, 121, 129
Repp, William, 21
Rettig, John, 119
Revans, Reg, 82
Rhodes, Dennis, 113
Rhodes, John B., 59
Rhodes, Susan R., 2
Rice, Joseph A., 17, 22
Richards, Gary , 20, 138
Richards, Paul, 22
Richardson, Elliot L., 59
Richmond, Robert L., 6
Ricker, Jr., John B., 74
Riley, Max V., 94
Rimler, George W., 78, 130
Rimmer, Murray, 81
Rinella, Richard J., 3, 13
Rippon Q.C. M.P., Rt. Hon. Geoffrey, 62
Riser, Elizabeth, 72
Risher, Howard, 39, 71
Ritterbach, George H., 34
Ritvo, Edward, 10
Roach, John M., 37, 56, 66
Roalman, Arthur R., 69
Robb, Donald O., 85
Robb, Warren D., 68
Robbins, Claire C., 3, 13
Robbins, Paula I., 11, 13, 40, 84, 95
Roberts, Edward B., 130
Robinson, John, 62
Robinson, Joseph A., 143

Robinson, Richard D., 59
Rodeghero, James A., 134
Roderick, David M., 32
Rogers III., Charles W., 65
Rogers, David, 118
Rogers, Robert S., 126
Roman, Murray, 88
Roney, Candace, 42, 59
Root, Franklin R., 66
Roseman, Edward, 11, 15, 32, 138, 139, 141
Rosen, Nancy J., 89
Rosen, Stephen S., 94
Rosenbaum, Bernard, 94
Rosenberg, DeAnne, 44, 142
Rosenberg, Larry J., 87
Rosenbloom, Arthur H., 91
Rosendahl, Iris D., 14, 42, 68, 121, 128, 137
Rosow, Jerome M., 44, 116
Ross, Edwin S., 83, 129
Ross, Eleanor M., 41
Ross, Ronald G., 33, 35, 50, 95
Rothschild, William E., 29, 49, 87, 108, 112, 113
Rothwell, Wade, 127
Rotondi, Jr., Thomas, 97
Rourke, Charles K., 96
Rowe, David L., 143
Roxe, Linda A., 15, 25, 40, 55, 58, 75, 93, 128, 130, 134, 140, 141
Rubenfeld, Stephen A., 102
Rubenfield, Stephen, 128
Rubinstein, Sidney P., 101
Ruby, James B., 50
Ruck, Jr., Frank J., 115
Rucks, Andrew C., 100
Rumack, Frederick W., 136
Runcie, John F., 121
Runzheimer, Jr., Rufus E., 24, 25
Russ, Zack, 132
Russo, Samuel F., 64
Rust, H. Lee, 13
Rustin, Randall, 34
Ryan, John L., 107, 137
Ryan, Joseph E., 90
Ryan, Thomas J., 66

Sachs, Randi, 38
Saffer, Brian H., 91
Salancik, Gerald R., 4, 98, 99
Salscheider, James, 24
Salton, Gary J., 79
Salveson, Melvin E., 106, 111
Salzman, Jeffrey, 52
Sambar, David H., 64
Sambridge, Edward R., 29, 35, 119
Samek, Michael J., 34
Sammet, Jr., George, 29, 119, 123
Sampson, Howard L., 85
Samuelson, Paul A., 52
Sandberg, Carl H., 14
Sanders, Bruce D., 12, 90, 98, 137
Sanders, George S., 36, 37, 49, 58, 78, 84, 87, 96, 112, 113, 124
Sanders, Norman, 33
Sanders, Wayne, 17
Sands, Ben F., 101
Sands, Saul, 112
Sanzotta, Donald, 56, 93
Sargent, Alice G., 44, 46
Sargent, Howard, 44
Sashkin, Marshall, 102
Sathe, Vijay, 16, 48, 95, 100
Sauer, Jr., James E., 86
Savage, James M., 75
Savage, Stuart J., 79
Sawhill, John C., 41, 42
Sawyer, Lawrence B., 6, 18, 36, 70, 78, 80, 85, 103, 105, 108
Saxberg, Borje O., 116
Sayles, Leonard, 19
Schachat, Robert, 20
Schaffer, Robert H., 122
Schaffner, Robert M., 117
Schary, Philip B., 63
Schein, Virginia E., 97
Schell, Erwin H., 76
Schiff, Michael, 14
Schlachtmeyer, Albert S., 40
Schleh, Edward C., 38, 72, 76, 109
Schleicher, J. Gordon, 15, 90
Schlesinger, Leonard, 101
Schlump, James D., 143

Schmertz, Herbert, 74, 117
Schmidt, Richard F., 109
Schmidt, Robert D., 63
Schmölders, Günther, 62
Schnake, Melvin E., 104
Schnake, M. E., 102, 134
Schnapper, Bette P., 54
Schneider, Benjamin, 103, 129
Schneirer, Dena B., 103
Schnitzer, Elliot M., 74
Schoeffler, Sidney, 125
Schoen, Donald R., 108
Schoenfeldt, Lyle F., 82
Schoenfeldt, Roger C., 134
Schork, John E., 110
Schrank, Robert, 66
Schuler, Randall S., 104
Schwartz, Eleanor B., 47, 139
Schwartz, Irving R., 13
Schwartz, Jonathan E., 89
Schwartzel, Heinz, 136
Schweizer, Jason, 98
Scobel, Donald N., 71
Scotese, Peter G., 7, 131
Scott, Barry, 82
Scott, Walter B., 101
Scotti, Marie, 126
Seaborg, Glenn T., 110
Seabury, Steve, 85
Searby, Daniel M., 63
Seely, Michael, 69
Segar, Alfred, 31
Segev, Eli, 106, 107
Seidel, Lena, 18
Seiden, Hank, 3
Seiler, George R., 80, 123, 125
Sekiguchi, Shiro, 61, 95
Selck, Thomas, 48
Seligman, Harold L., 31
Seng, Roger W., 126, 127
Serenbetz, Warren L., 39
Sethi, S. Prakash, 52, 65, 7
Severiens, Jacobus T., 112
Shaffer, Robert H., 115
Shafton, Robert M., 8
Shagam, Jerome I., 65
Shaner, Karl L., 116
Shaner, Michael C., 137
Shanklin, William L., 89
Shapiro, Alan C., 64

Shapiro, Benson P., 88
Shapiro, Irving S., 51
Sharp, Arthur G., 21, 127
Sharwell, William G., 76
Shaver, Ann V., 2
Shaw, John C., 120, 129
Shaw, Malcolm E., 45, 72, 83
Shaw, Robert J., 68
Shay, Philip W., 78
Sheehan, Don, 127
Sheldon, Alan, 98
Sheldon, Garrett L., 33
Shelton, Jack K., 31
Sheppard, I. Thomas, 47, 65
Sherman, George, 142
Sherman, V. Clayton, 17, 54, 85
Sherony, Bruce C., 8
Sherwood, John J., 29, 37
Shetty, Y. Krishna, 80, 114, 115
Shiff, Robert A., 94
Shimada, Justin, 120
Shirk, Charles A., 114
Shores, David L., 57, 99
Shulman, Joel J., 22
Sibson, Robert E., 24, 27, 28, 40, 71, 104
Sidwell, P. Philip, 11
Siegel, Alan, 22
Siegel, Jerome, 39, 75, 138
Siemens, Warren D., 125
Sikula, Andrew F., 104
Sikula, John P., 104
Silber, Mark B., 18, 47, 53
Sillavan, Dick, 31
Silver, Donald F., 41
Silver, M. S., 142
Silverman, Buddy Robert Stephen, 27
Simon, John R., 29
Sinason, H. Henry, 119
Sinclair, David R., 74
Sinclair, Don, 83
Sindell, P. S., 131
Singhvi, Surendra S., 48
Singleton, John P., 45, 79
Sirc, Ljubo, 62
Sirny, Rudolf E., 12
Sirota, David, 5
Siwinski, Wlodzimierz, 60
Skibbins, Gerald J., 131
Slevin, Dennis P., 139
Slijper, Martin T., 141

Smiddy, Harold, 14, 36, 77, 78, 80, 81, 85, 92, 96, 97, 107, 108, 123
Smith, Charles A., 24
Smith, Edward B., 28
Smith, Frank J., 5
Smith, George S., 94, 136
Smith, Howard L., 14, 38, 85, 139
Smith, Howard R., 94, 135
Smith, H. Dean, 30
Smith, J. G., 131
Smith, Marshall, 123
Smith, Martin R., 6, 95, 120
Smith, Michael, 102
Smith, Mike, 90
Smith, Robert D., 129
Smith, Robert F., 90
Smith, Robert H., 128
Smith, Sidney S., 113
Smith, Terry L., 15
Smith, Theodore A., 111
Smith, Ward C., 31, 112, 129
Smith, William M., 98
Smykay, Edward W., 39, 88
Soat, Douglas M., 98
Sobiech, Georgia, 86
Soltanoff, Louis, 125
Somerville, James D., 81
Sommers, William P., 124
Sondak, Arthur, 100, 133
Sorcher, Melvin, 4
Sorensen, Jane, 47
Sorensen, Peter F., 79
Souerwine, Andrew H., 10, 11, 12, 13
Spader, Peter H., 43
Spechler, Jay, 16, 97
Spencer, Edson W., 124
Spiegen, Don, 92
Spinanger, Arthur, 14
Spooner, Peter, 77, 81, 131, 132
Springate, David J., 64
Springer, Philip, 24, 42
Spurr, Daniel, 68
Stack, Ruth H., 50, 55
Stamps, Paula L., 4, 92
Stanek, Lou Willet, 47
Stanton, Erwin S., 38, 68, 121, 128
Staples, Jeffrey, 88
Starchild, Adam, 50, 105, 137

Staudohar, Paul D., 28
Staw, Barry M., 95
Steele, James W., 103
Steers, Richard M., 2
Steffens, John L., 41, 105
Stein, Barry A., 70
Stein, Judith, 22
Steinberg, Samuel H., 134
Steinbrecher, David D.,
    55, 73, 83, 142
Steiner, George A., 107,
    131
Steinhauser, Larry, 122
Steinthal, Nicholas, 64
Stephenson, George, 35
Sterling, Lionel N., 48
Stern, Allan D. R., 12
Sterne, Michael, 89
Stessin, Lawrence, 55
Stevenson, Adlai E., 60
Stewart, Rosemary, 77
Stewart, Wendell M., 39
Stiegler, Christine B., 17
Stillian, Gabriel, 17
Stillman, Nina G., 74
Stimac, Michele, 14
Stinson, John W., 102
Stinson, Jr., Milton E., 14
Stockard, James G., 76,
    81, 118, 134, 139
Stoeberl, Philipp A., 8
Stokes, Douglas M., 28
Stolz, Karen, 12
Stone, Morris, 4
Storer, Andrew F., 119
Stormes, John M., 56
Stout, Russell, 95
Stover, Robert W., 122
Stratton, William E., 133
Streidl, J. William, 79
Student, Kurt R., 53, 57
Stumm, David A., 127
St. John, Robert L., 43
Sugarman, Jule M., 118
Sullivan, Dawn B. H., 27
Sullivan, Frederick L., 16,
    24, 31, 137, 142
Sullivan, James J., 26
Sullivan, Joan A., 81
Sullivan, John F., 98
Sullivan, John P., 81
Sullivan, Travis D., 47
Summer, Claire, 33, 34
Susser, Peter, 91
Sussman, John A., 44
Sussman, Lyle, 18
Sutton, Harry L., 31

Suver, James D., 48
Swanson, Carl L., 7, 65
Swart, J. Carroll, 55, 121
Swart, William W., 113
Sweeney, Allen, 125
Swenson, Dan H., 22
Sylvia, Robert A., 34
Symonds, Curtis W., 47,
    111, 125
Szilagyi, Jr., Andrew D.,
    79, 94, 141
Szuprowicz, Bohdan O.,
    61, 62, 67

Tade, George T., 22
Taetzsch, Lyn, 46
Taffi, Donald J., 106, 130
Tagliaferri, Louis E., 31
Tagman, Jr., Charles T.,
    59
Taliaferro, Brook, 45
Talpaert, Roger, 77
Tanner, W. Lynn, 50
Taracena, Mario, 133
Tashenberg, C. Bradley,
    33, 36
Tausky, Curt, 70
Tavernier, Gerard, 18, 19,
    41, 101, 113, 122,
    139
Taylor, Henry M., 53
Taylor, M. Elliott, 117
Taylor, Susan G., 40
Teague, Carroll H., 137
Teague, Frederick A., 27
Tedd, M. T., 140
Tehan, Cynthia C., 91
Teller, Edward, 42
Teplitz, Charles J., 134
Tercek, John F., 40
Teriet, Bernhard, 55
Terrell, Richard L., 52
Thackeray, John, 131
Thayer, Robert, 3
Theriot, Lawrence H., 62
Thierauf, Robert J., 6, 48,
    57, 84, 87, 106, 113,
    121, 123
Tholt, Mary E., 53
Thomas, Richard E., 124
Thomas, William C., 13
Thompson, Duane E., 103
Thompson, Frederick T.,
    122
Thompson, Ken, 5, 9, 37,
    80, 93, 102, 104, 108,
    135

Thompson, Paul H., 13,
    83
Thomsen, David J., 25,
    38, 70
Thomson, Harvey A., 46
Thorne, Betty J., 91
Thornton, III, George C.,
    12
Thornton, Robert J., 25
Thurber, Le Grand L., 121
Thurman, Thomas N., 89
Thylin, Roy D., 51
Tibbetts, H. M., 6, 87
Tichy, Noel, 58
Tidwell, Gary L., 138
Tijunelis, Donatas, 9, 83,
    125
Till, Paul H., 29, 51, 74
Timbrell, David Y., 136
Timm, Paul R., 19
Tita, Michael A., 29
Titus, Parvin S., 113, 133,
    143
Todd, John, 80
Toffler, Alvin, 133
Tombari, Henry A., 26, 90,
    122
Tomeski, Edward A., 35
Toth, Edward R., 92
Touhey, John C., 50, 105
Townshend, Rolph, 61
Tracey, William R., 9, 31,
    40, 43, 45, 57, 71, 80,
    81, 84, 94, 96, 98,
    104, 108, 110, 115,
    128, 139, 140
Trapani, Cosmo S., 106
Trautman, Lawrence J., 7,
    17, 48, 130
Tregoe, Benjamin B., 109
Trestman, Frank D., 14
Trilli, Harvey J., 67
Troisi, Angelo M., 138
Trollop, Glyn, 83
Trotman, Elizabeth, 3, 7
Trotzky, Evelyn, 119
Troughton, George H., 33
Trueblood, Roy, 30
Truell, George F., 56, 99
Tubbs, Steward L., 19
Tucker, Stephen L., 88
Tudhope, R. A., 141
Ture, Norman B., 65
Turner, T. S., 129
Turney, John R., 101
Tushman, Michael, 98
Twine, Edgar H., 131

Ueda, Taizo, 61
Ueda, Yoshio, 62
Ulery, John D., 69, 113
Umstot, Denis D., 70
Unni, V. K., 82
Uris, Auren, 30, 45, 52
Urwick, Lyndall F., 76
Utley, Jim A., 129
Utterback, James M., 112

Valaskakis, K., 131
Valentine, Raymond F., 68, 128
Van Riper, Robert, 117
Van Vorst, James R., 118
Van Zanten, G., 40
Vance, Stanley C., 7, 8, 43
Vandermyn, Gaye, 30
Vanderslice, Thomas A., 41
Vardaman, George T., 20, 21, 22, 127
Vaught, Bobby C., 73
Vavra, Sandra A., 57
Velmans, Loet A., 59
Venuto, Peter B., 47, 108
Vernon, Raymond, 60
Vertinsky, Alan, 88
Vicars, William, 79
Vieceli, Louis, 122
Villere, Maurice F., 21
Vles, Joseph M., 33, 51
Vogel, David P., 120
Von Bergen, Jr., Clarence W., 32
Von der Embse, Thomas J., 92
Vora, Jay A., 109
Voros, Gerald J., 3, 6, 9, 18, 23, 29, 52, 68, 69, 71, 108, 117
Vough, Clair F., 31, 70, 73, 90, 107, 115, 116, 120, 144
Vroom, Victor H., 71
Vyssotsky, Victor A., 33

Waddell, William C., 5, 30, 44, 72, 78, 79, 81, 96, 107, 108, 114, 133
Wagel, William H., 12, 13, 23, 26, 42, 44, 55, 57, 81, 122
Wagner, Paul A., 88
Walker, Alfred J., 34
Walker, James W., 11, 82, 86, 95

Walker, Joseph J., 4
Wall, Anders, 48
Wallace, Les, 103
Wallack, Stuart J., 138
Wallendorf, Melanie, 89
Wallfesh, Henry M., 74, 95, 110
Walsh, Edward K., 51
Walsh, Richard J., 16, 55, 91
Walters, Timothy G., 59
Walton, Richard E., 101
Walvoord, R. Wayne, 67, 89
Ward, Kenneth G., 76
Warren, Carl, 33
Warren, Thomas L., 22
Wasem, George, 88
Washing, Harry A., 4
Wasserman, Norman, 20
Waters, James A., 43, 83
Waters, William, 95, 105
Watkins, Larry E., 85
Watt, William J., 119
Way, Jr., Howard, 39
Weaver, Richard F., 133
Webber, Ross Arkell, 5
Weber, James, 43
Weber, Robert A., 127
Wehrenberg, Stephen B., 138
Weick, Karl E., 98
Weidenbaum, Murray L., 74
Weihrich, Heinz, 21, 79, 103
Weil, Frank A., 66
Weiner, Nan, 58
Weintraub, Victor, 108
Weis, William L., 53
Weisbord, Marvin R., 30, 35, 45
Weisman, Matthew C., 141
Weiss, Alan Jay, 19, 45, 46, 57, 73, 135
Weiss, Allen, 20, 21, 22, 23
Weiss, Bernard, 102
Weiss, Donald H., 30
Weiss, Eric A., 117
Weiss, Rhoda E., 86
Weitzul, James, 138
Welch, Joe L., 56
Wellbank, Harry L., 12
Wells, Beth, 21

Welsh, A. N., 46
Welsh, John A., 130
Wentworth, Felix, 39, 61, 141
Werner, Gerald C., 96
Werner, William L., 6
Wesley, Ann Marie, 9, 102
Wessner, Kenneth T., 80
Whalen, P. J., 35
Wheelen, Thomas L., 49
Wheeler, Richard O., 59
Wheelock, Keith, 123
White, Jerry F., 130
White, Norman A., 41, 42, 63
White, Phillip D., 36, 119
White, William L., 26, 28, 40, 65, 104
White, Jr., Willis S., 51
Whitson, D. R., 66
Whittier, David B., 71, 134
Whitworth, Hall B., 89
Wicker, John, 17, 97
Widgery, Robin N., 19
Wiebe, Frank A., 30, 42
Wieland, George F., 99
Wijting, Jan P., 40
Wilkie, William L., 89
Wilkinson, Glen A., 7
Williams, III, Alexander H., 91
Williams, Derek W., 2
Williams, Harold M., 51, 132
Williams, Harry E., 120
Williams, Whiting, 94
Williamson, Denny, 104
Williamson, Jr., T. D., 66
Wilmotte, Raymond M., 36
Wilson, Donald, 31
Wilson, Ian H., 121, 144
Wilson, Ian R., 61
Wilson, James A., 54
Wilson, Janice, 90
Wilson, Richard L., 109
Wilson, Terry, 123
Wilterding, Jim A., 141
Winans, Patricia A., 23
Winchester, Mark B., 60
Wing, Jan, 90
Wingett, Peter J., 59
Wining, Jean W., 18
Winkler, Charles, 84
Winters, Kenneth T., 57
Wise, Joseph, 116
Witchel, Sam, 1
Witkin, Arthur A., 68

Wohl, Ronald H., 102
Wolf, James F., 10
Wolf, John, 52
Wolff, Joel C., 39, 114
Wolz, William T., 68, 129
Wood, Jr., D. Robley, 130
Wood, Ivan, 74
Wood, Marion M., 18
Wood, Philip, 65
Wood, Robert J., 117
Woodruff, Robert L., 44
Woodrum, David L., 7, 96, 137
Woodrum, Robert L., 39
Woods, Gary L., 83, 118
Woodworth, Warner, 99
Wooldrege, William D., 82
Woolf, Donald Austin, 4
Woolston, Susan W., 58, 96, 110, 114, 118, 124
Wooten, Bob, 104
Wooters, J. Dukes, 86, 87
Worrell, Allan K., 25
Worthy, James C., 57, 76
Wortman, Leon A., 50
Wright, Bruce J., 9
Wright, Jr., Norman H., 90

Wright, Peter, 31
Wriston, Walter B., 67
Wu, Rong-I, 65
Wunderli, Earl M., 75
Wunnenberg, Jr., C. A., 39
Wyatt, H. E., 63

Yamashita, Yoshimichi, 61
Yanda, M.D., Roman L., 29, 118
Yates, Don, 99, 101
Yates, Helen, 123
Yates, Jere E., 54
Yaworsky, George M., 49
Yeargain, John, 31
Yerys, Arlene, 127, 143
Yeutter, Clayton K., 66
Ylvisaker, William T., 82
Yockey, Donald J., 66
Yoder, Dale, 57
Yoon, B. Man, 35
Yorks, Lyle, 70, 93, 121
Youker, Robert, 96
Young, Richard T., 2, 94, 114, 123, 127, 142, 143

Youngblood, Stuart A., 138
Youngs, Donald L., 66
Yrle, Augusta C., 18

Zachmann, William F., 100, 114
Zalar, Dennis A., 87, 92
Zaltman, Gerald, 88, 118
Zeldman, Maurice I., 32, 116, 127
Zenger, John H., 44
Zepke, Brent E., 4, 75
Zierden, William E., 32, 52, 72, 134, 135
Zimet, Melvin, 77
Zimmer, Arno B., 38, 53, 74, 84
Zimmerman, John W., 109
Zippo, Mary, 2, 5, 24, 29, 39, 40, 41, 52, 54, 55, 58, 93, 95, 102, 113, 114, 115, 116, 120, 121, 122, 128, 131, 138
Zivan, Mark S., 56
Zoffer, H. J., 40